T0239086

Building the SharePoint User Experience

Bjørn Christoffer Thorsmæhlum Furuknap

Apress®

Building the SharePoint User Experience

Copyright © 2009 by Bjørn Christoffer Thorsmæhlum Furuknap

All rights reserved. No part of this work may be reproduced or transmitted in any form or by any means, electronic or mechanical, including photocopying, recording, or by any information storage or retrieval system, without the prior written permission of the copyright owner and the publisher.

ISBN-13 (pbk): 978-1-4302-1896-8

ISBN-13 (electronic): 978-1-4302-1897-5

9 8 7 6 5 4 3 2 1

Trademarked names may appear in this book. Rather than use a trademark symbol with every occurrence of a trademarked name, we use the names only in an editorial fashion and to the benefit of the trademark owner, with no intention of infringement of the trademark.

Lead Editor: Ewan Buckingham
Technical Reviewer: Sahil Malik
Community Reviewers: Gil Stav, Tom Resing, Barb Troyer, Martin Opheim Smedsrud
Editorial Board: Clay Andres, Steve Anglin, Mark Beckner, Ewan Buckingham, Tony Campbell,
  Gary Cornell, Jonathan Gennick, Michelle Lowman, Matthew Moodie, Jeffrey Pepper,
  Frank Pohlmann, Ben Renow-Clarke, Dominic Shakeshaft, Matt Wade, Tom Welsh
Project Manager: Sofia Marchant
Copy Editor: Kim Wimpsett
Associate Production Director: Kari Brooks-Copony
Production Editor: Kelly Winquist
Compositor: Regina Rexrode
Proofreader: April Eddy
Indexer: Julie Grady
Artist: April Milne
Cover Designer: Kurt Krames
Manufacturing Director: Tom Debolski

Distributed to the book trade worldwide by Springer-Verlag New York, Inc., 233 Spring Street, 6th Floor, New York, NY 10013. Phone 1-800-SPRINGER, fax 201-348-4505, e-mail orders-ny@springer-sbm.com, or visit http://www.springeronline.com.

For information on translations, please contact Apress directly at 2855 Telegraph Avenue, Suite 600, Berkeley, CA 94705. Phone 510-549-5930, fax 510-549-5939, e-mail info@apress.com, or visit http://www.apress.com.

Apress and friends of ED books may be purchased in bulk for academic, corporate, or promotional use. eBook versions and licenses are also available for most titles. For more information, reference our Special Bulk Sales–eBook Licensing web page at http://www.apress.com/info/bulksales.

The information in this book is distributed on an "as is" basis, without warranty. Although every precaution has been taken in the preparation of this work, neither the author(s) nor Apress shall have any liability to any person or entity with respect to any loss or damage caused or alleged to be caused directly or indirectly by the information contained in this work.

The source code for this book is available to readers at http://www.apress.com.

This book is entirely dedicated to the most beautiful woman in the universe, my wife Lena. Lena, without your support, your love, and your endless patience, I could never have written this book or been as happy as I am today.
I love you.

Contents at a Glance

Contents

PART 1 ▪▪▪ Setup and Basics

PART 2 ▪▪▪ Dissecting the Default User Experience

PART 3 ■■■ Building an Empire

About the Author

**BJØRN CHRISTOFFER THORSMÆHLUM FURUKNAP** is a senior solutions architect, author and editor of *Understanding SharePoint Journal*, speaker, and passionate SharePointaholic. He has been doing software development professionally since 1993 for small companies as well as multinational corporations. He has also been a teacher at a college-level school, teaching programming and development to aspiring students, a job that inspired him to begin teaching what he has learned and learns every day.

In 2007, Bjørn began writing online in his blog, before he moved on to writing for online magazines and eventually starting his own periodical called *Understanding SharePoint Journal* in 2009. These days he spends more time writing, speaking, answering questions, and providing advice than making any real progress or money.

About the Technical Reviewer

SAHIL MALIK has been a Microsoft MVP and INETA speaker for many years; he is the author of many books and numerous articles, as well as a consultant and trainer who delivers training and talks at conferences internationally. His talks are full of humor and practical nuggets and tend to be very highly charged, fast moving, and interactive. Sahil likes to maintain a balance and learn as much as possible about all the Microsoft technologies, thus completely ignoring balance in his personal life. He still thinks COM was cool. You should check out his site at http://blah.winsmarts.com.

Acknowledgments

Yeah, this is it. I suddenly realize how far along this book has come now that I have to sit down and think back about who actually made this piece of work possible.

Of course, I'd like to thank myself. Without me, this book would never have happened. Through seemingly endless hours of writing, researching, and fighting for space, I have shown me that I had what it took to make it through. Thank me, I've been wonderful.

OK, time to get serious.

No person has meant more to completing this book than my wife Lena. I mean, I've spent the last nine months writing almost every day for more hours than I care to count, but Lena has still been patient and has supported me, encouraged me, cooked me dinner, cleaned the house, and done absolutely everything that anyone can dream of in a partner. This really isn't a book written by me; it is a book created by us, and her name should be on the cover, above mine.

Second, I would like to thank the SharePoint community. You have my deepest respect for your effort, your attitude, and the willingness to share and help anyone, regardless of level or experience. Thanks to you people, you have taught me more about SharePoint than I thought was possible to learn in a lifetime.

Writing a book, though, is not a solo effort. The Apress team, the technical reviewer, and the community reviewers have contributed massively to ensure that this book made it past the first chapter. Specifically, I would like to mention Sahil Malik, the technical reviewer; Sofia Marchant, the project manager; and Kim Wimpsett, the copy editor—thank you all for your massive help during the previous months.

Phew, I think that's about as much seriousness as I can take.

I'd like to thank my sister's dalmatian: Spot, the dog. You are my absolute favorite nephew.

Honorable mention also goes to the pizza guy, the artists on my Spotify playlists, Aleister Crowley, Santa Claus, Ikea, the seven dwarfs, and whoever figured out that coffee was a good idea. Writing just isn't the same without coffee. As for the other honorable mentions, well, you'll just have to imagine something. ☺

Oh, and of course, Arno Nel of *SharePoint Magazine*, who gave me a chance to write in public and start a career path that so far has left me flat broke and with more people hating me than I knew existed before I started writing—thanks a lot, dude. I'll bring a bat to thank you in person next time we meet.

The biggest thanks go to you, however, the reader of this book. Ultimately, I wrote this for you and no one else. Thank you, from the bottom of my heart, for reading what I write. You make it all worthwhile.

Introduction

It was a dark autumn night when private investigator AJ was sitting in his office, looking forward to the next day's bottle of bourbon. He wasn't much looking forward to anything; rather, it would be more correct to say he hated his life a little bit less when he got a few shots of bourbon. Today's bottle was empty, and reality had started to crawl up his spine.

You may very well wonder what this has to do with SharePoint. The answer is absolutely nothing! However, it has something to do with what you are about to read.

You are about to embark on a journey into the deepest secrets of SharePoint, a journey that will not only teach you about the architecture and user experience of SharePoint but also take you along a journey of exploration and of building an empire.

The first part of this book will deal with basics—what you need in order to get the most out of the remaining parts of the book.

The second part will deal with exploration. Think of it as a guided tour through SharePoint Land where I will explain and show you the sights to see. Beware, though, because there will be dangers aplenty.

In the third part of this book, you will start building an empire that will stand the test of time. You will construct your own SharePoint solution and put some of your newly acquired knowledge into practical use.

Before we get going, however, I'd like to offer some advice.

This is not a reference book. I have worked very hard to include only the good stuff, and I have left out all the mindless references and tables. Because of this highly condensed format, I'm recommending that you read as much as possible of the content rather than just skimming it.

Second, don't take anything too seriously. I'm certainly not. If you are deeply offended by something in this book, consider it a joke. And that leads to the final piece of advice....

Have fun!

PART 1

Setup and Basics

■ ■ ■

CHAPTER 1

Checking Your Gear for Departure

Making Sure Your Setup Is in Order

Before we start our journey, we need to make sure we have our gear in order. First, we are going to set up a common development environment in which we can experiment. This ensures that the results we get are the same and that we can explore the same files.

Second, I will introduce you to some very nice tools that will help speed up and improve your development experience. Although many such tools are available, I have found the tools I mention in this chapter to be a very valuable addition to my setup. And, best of all, they are all free.

Finally, I'll suggest a site setup that includes all the basic site definitions that ship with Windows SharePoint Service (WSS). Following this setup is important if you want to make sure you see the same results as shown in this book. I have used this site setup for all the screenshots throughout the book.

Setting Up Your Environment

Your development machine needs to run Windows Server 2003 R2. I know people would really like to develop on Windows XP, but unfortunately, until pigs fly, there will be no official Share-Point support on Windows XP. And, since the wonderful object model works only locally, we actually need to also run Visual Studio on that server.

Most of us, however, have Windows XP running on our workstations, and very few of us walk around with a server under our arm. We also know that developing on a server is usually a bad idea since, well, we tend to make mistakes, and taking down a server is a bit more serious than rebooting a laptop.

I have read a lot of blogs by people cursing Microsoft for making it so difficult to develop for SharePoint, but more often than not, these arguments are based on laziness rather than an actual problem. People have developed and recommended different techniques for circumventing the server requirement, but I have a better suggestion, one that not only saves you time and frustration but also gives you a lot of added benefit.

I run all my development on virtual machines. With advances in virtual machine technology, running an isolated machine to do development work is easier than ever. And Windows Server 2003 runs quite comfortably on a gigabyte of RAM, and with cheaper and cheaper RAM prices, most people should be able to upgrade to an extra gigabyte or two to save their laptop from undue reinstalls and general messiness.

Using an isolated virtual machine with Windows Server 2003 and Visual Studio has monumental benefits to us as developers. We can tailor a single virtual machine for each development project and just offload the different virtual machines to an external hard drive when we do not need them. If we wreck our setup, snapshots make it easy to restore a previous state without needing to reinstall and set up from scratch. With some virtual machine software, we can take multiple snapshots and snapshot branches so that we can jump back and forth between different setups in a, well, snap. We can even take a snapshot before a particularly dangerous operation, and if everything blows up, it will take just seconds to get back to the predisaster state.

Besides, Microsoft now gives us all the software we need free of charge. If you do not have an MSDN subscription, you can easily download evaluation or Express versions of Windows Server 2003, Visual Studio 2008, SharePoint Designer, and Microsoft Virtual PC.

So yes, you need Windows Server 2003. Yes, you need to run Visual Studio on that server. No, that is not a bad idea, a bad development experience, or even the slightest bit of a problem. If you haven't done so already, you should now set up that server and install Visual Studio and SharePoint Designer.

Tip If you have problems installing and setting up a server machine, Microsoft provides preinstalled virtual machine VHD images for you to download at `http://www.understandingsharepoint.com/url/10029`.

Tip Have an external storage location available for storing your project files. That way, a snapshot restore will not delete the files that you worked so hard to create. For instance, you can use a USB key, an external hard drive, a share on your host machine, or, if your virtual machine software supports it, a static or an independent virtual drive. Put your project files, for example, from Visual Studio, on that external storage location, and if by chance your virtual machine is destroyed, you still retain all your hard work.

Your first objective is to configure Visual Studio so it will recognize the CAML code we want to explore. Although not strictly necessary for this part of the book because we will mostly be looking and not touching, I find it useful to have IntelliSense so that I can check the syntax and subelements of a particular XML element. If you prefer another XML editor, feel free to figure out how to configure similar functionality if you like.

To configure Visual Studio 2005 to automatically recognize well-formatted CAML files, you need to create an XML file in the `C:\Program Files\Microsoft Visual Studio 8\Xml\Schemas` folder. You can call the file anything you like, for instance `SPCAML.xml`. Next, paste the following code into that file:

```
<schemacatalog xmlns="http://schemas.microsoft.com/xsd/catalog">
  <Schemahref="C:/Program Files/Common Files/Microsoft Shared/web server ➥
extensions/12/TEMPLATE/XML/wss.xsd"
    targetNamespace="http://schemas.microsoft.com/sharepoint/" />
</schemacatalog>
```

We're telling Visual Studio that our file is a schema catalog and then pointing a particular schema, the WSS schema file specified in Schemahref, to a particular namespace, as specified in the targetNamespace attribute. Effectively, this means that when Visual Studio encounters an XML file with that namespace, it will automatically use the specified WSP schema file and give us IntelliSense.

This will get you far with your own files, but unfortunately, Microsoft doesn't always use this namespace in its files. If you open any of the built-in WSS CAML files, such as an onet.xml file, your IntelliSense will not work. To fix this, you can manually set the schema to be used by opening the XML file in Visual Studio and setting the proper schema file in the Schemas property. Just browse to the address listed in the Schemahref element listed previously, and you should get IntelliSense to work.

Tip You can use the same technique described earlier to create schema catalogs for your own, custom XML files if you have an XSD schema file that you would like to use.

You should consider creating some test users so that you can explore how the user experience is for different kinds of users. One of the most common reasons why projects have problems in production that were not seen during development is that developers love doing their work as administrators. This is a good thing and even a requirement when you need to do things such as deploying assemblies, updating web.config files, or creating files in the [12] structure, which are impossible to do if you are a normal user. However, testing your solution using different user accounts will help prevent problems that are not seen if you are running as an administrator, and it also helps cool down our bloated developer egos to experience life as a normal user from time to time.

Before we begin our site setup, your final objective will be to gather and install a set of useful and free tools. These tools help you with different aspects of SharePoint development and are useful for exploring properties of SharePoint objects not usually visible through any web interface.

The following are the tools you will want:

- SharePoint Manager 2007 (http://www.codeplex.com/spm/)

- .NET Reflector (http://reflector.red-gate.com/)

- WSPBuilder and Visual Studio Extensions for WSPBuilder (http://www.codeplex.com/wspbuilder/)

These tools may seem simple enough, but I do not think having tools should be our primary strength. You are here to learn the deeper secrets of SharePoint, and doing so with a "click here to solve all your problems" tool is difficult. I would have preferred just recommending you a battery, two wires, and a nail, but I realize that manually magnetizing your hard drive with the correct bits may be a bit too hard-core, even for me.

The tools I recommend here do not spoil the fun of discovery, but they do save you tons of time when you need to quickly glance over all the properties of a list, create and deploy a list template within five minutes, or figure out how exactly a particular poorly documented feature works. And there will be plenty of the latter.

SharePoint Manager 2007

SharePoint Manager 2007, or SPM for short, is a tool developed by Carsten Keutmann, who is also responsible for the WSPBuilder tool. SPM gives you a visual interface to the object model of SharePoint, allowing you to explore what properties are available, see how a site is structured, discover "hidden" files and folders, and do a ton of other stuff. Figure 1-1 shows the basic view of SPM.

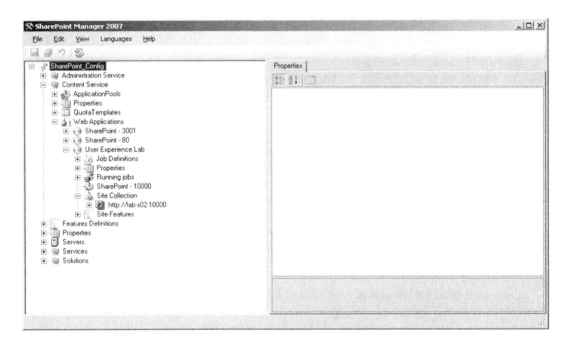

Figure 1-1. *SharePoint Manager 2007*

■**Tip** When you start SPM, select View ➤ Object Model, and make sure you have set it to display the Full object model if you want all the details. And you do.

Benefits of SharePoint Manager 2007

With SPM, you can browse your entire SharePoint installation, including servers, sites, services, lists, items, and anything else. But that is only the beginning. SPM also allows you to modify the properties of all those objects, which gives you a wonderful opportunity to test how different properties affect your sites. When you click an item in the list, the right pane of SPM shows all the properties. Properties in black are editable, while properties in gray cannot be edited. Which properties are editable is a SharePoint thing, however, so don't blame SPM if you cannot change the parent web of a site.

Figure 1-2 shows the typical SPM experience and how editing properties works.

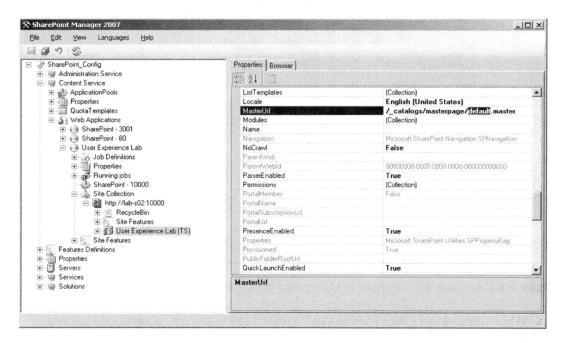

Figure 1-2. *Editing properties in SPM*

Another absolute killer feature of SPM is SharePoint feature handling. SPM lists all feature definitions of your farm, conveniently organized according to scope. Within each site, site collection, and web application, there is a Features node. Right-clicking a feature in that node allows you to activate or deactivate a feature without visiting the web interface. Even hidden features are listed. Figure 1-3 shows the feature deactivation of the hidden Basic Web Parts feature.

Feature handling does not stop there. Near the bottom of the node tree of SPM are all the features that are located in the [12]\TEMPLATE\FEATURES folder, whether they are installed or not. The right-click options give you the chance to install a feature by simply clicking your mouse. If you are fed up with writing STSADM commands or visiting the Site Settings page each time you update your feature, use SPM instead.

⬛Note [12] refers to the 12 hive, the installation folder of SharePoint. This is usually at C:\Program
Files\Common Files\Microsoft Shared\web server extensions\12.

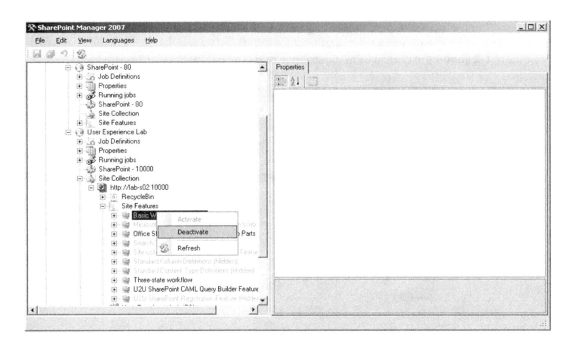

Figure 1-3. *Deactivating a feature in SPM is as easy as clicking.*

When you click web items such as a site, a list, or a view, you get an additional tab in the
right pane, called Browser. This is simply a browser view of the object as it would appear if
you had opened the object in your normal web browser. A cool trick is that since SPM shows
hidden objects, you can see how the hidden views will look without exposing them to users.

⬛Tip Did you know that in the document libraries in WSS there are two "secret" features? Open a docu-
ment library, such as the Shared Documents library, in SPM, and check out the views. There will be a Merge
Documents view as well as a Relink Documents view. Open these in the Browser pane to see how they look.
These views are tied to MOSS functionality and will not be covered in this book.

But wait, there's more! If you are viewing a list in SPM, you also have a grid view of the list where you can make basic data input or edits. It's nothing fancy, but it's useful if you just want to make quick edits to a list item or if you are testing feature receivers and get tired of reloading the web interface for editing, deleting, or adding items. Direct editing in SPM can also be useful if you have hidden columns that do not appear in the web user interface.

The final feature I want to mention in SPM is schema output. Whenever you select an object that is defined by a CAML schema, SPM will display a Schema Xml tab and occasionally a CAML tab. These tabs contain the XML code for an object. You can more or less copy and paste this code into your own feature. Suddenly you have designer support for your CAML code; just design whatever object you want in the web interface, and then copy the CAML XML code from SPM.

Note that the XML you get from SharePoint through either SPM or other tools might not necessarily be immediately usable inside a feature. Some elements, such as fields, can be copied and pasted directly, while custom views require a bit of rewriting. In Appendix A, I will cover this in more detail and show you some examples of how you would extract CAML code for reuse in your own feature.

Danger, Will Robinson!

There are some things you need to know about SPM, however. All is not well in the state of Denmark apparently, because some of these things will kill your SharePoint server.

■**Note** Carsten Keutmann is Danish. And a genius.

First, let's talk about the minor stuff. SPM does not handle data refresh well. If you delete a list outside of SPM while SPM is open, the list will still be visible in SPM, even if you hit the Refresh button. Actually, this depends a bit on what you modify or delete and also what object in SPM is currently selected when you hit Refresh. This is a minor inconvenience.

Second is exception handling. Although SPM is as stable as the pyramids, meaning it might be less in use in 4,000 years but will still draw a massive amount of tourists, exceptions from SharePoint are just displayed to the user with no stack trace, inner exceptions, or anything like that. In addition, because of the refresh issue mentioned earlier, you might not even get the right exception. Again, it's just a minor issue, but it might catch you off guard and cause some bewilderment.

The third issue is a major one. Never, ever delete a site or site collection in SPM. Doing so will mess up your system. And I mean big time. Also, if you use SPM to delete anything, make absolutely sure that you *first* select the item using a normal left-click before you right-click to delete the item. SPM will delete whatever you clicked prior to right-clicking. That might be your entire SharePoint configuration database. And that will be bad.

Take a look at the sidebar "Dead SharePoint System: A Recovering SPM Deleter" for how to restore your SharePoint server without having to reinstall your entire computer.

DEAD SHAREPOINT SYSTEM: A RECOVERING SPM DELETER

I have done this a few times. Not just from messing around with SPM but from sheer stupidity. "Done what?" you ask. I've done something that broke my SharePoint installation, such as deleting the configuration database or corrupting that database to the extent where recovery was not possible.

The problem, especially if you don't have proper backups, is that there is no way to recover SharePoint. If you try to run Central Administration, the corrupted or missing SharePoint database will spoil the fun. If you try to run the SharePoint Products and Technologies Configuration Wizard, it will croak and complain that SharePoint is not correctly installed, or it will simply throw an exception and let Dr. Watson promise you that Microsoft will be notified if you hit a button. You don't get much help there.

So, you start the uninstallation of SharePoint, which fails, because SharePoint does not know how to uninstall itself without having access to the configuration. The same thing applies if you try to reinstall the installation using any supported method. All seems lost; you cannot set up a new configuration database, you cannot get rid of SharePoint, and you cannot reinstall and repair.

Before you start looking for your Windows Server installation discs to scratch your system, however, do read on.

What if there is a network problem and you cannot access the database at all? In that case, the Share-Point configuration wizard will allow you to disconnect from the database and connect to another database. This provides you with an opportunity to get SharePoint up and running even if you are not able to pull the network cable to simulate a network outage.

Simply stop the SQL Server instance, and rerun the configuration wizard. SharePoint will complain that it is unable to detect whether the server is part of a farm and allow you to disconnect from the database server. Next, delete the corrupt SharePoint databases, restart the database server, and run your configuration wizard again. You can then use any restore tool to restore your old content databases into the new SharePoint farm.

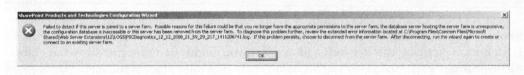

Despite the issues, SharePoint Manager 2007 still remains my favorite SharePoint tool. Using SPM saves me hours of development time.

.NET Reflector

.NET Reflector is not a SharePoint tool per se, but it is still incredibly useful for developers. .NET Reflector allows you to see the source code of .NET code. That's right, campers; SharePoint is a .NET application, so you can see the source code of SharePoint as clear as the sky on a sunny day. Or at least you can see a lot of it; some code in SharePoint is obfuscated, and reflection will not work.

After you have started .NET Reflector, you need to load whatever assembly you want to inspect, and a prime candidate is the Windows.SharePoint.dll file located in the [12]\ISAPI folder. Either open the assembly from the Open menu or drag and drop the assembly from a folder into the .NET Reflector window. Click the expand icon (the small plus sign) in front of the assembly name, and you can keep browsing down into the namespaces and classes inside the assembly. Double-click a property or method, and a second pane opens showing the source code of the method. You can also right-click an entire class and choose Disassemble to open an entire class for inspection. Figure 1-4 shows .NET Reflector with a disassembled SharePoint class.

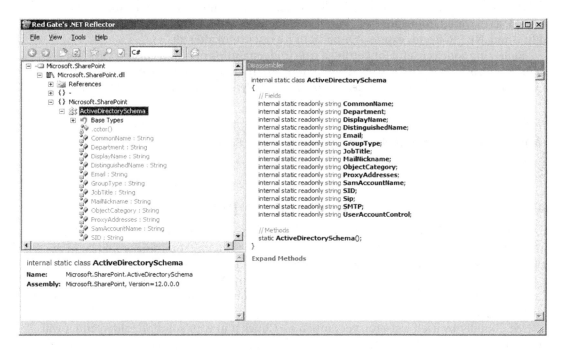

Figure 1-4. *.NET Reflector*

One particularly useful feature of .NET Reflector is that it will give you the four-part strong name of a strong-named assembly. Open the assembly in .NET Reflector, and look in the lower yellow section of the window.

When you browse through the code in .NET Reflector, you can click methods and properties to go directly to the code for that method or property. If the linked code is located in another assembly, .NET Reflector will prompt you for the file location and make a qualified guess if the assembly can be located in the GAC.

Other particularly useful features are the Back and Forward buttons. You may be digging through countless levels of method calls to get where you want, but it is easy to lose track of where you started. Using the Back and Forward buttons, you can navigate to previous code just like you would in a web browser.

The next cool feature of .NET Reflector is the ability to bookmark code. If you are working a lot with a certain class or assembly, you can add a bookmark to the code, and .NET Reflector will jump right to that code with the click of a mouse. If you close the assembly in which you have placed a bookmark, .NET Reflector will open the assembly for you if you click the bookmark.

The final feature I want to address here is the support for plug-ins in .NET Reflector. There is a CodePlex project that holds a range of .NET Reflector plug-ins to extend their functionality. One useful plug-in is the AutoDiagrammer, which shows the assembly classes in a Visual Studio–like class diagram.

There is only one thing truly annoying about .NET Reflector. It is a free tool, and that is great, but it still expires and requires regular updating. What happens is that at times when you start .NET Reflector, it will tell you that it has expired and needs to be updated. You are asked whether you want to update, and if you don't update, then .NET Reflector will be deleted, as in wiped from your disk. This is incredibly useful for that time when you are offline and .NET Reflector expires. Or perhaps it's not useful after all.

Reflecting code is useful for getting a true understanding of how a complex system like SharePoint works. A lot of the truly deep material in this book was discovered using Reflector. If you haven't taken the time to reflect in anything lately, doing so will pay off in the long run.

Note I am beginning to sound like a marketing person here. Sorry.

WSPBuilder Extensions for Visual Studio

Authoring SharePoint solutions is a tedious task if done manually. If there was a list of most annoying software development tasks, creating DDF files for WSP building would be in the top spot, perhaps even the top two spots, with a guest appearance at the number 3 spot.

That all ended when WSPBuilder saw the light of day. Again, the awesomely cool guy Carsten Keutmann steps up to the plate to receive honors for making SharePoint development a whole lot less painful.

WSPBuilder by itself is useful, very much so. Chuck it in your solution folder, and it will magically create a WSP file for you, no questions asked. If you want to configure, you have more options than grains of sand in the Sahara. That's all great, but it is not even close to the coolness of WSPBuilder Extensions for Visual Studio.

WSPBuilder Extensions for Visual Studio… I'll just refer to the product as WSPBuilder. WSPBuilder integrates with Visual Studio in several ways. First, it creates a range of new solution and project templates for you so you can easily create SharePoint features such as event handlers, web parts, custom field types, features with receivers, and workflows. See Figure 1-5 for the project types you can add.

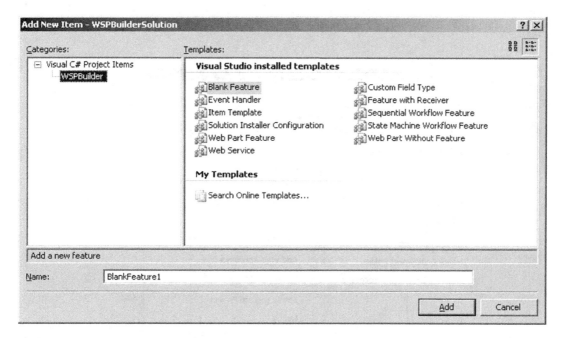

Figure 1-5. *WSPBuilder project types*

Adding one of these projects to your solution will not only add the required files, but it will set up your feature.xml file, create a signing key and sign your assemblies, and add the strong name to the feature files where required. This task alone takes several minutes if done manually and is also error prone and annoying.

To make WSPBuilder even cooler, you also get a new menu item under Tools that is a massive time-saver. The WSPBuilder menu item includes tasks such as building the WSP file; deploying, retracting, and upgrading the solution; attaching to the IIS worker process for debugging; recycling the application pools; copying files to [12] or the GAC; and creating a complete deployment folder with both batch files and setup files needed to deploy on another computer.

The menu items are also available on the right-click menu of the Solution Explorer in Visual Studio (see Figure 1-6).

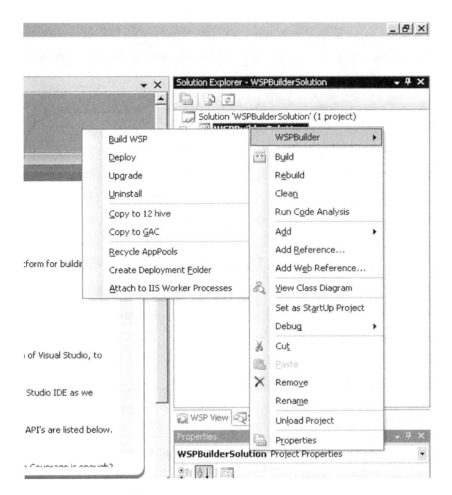

Figure 1-6. *WSPBuilder integration menu*

I do most of my SharePoint development using WSPBuilder, especially when I need to attach the debugger to code such as when developing event receivers or when creating code-behind classes for custom pages.

The tools I have mentioned here are the tools I use. However, there are plenty of other tools that can accomplish the same or similar things.

I prefer not to recommend any particular tool too much. I will talk a bit more about this in a later chapter, but in short, I recommend you take the time to evaluate different alternatives to find out which tools you prefer.

Setting Up Your SharePoint Environment

At this point, you should have the following environment set up:

- Windows Server 2003, any edition

- Windows SharePoint Services 3 with SP1 and otherwise fully patched

- Visual Studio, either 2005 or 2008

- SharePoint Designer 2007

- IntelliSense set up for Visual Studio

- SharePoint Manager, .NET Reflector, and WSPBuilder

Tip We will be working a lot with the 12 hive. Although it's not required, I recommend you create a short-cut to the root of the hive for easy access. I recommend adding a shortcut to the Start menu or adding a toolbar to the Windows taskbar. To do so, right-click an empty section of the taskbar, click Toolbars, and then select New Toolbar. Browse to the [12] folder, and click OK.

For your development machine, you might also want to grab a copy of Microsoft Office. Although you would never put this on your production server, having Office installed in your development environment makes it that much easier to test Office integration. Also, you get access to the grid view of lists, which makes updating multiple items at the same time a lot easier.

This is completely optional, however, and since Office costs a good chunk of money, you might want to skip this part.

Site Setup

Now that we share a basic set of tools, it is time to begin our adventure. Having established that you already know how to set up a basic web application in SharePoint, there should be no problem for you to do so now. I will give you step-by-step setup instructions in a moment, so for now, focus on understanding the site hierarchy and our setup.

Our SharePoint site setup will be rather simple. We want a root site based on the Team Site definition that ships with WSS. On that site, we will create multiple subsites based on each of the major site definitions that are available out of the box, namely, a meeting workplace, a wiki site, and a blog site. We will use these particular sites because they offer us a wide variety of user experience elements that we should learn.

Note Do not skip this setup. It may seem trivial, but it ensures that we will get the same results in later exercises.

---

1. Create your web application any way you choose using any port number. For my examples, I have a server called LAB-S02, and I use port number 10000. When you see a reference to `http://lab-s02:10000/`, you know to which site I am referring.

2. Create a new site collection in the root of your new web application. Choose the Team Site template, and fill in the remaining fields as you want.

3. Open your new site, and create three new subsites using the following site templates. Name them whatever you like; I have placed the names I use in parentheses.

   - Basic Meeting Workplace (Basic Meeting Lab)

   - Wiki (Wiki Lab)

   - Blog (Blog Lab)

At this point, you should have a site that resembles Figure 1-7.

Figure 1-7. *Initial site structure*

This setup will allow you to test the same code that will be used in later chapters of this book and get the same results. You may of course skip or change the setup, but do so only if you feel sufficiently confident that you know what the consequences are.

Virtual Machine Snapshot

We are just about ready to start diving in, so it makes sense to take a snapshot of your virtual machine now. That way, if you really mess up your installation later, you can easily come back to this state with all the setup completed. Just remember to put all your hard work on an external storage medium so a snapshot restore does not delete your files.

Tip If you are using a virtual machine software package that does not support snapshots, you may chose to power down your virtual machine and back up the VM folder or disks.

Remember to activate your software before you take a snapshot.

That's a Wrap

OK, we now have a working environment in which we can start developing. You should also have learned a bit about how to use the set of tools that I use most frequently for making the SharePoint development experience a lot better.

Remember that tools can remove the learning experience and that you should learn how to develop without tools first. Once you know how to create a certain piece of code, using tools is a good approach to save time. Even so, I still sometimes go back and create features from scratch, in Notepad, just to make sure I remember the right syntax.

Going forward, we are going to explore a couple of topics outside the main focus of this book, namely, XML and SharePoint Features. You should have at least a cursory knowledge of these topics already, but getting a refresher is always useful.

In the meantime, pat yourself on the back for having taken the first step toward a better understanding of SharePoint and the user experience.

■ ■ ■

CHAPTER 2

Taking a Crash Course in XML
Reviewing the Simple Stuff
Needed to Work with SharePoint

SharePoint uses Extensible Markup Language (XML)—or, to be more specific, the Collaborative Application Markup Language (CAML). We will spend a lot of time working with CAML, but it will be a lot easier to understand if you have the basics of XML down first.

Feel free to skip along your merry way to the next chapter if you can tell me what the difference is between an element and an attribute and when you should use one or the other.

If you have never worked with XML, either you have been living in a cave for the past ten years or you have worked very hard to avoid XML. It is time to either get you out of that cave or turn some of that avoidance effort into a learning effort.

If nothing else, I hope to show you in this chapter that XML is quite simple and that any fear you have for XML will be nothing compared to what you will face later in the book. So, take this time to relax and get some cheap knowledge that will be applicable outside of SharePoint as well.

There will be plenty of terror later. Mu-ha-ha-ha-ha....

XML: A Definition

What you see here is an XML document, albeit a rather crude and simple one:

```
<?xml version="1.0" encoding="utf-8" ?>
<xml>
  <definition>XML is a metalanguage used to describe data</definition>
  <usages>
    <usage>Use XML to describe your data and to ensure you store,
      transfer, and receive data in the proper format
    </usage>
    <usage>XML defines nothing; you must make up your own tags</usage>
    <usage>Syntax is important; XML is not forgiving for minor errors.
      See <![CDATA[<a href="#syntax">syntax</a>]]> for more information.
    </usage>
  </usages>
```

```
<acronym abbreviation="XML">Extensible Markup Language</acronym>
<syntax>
  OK, I think you get the point; we'll get to syntax later.
</syntax>
</xml>
```

In the previous XML document, you will notice the similarities to Hypertext Markup Language (HTML), but don't let that fool you. Besides the < and > to define tags and the use of attributes to add information about the tags, there is very little commonality between the two languages.

XML is all about data and nothing else. True, you can use a derivative language called Extensible Stylesheet Language (XSL) to format the data, but XML itself cares nothing for presentation or how you use the actual data. This also means that an XML document by itself is rather pointless. You need some kind of processor to actually make use of the data.

The *extensible* part of the name means that you can create "dialects" of XML. As long as you adhere to the rules of XML, your dialect language is considered XML as well. The benefit is that you can use any XML editor or reader on your dialect XML files and the editor and reader will understand your document. An example of this is the CAML dialect in SharePoint or Extensible Application Markup Language (XAML) used in Windows Presentation Foundation and workflows.

The good thing about XML is that it is completely open. If you think back about a decade or two and try to remember which word processor you used to write that very important contract, you are likely to find that, even with your most trusted storage medium, the file is simply unreadable because the software used to interpret the file is gone.

XML has the shelf life of plutonium. No matter how long it takes before you need to reopen your very important file, you can always crack the file open with a text editor to extract everything you need. The original program used to author the file may have been pushing daisies for the last 20 years, but you can still get to your data.

XML Syntax

The syntax of XML resembles HTML, so if you are familiar with HTML, you should easily understand the syntax of XML as well. However, although HTML is a very loose language, XML follows strict syntax rules. In fact, XML interpreters are forbidden by the standard to attempt to interpret errors in a document.

So, to make sure that you know the rules, I'll walk you through the syntax of XML.

Note The good thing about a strict language, such as XML, C#, or mathematics, is that as long as you follow the rules, you always get the same result, and you don't make mistakes. This is very unlike loose or natural languages such as English or HTML where one thing may mean something completely different to two different people or browsers.

Elements

XML consists of elements, often referred to as *tags*. An element looks like this:

```
<element></element>
```

Anything inside those elements is considered data. That data can comprise new elements, referred to as *child elements*, or it can contain literal data such as the string "Hello, world!"

Here's one example:

```
<element>
 <childtag></childtag>
</element>
```

And here's another example:

```
<element>Hello, world!</element>
```

If your element does not contain any data, you can shorten the start-tag and end-tag combo. For instance, the following:

```
<element></element>
```

is exactly the same as this:

```
<element/>
```

Unlike HTML, XML is very case sensitive. In other words, the following:

```
<Element>
```

is not the same as this:

```
<element>
```

Also, unlike HTML parsers such as browsers, XML parsers are forbidden to try to fix such errors and should instead return an error to the user.

■**Note** Having an empty element such as `<tag/>` may seem pointless, but consider how you would store NULL data in your file, and it may make more sense.

You can also have multiple and similar child elements in a tag:

```
<element>
 <childtag>child data 1</childtag>
 <childtag>child data 2</childtag>
...
 <childtag>child data n</childtag>
</element>
```

You can use attributes, described later in the chapter, to identify each child element uniquely. Having unnumbered tags such as the previous example does have its advantages, however. Consider a simple document stored as XML:

```
<book>
 <chapter>
  <heading>Chapter 1</heading>
  <paragraph>Lorem ipsum dolor sit amet, consectetuer adipiscing elit.</paragraph>
  <paragraph>Maecenas porttitor congue massa.</paragraph>
  <illustration>
   <file>illustration1.tif</file>
   <caption>Illustration 1</caption>
  </illustration>
  <paragraph>Fusce posuere, magna sed pulvinar ultricies, purus lectus…</paragraph>
 </chapter>
</book>
```

If only books were that simple….

XML Declarations

XML also requires, or at least strongly encourages, you to declare the version of the XML standard. This should be considered mandatory and should be the first element in your document:

```
<?xml version="1.0"?>
```

In addition, the ?xml declaration may contain information about encoding and whether or not this document uses an external Document Type Definition (DTD):

```
<?xml version="1.0" encoding="UTF-8" standalone="no" ?>
```

Note DTDs are not covered in this chapter, but we will explore a more powerful alternative for XML validation, the XML Schema language (known as XSD).

The reason why DTDs are not covered is that XSD is used by SharePoint to validate files. XSD is also more developer friendly and is based on XML, while DTD uses a more obscure syntax that requires a lot more explaining. This is a crash course focused on SharePoint, remember? I'm not aiming to make an XML guru out of you, at least not in this book.

This declaration must be placed on the first line and at the first character of your document (in other words, no blank spaces or lines should appear before the declaration). The declaration is referred to as the *XML declaration.*

Here is an example of a complete and well-formed XML document, meaning the document follows the correct XML syntax and will be read correctly by any XML interpreter:

```
<?xml version="1.0"?>
<element>
 <childelement></childelement>
</element>
```

Attributes

In addition to data, your elements can contain *attributes*. Attributes are often used to "configure" your element, but you can use attributes to store data as well.

Attributes are added inside your start tag and contain an attribute name and value pair:

```
<element attributename="value"></element>
```

You can have multiple attributes as well; just make sure you always enclose the values with quotes (""):

```
<element attribute1="value1" attribute2="value2"/>
```

As with element names, attribute names are case sensitive. In other words, the following two elements are not the same:

```
<element Attribute1="value1" Attribute2="value2"></element>
<element attribute1="value1" attribute2="value2"></element>
```

Although this may or may not be valid XML depending on the schema, `Attribute1` and `attribute1` are not the same attribute.

Namespaces

Namespaces in XML ensure that multiple element names are not in conflict. If you have multiple elements with the same name but different meanings, you couldn't validate the XML document without some way to separate the similar elements.

Take a look at this example:

```
<book>
 <author>
  <name>Bjørn Christoffer Thorsmæhlum Furuknap</name>
  <title>Senior Solutions Architect</title>
 </author>
 <chapter number="1">
  <title>Checking Your Gear for Departure</title>
 </chapter>
</book>
```

Notice the two `title` elements. Having two `title` tags presents a problem in addressing the right `title` tag. You can solve this problem by prefixing elements that belong to a certain data group. Take a look at this improved example:

```
<book>
 <author>
  <a:name>Bjørn Christoffer Thorsmæhlum Furuknap</a:name>
  <a:title>Senior Solutions Architect</a:title>
 </author>
 <chapter number="1">
  <c:title>Checking Your Gear for Departure</c:title>
 </chapter>
</book>
```

Now, rather than just having `title` as the element name, you have `a:title` for the author title and `c:title` as the chapter title.

Each of the prefixes `a` and `c` is tied to a namespace. The good thing is that it's simple to define these namespaces and the connected prefix. To get a namespace and tie it to a prefix, you add an attribute to the element or an ancestor element where you intend to use the prefix:

```
<book xmlns:a="http://understandingsharepoint.com/userexperience/author"
      xmlns:c="http://understandingsharepoint.com/userexperience/chapter">
...
</book>
```

The format of the namespace declaration is quite simple but can be confusing, especially since there seems to be a URL in there.

The first part, `xmlns`, is just to say that this is a namespace declaration. The second part, separated from `xml` by a colon, states which prefix you will be using. The third part is the name of the namespace and has nothing to do with the web address it resembles. You might as well have written this:

```
<book xmlns:a="http://Randomtext.com/Author"
      xmlns:c="http://ThisIsAnotherRandomText.com/Chapter">
...
</book>
```

As long as the namespace name is a URI (or an empty string, which rarely makes sense), you should be OK.

You can add the namespace declaration to any element that is an ancestor to the element using the namespace, but you can even define the namespace on the element itself. All the following are valid declarations of namespaces for the a prefix:

```
<book xmlns:a="http://understandingsharepoint.com/userexperience/author">
 <author><a:name>Bjørn Christoffer Thorsmæhlum Furuknap</a:name></author>
</book>
```

```
<book>
 <author xmlns:a="http://understandingsharepoint.com/userexperience/author">
  <a:name>Bjørn Christoffer Thorsmæhlum Furuknap</a:name>
 </author>
</book>
```

```
<book>
```

```
<author>
  <a:name xmlns:a="http://understandingsharepoint.com/userexperience/author">
  Bjørn Christoffer Thorsmæhlum Furuknap
  </a:name>
 </author>
</book>
```

Storing Markup in Markup

There is a problem, though. What happens if you want to store other markup, such as HTML, inside an XML document? You could translate the markup < and > into < and >, respectively, before you store the data, but that gets you only part of the way. What about storing a binary file over which you have no control? A C# method function might contain < and > as comparison operators. Consider the following C# method that you might want to store:

```
<Method Name="IsInRange">
public bool IsInRange(int min, int max, int value)
{
    if (value < max && value > min)
    {
        return true;
    }
    else
    {
        return false;
    }

}
</Method>
```

Storing the method in an XML document will lead the XML parser to recognize an XML start tag, <max && min>, which is neither valid XML nor has a matching end tag. The result is that the parser will croak.

The solution comes in the form of a strangely formatted element called CDATA, short for *character data*. What the CDATA element does is turn off parsing of content as XML.

The format of the CDATA element is as such:

```
<![CDATA[content]]>
```

in which *content* is what should not be parsed as XML.

You can add line breaks, more XML, other markup, binary data, or generally whatever you like, as long as it does not contain the sequence]]>.

To store your C# method, you would do something like this:

```
<Method Name="IsInRange">
<![CDATA[
public bool IsInRange(int min, int max, int value)
{
    if (value < max && value > min)
```

```
    {
        return true;
    }
    else
    {
        return false;
    }


}
]]>
</Method>
```

You may actually find yourself in the position where you need to store]]> as part of the CDATA element. What if you wanted to store the entire Method element shown previously inside another XML element, for instance, to show as an example in a book?

To store a CDATA element inside another CDATA element, you should just split the final]]> sequence into two CDATA elements, right before the final >:

```
<Example>
 <![CDATA[
<Method Name="IsInRange">
<![CDATA[
public bool IsInRange(int min, int max, int value)
{
    if (value < max && value > min)
    {
        return true;
    }
    else
    {
        return false;
    }


}
]]]]><![CDATA[>]]>
</Method>
</Example>
```

The magic happens in the line]]]]><![CDATA[>]]>. If you break it down, you will see that the first two characters,]], are the beginning of the end of the inner CDATA element. Then you finish the first and outer CDATA element with the]]> sequence before you start a completely new CDATA element to hold the final > of the inner CDATA element.

Voilà! You have a valid XML element containing another CDATA element. You might also have a headache.

Despite all these syntax rules and possibilities, you still have no way of knowing what you should put into the XML document. For that we turn to…

XML Validation

There is a difference between having a *well-formed* XML document and having a *valid* XML document. This relates to the issue of the XML schema. A *schema* defines how an XML document should be built—no, not which program is used to create the file but what it contains.

There are two "competing" standards for defining an XML document schema, DTD and XSD.

As I mentioned earlier, I won't be covering DTDs in this book. Simply put, I find DTDs to be more restrictive, and not in the good way, and less powerful than XSD. Also, since Share-Point uses XSD for the CAML schema, focus should be on XSD.

Note Strictly speaking, you must have a DTD to have a valid XML document.

XSD

An XSD file defines what you are allowed to put into your XML document. Although a schema is not required in order to have a well-formed XML document that adheres to the syntax rules of XML, having a schema means you are able to verify that the document contains what it should and in the correct amount, that is, how many times an element can or must be present. And an XML schema also enables simple data validation such as giving you a boundary for integer values or the valid values in an enumeration.

An XSD schema is just an XML file and nothing more. The XSD file uses a namespace with a prefix of XS and a name of http://www.w3.org/2001/XMLSchema. This, again, has nothing to do the web page at http://www.w3.org/2001/XMLSchema. You might begin to see the confusion here.

The XSD file defines which elements and attributes are allowed in an XML document. A good XSD file will limit the chances of making data structure mistakes in your XML document and can even limit, to some extent, errors in the data. This is accomplished by defining validation rules that are applied to elements and attributes.

The XSD schema file defines which elements are allowed at a certain level in the hierarchy and defines the actual data types that you can use. That's right—not only can you restrict a certain attribute to be a string, but you can ensure that any child elements of an element adhere to strict data formatting rules that you define.

XSD is fun, at least when you have a good schema editor and understand the basics.

The SharePoint XSD

To make heads or tails of this, we will look at how the wss.xsd file is used to validate CAML. Since we will explore a simple feature file in Chapter 3, we'll take a quick look at how a feature is defined in the wss.xsd schema.

First, using Visual Studio or any other XML editor (or even Notepad in a pinch), open the file [12]\TEMPLATE\XML\wss.xsd. If using Visual Studio, you will want to right-click the file and select View Code to see the gory details rather than the pretty visual rendering.

Then, scroll down to around line 683 to find these two lines:

```
<xs:element name="Feature" type="FeatureDefinition">
</xs:element>
```

Tip If you do not find the correct lines at the numbers I specify, search for the string. Microsoft may update these XSD files at times, so your version may be different.

Notice that this looks surprisingly much like XML. As I said earlier, XSD is just XML, nothing more. Now you know you can trust me.

The xs: prefix tells us that this is tied to a namespace. You can verify which namespace it is by looking at the first element in the XSD file, the element named xs:schema; there you will find the attribute xmlns:xs="http://www.w3.org/2001/XMLSchema".

The name element is the element name, go figure, and it tells the schema parser that this is an element. You can also learn from the element element that the name of the element is Feature and that it has a type of FeatureDefinition.

From this information, you can deduce that there at least is the possibility of adding an element named Feature, which should be of type FeatureDefinition from a schema file.

Tip If you are familiar with creating features, element files, or site definitions using Visual Studio, you can find all the root elements of a CAML file as xs:element in the wss.xsd file.

But what does this really tell us? I mean, a feature is way more complex than just being a single element, right?

That is where the type comes in. In XSD, the type attribute refers to one of several data types. These data types include basic types such as strings, integers, dates, and booleans, but you can also define your very own data types.

In the Feature element, we have a type of FeatureDefinition. If you search a bit in the wss.xsd file, you'll find, at around line 654, an element beginning with this:

```
<xs:complexType name="FeatureDefinition">
```

This element again uses the xs prefix but has an element name of complexType. The FeatureDefinition complex type is a data type definition that consists of several attributes and several child elements. You may recognize the attributes from our examination of features.

I'll include some of the lines here for easy reference in case you are reading this book on a bus:

```
<xs:complexType name="FeatureDefinition">
 <xs:all>
  <xs:element name="ElementManifests" type="ElementManifestReferences"➥
```

```
  minOccurs="0" maxOccurs="1" />
 <xs:element name="Properties" type="FeaturePropertyDefinitions"➥
  minOccurs="0" maxOccurs="1" />
 <xs:element name="ActivationDependencies" minOccurs="0"➥
  maxOccurs="1" type="FeatureActivationDependencyDefinitions" />
</xs:all>
<xs:attribute name="Id" type="UniqueIdentifier" use="required" />
<xs:attribute name="Title" type="LocalizableString" />
<xs:attribute name="Description" type="LocalizableString" />
<xs:attribute name="Version" type="FeatureVersion" />
<xs:attribute name="Scope" type="FeatureScope" use="required" />
<xs:attribute name="ReceiverAssembly" type="AssemblyStrongName" />
<xs:attribute name="ReceiverClass" type="AssemblyClass" />
… (snipped for the sake of brevity)
```

Each of these attributes and child elements constitutes the schema we need to validate that our feature adheres to the specification.

The outer element xs:ComplexType means we have a type that comprises other attributes and elements. You can also see the xs:all element, which says that we can include all child elements within the xs:all element.

Each of the child elements inside this xs:all element has a minOccurs attribute and a maxOccurs attribute. Although not required, these attributes define how many times a child element can occur. For the three child elements here, we can have zero or one occurrence of the element, meaning they are all optional but cannot be included more than once.

Note also that each of the child elements has a different type, defined elsewhere in the wss.xsd file. Feel free to look them up to see more examples of how XSD works.

Next we have a set of xs:attribute elements, and, you guessed it, these list which attributes are allowed in the Feature element.

If you are using an XML editor, you can connect your XML document, such as your feature.xml file, to the schema document wss.xsd to get IntelliSense support. I explained how to set this up using Visual Studio in Chapter 1.

Tip There is a wonderful XSD tutorial at http://www.w3schools.com/schema/ that explains far more details than I can fit here.

CAML

So, what if you want to lead the CAML to the water *and* make it drink? CAML is what I referred to earlier as an XML *dialect*. Dialects are implementations of XML and, simply put, are just a set of references and schemas to define how to create an XML document that will be used in a certain fashion. But there is more to CAML than just XML documents.

The truth is, any use of the start-tag/end-tag notation that adheres to the XML syntax rules can be considered XML. The implementation is not just limited to XML documents. In SharePoint, for instance, you would use a CAML string to retrieve data from an SPQuery object:

```
SPQuery query = new SPQuery();
query.Query = @"<Where><Eq><FieldRef Name='Title'/><Value Type='Text'>➥
                My title</Value></Eq></Where>";
SPListItemCollection items = list.GetItems(query);
```

Even though there is no XML declaration, this is XML all the same. This means you have the best of both worlds. First you have the rigidity and strong typing of an XML document, supported by a good editor. Then you can pull only the parts you need when you use XML in other forms, such as in a CAML query in an SPQuery object.

Of course, this can be a bit cumbersome. Writing the CAML by hand without validation tool support can be a nasty experience, especially for more complex queries. This is where tools come into play. Normally I do not recommend any particular tools, because I think you should find the tools you like and learn them. However, since authoring CAML can be frustrating, I'll mention a few of these tools now that we are in the desert. (Get it? Desert? Lots of CAMLs? Oh, I crack myself up.)

■ **Note** We will dive into CAML details throughout the book. And I mean *deep* dive. Think scuba gear.

CAML.net

I don't believe I am alone when I say that I hate writing HTML code by hand. Writing XML is even worse, especially if you have no IntelliSense to help you get things right. Unless you have Forrest Gump tendencies, you will have serious problems keeping track of all the elements, nesting tags, syntax, and field type references. Doing so inside a string is likely to make your head implode.

The first tool I want to mention is John Holiday's CAML.net. CAML.net is a free tool available from CodePlex. You can download it at http://www.codeplex.com/camldotnet. Feel free to mention Mr. Holiday in your prayers for his wonderful contribution to your CAML authoring sanity.

What this tool does is…let me rephrase that a bit. CAML.net is an assembly—a DLL, nothing less—that you reference in your project. When you do, you get to use the wonderful class

CAML, which takes much of the pain of writing CAML code out of the equation. For example, the following:

```
query.Query = @"<Where><Eq><FieldRef Name='Title'/><Value Type='Text'>➡
            My title</Value></Eq></Where>";
```

magically turns into this:

```
query.Query =
    CAML.Where(
        CAML.Eq(
            CAML.FieldRef("Title"),
            CAML.Value("Text", "My title")
        )
    );
```

which is a lot easier to read, not to mention easier to write.

Suddenly you have strong typing for inline CAML code, including IntelliSense support. Your days of misspelling queries or forgetting an ending tag in a complex query are over.

This is all good, but it doesn't really give you anything unless you know the CAML query in advance. As you will see in later chapters, defining views can be a bit complex. Having a tool to help us create the views would be great.

U2U CAML Query Builder Solution

U2U CAML Query Builder, or CQB for short, is a SharePoint add-in that allows you to get the CAML query of a view. The solution adds a custom action to the Actions menu on every list in your site collection. The custom action leads to an application page that contains the functionality of the solution.

Note Custom actions will be covered in Chapter 5.

You define the view almost as you would define any other view in the web interface. Then CQB displays the CAML code for the view for you to use in your code.

CQB even allows you to create C# and VB .NET code for the view, including a wrapper class that you can plug into your class. Figure 2-1 shows an example of how the CQB can create CAML queries for you.

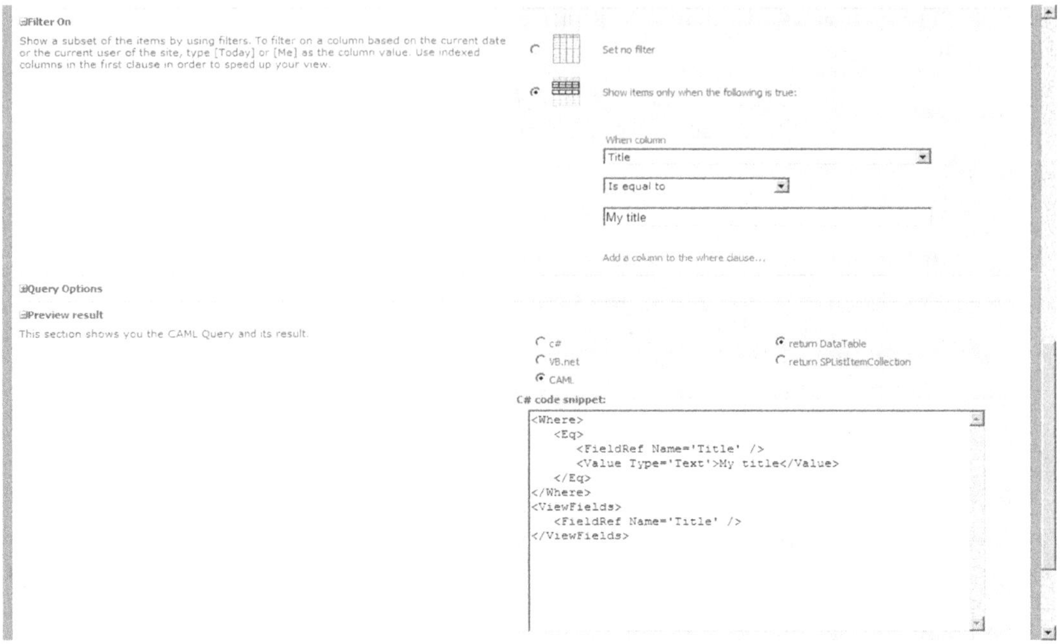

Figure 2-1. *U2U CAML Query Builder query result*

Going from CAML to CAML.net is trivial if you prefer to work with an object model approach.

U2U CAML Query Builder is a nagware tool, available from `http://www.u2u.net`. However, registration is just €10.

U2U also has a powerful Windows version of its Query Builder tool available from the same site. It's even more flexible but lacks the SharePoint integration, so I will hide behind my statement of not focusing too much on tools and instead leave the exploration to you.

XSLT

There is another technology that you might want to investigate, and I'll tell you why in a moment. Extensible Stylesheet Language Transformations (XSLT) is used to convert XML into something else. XML by itself is about as useful as square wheels, so most of the time you'll actually want XML to be something other than XML.

XSLT enters the scene and answers all our prayers. And, if you don't pray, it will still be very helpful. Basically, XSLT is an XML-based language, just like XSD, that tells an XSLT processor how to convert your XML to another language.

Now, XSLT is a somewhat complex language. First, there are two main versions, 1.0 and 2.0. Second, there are numerous XSLT processors, and each varies slightly in how they interpret the standards. Third, XSLT requires a different method of thinking than your regular run-of-the-mill parse-from-the-top thinking to which you might have become accustomed.

For example, XSLT relies heavily on the notion of templates to transform XML. Templates are called from anywhere in the XSLT file, whenever a certain element is matched in the XML file. This means you will need to think more like an event-driven parser.

XSLT is somewhat important to SharePoint version 3 in that the DataForm web part relies on using XSLT to transform XML from a query into HTML for display. If you want to manipulate the DataForm web part results, learning XSLT is an absolute must.

However, there is an even more important reason why you should learn XSLT. Starting with the next version of SharePoint, XSLT will replace CAML as the main rendering language for views. CAML will still be used extensively in other areas of SharePoint, but view rendering will change. And, even though the next version of SharePoint will support XSLT to a much greater extent, SharePoint 3 still relies on CAML. Chapter 7 deals with CAML as a rendering language and is thus useful if you plan on working with SharePoint 3.

If you want to learn more about XSLT, I recommend the book *Beginning XSLT: From Novice to Professional* by Jeni Tennison (Apress, 2005). You can also stop by http://www.understandingsharepoint.com/training for a six-part introduction course to XSLT.

</Thoughts>

Although this chapter was nowhere near a complete examination of XML, I do hope you have at least gotten a glimpse of what XML can do. And that is nothing, really, since you need to do all the hard work yourself, or at least use a decent XML parser.

However, basic knowledge of XML is vital to understanding CAML—and understand CAML you must if you are to have any chance of surviving our journey. If you have read this chapter from start to finish, you should have all the knowledge you need to both read and explore the different CAML files used later in the book.

If you want to explore XML further, I suggest picking up a copy of *XML by Example (2nd Edition)* by Benoit Marchal (Que, 2001), or check out the resources available at W3Schools.com. Keep in mind that although XML at the level on which we have used it so far is useful, becoming an XML guru is almost as daunting a task as learning SharePoint.

CHAPTER 3

∎∎∎

Exploring Feature Basics and Not-So Basics

Getting Down with the Feature Framework of SharePoint

Listen carefully. I shall say this only once…well, I will probably repeat myself endlessly during the course of this book, but I will say it now anyway: use features as much as possible.

There! Said and done. And now you are probably expecting an explanation. OK, I will give you one later, but first let's take a look at what's in store for this chapter.

This chapter will show you several aspects of the SharePoint feature framework and make sure we are on a level playing field regarding features. You will learn the basics and a few more advanced techniques of authoring features, and then, oh yes, I will tell you exactly why I think features are more important than water in a desert.

We need to have a starting point for our feature bonanza, so let's start with something simple.

Creating a Basic Feature in Visual Studio

Creating a feature from scratch is not just a good learning experience; it is downright required in some cases. If you are using tools such as WSPBuilder, Visual Studio Extensions for WSS, or STSDEV, you may be tempted to skip this section. Fine, go ahead, but don't blame me the day you are given a third-party feature that has an error and you need to debug the files by hand.

If, on the other hand, you choose to use tools only because you have created so many features by hand that you have worn out the F, E, A, T, U, and R keys on your keyboard, feel free to skip ahead and blame whomever you want.

Later in this book I may ask you to create a feature and add something to the elements file. When I say that, here's what I want you to do:

1. Create a new project in Visual Studio. I prefer using the class library project since I can attach deployment to the Build actions and then just hit Build to deploy the feature.

2. Add a new folder to the project, and call it Feature. Then add a subfolder to the Feature folder, and give it a name you like, such as MyFeature. The MyFeature folder will become the feature folder. The reason we add this folder structure is that we will automate copying our feature files into the [12]\TEMPLATE\FEATURES folder.

3. Add a new text file to the project, and rename it to setup.bat. We will put our deployment code in this file and run it whenever we build the solution.

4. Open the project properties, and go to the Build Events tab. In the post-build events, enter the following:

```
cd $(ProjectDir)
setup.bat
```

This will automatically run setup.bat when we build our solution.

5. Open the setup.bat file, and enter the following:

```
@SET FEATURES="c:\Program Files\Common Files\Microsoft Shared\➡
web server extensions\12\TEMPLATE\FEATURES"
@SET FEATURENAME=[Your feature name]
@SET STSADMEXE="c:\Program Files\Common Files\Microsoft Shared\➡
web server extensions\12\bin\stsadm.exe"
%STSADMEXE% -o deactivatefeature –name %FEATURENAME%-url http://localhost/
%STSADMEXE% -o uninstallfeature –name  %FEATURENAME%
xcopy Feature /E /Y %FEATUREDIR%
%STSADMEXE% -o installfeature -name  %FEATURENAME%
Rem %STSADMEXE% -o activatefeature –name  %FEATURENAME% –url http://localhost/
```

In the previous code, substitute [Your feature name] in line 3 with the folder name you chose in step 2, and substitute http://localhost/ with the URL of your site. Mine is http://lab-s02:10000/ or http://localhost:10000/.

6. In the MyFeature folder, add an XML file, and name it Feature.xml. Open the file, and add the following code:

```
<Feature   Id="[Create guid]"
           Title="MyFeature"
           Description="My description"
           Version="12.0.0.0"
           Hidden="FALSE"
           Scope="Web"
           DefaultResourceFile="core"
           xmlns="http://schemas.microsoft.com/sharepoint/">
  <ElementManifests>
    <ElementManifest Location="elements.xml"/>
  </ElementManifests>
</Feature>
```

Substitute [Create guid] with a unique GUID. And yes, you can substitute the Title and Description attributes as well.

7. Still in the MyFeature folder, add a new XML file, and name it elements.xml. Add the following code:

```
<Elements xmlns="http://schemas.microsoft.com/sharepoint/">
</Elements>
```

The actual contents of the Elements element will vary, so leave it empty for now.

That's it. Using this feature as a template, you should have few problems when you need to create a feature to test something. Oh, and again, if you use tools, most of this may be unnecessary, but you should still know how to do this by hand if required. Now it is time to learn what you just created.

What Are SharePoint Features?

A SharePoint *feature* is a technical term not to be confused with a feature in the software. Think of a SharePoint feature as a deployable set of content, functionality, files, and so on, that you can activate or deactivate on demand. Think plug-in.

■**Tip** The dual meaning of the term *feature* will be confusing. Prepare yourself.

Site or farm administrators can activate and deactivate these features as they please, thus adding or removing functionality on demand.

The Site Settings page has links for activating site-scoped and web-scoped features. The link for site-scoped feature management, called "Site collection features," is present only on the root site in a site collection. The link for web-scoped feature management, called "Site features," is present on all sites. Figure 3-1 shows both.

Application-scoped features cover all site collections and all sites within a single SharePoint web application, while a *farm-scoped* feature covers everything within a single SharePoint farm. The management of farm-scoped and application-scoped features is done through the Central Administration web site.

Oh, you're wondering what scope means? I'll tell you in a little while.

Figure 3-1. *Feature management links*

A feature usually consists of at least two files located in a folder under the [12]\ TEMPLATE\FEATURES folder. Contrary to popular belief, these files do not need to have special names; only convention states that they should be called feature.xml and elements.xml. So, for ease of reference, I will call these files just that.

The first file, feature.xml, contains the metadata of the feature such as the identifier, title, description, and scope. The second file, elements.xml, contains the content of the feature, such as the list instances, fields, list templates, content types, and so on, that the feature is installing or adding.

Features are activated and deactivated through the web interface. You can also activate or deactivate a feature simply by adding the feature definition to the Features collection of an SPWeb, SPSite, or SPWebApplication:

```
SPWeb web = SPContext.Current.Web;
web.Features.Add([YOUR FEATURE GUID HERE]);
```

This is useful if you want to create your own interface for feature management or activate multiple features at once using a feature event handler. We will use this technique in Part 3 when we create our own site setup experience.

It may seem logical, based on the previous pattern, that to add farm-scoped features you simply add a feature GUID to the SPFarm object. However, the SPFarm object does not have a Features collection. Instead, the Features collection for a farm is located inside to the SPWebService object. For example, to get the farm-scoped features activated for a given site, you might use the following code:

```
SPFeatureCollection features = site.WebApplication.WebService.Features;
```

Although a feature is usually comprised of at least two files, you can in theory have a feature with only a single feature.xml file and no elements file at all. This is useful if you intend to use the mentioned feature event handlers to deploy the actual content of the feature using code.

Note Feature event handlers will be covered in the "Advanced Feature Concepts" section of this chapter.

Now, let's clear up that scope question of yours.

Feature Scope

Features are *scoped*, meaning you can have a feature activated at the farm, web application, site collection, or site level. When a feature is activated at a scope, it also affects subscopes, so if you use a web application–scoped feature to add a custom action somewhere, then every site collection and every site beneath the web application will have the same custom action.

It's a bit confusing, perhaps, but when scoping features, the WSS 2–style names are used. That is, *site* is used for site collections, and *web* is used for web sites. This is very strange, especially since features were introduced in WSS 3 and didn't even exist in WSS 2.

For the sake of being consistent with other information, I will use the WSS 2 names for the scopes, that is, web-scoped, site-scoped, web application–scoped, and farm-scoped.

The scoping of a feature is important, because scoping defines which types of elements can be deployed with a feature. For instance, content types, to be covered more in Chapter 8, make sense only in a site-scoped feature, since content types are stored in the site collection.

This does lead to a bit of a challenge when you want to add a web-scoped list template where you add some custom fields, which are site-scoped. One way to solve this is to have two separate features. You can then use feature activation dependencies to make sure the fields are activated before the list template. You'll learn more about that a bit later in the chapter.

Tip You can find an online table of all feature elements by scope at www.understandingsharepoint.com/url/10025. Or just google *feature elements by scope*.

Advanced Feature Concepts

Although features can be as simple as adding a list or a field, features offer far more bang for the buck than any other SharePoint…feature. I told you it would be confusing.

The following sections contain some slightly more advanced feature topics for your reading pleasure.

Feature Event Handlers

Another powerful feature of features is the ability to add *event handlers* directly to the feature so that you can have code executed when the feature is activated, deactivating, installed, or uninstalling. Note the subtle differences in word stemming. The FeatureActivated event happens asynchronously, while the FeatureDeactivating event is synchronous. The events ending in ed happen after the fact, while the ones ending in ing happen during the fact.

To add an event receiver to your feature, you simply add the `ReceiverAssembly` and `ReceiverClass` properties of your receiver to the `Feature` element in `feature.xml` as such:

```
<Feature  Id="[Create guid]"
          Title="MyFeature"
          ReceiverAssembly="[YOUR STRONG NAME HERE]"
          ReceiverClass="[YOUR CLASS NAME HERE]"
          Description="My description"
          Version="12.0.0.0"
          Hidden="FALSE"
          Scope="Web"
          DefaultResourceFile="core"
          xmlns="http://schemas.microsoft.com/sharepoint/">
```

Your class should inherit from the `SPFeatureReceiver` base class. When writing your class, you have access to the site, site collection, web application, or farm on which the feature is activated or is deactivating through the `properties.Feature.Parent` property. This property returns only an object type, however, so you would need to cast the parent to a class matching the respective scope. For a web-scoped feature (remember, that means it is activated on a site in WSS 3 terms), you could write something like this:

```
public override void FeatureActivated(SPFeatureReceiverProperties properties)
{
  SPWeb web = (SPWeb)properties.Feature.Parent;
}
```

Since you have access to the parent object, you can do virtually anything in the event handler itself, including anything you would normally do in the CAML in the `elements.xml` file such as creating list instances, adding fields or content types, provisioning pages, and so on. In fact, you can usually do plenty more in a feature event handler than you can with a CAML elements file. For example, you can have a feature create subsites or add SharePoint user groups in code, but not in CAML. Creating custom views, however, is one thing you would probably want to do in CAML rather than in code, especially if you are looking to make your views a bit more complex than the default experience.

Feature event handlers are very powerful. As an exercise for yourself, you should try once to do an entire site creation process in code, just to see how the different parts of a site can be created. I will cover the CAML part of site creation in Part 3 of this book and also talk about how you can use code to set up features in a site in Chapter 14.

Feature Activation Dependency

Some features may *depend* on each other. For instance, you may have a feature to deploy a customer list. That list may be useless unless you have activated a customer management interface through another feature.

You may think that you could put these two features into a single feature, and you might be right. Even if separating features is preferable for the sake of flexibility, tightly coupled features might be put together.

There is another problem, however, and that is the problem of scope. If you are going to add a content type–enabled list to a web, you first need to add the content type, which is site-scoped, and then add the list, which is web-scoped. The problem, of course, is that a feature can have only a single scope, so you are forced to have two separate features.

If you have two separate features, both must be activated for the full feature to work properly. And you need to activate the features in a specific order, lest errors be abundant.

But…was it the content type first and then the list, or was it the list first and then the content type? And even if you can cheat and look back now, how about a year from now, or when you hand over the site to a completely new administrator?

Enter `ActivationDependencies`—your ticket to activation chain nirvana. By setting one or more activation dependencies, you can make sure that other features are activated before this feature can be activated:

```
<ActivationDependencies>
  <ActivationDependency FeatureId="CF54600B-0050-4702-BA19-E901653E6FD9"/>
  <ActivationDependency FeatureId="1DF77300-CA9F-4689-BC37-738CD08B6327"/>
</ActivationDependencies>
```

You can have as many or as few activation dependencies as you like, or you can have none at all.

■ **Caution** Avoid circular dependencies, where feature A depends on feature B, which depends on feature C, which depends on feature A. Actually, you might want to try that once, but be warned that it might get messy and you will not be able to activate any of the features.

Resources

Although not strictly a feature-specific technology, *resources* are very useful for creating dynamic user experiences using features. You may already have seen resources in action; whenever you happen upon a string that looks like `$Resources:wss,fldedit_changesitecolumn`, you'll see how resources can be used.

Resources are XML files that contain a key and value mapping, just like a hash table. Because the XML files are separate from the feature or solution, you can change the resource file and thus change which values the keys represent. This is very useful for creating language packs or in any other scenario where you want to have dynamic values.

There are two types of resources: *runtime resources*, which are just normal ASP.NET resources, and *provisioning resources*, used in CAML when provisioning sites, pages, lists, and anything else you would provision outside of ASP.NET. Resource management in ASP.NET is outside the scope of this book, but I'll explain at least the basics of provisioning resources.

To make sure anyone who does not read all the text will be utterly confused, I will from here on refer to provisioning resources only as *resources*.

Resources, despite being seldom used, are actually quite simple. The format of a resource file is just very simple XML. You have a `data` element with a `name` attribute and a child `value` element. In addition, you can have a child `comment` element to ease understanding. All this is stored in a root element, conveniently named `root`. Here is a simple resource file:

```
<?xml version="1.0" encoding="utf-8"?>
<root>
  <data name="MyKey">
    <value>MyValue</value>
  </data>
</root>
```

■ **Note** Because resource files are very well explained in various ASP.NET books and documentation, I will skip explaining all the various authoring steps.

Features can use such files by referencing the resource file and the key directly in the feature CAML code. Remember that $Resources:wss,fldedit_changesitecolumn string we looked at earlier? This string reference has three parts. $Resources states that we will be using a resource reference rather than a regular string, wss is the first part of the resource file name (such as wss in wss.resx), and fldedit_changesitecolumn is the key name to use.

If you have defined a default resource file, you need not include the file name part of the resource reference, so you can just use $Resources:keyname in your CAML file.

Placing resources is also important. You can place resources either in the feature itself or in the [12]\Resources folder. If you place your resources in the feature folder, as we will do in a short exercise in a moment, name the resource file Resources.resx, and set the DefaultResourceFile to _Res to be able to omit the file name part of the resource name.

The true beauty of resources is perhaps in the automatic handling of multiple language localizations. By adding .resx files with the culture between the file name and .resx, Share-Point will automatically use the localized version of the resource file. For instance, if you want to have localized strings for US English and the two Norwegian languages Bokmål and Nynorsk, you could add the resource files listed in Table 3-1 to your feature.

Table 3-1. *Sample Resources Files and Cultures*

File Name	Culture	Description
Resources.resx	None/default	Default file used if no culture defined
Resources.en-US.resx	en-US	US English
Resources.nb-no.resx	nb-no	Norwegian Bokmål
Resources.nn-no.resx	nn-no	Norwegian Nynorsk

■ **Note** Yeah, Norway has two languages. Actually, we have four. That is almost one language per person. In addition, everyone learns at least two foreign languages and understands every Scandinavian language. Chances are, if you are in Norway and speak your native tongue, people will understand.

To test all this, follow this procedure:

1. Create a blank feature, as explained in the first section of this chapter.

2. In your MyFeature folder, create a folder called Resources, and in that folder create a new resource file called Resources.resx.

3. Open your Resource.resx file, and add the two keys and values shown in Table 3-2.

Table 3-2. *Resource File Keys and Values*

Key	Value
featuredescription	Description from resource
featuretitle	Title from resource

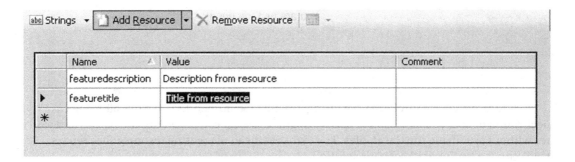

4. In your feature.xml file, modify the Description attribute to $Resources: featuredescription; and your Title attribute to $Resources:featuretitle;. Modify your DefaultResourceFile attribute to _Res. Your feature element should now look like this:

```
<Feature  Id="[Create guid]"
          Title="$Resources:featuretitle;"
          Description="$Resources:featuredescription;"
          Version="12.0.0.0"
          Hidden="FALSE"
          Scope="Web"
          DefaultResourceFile="_Res"
          xmlns="http://schemas.microsoft.com/sharepoint/"/>
```

For this example, don't worry about the lack of an elements file. We won't actually deploy anything; we're just checking that our resources are used properly.

5. Build and deploy your feature. If you followed the recipe in the beginning, this should be as easy as hitting Build in Visual Studio.

6. Verify on the Site Features page of a site that your feature now retrieves its title and description from the resource file.

Using resources to provision your string is highly recommended. Besides allowing easy localization of text, you can also very easily upgrade resource files and update names and values without modifying the CAML files. The extra overhead of creating resource files repays itself after the first upgrade of your solution.

Strong buy!

Tip Never take stock tips from me.

Feature Stapling

Features can be activated through the web interface or through code, but we also have another powerful option called *feature stapling*.

Feature stapling allows you to add a feature to an already existing site definition. You may think this would be a complete waste of time, because you can simply add the feature into the site definition using far less code than having a feature staple, but when I tell you that Microsoft does not support modifying a site definition in any way after a single site has been provisioned from that site template, you may reconsider.

That's right, folks. Write up a fancy site definition, like we will later in the book, and once you have created even a single site from that site definition, Microsoft will refuse to support your solution if you modify a single bit of that definition. So don't—at least not in production environments.

So, what if you made a mistake and forgot to add a feature or you create a "golden goose" feature that you desperately need in all of your sites? Well, you can always manually activate the feature for all sites. It would just take 30 seconds per site, and with only 10,000 sites that would not set you back more than, oh, the better part of a month?

Or, you could turn to *feature stapling*. Feature stapling will be discussed in more detail in Chapter 5 when we investigate how to modify the default user experience, but in short, feature stapling allows you to attach a new feature to an existing site definition without modifying the site definition at all.

Combine this with good resource usage, and you can actually do quite a bit of modifying the site definition without breaking your supportability.

■ **Note** Feature stapling will be discussed more in Chapter 5, but you need some more knowledge before exploring the details. Keep reading—your patience will be rewarded.

Site Definitions vs. Features

There are two dominant schools of thought when it comes to features and site definitions.

It all comes down to what you put into your site definitions, really. Site definitions are the core building block of new sites; they define the content that will be present when you create a new site. You can add stuff such as lists, libraries, views, pages, folders, and data using nothing but site definitions. In fact, until WSS 3 came along, everything revolved around creating site definitions, because the feature framework did not exist.

That has all changed since the introduction of the feature framework in WSS 3, and we should embrace the change, but as I said, there are two schools of thought on how far that embracing should go. Do we just pat each other on the back to recognize each other's existence, or should we go all in and French kiss on the first date?

First there are those who think that features are cool, but you can do most of what you want in a site definition. Rather than having to maintain perhaps as much as 20 rather similar features to create different sites, you can put the common denominators in a site definition and save yourself time.

This makes sense if you create one-off sites that are basically similar every time. Consider a specific legal document tracking solution in which all the required functionality is set in stone once the site is created. Why would you want to create features that need to be activated after the site has been created? Even if you could automatically activate the features when the site is created, all you accomplish by moving everything into features is overhead to account for a situation that will never happen.

Reuse is good, and features provide good reuse facilities, but if your requirements are specific enough, chances are your reuse will be limited or nonexistent. And even allowing features to be added could be a problem, since features can modify existing functionality, and in a solution where trackability and accountability is paramount, modifying how data works or is stored is not a good thing.

If you should find out you were wrong to abandon features from the beginning, it is possible to use feature stapling to add a feature to an already existing site definition. Any new site will automatically have your new feature added, and you can always activate features manually for the sites already provisioned.

Then there are those who say that the best site definition is an empty site definition—empty as in absolutely nothing...no pages, no lists, no features, no nothing. Then, use features to put together the site you want, including adding master pages, lists, libraries, and so forth, only after the basic site has been created.

I tend to lean toward the latter method. Features are much more powerful and flexible than site definitions. You can do pretty much everything you can in site definitions using a feature, and what you can't do directly in a feature can always be done using a `FeatureActivated` event receiver.

In theory, you could have a single feature activate everything you need for a site, including adding subsites, activating other features, dynamically creating data, and so on. You'd lose the benefit of features, however, since one of the most important reasons to use features is to have granular control over what gets added. You would basically be back at the site definition level.

What most people of the "simple site definition" camp seem to champion is that features should add only what you need. Add a list template as a feature, but add the list instance based on that template as a separate feature. This makes sense from a granularity point of view but means you would have to activate a whole lot of features to get some basic functionality going.

You could balance the two approaches and have "packs" of features. For instance, create a "publishing pack" to add the lists, templates, pages, and content types you need to create functionality for a publishing site. This is what Microsoft does in essence in MOSS. That's fine if you want the whole pack, but it's not so fine if all you really want is a useful content type or a page from that pack.

My point here is that you need to weigh the benefits of granularity against the overhead of creating multiple features. There is no clear-cut answer that works in every situation, and the debate of what is better—having multiple features, feature packs, or just sites—is rather pointless from a general point of view. Your best approach is to evaluate the needs of the solution and not be overly religious about one particular point of view.

Featured Finale

Features are cool, features are great, love your features, use them as much as possible.

It may seem strange to recommend building your entire solution based on something that is little more than a plug-in to an existing architecture. However, keep in mind that SharePoint is an evolving technology. The `Feature` is a great new addition to the version 3 editions of SharePoint; it provides us with a great option for building scalable solutions far better than what was possible in previous versions of SharePoint.

Now that we have gone through this rather short introduction to some basic topics of SharePoint development, it is time to shift focus. Going forward, we will be spending most of our time with the user experience in mind. We want to explore how sites are built and what opportunities await us.

Oh, and there will be dragons and monsters.

PART 2

Dissecting the Default User Experience

∎ ∎ ∎

CHAPTER 4

Excavating the Site
Overview of the Default SharePoint Interface from a Technical Point of View

As our journey to the center of the user experience begins, you'll get an overview of the area we are about to explore. The odd bit here is that we actually create the land to explore ourselves. We do that on a very high level at first, so in order to understand what actually happens during the process, you need to pay attention.

In this chapter, we will start exploring the different aspects of that site and see how and where these elements are defined.

So, without further ado, let's get started.

The Plan for Exploration

The story begins with a little boy named Frank, who wanted nothing more than a new bike for Christmas. Why he wanted a bike in the middle of the winter is beyond me, but Frank dreamed of nothing but riding his new bike down the snowy streets of his hometown.

Oh, sorry, wrong story. Never mind, here's the right one: Figure 4-1 shows you the sights of your journey.

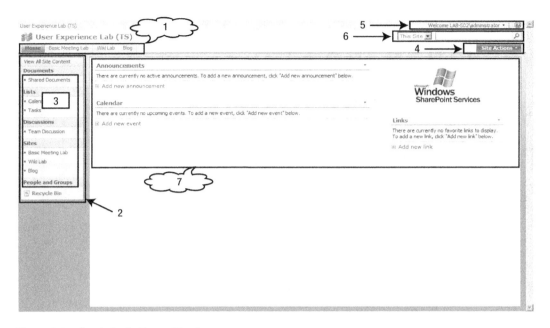

Figure 4-1. *The default Team Site front page*

Of course, no screenshot with annotations is complete without some descriptive text. Figure 4-1 shows the front page of a Team Site, and each of the numbered elements represents a different part of the user interface that you will explore during the course of this book. They are as follows:

1. The top navigation bar

2. The QuickLaunch menu

3. The lists

4. The Site Actions menu

5. The personal actions menu

6. The search area delegate control

7. The content area

The front page is just a single page in the SharePoint site. Other pages, while utilizing many of the visual elements shown here, contain other unique elements. Each page is therefore a separate "map," and I could spend days going over each map and pointing to certain visual elements. I won't do that. Instead, you should try to understand the root elements that constitute a site as we go through the chapter. This will give you a far better chance at understanding the architecture of a site rather than just memorizing the positions of elements. In turn, this means you will be better equipped to create a new site or even just modify an existing site.

If you find yourself unsure of where a certain section of this chapter is leading, just bear with me for a few pages. Chances are that all will become crystal clear very soon.

Mission Objective

Our current mission is easily defined. We are going to look at different aspects of the default sites and investigate where and how the different elements of that site are defined. Although simple enough in theory, as you shall soon see, this task may not be as simple as this description may indicate.

A site consists of several pieces. There are site definitions, lists, content types, fields, forms, custom application pages, style sheets, images, and templates. And that's not even an exhaustive list. What you see on the front page in Figure 4-1 is just a subset of these elements. What you see when you open a new item form is also a subset of elements. In this part of the book, you'll learn what these elements are, how you can find their definitions, and how you can create your own elements to tailor your own customized user experience.

To understand these elements, you need to learn the basics of SharePoint site definitions, lists, master pages, content types, and fields. Here is a short description of each of these elements:

- A *site definition* consists of several files and depends on even more files. At the very least, a site definition will have a `webtemp.xml` XML file and an `onet.xml` XML file. In a site definition you will find the content of a new site. Think of it as an index to what a site should contain.

- *Lists* make up the primary storage facility of SharePoint and arguably are the most important aspect of SharePoint. At its core, a list is no more than a database table on steroids, but it can be as complex as the cure for cancer. Lists contain columns but can also contain other elements to customize the user experience, such as content types and custom list forms to create or maintain data in a list.

- *Master pages* in SharePoint are very much like master pages in ASP.NET, with a few noted exceptions that I will cover later in this chapter. I will assume that you know what a master page does, so besides exploring some of the contents of the default master pages, I will not spend a lot of time on this topic.

- If lists are the most important concept of SharePoint, *content types* are by far the coolest. Basically, a content type is just that, a type of content, such as an article, an item, a document, or just about anything else. Content types encapsulate data, behavior, and visual appearance, and they can have a massive impact on the user experience. I will cover content types in much greater detail in Chapter 8.

- A *field* is the atomic storage unit of SharePoint. Actually, a field is just the template of a column that does the storage. Fields make it possible to customize the user input and visual representation of information, and I will spend quite a lot of time on this in Chapter 9.

Now that you know where you are going, you can pack up your camp, wave goodbye to your loved ones, and start your trip. My name is Bjørn Furuknap, and I will be your guide on this ride. Please keep your hands inside the vehicle at all times, do not feed the wild animals, and remain seated until the book has come to a full and complete stop.

Exploring Site Definitions

So far, this chapter has been fairly straightforward, but now it is time to get serious.

As you have probably figured by now, this book is not about giving you recipes for a quick fix of SharePoint customization. This book does not trust the official documentation. You are not here to read yet another explanation of how to provision a file, although I will cover that later.

You are here to dig—to find the real truth of how SharePoint works. You want to see solid proof; you want to expose every flaw or implementation mistake. It is time to take your understanding of the SharePoint user experience to the extreme.

The [12] Hive TEMPLATE Folder

Most of what defines the user experience resides in the TEMPLATE folder of the [12] hive (see Figure 4-2). Within that folder lies a wealth of customization options, but there are also lethal traps, so you need to know where to step.

■ **Tip**   The 12 hive, usually located at C:\Program Files\Common Files\Microsoft Shared\ web server extensions\12, is referred to as [12] in this book.

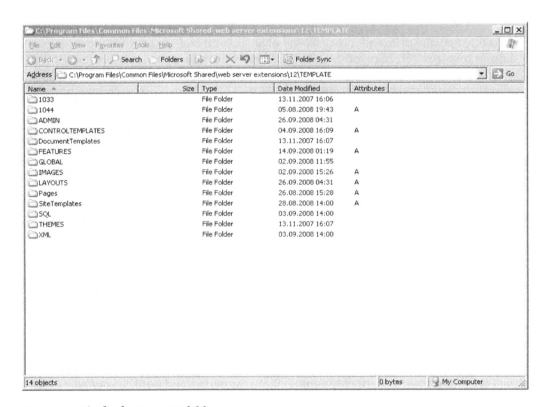

Figure 4-2. *The* [12]\TEMPLATE *folder*

You may notice that the folders in Figure 4-2 include a folder named 1044, which may not be present in your [12]\TEMPLATE. That 1044 folder contains site template information for a language pack, which in this case is the Norwegian language pack. The number 1044 is the locale identifier (LCID). 1033 is the LCID of English, and you may have other folders that represent the LCID of the language packs you have installed.

More to the point, the LCID-related folders contain three subfolders out of the box, called STS, Workflow, and XML. For now, you want to go into the XML folder to find the starting point of your site exploration, the webtemp.xml file.

Note The STS folder and the Workflow folder contain templates for documents and some workflow definitions, including the actions for editors such as SharePoint Designer. I will not cover these subfolders in this book.

---

webtemp.xml

The webtemp.xml file, located in the [12]\TEMPLATE\[1033]\XML directory, is the default site template file that ships with WSS. When you develop your own site later in this book, you will create your own webtemp.xml file, and if you install third-party site definitions, these will typically also create their own webtemp.xml files. These extra webtemp.xml files will be named webtempXXXXX.xml, where XXXXX is anything you like. SharePoint searches for anything beginning with webtemp and ending in .xml to find web templates.

Caution If you care about getting support from Microsoft, do not modify the webtemp.xml template that comes with SharePoint. The only thing you are allowed to change is the Hidden attribute of Configuration elements. If you don't care about supportability, go bananas, and do what you want.

Just one more thing...

Caution The previous caution applies to all files that ship with SharePoint. With the noted exception of the Hidden attribute, Microsoft will refuse to help you if you modify any included file in any fashion.

...and I nearly forgot:

Caution Oh, who am I kidding? You are a developer; you thrive on breaking things to find out how they work. Just don't tell anyone what you do on your unsupported lab environment, and you can go bananas and modify anything you like. Seriously, though, there is a very good reason why you do not want to mess up the files that ship with SharePoint in a production environment. At any time, as part of a product upgrade, patch, or service pack, Microsoft may choose to overwrite any file that ships with SharePoint. If you have made modifications to those files, you'll lose your changes.

Open the default `webtemp.xml` file in your XML editor now. Depending on your LCID, you should see something along the lines of Figure 4-3.

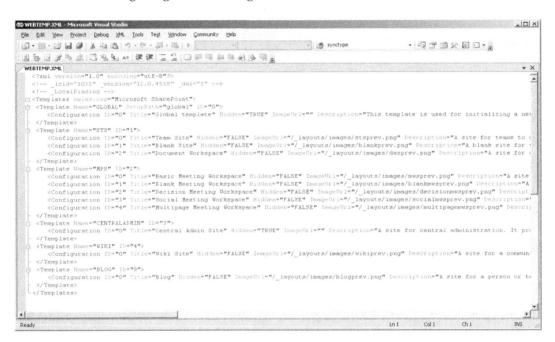

Figure 4-3. *Default* `webtemp.xml`

As you can see, `webtemp.xml` contains only `Template` elements that in turn contain `Configuration` elements. Each of these configurations is a site definition. When you used the Team Site, Basic Meeting Workspace, Wiki, and Blog site definitions in earlier chapters, SharePoint found these site definitions in this file.

There is some confusion about terminology when it comes to site templates and site definitions. Basically, a *site template* is made by selecting the Save Site As Template option of the Site Settings page and is thus based on an existing and customized site. A *site definition*, by contrast, is the original definition of a site. If you compare the two to programming, think of a site definition as the class and the site template as the object, in other words, an instance of the class.

To make this even more confusing, the `Template` element of a `webtemp.xml` file has nothing to do with site templates but is rather a *site type,* for instance, a team site (STS), a meeting site

(MPS), or any number of custom types. The types do not follow any particular pattern, so you can create your own types by just setting the name of one of the Template elements. Yes, this is confusing.

When you want to reference a specific template (for example, if you want to programmatically create a new site), you need to use both the template name and the configuration ID and separate them with a number sign (#). The full reference for a Basic Meeting Workspace is MPS#0, which is the parameter you need to pass to a method in code:

```
SPWeb newWeb = web.Webs.Add("NewMeetingSite",➥
 "My Basic Meeting Workspace", "My description", 1033, "MPS#0", false, false);
```

You can hide a specific configuration by setting the Hidden attribute to True. This means the configuration will not appear in the default web interface. You can still create sites based on the configuration by using code or when you create your own site creation web interface. For example, you might want to do this when you want only certain site definitions to be available to users when they are creating new sites.

Setting the Hidden attribute is also the only modification that Microsoft allows without breaking supportability. If you intend to modify the file, at least make a backup and name it something other than webtempXXXXX.xml so that if you need support from Microsoft, you can restore the original file quickly.

Besides Hidden, the other attributes of the Configuration elements in the default webtemp.xml file, the Title, ImageUrl, and Description, should be rather self-explanatory, but several attributes of the Configuration elements are both useful and powerful. One of them, DisplayCategory, is used in the default webtemp.xml file configurations.

If you look toward the end of each Configuration element in Figure 4-3, you will see the DisplayCategory attribute. This attribute determines under which tab of the "Select a template" tabs the site definition should appear (see Figure 4-4).

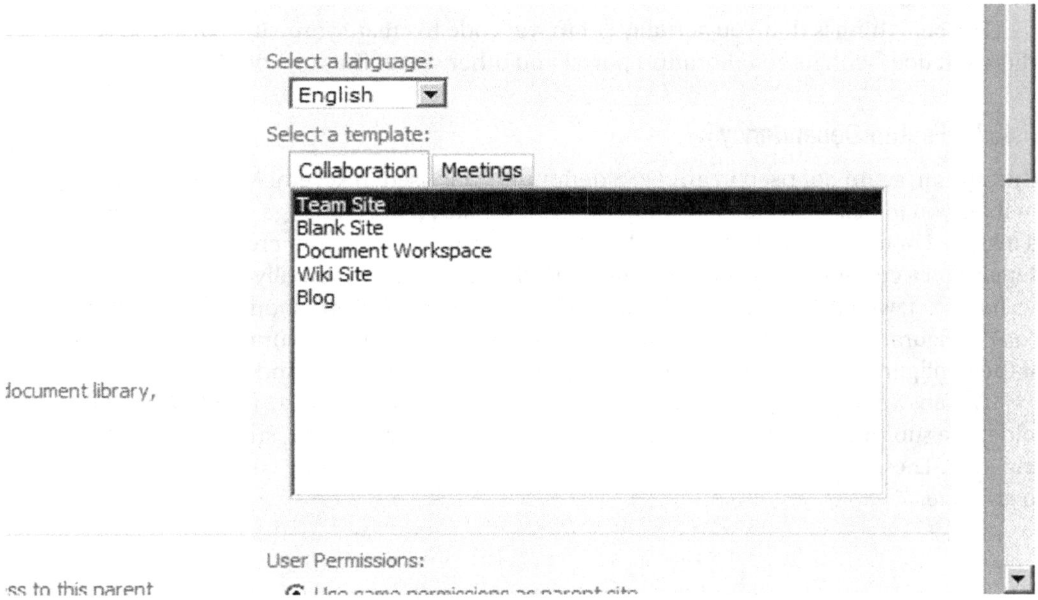

Figure 4-4. *Creating a new SharePoint site page*

The DisplayCategory values are arbitrary names that you can either create or modify by just changing the value. If you change the value, the site template will move to the new tab, and if the new tab does not exist, then SharePoint will create it for you.

Note If you use the Save Site As Template option of the Site Settings page to create a site template, SharePoint puts your saved template under the Custom tab.

Some attributes of the Configuration elements are not used in any WSS site definitions; they're used in some MOSS definitions, so if you have access to a MOSS site, you can see the attributes in action there. I do want to point out the general usage of these attributes here and provide a few sample scenarios.

ProvisionAssembly, ProvisionClass, and ProvisionData

If you have ever created a MOSS collaboration portal, you may have been puzzled that this actually results in multiple sites created from a single site definition. If you are as adventurous as me, you may even have dug into the webtempsps.xml file to see what happens. What you would have found is that the SPSPORTAL type (template, which isn't a template) and its child Configuration element sets ProvisionAssembly, ProvisionClass, and ProvisionData.

So, what do these attributes do? The short answer is that they create your site. The longer answer is that rather than going to an onet.xml file, which I will cover shortly, to find configuration information from the site, setting ProvisionAssembly and ProvisionClass will cause SharePoint to run that class from that assembly for the provisioning of your site. ProvisionData is just an additional and optional value that you can use to store data for the provisioning.

The cool thing is that you actually get to run code to create your site—or sites, as Microsoft does with its collaboration portal and other site definitions of MOSS.

VisibilityFeatureDependency

This option, again not used in any WSS definitions but used in several MOSS definitions, enables you to display a site definition in the new SharePoint site page only if a certain feature is installed or activated. This means that you can prevent users from creating new sites that depend on a certain feature being installed until that feature is actually available. Now that we have reviewed the webtemp.xml configurations, a few questions should pop into your mind. The configuration section of the default webtemp.xml file is rather minimal, so where is the rest of the configuration? Where are all the lists, the views, the features, and the content?

The answer to that question lies in the SiteTemplates folder of [12]\TEMPLATE. In that folder are subfolders that match the template names in webtemp.xml, such as STS, MPS, Blog, and Wiki. These folders hold the actual content of the site definition, so your next step will be to go there.

onet.xml

Open the STS folder under [12]\TEMPLATE\SiteTemplates. You should see two files and an XML folder. Open the XML folder and then the onet.xml file. In Figure 4-5, I have closed the second-level elements to give you a better overview of the onet.xml file.

```
<?xml version="1.0" encoding="utf-8"?>
<Project xmlns="http://schemas.microsoft.com/sharepoint/"
         Title="$Resources:onet_TeamWebSite;"
         Revision="2"
         ListDir="$Resources:core,lists_Folder;"
         xmlns:ows="Microsoft SharePoint">
  <!-- _locID@Title="camlidonet1" _locComment="{StringCategory=HTX}" -->
  <NavBars>...
  <ListTemplates>...
  <DocumentTemplates>...
  <Configurations>...
  <Modules>...
  <ServerEmailFooter>$Resources:ServerEmailFooter;</ServerEmailFooter>
</Project>
```

Figure 4-5. onet.xml

Tip Closing the second-level elements makes the file look a lot less scary.

Now you are getting somewhere. The onet.xml file holds a lot more information about your configurations, although not everything. You need to explore this file in greater detail on your path toward SharePoint enlightenment.

First, however, you need to know how SharePoint finds this file. The rule is that if you create a Template element in a webtemp.xml file, you need to have a folder in the [12]\TEMPLATE\SiteTemplates folder that matches the Name attribute of the Template element, and that folder should contain an XML folder, which in turn should contain an onet.xml file. If you create a Template element called MyDefinition, for example, you need to create a file called [12]\TEMPLATE\SiteTemplates\MyDefinition\XML\onet.xml. Your onet.xml file should contain the main content of your site definition.

Tip I will cover site definitions more in Part 3, but in short, my recommendation is that you should add functionality as features rather than building a site definition so large it will require its own ZIP code. Site definitions can seem like a great idea in the beginning but are tricky and can be very cumbersome.

For now you will focus on exploring the existing STS folder's onet.xml.

Project

The Project element contains some very useful attributes that you can use to modify how pages in a site work. These attributes affect every site configuration of the site, which can be a good thing or a bad thing, depending on what you want to do. I will cover site configurations in a moment, but first it is time to discover a little quirk.

The AlternateCSS attribute is extremely useful for the designers of site layouts and thus important to you as a developer. The AlternateCSS attribute defines an extra CSS style sheet URL that will be included after the default core.css of SharePoint.

This is important, and I'll tell you why. SharePoint includes a method of adding CSS URLs to a master page using the CSSLink and CSSRegistration ASP.NET tags. Your master page should always include a CSSLink tag and will render any CSS URLs added with the CSSRegistration tag. And then CSSLink adds the core.css default style sheet. This means trouble if you want to override styles that reside in core.css, since core.css is always rendered last and thus takes precedence over your own shiny new and beautiful CSS styles.

You could instead use the AlternateCSS method to add a CSS URL to your page, and the AlternateCSS URL will be rendered after the core.css link. Another benefit is that you do not need to modify the master page you have created just to change the CSS styles.

Of course, there are other options for getting a CSS file placed where you want, but AlternateCSS is a valuable tool.

With the explanation of AlternateHeader comes that quirk I mentioned. You see, the wss.xsd file contains an error. The Project element in wss.xsd does not have the AlternateHeader attribute defined at all. In fact, several attributes are missing. In turn, you get another attribute that does not serve any purpose, called AlternateUrl. You will notice this if you try to use IntelliSense to create or modify a Project element. Do not despair, because AlternateHeader works even if you get a validation error in Visual Studio.

But what does it do? Ah, an excellent question. You could check the documentation, and you would be promised that AlternateHeader should be set in order to replace the header of a site page with the contents of any ASPX page residing in the [12]\LAYOUTS\ directory. Sadly, that promise would not be fulfilled. Here's what really happens....

AlternateHeader replaces the top navigation of application pages with an ASPX page of your choice. Yup, just set the AlternateHeader to point to any file in the [12]\LAYOUTS\ [LCID] folder, and poof goes the top navigation bar and in goes your ASPX page of choice. This incredible feat of engineering is accomplished using a call to Server. Execute(alternateHeader) in [12]\TEMPLATE\CONTROLTEMPLATES\TopNavBar.ascx, so in theory you could add other things than ASPX as well. (Yes, I am being ironic when I refer to this as a great or even useful feature!)

■**Note** Pages that reside in the [12]\LAYOUTS directory are often referred to as *application pages*.

I have been working really, really hard to come up with a somewhat useful scenario for this functionality, but frankly, I can't. Actually, it was rather useful in the old version of SharePoint, a.k.a. WSS 2 and SPS 2003, where `AlternateHeader` would replace the whole header of a page, but for some reason Microsoft chose to put the code to run `AlternateHeader` inside a control called `TopNavBar.ascx`.

The only thing I can think of is using it if you create functionality that utilizes this attribute. For instance, you could mimic the `TopNavBar.ascx` functionality but expand the scope to include both regular pages and probably a wider area than just navigation. That way, you could use a single master page and customize the header by changing only the site definition.

But then again, that would be a very corny way of accomplishing a rather trivial task. Not just that, but changing the site definition after any site has been created from that site definition is not supported, so this would be possible only when you first create your site definition. I vote to place `AlternateHeader` very high on the "least useful" list of SharePoint features. It may have been a great idea in theory, but it's definitely not so great in practice.

`CustomJSUrl`, on the other hand, can be quite useful and should hold the URL of a JavaScript file. There is an ASP.NET tag that is present in all default master pages called `CustomJSUrl` that will render a script tag that adds the value of the `CustomJSUrl` attribute to the page. If you want to add custom JavaScript to a master page and use a site definition to control which script file should be used, then `CustomJSUrl` is the way to go.

Note `CustomJSUrl` is not present in the `wss.xsd` file either, so it will not show up in IntelliSense. Oh, bother....

I have a strange hobby: I taunt designers. Now, it's not nasty bullying or anything bad like that; it's just some gentle encouragement that they should start doing actual development rather than drawing pretty pictures in Photoshop all the time.

If I am unable to taunt my designer (or when they get fed up with my kind and loving suggestions), I turn to `DisableWebDesignFeatures`. `DisableWebDesignFeatures` allows you to specify several features that will be disabled when editing a site using tools such as SharePoint Designer. For instance, I can set `DisableWebDesignFeatures` to `wdfopensite`, which will give anyone trying to access the site with SharePoint Designer a nice message that they cannot gain access (see Figure 4-6).

You can set various limitations, and you can set more than one at a time by separating each value with a semicolon. The names and documentation available from MSDN (`http://www.understandingsharepoint.com/url/10027`) or the SDK are quite good, so I will just refer you to those; however, note that this can be a very useful feature for users, perhaps more from a security perspective than from a user experience perspective.

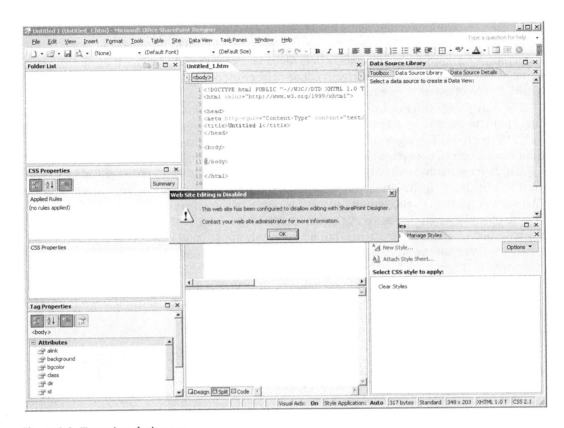

Figure 4-6. *Taunting designers*

The ListDir attribute defines where new lists get created. Usually this is for lists for English sites, but the value is actually set from a resource value. In any case, this is of little relevance to the user experience, so you should just leave it as is. Just know that you could change it if you wanted.

SiteLogoUrl sets the default logo used for new sites. You can always set this manually using the web interface later, but if you want a site to have a certain logo out of the box, then set this attribute to the URL of the image. You could also put the logo in the site definition itself and provision the image file using a module. For more on modules, be patient; I will get to them later in the chapter.

Note   I am getting a bit tired of repeating myself, but SiteLogoUrl is not in the wss.xsd file either.

OK, now it is time to investigate the content of the Project element. This is where the really good stuff lives.

NavBars

The NavBars section contains, well, the nav bars. What is a nav bar? you ask. Good question. Nav bars are the main navigational elements of a SharePoint site. You should be familiar with the top nav bar, which is the navigational bar over the main content area of a Team Site that holds links to the subsites of our site collection. It is marked 1 in Figure 4-1.

However, there are plenty of other nav bars as well. In the STS folder's onet.xml file, you'll find six nav bars, which consist of the top nav bar and a nav bar for each of the headings in the QuickLaunch menu. When you add a new library, list, discussion board, or site to your site, SharePoint optionally adds a link to the respective nav bar. You can also add your own links using either declarative syntax or code. You can even modify the nav bars in real time or create an entirely new nav bar if you are so inclined.

Nav bars are cool when you get the hang of them. You have great control over their appearance and behavior, and you can use both the built-in nav bar and your own nav bar to customize and create new navigational options. You will explore modifying the NavBars section in more detail in Chapter 15.

ListTemplates

If you open the ListTemplates section, you will find…nothing? How strange that there are no list templates defined for your site, especially since you know that there must be list templates defined somewhere. The answer to this mystery is that the list templates that are available for the Team Site are defined in features, not in the site definition.

So, what is a *list template*? Well, as the name implies, it is a template for new lists, defining the fields, views, settings, and forms that a new list should contain. When list templates are defined for a site, either through the site definition or through features, the list template appears on the Create page of SharePoint.

I will cover lists and list templates in much more detail in Chapter 7.

DocumentTemplates

The DocumentTemplates section defined in the onet.xml file contains the list of templates available for a new library. You may have noticed that when you create a new document library you are given an option to attach a default document template. The list from which you choose is composed of the DocumentTemplate elements of the site definition. Figure 4-7 shows the default document templates for the English Team Site definition.

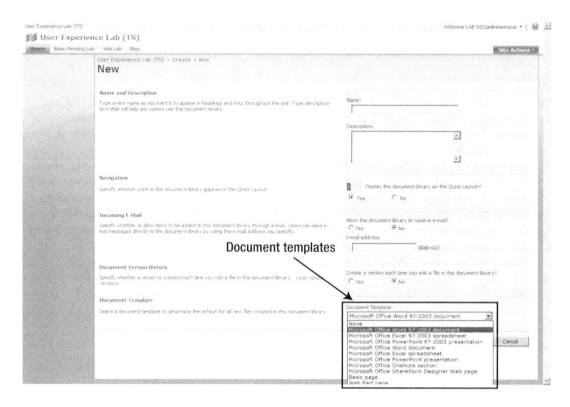

Figure 4-7. *Default document templates*

Why is this cool? Well, it allows you to create a set of templates customized to your solution; for example, you can have Microsoft Word template documents with your company's letterhead or Microsoft PowerPoint presentation templates that follow a predetermined format, or you can precreate web pages with a custom layout that you use for new pages. You are not limited by the Microsoft Office suite of document templates either—you can add document templates from any application.

Note that if you add a new document template type, for instance a PDF file, you may want to add a document icon so that the new document will not display an unknown document type icon. To do so, go to the [12]\TEMPLATE\XML folder, and open the docicon.xml file. Here, add an entry under the ByExtension section as such:

```
<Mapping Key="pdf" Value="pdficon.gif""/>
```

Exchange the Key and Value values shown here with your specific information. Next, add the .gif file of your document template type to the [12]\TEMPLATE\IMAGES folder.

■**Caution** Changing any Microsoft-provided file, including the docicon.xml file, is not supported. Unfortunately, there are no other solutions. If you decide to change any such file, make sure you back up the original file first.

Configurations

Hang on a minute. This is oddly familiar. Why are there configurations both in webtemp.xml and onet.xml? The short answer is that the configuration section of webtemp.xml is used to describe the site definition on the New SharePoint Site web page as well as provide metainformation about how the site gets provisioned. The configuration of webtemp.xml is what contains the content of the site definition.

For the long answer, read the sidebar "Configuration Shakedown: webtemp.xml vs. onet.xml."

CONFIGURATION SHAKEDOWN: WEBTEMP.XML VS. ONET.XML

The configurations of webtemp.xml and onet.xml are different in several ways. The webtemp.xml file's configurations are normally used to describe the site definition for the New SharePoint Site page, in addition to providing information about how the site should be provisioned. The configuration section of onet.xml, on the other hand, contains the actual matter of the definition.

There is some confusion regarding the two different Configuration elements. First, the documentation lists only a single Configuration element, which should indicate that an attribute or a property could be set in either configuration. However, if you look at the wss.xsd schema or just use IntelliSense in the onet.xml file, you will notice that several of the attributes from the documentation, such as the ProvisionAssembly and ProvisionClass attributes discussed earlier, are not present. These attributes would thus not work if put in the configurations of onet.xml.

Because there is no XSD schema for webtemp.xml files, at least not that I know of, it is difficult to check the actual schema for the webtemp.xml configurations. From testing, I have determined that there are also properties that are allowed in the onet.xml configurations that do not work as expected in webtemp.xml. For instance, setting the MasterUrl property of a webtemp.xml configuration does not work, while doing the same thing in onet.xml will produce the expected result.

The configuration section of the onet.xml file is what defines the actual content of your site definition. As such, it warrants closer scrutiny. This is an overview of sites, after all.

The Configuration element has several attributes, and besides reading the documentation and guessing, the easiest way to get an overview of these attributes is by using IntelliSense in Visual Studio. You have gotten that working now, haven't you? If not, this would be a great time to go back to Chapter 1 and set it up.

When you hit Ctrl+spacebar inside an empty `Configuration` start tag, you should see an IntelliSense pop-up, as shown in Figure 4-8.

```
<ListTemplates>...
<DocumentTemplates>...
<Configurations>
  <Configuration
  <Configurati    CustomMasterUrl    "NewWeb" />
  <Configurati    Description        Default">
    <Lists>        Hidden
      <List Fe     ID               1-E717-4E80-AA17-D0C71B360101"  Type="101"  Title="$Resources:core,shareddo(
      <List Fe     ImageUrl         1-6A49-43FA-B535-D15C05500108"  Type="108"  Title="$Resources:core,discussi(
      <List Fe     MasterUrl        1-D1CE-42de-9C63-A44004CE0104"  Type="104"  Title="$Resources:core,announce(
        <Data>     Name
        <Row       Title
         <R        Type
              <Field Name="Title">$Resources:onetid11;</Field>
              <Field Name="Body">$Resources:onetid12;</Field>
              <Field Name="Expires">&lt;ows:TodayISO/&gt;</Field>
            </Row>
          </Rows>
        </Data>
      </List>
      <List FeatureId="00BFEA71-2062-426C-90BF-714C59600103"  Type="103"  Title="$Resources:core,linksList
      <List FeatureId="00BFEA71-EC85-4903-972D-EBE475780106"  Type="106"  Title="$Resources:core,calendar]
      <List FeatureId="00BFEA71-A83E-497E-9BA0-7A5C597D0107"  Type="107"  Title="$Resources:core,taskList.
    </Lists>
    <Modules>
      <Module Name="Default" />
    </Modules>
    <SiteFeatures>
      <!-- BasicWebParts Feature -->
      <Feature ID="00BFEA71-1C5E-4A24-B310-BA51C3EB7A57" />
      <!-- Three-state Workflow Feature -->
      <Feature ID="FDE5D850-671E-4143-950A-87B473922DC7" />
    </SiteFeatures>
    <WebFeatures>
      <Feature ID="00BFEA71-4EA5-48D4-A4AD-7EA5C011ABE5" />
      <!-- TeamCollab Feature -->
      <Feature ID="F41CC668-37E5-4743-B4A8-74D1DB3FD8A4" />
      <!-- MobilityRedirect -->
    </WebFeatures>
  </Configuration>
  <Configuration ID="1" Name="Blank">
```

Figure 4-8. *IntelliSense for* `onet.xml` *configuration*

I will go through each of the `Configuration` attributes now to show how they relate to the user experience.

`MasterUrl` and `CustomMasterUrl` are related and behave much in the same way. The concept of master pages in SharePoint is quite similar to that of ASP.NET. There is a notable difference, though, and it relates to how the master pages are being set.

In a SharePoint ASPX page, you can set master pages just like you do with any normal ASP.NET page, but you can also set the master page to the master page for the site. SharePoint handles this using a token that references either the default master page or the custom master page. A SharePoint page might set a master page using either of the following syntaxes:

```
<%@ Page language="C#" MasterPageFile="~masterurl/default.master" [...]
<%@ Page language="C#" MasterPageFile="~masterurl/custom.master" [...]
```

The entire string ~masterurl/default.master or ~masterurl/custom.master is replaced with the value of the MasterUrl or CustomMasterUrl attribute set for the site. The cool thing about this is that you can change which master page is used for a site and all the pages using the site master page without changing the pages themselves.

Oh, you may be wondering, "Why is changing the masterpagefile property of a page a bad thing? Why not just modify the master page rather than setting a different master page?" Your questions are valid, and the problem relates to the concept of customizing pages in SharePoint, which is the feature formerly called *ghosting* and *unghosting*. An extremely short explanation is that if you modify a page, including a master page, that page is copied from the site definition and into the database (customizing or unghosting it), preventing updates to the page from the site definition.

For a more exhaustive explanation, I recommend reading Andrew Connell's article in the SDK or on MSDN at http://www.understandingsharepoint.com/url/10028. If you are unfamiliar with this feature, I highly recommend you read up on it because it is an important concept of SharePoint.

The Hidden attribute may seem to refer to whether the site should appear on the new SharePoint site page. The Description, Name, and ImageUrl attributes might seem self-explanatory. Unfortunately, this is not the case, leading again to the confusion of how configurations actually work.

You see, setting the Hidden attribute to True in onet.xml doesn't hide the definition, as you might think. Only the webtemp value is actually used in the web interface. Not even if you completely remove the Hidden attribute in webtemp.xml will the onet.xml value be used. The same applies for Name, Description, and ImageUrl. None of these is used in onet.xml, even if the schema allows them. Setting the attributes in webtemp.xml produces expected results for all these attributes. See Figure 4-9 and Figure 4-10 as well as the sidebar "Configuration Shakedown: webtemp.xml vs. onet.xml" for more information.

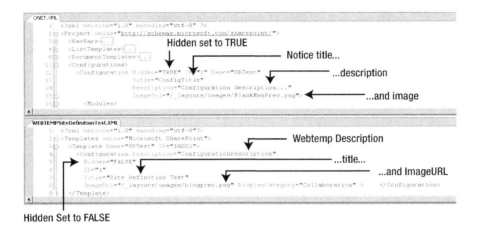

Figure 4-9. *Sample configuration attempt in* onet.xml

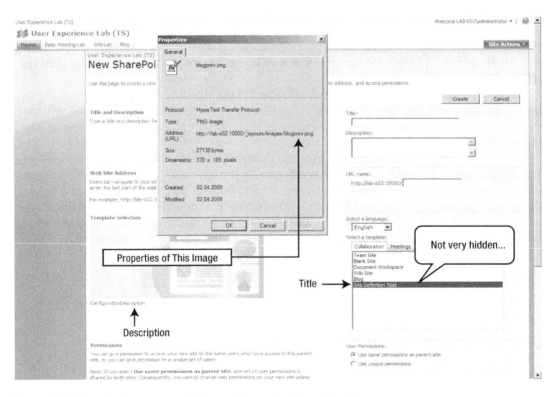

Figure 4-10. *Result of attempt to hide configuration in* onet.xml

You may have noticed that when you create a Team Site, you also get a bunch of lists and libraries created for you. If you haven't noticed, take a look at the fancy screenshot I made for you earlier in the chapter (Figure 4-1). It's the one with all the notations, remember? Check out element 3 there, which is right in front of the QuickLaunch menu. Those are lists, and the lists there get created using the List elements.

You can also add items to a list using the Data child element of the list. You should see an example of this for the announcements list, the list with a Type attribute of 104 and a FeatureId attribute of 00BFEA71-D1CE-42de-9C63-A44004CE0104. If you ever wondered where the "Get Started with Windows SharePoint Services" message gets created, now you know.

Note You will see several references to values containing the term $Resources while you explore the built-in sites. This syntax is used to get information from a resource file. (Resource files were covered in Chapter 3 in case you haven't read that yet.)

I will cover lists and list templates in much more detail in the next chapter, so if you are wondering where that Guid and the type are defined, you will learn that there.

Modules are collections of files, such as master pages, web pages, images, templates, and other files you want to put into your SharePoint site. Within the Configuration element, you usually only reference and customize modules that are defined elsewhere, either in the onet.xml file itself or in features. You can, however, define and customize complete modules within each Configuration element.

Note Modules require a bit of explaining, so I will cover them in greater depth in the "Modules" section a bit later in the chapter.

ExecuteUrl is another often overlooked feature. ExecuteUrl allows you to send a user to a page after the site has been created. If it's omitted, you are just sent to the default.aspx page of your new site, but you can override this with the ExecuteUrl attribute.

The thing to note, however, is that the address is relative to the site you create, so the page you want to display must be provisioned with the site. Also, for very natural reasons, the page gets displayed only when a site is created through the web interface, not through code.

Besides that, I think this is a very powerful feature, and I use it to create special instruction pages for new sites that get displayed when a site is created. I do this by creating a module that provisions the instruction pages into a library and then sends the user to the first page of that library.

WebFeatures and SiteFeatures state which features should be activated with the site definition. The only difference between these two elements is whether they refer to features that are web- or site-scoped. Each of these elements contains one or more feature elements that reference an existing and installed feature. Note that if you try to activate a feature that is not installed, you will get an error on site creation.

If you look at the configuration with ID 0 in the STS folder's onet.xml, you will see that it activates four features. One of these features in turn activates other features. And because these features are important to understanding the default out-of-the-box experience, I'll cover them in a bit more depth.

■**Note** The commenting is a bit off in the STS folder's onet.xml file because the descriptive comments appear above the feature element for site features and below the feature element for web features.

Team Site Default Features

The default features that are activated in the default Team Site definition are responsible for setting up quite a lot of the content that you would normally consider built in. The truth, however, is that there are extremely few built-in features at all; most of what you see in a Team Site is added using features.

Table 4-1 lists the four features in the default Team Site configuration.

Table 4-1. *Default Features for SharePoint Team Site Definition*

Name	GUID	Folder	Purpose
Basic Web Parts feature	00BFEA71-1C5E-4A24-B310-BA51C3EB7A57	BasicWebParts	Installs eight web parts, including Content Editor web part, Page Viewer web part, and User Tasks web part.
Three-state Workflow feature	FDE5D850-671E-4143-950A-87B473922DC7	IssueTrackingWorkflow	The only workflow included by default in the WSS installation. Tracks state on an item.
Team Collaboration Lists feature	00BFEA71-4EA5-48D4-A4AD-7EA5C011ABE5	TeamCollab	Responsible for installing most of the lists and list templates through activating other features. See the following discussion.
Mobility Redirection feature	F41CC668-37E5-4743-B4A8-74D1DB3FD8A4	MobilityRedirect	Using a module, installs a simple default.aspx file in the /m folder of a site; used for redirecting mobile users such as phones and PDAs.

One of these features is worth a bit of extra attention, and that is the TeamCollab feature. That feature is responsible for creating all the default list templates that you normally see when you go to the Create page of a site. The TeamCollab feature does not create anything, but it does contain several ActivationDependency elements that activate a range of features.

To investigate this, go to the [12]\TEMPLATE\FEATURES\TeamCollab folder, and open the Feature.xml file there (see Figure 4-11).

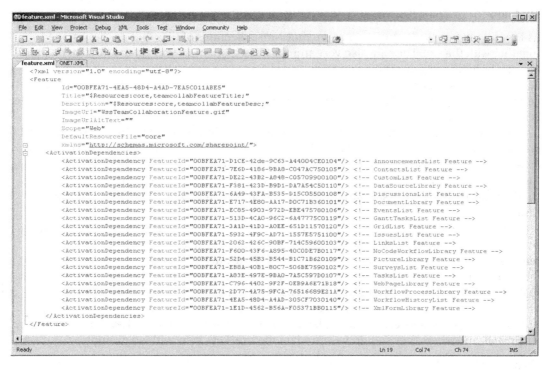

Figure 4-11. *TeamCollab* feature.xml

As you can see, there are ActivationDependencies elements for most of what are considered standard list templates, such as the announcements list, the document library, the links list, and the tasks list templates. So, when you activate the TeamCollab feature, you also activate features to install all these templates and make them, at least some of them, available from the Create page.

Several of the list templates that are activated here are not visible, however. That is because the list template is set to be hidden. That means the list must be created using other means, usually through code or another feature.

▓ **Note** I will cover lists and list templates in much greater detail in Chapter 6.

And that concludes your exploration of the configuration section. That wasn't so bad, was it? You will return to the configuration section and get plenty of exercise when you build your own site in the last part of this book. For now, let's move onward.

Modules

As I mentioned earlier in this chapter, *modules* are collections of files that are provisioned together with the site. They are also very strange beasts, but once you get to know them, modules are friendly and powerful helpers.

A module is the primary method of adding one or more files to a site. For instance, the default.aspx page that is the default startup page is provisioned using a module. That module is named…take a guess…Default.

Just for a second, go back to the Configuration element with the Id attribute set to 0, and check under the Modules element. You will see a single Module element with a single attribute, Name="Default". That Module element is just a reference to a complete module definition. This means that you can define a module to instantiate the default.aspx page and then reference that module in many other site configurations without having to re-create the module each time.

The module definition is usually placed either in the site definition itself (if so, it is placed in the Modules section of the Project root element) or in features, which means you can use features to install files to libraries or elsewhere on a site after you have set up a site. So if you want to create an application page or add some report templates to a library, you can create a feature with a module to accomplish that task. We will try that in Part 3 of this book.

The module syntax requires a bit of explanation. The Module element has several attributes that are used to determine how files should be provisioned, where they are stored before the install, and where they should be stored on the site. Let's start with an example:

```
<Module Name="Default" Url="" Path="">
  <File Url="default.aspx" NavBarHome="True">
  </File>
</Module>
```

There are at least two parts to a module: the Module element itself and one or more file elements. As I mentioned in the beginning of this section, modules are collections of files, so you can add more than one File element as well.

A Module element has several attributes that affect the entire file set. The Name attribute gives the module a name and is the only required attribute. You use this name when you want to reference the module from a configuration where you want the module provisioned.

RootWebOnly tells the module to provision the files only if the module is provisioned on the root web of a site collection. This is useful to create files that should be available for an entire site collection, such as design elements, common master pages, or templates.

The Path and SetupPath attributes are similar in behavior. Both attributes let the module know where to look for the source files used in provisioning the site. The difference is that Path is relative to the site definition itself, while SetupPath is relative to the [12]\TEMPLATE folder.

The URL attribute tells the module where to store the files on the site. You would typically set this to a list or library or just leave it empty to store files in the root of the site. Note that if you do not specify a Path or SetupPath attribute, then Url behaves like Path and is used to find the files to be provisioned relative to the site definition folder.

Tip You can use the Url attribute to create folders in your libraries. When you add a Module element with a Url attribute set to a folder within a library, SharePoint ensures that the folder exists. If you just add an empty Module element, you get an empty folder.

File

The simple point here is that each File element in a given Module element represents one file that will be installed when the module is activated either in a site definition or as part of a feature. For each of the File elements, you need to specify at least the Url attribute, which will be the path to which the file will be provisioned.

Each File element can contain a set of subelements that can be used to set properties for the file as well as install web parts to the file if the file is a web part page. The subelements of the file modules are AllUsersWebPart, View, NavBarPage, and Property. We will return to these a bit later in the chapter.

As is the case for Module, the Url attribute serves a double purpose if it is the only attribute set, setting both the final URL of the file in the site and the path and name of the file to be installed. Thus, in the previous example, the file will be named default.aspx on the site and is also called default.aspx in the site definition installation folder. You can verify this if you look in the site definition folder of the STS definition at [12]\TEMPLATE\SiteTemplates\STS. You'll see a file named default.aspx there.

Although this is usually sufficient for simple scenarios, you may want more control over the naming of the files in the site definition folder. To accomplish this, you may specify the file installation path using the attribute Path of the File element. This Path attribute may include folders, so if you want to put your pages in a folder named ApplicationPages and give the file a descriptive name, you could do something like this:

```
<File Path="ApplicationPages/EMailForm.aspx" Url="Mail.aspx" NavBarHome="True">
```

Note that the name of the file in Path and the name of the final URL are different. You must also be aware that the Path attribute is relative to the site template folder or the feature folder, depending on whether the module of the file is defined in a site definition or in a feature.

If you want your page to be provisioned to a specific folder on the site, you can also include the folder name in the Url attribute as such:

```
<File Path="ApplicationPages/EMailForm.aspx" Url="Myfolder/Mail.aspx"
NavBarHome="True">
```

If the folder, Myfolder in this case, does not exist, then SharePoint will create it for you. If the folder does exist, then your file will be added to that folder. This is useful if you want to have a feature add a new page to an existing library, for instance. You will use this technique in Chapter 7 to create a new view page for a list.

Note A folder is not the same as a list. Although most lists have a folder, not all folders correspond to a list.

So, what happens if you add a file that already exists, for instance, if you attempt to add an `AllItems.aspx` to an existing document library or list? Luckily, there is a setting in the `File` element called `IgnoreIfAlreadyExists` that, when set to `True`, will prevent a file overwrite.

The final attribute of the `File` element that requires a bit of explaining is the `Type` attribute. You can set this attribute to one of two values, `Ghostable` or `GhostableInLibrary`. Although they do behave somewhat similarly, there are important distinctions. If you set the `Type` attribute to `GhostableInLibrary`, you tell SharePoint that the file should be cached in a library and that you should be able to work with the file as you would any other file in a library. If you go to the master page gallery of a site, you will notice that each master page is a file like any other in a library. This is because they are provisioned as `GhostableInLibrary` rather than just `Ghostable`.

A `Ghostable` file, like `default.aspx`, is not part of a library. `GhostableInLibrary` files have version history, have Created By and Modified By columns, and can have any other column that the library provides. A `Ghostable` file does not. A `GhostableInLibrary` file can be checked out, approved, deleted, and anything else a library file can. A `Ghostable` file cannot. Basically, if you want to work with a module-provisioned file through the web interface, use `GhostableInLibrary`.

WHAT, NO NAVBARHOME?

Astute readers may have noticed that we skipped the `NavBarHome` attribute. You are right.

If you are thinking about setting the `NavBarHome` attribute to a different page than `default.aspx` in order to create a cool new page at a different address, save yourself some frustration because it will not work. The documentation states that `NavBarHome` should be set to `True` on the file that should be linked to in the Home tab of the top navigation, but it doesn't work.

In fact, the Home tab is hard-coded to be set to either `default.htm` or `default.aspx`, in that order. If neither exists, no Home tab will appear. These two names are hard-coded in the SQL statements that input fields in the `WelcomeNames` table of the SharePoint content database. The only way to add new names or modify the order is to modify the `WelcomeNames` table in the database.

So, how do tools such as SharePoint Designer know how to "set page as home page" when you right-click on a file? They don't; they just assume that your home page is called `default.aspx` and rename the file to that.

To make matters even worse, the `WelcomeNames` table is shared across the entire content database, including all site collections in the web application. Modifying the `WelcomeNames` table will affect all sites within a web application.

Don't do that.

As I mentioned earlier, the File element can also have subelements. These are all optional, and some work only with web part pages. Since working with web parts is such an important aspect of SharePoint user experience development, I want you to fully understand how these subelements work. There is a whole separate section on working with web parts in site definitions later, called "Working with Web Parts in a Site Definition." The knowledge gained from that section is applicable to many other situations, so although you think you may never add web parts in a site definition, read the section.

Oh, but you're not getting away from the other subelements either. You will now look briefly at the NavBarPage and Properties elements.

NavBarPage is one of the elements that causes quite a bit of confusion in online forums, so I will explain here how the element actually works. The element has three attributes: Id, Name, and Position. The documentation from Microsoft states, at least at the time of this writing, that Id refers to the ID of the page. Rubbish, I say! Rubbish!

The Id attribute actually refers to the nav bars defined in the site definition, not the page. The top link nav bar has an Id attribute of 1002, meaning that if you want to add a link from the file to the top link nav bar, you set the Id attribute of NavBarPage to 1002. If you want to add the link to the Lists nav bar in the QuickLaunch menu, that Id attribute is 1003. If you create your own nav bars, and you will do that later, then you add your own nav bar's Id attribute. It's as simple as that.

The Name attribute is the name of the link, for instance Home, so no big mysteries there. The Position attribute is also quite simple in theory, but it doesn't quite work as expected, or at all, for that matter. The MSDN and SDK documentation state that Position is simply an ordering number that goes from 1000 (the first position; can also be substituted by Start) to 2000 (or End). Take a look at the following code for an example of how to use NavBarPage to set multiple links to the same page:

```
<!-- Link to Home (default.aspx) as the first (leftmost) link in top navbar -->
<NavBarPage Name="First" ID="1002" Position="Start" />
<!-- Extra link to Home as the last link in top navbar -->
<NavBarPage Name="Last" ID="1002" Position="End" />
<!-- Extra link to default.aspx as the second link in top navbar -->
<NavBarPage Name="Second" ID="1002" Position="1002" />
<!-- Link to default.aspx as the last (bottom) link in Lists in quicklaunch -->
<NavBarPage Name="List last" ID="1003" Position="End" />
<!-- Link to default.aspx as the middle link in Lists in quicklaunch -->
<NavBarPage Name="List middle" ID="1003" Position="1001" />
<!-- Link to default.aspx as the first (top) link in Lists in quicklaunch -->
<NavBarPage Name="List first" ID="1003" Position="Start" />
```

Now, wouldn't it be nice if the order of the links in the top bar would be First, Second, Last? And if the links in the lists section of the QuickLaunch menu would be List First, List Middle, and List Last?

Turns out, it won't, at least not from this code. The Position attribute does not behave as you would expect. The End position refers to the last element at the time the NavBarPage element is created. In the previous example, End refers to the first element after Start when it is created.

You can use the Properties element of a file to set custom properties on the file, such as columns if you're storing the file in a library.

Working with Web Parts in a Site Definition

AllUserWebPart will add a web part to a web part page. It is deceptively simple on the surface, exposing only two rather self-explanatory attributes, WebPartOrder and WebPartZoneId. The WebPartZoneId attribute is the ID of the web part zone in the web part page. If you take a look at the Default.aspx file that resides in the site definition folder for STS, or Figure 4-12, you will see two web part zones defined in the Main placeholder, one with the ID Left and one with the ID Right. If you were to insert an AllUserWebPart element into the Default.aspx file via the File element, one of these IDs would fit snugly in the WebPartZoneId attribute.

Figure 4-12. WebPartZone *setup in STS* Default.aspx

The WebPartOrder attribute states where in the WebPartZone the web part should be placed. Although 1 is usually the first web part in the zone, if you have more than one web part with the same WebPartOrder, they will be added in the sequence they are defined.

That was the easy part. You, being an observant reader, will likely have noticed a rather important omission: the actual web part code. You know where the web part should go and in which order, but frankly you have no idea what web path should be added. And the answer may be a bit different from what you'd expect.

If you have tried adding a subelement to the AllUsersWebPart element already, you may have noticed there are no subelements defined in the WSS schema. That is because, amazingly enough, there are no subelements to AllUsersWebPart defined in the schema. So, to add your actual web part code, you need to do something else. If you have looked at the module definitions of the STS site definition, you already know the answer. You need to put your code in a CDATA element.

Tip If you forgot what a CDATA element is or you didn't read Chapter 2, you should read that chapter now. Basically, it is character data that is not parsed as XML even though it resides in an XML file.

Once you know what to put in the CDATA, then adding web parts using AllUserWebPart is a breeze, and when I tell you that it is quite simple in theory, then you might be tempted to just skip ahead. You know you will regret it, so please, read on.

Simply put, what you put into the AllUsersWebPart CDATA element is just the web part markup needed, but it's ASP.NET. It can be as simple as adding a WebPart tag, which is what is done in the following code, which was taken from the STS default module, or it can be as complex as rocket science, depending on the requirements of the web part:

```
<WebPart xmlns="http://schemas.microsoft.com/WebPart/v2" ➡
xmlns:iwp="http://schemas.microsoft.com/WebPart/v2/Image">
 <Assembly>Microsoft.SharePoint, Version=12.0.0.0, Culture=neutral, ➡
 PublicKeyToken=71e9bce111e9429c</Assembly>
 <TypeName>Microsoft.SharePoint.WebPartPages.ImageWebPart</TypeName>
 <FrameType>None</FrameType>
 <Title>$Resources:wp_SiteImage;</Title>
 <iwp:ImageLink>/_layouts/images/homepage.gif</iwp:ImageLink>
 <iwp:AlternativeText>$Resources:core,sitelogo_wss;</iwp:AlternativeText>
</WebPart>
```

If you ignore the iwp: tags for a moment, you will recognize fairly common properties of an assembly as well as FrameType and Title. The latter two are web part properties, while Assembly and TypeName should be familiar to any .NET developer, even though TypeName has replaced Class.

Note The FrameType property is considered obsolete in WSS 3. Use ChromeType instead.

This syntax works only for WSS 2 web parts, meaning you can use it only with web parts that inherit from a class such as Microsoft.SharePoint.WebPartPages.WebPart. If you want to add WSS 3 web parts, which are nothing more than ASP.NET 2.0 web parts, you must use a different syntax. All this gets very confusing, and I can understand if you get a bit frustrated. There is a simple solution, however.

You see, the code you need to add to AllUsersWebPart is the same code that resides in a .dwp file from WSS 2 or a .webpart file from WSS 3. Not only that, but if you have the web part installed, there is an easy way to get the XML from within SharePoint. Go to the web part gallery of your root site—you know, the one you set up earlier in this chapter. You will see several web parts in the library, similar to Figure 4-13.

Figure 4-13. *Web Part Gallery*

Click the Edit icon, and you will get the properties for the web part, as shown in Figure 4-14.

Figure 4-14. *Web part properties*

Now, click the View XML link in the toolbar, and you will be given the XML you need to add the web part to the `AllUsersWebPart` element. You can use the same technique regardless of whether you have a WSS 2–style `.dwp` web part or a WSS 3–style `.webpart` file.

This will only get you a nonconfigured web part, however, meaning that although you can add an `ImageWebPart`, you will not get to set which image should be displayed unless you add the markup yourself. Again, there is a simple solution.

You can export a complete web part file if you add the web part to a web part zone. That export will include custom configurations, such as which image is displayed in an `ImageWebPart`. To do this, start by adding the web part to a web part page, and configure it as you want it to be in your `AllUsersWebPart` element. Then, from the web part menu—you know, the little arrow in the top right of the web part—click Export. You will get a web part file that you can open in your favorite editor and insert into the `AllUsersWebPart` CDATA section.

If you do not see an Export option in the web part menu, there may be at least two reasons. The first is that the web part is marked as not exportable. The second is that your web application does not allow exporting. You can solve the first problem by setting the `ExportMode` property of the web part to `All` or `NonSensitiveData`. How? Use SharePoint Manager 2007, write a code snippet to do it, use the web interface, and modify the web part from there. You have a ton of options; just pick the one you like.

To fix the second problem, open the `web.config` file, usually stored in `C:\Inetpub\wwwroot\wss\VirtualDirectories\[portnumber]`. In that file, locate the `system.web` element and then the `webParts` element. To the `webParts` element, add an attribute called `enableExport="True"`. Then reset your web application.

EXPORTING LISTVIEWWEBPARTS?

There is actually a third reason why you might not be able to export a web part. `ListViewWebParts`, such as the Announcements or Calendar web part in the `STS` folder's `default.aspx` file, cannot be exported. At least that's what Microsoft wants you to believe.

Microsoft is sort of right. Even if you use code or SharePoint Manager 2007 to set the `ExportMode` property for a `ListViewWebPart` element to `All`, the web part will not allow you to export it. There is a perfectly good reason for this. `ListViewWebPart` elements are tied to the underlying list and views by GUID, and the GUID is unique for each view and each list in each site. Thus, exporting the web part makes no sense since you would not be able to use it on another site.

The thing is, I don't care what Microsoft thinks is reasonable. There may be situations where I still want the code. Perhaps I want to take a backup of a web part before removing it from the page. Perhaps I want to manually edit the file for a new site. Perhaps I want to study how `ListViewWebPart` works. Perhaps I even want to add it to an `AllUsersWebPart` element.

I want that code, and if you do as well, here's how to get it....

Open the web page hosting the web part in Microsoft SharePoint Designer 2007. Then, select the web part in Design mode. Now, switch to Split view, and you should see the web part code marked. Copy the code, and use it as you see fit.

Note that you will likely not get much practical use out of the code, because it is far too tied to the underlying list and the views of that list, and in any case, setting up a list view from scratch is a lot easier than trying to force a copied web part to behave.

But you should know you have the option.

We still have one web part element to explore, the View element. Views can be very simple but can also be very complex. The basic functionality is to add a view of data in a list. If you check out the Default module for the STS folder's onet.xml, you will see some really simple samples.

Views can be much more than simple displays, but because they are so tightly coupled to lists, I will postpone the deep dive into views for now and return to them when I talk about lists in Chapters 7 and 8.

Components

Two more elements in the site definition deserve at least a mention. These elements both reside in the Components section, but they are very rarely used, so a thorough examination is beyond the scope of this book.

ExternalSecurityProvider is used to return security information to a crawler.

FileDialogPostProcessor could have been a really nice feature, but its implementation is quite complex. FileDialogPostProcessor references a component that will be triggered, for the entire site, when a file open or file save dialog box is used to show a web interface to the user. For instance, when you save a Word document to a SharePoint site, you get a minimal web view of that site to allow you to browse to different libraries and select folders where you want to store the file.

FileDialogPostProcessor is used to modify that web interface. Unfortunately, you can modify only an existing interface, and even if you wanted to go in that direction, I wouldn't be able to take the time here to go over a detailed enough scenario and implementation. Sorry!

What's the Global Site Configuration?

You need to explore one more concept to fully understand what makes up a site. You see, even with all the details you have seen so far, there are still things I have not explained. For example, from where do you get the default master page? You know you get a default master page, but you have found no trace of it in either the webtemp.xml or onet.xml file. And speaking of master pages, how does the actual master page library get created? Or the web part library, for that matter?

The answer to these questions, and more, is in what is called the *global site configuration*. The global site configuration is a "hidden" base configuration that is applied to all new sites. The global site configuration is applied before your selected and visible site configuration and contains settings that are required by all sites, regardless of how complex or simple your own site configuration may be.

The global site configuration is stored in [12]\TEMPLATE\GLOBAL\XML\onet.xml, so open that file now. In Figure 4-15 I have closed the BaseTypes element, but it should show you the outline of the site configuration.

```
   1    <?xml version="1.0" encoding="utf-8"?>
   2    <Project Title="$Resources:onet_TeamWebSite;" ListDir="$Resources:core,lists_Folder;" xmlns:ows="Microsoft SharePoint">
   3      <NavBars>
   4      </NavBars>
   5      <ListTemplates>
   6        <ListTemplate Name="mplib" DisplayName="$Resources:MasterPageGallery;" Description="$Resources:global_onet_mplib_des
   7        <ListTemplate Name="users" DisplayName="$Resources:userinfo_schema_listtitle;" Description="$Resources:global_onet_
   8        <ListTemplate Name="webtemp" DisplayName="$Resources:core,sitetemplategalleryList;" Description="$Resources:core,si
   9        <ListTemplate Name="wplib" DisplayName="$Resources:core,webpartgalleryList;" Description="$Resources:core,webpartga
  10        <ListTemplate Name="listtemp" DisplayName="$Resources:core,listtemplategalleryList;" Description="$Resources:core,l
  11      </ListTemplates>
  12      <BaseTypes>...
2589      <Configurations>
2590        <Configuration ID="0" Name="Default" MasterUrl="_catalogs/masterpage/default.master">
2591          <SiteFeatures>
2592            <Feature ID="CA7BD552-10B1-4563-85B9-5ED1D39C962A" />
2593            <!--Fields-->
2594            <Feature ID="695B6570-A48B-4A8E-8EA5-26EA7FC1D162" />
2595            <!--Ctypes-->
2596          </SiteFeatures>
2597          <WebFeatures>
2598          </WebFeatures>
2599          <Lists>
2600            <List Title="$Resources:core,MasterPageGallery;" Type="116" Url="_catalogs/masterpage" />
2601            <List Title="$Resources:core,userinfo_schema_listtitle;" Type="112" Url="_catalogs/users" RootWebOnly="TRUE" />
2602            <List Title="$Resources:core,sitetemplategalleryList;" Type="111" Url="_catalogs/wt" RootWebOnly="TRUE" />
2603            <List Type="113" Title="$Resources:core,webpartgalleryList;" Url="_catalogs/wp" RootWebOnly="TRUE" />
2604            <List Type="114" Title="$Resources:core,listtemplategalleryList;" Url="_catalogs/lt" RootWebOnly="TRUE" />
2605          </Lists>
2606          <Modules>
2607            <Module Name="DefaultMasterPage" />
2608          </Modules>
2609        </Configuration>
2610      </Configurations>
2611      <Modules>
2612        <Module Name="DefaultMasterPage" List="116" Url="_catalogs/masterpage" RootWebOnly="FALSE">
2613          <File Url="default.master" Type="GhostableInLibrary" IgnoreIfAlreadyExists="TRUE" />
2614        </Module>
```

Figure 4-15. *Global site configuration* onet.xml

You will recognize most of the elements in the global onet.xml file, with the noted exception of the BaseTypes element. I will talk more about BaseTypes a bit later, so for now, let's go over the elements you have seen before to learn how the global site configuration fits into the big picture.

In the ListTemplates element, you'll find all the list templates for required lists such as the master page library (mplib), users list (users), and web template library. As you will learn in Chapter 6, the actual schemas of these lists and libraries are stored in files called schema.xml that are stored in directories named after the Name attribute of the ListTemplate element. In the case of the global site definition, these directories reside in the [12]\TEMPLATE\GLOBAL directory, so if you ever need to explore these schemas, that is where you will find them.

The actual global site configuration is the single Configuration element in the onet.xml file. This configuration is responsible for setting up the default fields and content types required by all SharePoint lists, as well as generating the actual lists and libraries to hold the master pages, users and groups, site templates, web parts, and list templates. In addition, the configuration provisions a Module element that contains the default master page. From the Module definition further down (line 2612 in Figure 4-15), you can see that the default.master file is deployed to the master page gallery from the same directory as the root of the global site definition, in other words, [12]\TEMPLATE\GLOBAL. If you open that directory, you will see the default.master file.

Oh, yeah, you can wreak havoc in that file if you want, and changes will be immediately applied to all default master pages, but such changes are not supported. Then again, you are still a developer, so I'm not going to imagine that you will leave that file alone in your lab or development environment.

BaseTypes

In the rather bulky `BaseTypes` element, you find the root definitions for lists. Every list must inherit from a `BaseTypes` element, either from the generic list, document library, discussion forum, vote or survey, or issues list, and this is where those base types are defined.

Inside each of the `BaseTypes` elements, you will find a schema resembling the normal list template schema. You will explore that schema in much more detail in Chapters 7 and 8, so for now I just want to point you to where the base type definitions are stored.

Note The `BaseTypes` element can be used only in the global site configuration, and since modifying that file is not supported, you are stuck with the default base types. No, you cannot work around this issue. Yes, I know you want to.

Mostly the base types contain columns, defined in the schema using the `Fields` element. These columns are the required columns such as Created By, Title, Version, and list-specific columns for the different base types. When you create a new list, you always get these columns added unless you explicitly remove them. You will learn how to do so in later chapters.

Resources, Helpful Hints, and the Future

OK, so where are we? Ah, yes, we have covered the site definitions and explored the options available to you when constructing new site definitions. If there has been a bit too much theory, rest assured you will get plenty of chances to do exercises when you get to Chapter 11.

In the meantime, I would like to share with you some tips and tricks for getting the most out of your site definition adventures:

- *Explore by touch*: When you work with an `onet.xml` file, you should try to add elements to see what options IntelliSense gives you. Try adding attributes to an element to see what values are acceptable. You could just memorize `wss.xsd`, but chances are you'll get much less headache from just playing around with `onet.xml`. Just remember to save a copy first in case you break something.

- *Explore by test*: Make yourself a new site definition, and use it to test the effects of different elements, attributes, and values. Feel free to copy one of the default `webtemp.xml` and `onet.xml` files and customize it to your heart's content. You will do plenty of that later, but I have found that trying while reading yields immediate results and knowledge.

- *Explore by search*: If you are wondering how a feature works, there is a big chance that the included site definitions include examples of how that feature should be implemented. If you search the `[12]\TEMPLATE` folder for files containing a certain element, you might find that ready-to-use examples exist in one of the built-in site definitions or features.

- *Explore by Google*: With the entire world at your fingertips, an online search may be just what you need if you still haven't figured out a certain syntax or feature. Chances are that someone else has experienced the exact same problem and blogged or written an article about it.

- *Explore by inquiry*: If you are really stuck, a whole range of online communities has experts that can help you. Feel free to come to the `UnderstandingSharePoint.com/justask` site and ask a question. I will be there and can help you out as well.

So, I have covered site definitions, but there is still a ton of things I need to cover before you can claim to understand the user experience. I will continue to dig down, and here are some of the things to come in the next few chapters:

- *Lists galore*: Chapter 6 will cover lists, list templates, and list forms, your ticket to user experience nirvana.

- *Content types*: These are really the coolest feature of SharePoint, especially to control behavior of information.

- *Fields and columns*: These are tiny pieces of information capable of ruining or creating the perfect user experience.

Next up, however, you will explore some of the options you have to modify the default user experience and what will break your supportability. In the next chapter, I will cover topics such as `CustomAction`, delegate controls, feature stapling, and control templates.

CHAPTER 5

■ ■ ■

Evolving the Default User Experience

Tips on What You Can Change Without Breaking Supportability

With the overview of a site completed, you should have a better understanding of how all the pieces of a site fit together. Although you still have a long road ahead of you (and some really cool places to visit!), you'll now explore what you can do to modify the default user experience with and without ruining the supportability. (In short, this means that Microsoft Support will not help you if you get into trouble...as if they would anyway—read more about this in the "Disclaimer" section.)

In this chapter, you will look at several methods for customizing the default user experience. By no means exhaustive, the techniques you will learn here will make you a potent tool on any SharePoint team.

The techniques you will look at here are `MenuItemTemplate`, `CustomAction`, control templates, feature stapling, custom application pages, and delegate controls. Each of these techniques may be powerful on its own, but when you combine them...well, let's just say that nuclear explosions become like gentle whispers between oysters—during a hurricane.

Disclaimer

Changing any file that comes with SharePoint will break your supportability. I briefly mentioned one exception in Chapter 4, which is that you can change the `Hidden` attribute of the default `webtemp.xml` file.

If you modify any other file, though, you can no longer call Microsoft Support and expect them to help you. Actually, you can expect it as much as you like, but they will ask you to restore your original file, which sort of voids the whole point of modifying it. And, to make matters even worse, Microsoft can, with the release of any update that you choose to install, overwrite any file it wants to overwrite, at any time, without warning.

This all seems to point in one direction: do not muck around in the default files. Now, I have been in this game long enough to know that saying this to a developer is like telling a kid to not look forward to Christmas. We developers grow and learn by taking things apart and seeing how they work, or do not work, when we try to put them back together. It is going against nature to tell a developer not to do something that looks the slightest bit fun.

So, I will dispense with all the bovine manure and give you some advice instead.

■**Tip** Muck around in the default files as much as you like. Do so in a lab or test environment, and do so with vigor. Bomb your SharePoint installation to smithereens, tear down any site on which you can lay your hands, and try to see whether you can get it back together again. Just don't expect this to work in production, so explore from a learning perspective, not from a production perspective.

Customizing Menus and Lists

In Chapter 4, specifically in Figure 4-1, you saw a fancy screenshot with a bunch of annotations that were like a map of the user interface. Figure 5-1 shows the relevant parts of that screenshot to save you from page-flipping madness.

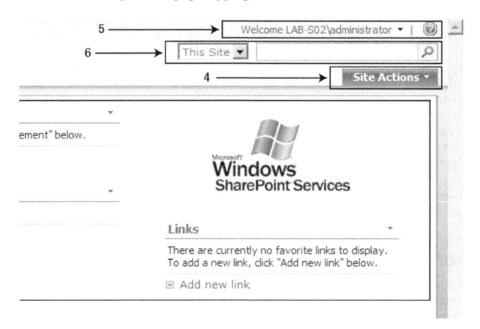

Figure 5-1. *Site and personal actions*

Elements 4 and 5 are the Site Actions and personal actions menus, respectively. I will get to element 6 later.

You may have noticed that the Site Actions menu changes with different site definitions, including the default Team Site and Meeting Workspace definitions (see Figure 5-2). And, if this can change based on what type of site definition you're using, there must be a way to modify that menu without breaking supportability.

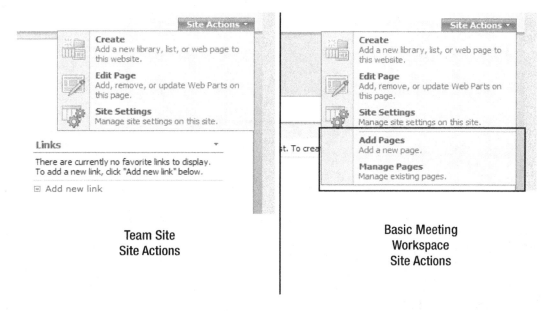

Team Site
Site Actions

Basic Meeting
Workspace
Site Actions

Figure 5-2. *Site Actions menu examples*

To modify the Site Actions menu, you should start by checking out the pages hosting the Site Actions menu to see how they get created. The Site Actions menu appears on every page, so it is safe to assume that it is defined in the master page rather than on individual pages. Let's open the `default.master` file that resides in the `[12]\TEMPLATE\GLOBAL` directory.

You could explore plenty of tags in the `default.master` file, but I'll detail some of these later; for now, I'll direct your attention to line 152 in `default.master`, which is the line starting with a `SharePoint:SiteActions` tag. I'm certain you can guess what that tag does, but you'll want to know how the tag works too.

■**Tip** If you want to use .NET Reflector to explore the `SharePoint:` tags, look at the `<%@Register Tagprefix="SharePoint"` tag at the start of the master page to find the correct assembly and namespace. In this case, that would be `Microsoft.SharePoint.WebControls` in `Microsoft.SharePoint.dll`.

Your first clues come from the child tags of the `SiteActions` tag, specifically the `FeatureMenuTemplate` tag. The tag is responsible for creating the menu. You will explore how it does this in a few moments, but first let's look at its child elements, as shown in Figure 5-3.

```
150   <tr>
151       <td class="ms-siteactionsmenu" id="siteactiontd">
152       <SharePoint:SiteActions runat="server" AccessKey="<%$Resources:wss,tb_SiteA(
153           PrefixHtml="&lt;div&gt;&lt;div&gt;"
154           SuffixHtml="&lt;/div&gt;&lt;/div&gt;"
155           MenuNotVisibleHtml=" "
156       >
157       <CustomTemplate>
158       <SharePoint:FeatureMenuTemplate runat="server"
159           FeatureScope="Site"
160           Location="Microsoft.SharePoint.StandardMenu"
161           GroupId="SiteActions"
162           UseShortId="true"
163       >
164       <SharePoint:MenuItemTemplate runat="server" id="MenuItem_Create"
165           Text="<%$Resources:wss,viewlsts_pagetitle_create%>"
166           Description="<%$Resources:wss,siteactions_createdescription%>"
167           ImageUrl="/_layouts/images/Actionscreate.gif"
168           MenuGroupId="100"
169           Sequence="100"
170           UseShort="true"
171           ClientOnClickNavigateUrl="~site/_layouts/create.aspx"
172           PermissionsString="ManageLists, ManageSubwebs"
173           PermissionMode="Any" />
174       <SharePoint:MenuItemTemplate id="MenuItem_EditPage" ... />
```

Figure 5-3. SiteActions *and its children*

MenuItemTemplate

You will quickly discover that the child MenuItemTemplate tags match the choices of the Site Actions menu, so there's no big surprise there. Those MenuItemTemplate tags have power, however, so you should take note of a few useful attributes. A really cool feature is the incredible control you have to filter which menu items are displayed. Specifically, using the attributes of a MenuItemTemplate, you can narrow down who gets to see a given item based on a wide array of filtering options. Note that some of the filtering attributes here are optional; if you do not set a filtering attribute, then the default value, specified for each attribute in the following text, is used.

First notice the PermissionsString and PermissionMode attributes. These attributes specify the permissions a user must have in order for the menu item to appear. The PermissionsString attribute holds one or more comma-separated string values that state which permissions the user needs. These values come from the SPBasePermissions enumeration. I could give you a complete list of all those values, but the official documentation does a great job, so I see no reason to just copy and paste that information here. Here are a few examples to show you what kind of permissions you could use (refer to the official documentation on MSDN at http://www.understandingsharepoint.com/url/10026, or search for *SPBasePermissions* in the SDK to get the complete list):

- AddAndCustomizePages

- ApproveItems

- CreateAlerts

- DeleteListItems

- ManageLists

- ManageWeb

- Open

- ViewPages

PermissionMode defines how these permissions should be evaluated; it can be either All to signify that a user needs every permission listed in the PermissionsString attribute or Any to signify that any permission is sufficient. If PermissionMode is not set, All is used as the default.

You can further refine the permission requirements using the PermissionContext attribute. By setting this value, you specify to which SharePoint objects or contexts the required permissions should apply. For instance, you can combine the Permissions string Open with the PermissionContext attribute set to RootSite to show a menu item only if the user has Open permissions on the site collection's root web.

The possible PermissionContext values are CurrentFolder, CurrentItem, CurrentList, CurrentSite, and RootSite. If PermissionContext is not set, CurrentSite is the default value.

In addition to user permission requirements, you can also filter menu items based on which features are activated; you just use the RequiredFeatures attribute to do this. For instance, if you have a feature to send an email from the current page, you can put a link to that page in a FeatureMenuTemplate element, such as the Site Settings menu, only if that feature has been activated. That way, you're not putting invalid links in the menu, and the link will automatically be removed if the feature is deactivated.

Then you have the AuthenticationRestrictions attribute, which can be set to either AllUsers, AnonymousUsersOnly, or AuthenticatedUsersOnly to specify which authentication method a user should use to see the menu item. That way, you can prevent a menu item from being shown to anonymous users or to authenticated users. For instance, you may want to hide a Log In to This Site menu item from authenticated users or hide a Log Out from This Site menu item from anonymous users.

The final filtering attribute I will mention here is the PageModes attribute. You can set this to Design, Normal, and All to filter when the menu item should be displayed. For example, you might want an Edit This Page link to appear only if you are in the Normal viewing mode of a page but not if you are already in the Design/Edit viewing mode.

Most of the other attributes of MenuItemTemplate are quite self-explanatory, but a few attributes require a bit more explanation.

The MenuGroupId attribute groups items together on the menu. To illustrate this, take a look at the Site Actions menu of the Meeting Workspace in Figure 5-2. The last two menu items, Add Pages and Manage Pages, are part of their own MenuGroupId, in this case 200, while the remaining and default menu items are part of the 100 MenuGroupId. These numbers are just arbitrary integers, by the way, but the groups do appear in numerical order.

The Sequence number of the MenuItemTemplate defines the order within the MenuGroupId in which items should appear. Again, this is just an arbitrary number, but menu items do appear in ascending order. Note that a menu item with Sequence set to 1 but part of MenuGroupId 200 will still appear after a menu item with sequence 5 that is part of MenuGroupId 100. In other words, the MenuGroupId attribute has priority over the Sequence attribute.

Note MenuGroupId is not the same as GroupId. I'll explain GroupId in a moment.

`MenuItemTemplate` has two attributes for handling the actual clicks on the menu item: `ClientOnClickNavigateUrl` and `ClientOnClickScript`. The `ClientOnClickNavigateUrl` attribute simply sets the URL to which the click will lead, while `ClientOnClickScript` contains a JavaScript call. The important thing here is to not use both attributes in the same `MenuItemTemplate`. If you do, as shown in Figure 5-4, only the attribute defined first will work. So if you need to have a JavaScript function called first and then have the user navigate to a URL, you must handle the URL navigation in script code.

```
<SharePoint:MenuItemTemplate runat="server" id="MenuItem_Create"
    Text="<%$Resources:wss,viewlsts_pagetitle_create%>"
    Description="<%$Resources:wss,siteactions_createdescription%>"
    ImageUrl="/_layouts/images/Actionscreate.gif"
    MenuGroupId="100"
    Sequence="100"
    UseShortId="true"
    ClientOnClickNavigateUrl="~site/_layouts/create.aspx"
    ClientOnClickScript="alert('Clicked!');"
    PermissionsString="ManageLists, ManageSubwebs"
    PermissionMode="Any" />
```

Script will not get called

```
<SharePoint:MenuItemTemplate runat="server" id="MenuItem_Create"
    Text="<%$Resources:wss,viewlsts_pagetitle_create%>"
    Description="<%$Resources:wss,siteactions_createdescription%>"
    ImageUrl="/_layouts/images/Actionscreate.gif"
    MenuGroupId="100"
    Sequence="100"
    UseShortId="true"
    ClientOnClickScript="alert('Clicked!');"
    ClientOnClickNavigateUrl="~site/_layouts/create.aspx"
    PermissionsString="ManageLists, ManageSubwebs"
    PermissionMode="Any" />
```

URL will not get called

Figure 5-4. *Conflicting* `ClientOnClick` *attributes*

FeatureMenuTemplate

You may be asking yourself why I'm spending so much time explaining the intricate details of a simple item in the Site Actions menu. The reason for this will become clear in a few moments, and it may even be one of those "aha!" moments for you. It was for me, at least; your mileage may vary.

The `FeatureMenuTemplate` tag wraps the four Site Actions menu items to create the Site Actions menu, but it also does far more than that. Two attributes are important: the `Location` attribute and the `GroupId` attribute. Combined, these two attributes define which menu to show:

```
<SharePoint:FeatureMenuTemplate runat="server"
    FeatureScope="Site"
    Location="Microsoft.SharePoint.StandardMenu"
    GroupId="SiteActions"
```

```
UseShortId="true"
>
```

The important thing to note here is that the two values are actually completely arbitrary string values despite looking like they may actually be connected to a namespace. You can create your own FeatureMenuTemplate element using whatever values you like. Take a look at the following sample code:

```
<SharePoint:FeatureMenuTemplate runat="server"
    FeatureScope="Site"
    Location="Microsoft.SharePoint.MyStandardMenu"
    GroupId="CustomSiteActions"
    UseShortId="true"
    >
```

If you replace the FeatureMenuTemplate of default.master with the previous code, your site settings will work just like before—at least until you want to add some menu items. We will get to that really soon, I promise.

Why are there two values, and how are they different? Both are grouping mechanisms that work quite similarly. They are usually used in unison to group similar menus.

Hold on…what do you mean by "group similar menus"? I thought we were talking about the Site Actions menu?

Ah, yes, it is time to show you why the FeatureMenuTemplate together with the MenuItemTemplate are so important to the user experience.

Ladies and gentlemen, I give you…Figure 5-5!

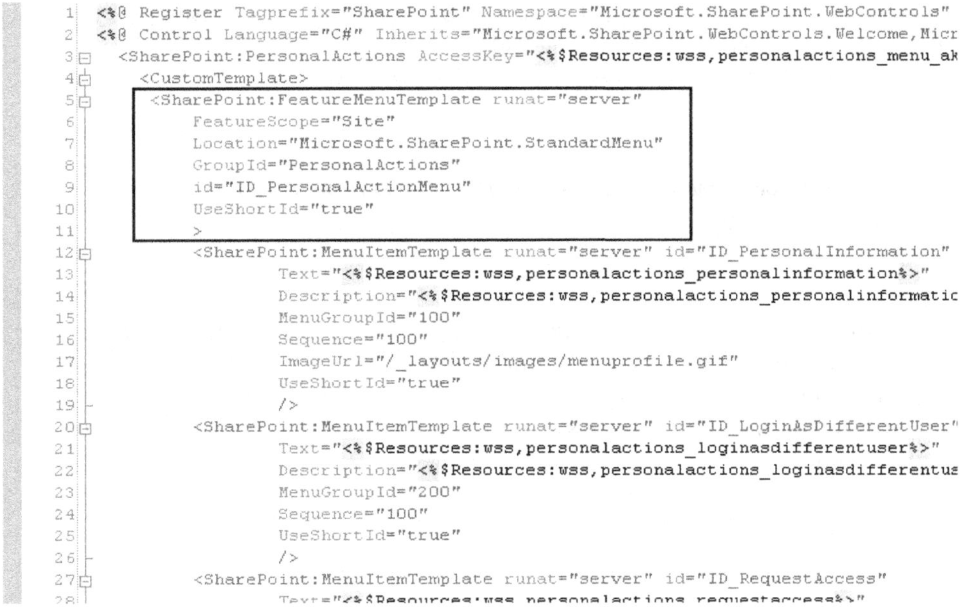

Figure 5-5. *Section from* welcome.ascx

What you see before you is a part of welcome.ascx, or the personal actions menu. As you can see, that menu is also based on the FeatureMenuTemplate but differs from the Site Actions menu in the GroupId attribute.

And, if you should happen to stumble upon an open DefaultTemplates.ascx file, scroll down to line 1795 to discover another FeatureMenuTemplate, inside the ToolbarActionsMenu template, as shown in Figure 5-6.

```
1791             runat="server"/>
1792         </SharePoint:FeatureMenuTemplate>
1793      </Template>
1794   </SharePoint:RenderingTemplate>
1795 <SharePoint:RenderingTemplate ID="ToolbarActionsMenu" runat="server">
1796   <Template>
1797     <SharePoint:FeatureMenuTemplate runat="server"
1798         FeatureScope="Site"
1799         Location="Microsoft.SharePoint.StandardMenu"
1800         GroupId="ActionsMenu"
1801         UseShortId="true"
1802         >
1803     <SharePoint:MenuItemTemplate
1804         ID="EditInGridButton"
1805         ImageUrl="/_layouts/images/menudatasheet.gif"
```

Figure 5-6. *Section from* DefaultTemplates.ascx

There are plenty of similar examples, so you should be beginning to see a pattern here. Quite a lot of menus in SharePoint are actually created using a FeatureMenuTemplate. Not all are, but many are.

Knowing that FeatureMenuTemplate contains MenuItemTemplate and that MenuItemTemplate can be highly targeted and context sensitive, you can now see how many menus behave and look differently depending on which user sees the menu. Why is there no Settings menu in a list when a user does not have the Manage Lists permission? It's simply because the items on the menu, in this case GroupId SettingsMenu and Location Microsoft.SharePoint. StandardMenu, all have the Permissions attribute set to ManageLists.

■ **Note** This is also how the Site Settings page shows only the links to which you have the proper permissions. I will get to that shortly.

However, all this information does not give you any information about how to create your own menu items, because you cannot actually modify any of these FeatureMenuTemplate tags to add more actions, right? Remember the disclaimer about modifying default SharePoint files? If you modify the files, you break your supportability. There must be another way to manipulate menu items.

Enter CustomAction....

CustomAction

CustomAction tags are defined in features so you can create, install, and activate a feature to modify different menus in SharePoint. The syntax matches that of MenuItemTemplate tags but differs in some key areas. Figure 5-7 shows an example of an elements file containing a CustomAction.

```
 1  <?xml version="1.0" encoding="utf-8" ?>
 2  <Elements xmlns="http://schemas.microsoft.com/sharepoint/">
 3    <CustomAction Id="MyCustomSiteAction"
 4                  GroupId="SiteActions"
 5                  Location="Microsoft.SharePoint.StandardMenu"
 6                  Title="My custom siteaction"
 7                  Description="Link to book blog"
 8                  >
 9      <UrlAction Url="http://www.understandingsharepoint.com/userexperience/"/>
10    </CustomAction>
11  </Elements>
```

Figure 5-7. CustomAction *sample*

Note that the CustomAction contains a GroupId attribute and a Location attribute that matches the values of the Site Actions menu's FeatureMenuTemplate. When activated, this feature will add a link to the Site Actions menu, linking the title "My custom siteaction" to the URL defined in the UrlAction child element, as shown in Figure 5-8.

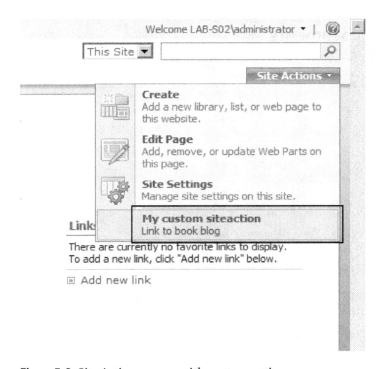

Figure 5-8. *Site Actions menu with custom action*

The CustomAction and MenuItemTemplate tags have some key differences. First, in the CustomAction tag, you have a different set of filtering options. There is no Permissions attribute like you have in MenuItemTemplate, and although you have a Rights attribute that closely resembles the Permissions attribute, Rights are always All, meaning that a user must have all the permissions you list in the value.

Second, you can use a CustomAction group to target specific content types, lists, or file types using the RegistrationType attribute. If you set that attribute, you must also set the RegistrationId attribute to match which content type, list template type, or file type you want to affect. For example, the following code will add an action to the EditControlBlock—you know, the drop-down menu that appears when you hover your pointer over an item—for folders only:

```
<CustomAction Id="MyCustomSiteAction"
              Location="EditControlBlock"
              Title="Open folder in Explorer"
              RegistrationType="ContentType"
              RegistrationId="0x0120"
              >
```

Figure 5-9 shows the result.

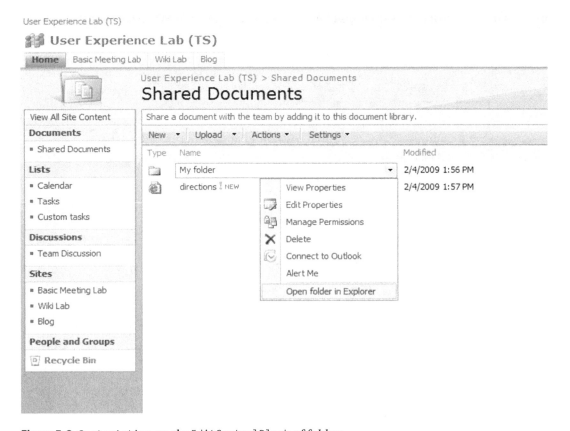

Figure 5-9. CustomAction *on the* EditControlBlock *of folders*

Tip Folders are actually just normal items with a content type inheriting from the root folder content type. We will get to that in Chapter 8.

Tip `CustomAction` honors the inheritance of content types, meaning that if you have a custom action connected to an existing type and you create a new content type based on that existing type, the new content type will also inherit the custom action.

Tip The drop-down menu you see in Figure 5-9 is called the `EditControlBlock`, ECB for short.

You may have noticed that the `UrlAction` child element is the only way to set an action through CAML. Although that may be correct, another option may quite possibly blow your mind. You can use the `ControlAssembly` and `ControlClass` attributes to manage the custom action through code.

What this means is that if you set these attributes to a valid class in a valid assembly, your class will get the chance to react to events when the custom action is added to the menu. You can use this to filter menu items at runtime rather than at design time, so this is an incredibly powerful feature. Here are some examples to show you how you could utilize this feature:

- You could have a menu item appear only during specific times of the day to ensure that certain actions, such as checking out documents, are permitted only during work hours and during the workweek.

- You could add a Ship This Order menu item only if the payment has been received from the customer.

- You could create a stock portfolio solution and have a Buy/Sell Shares in This Company menu item only if the P/E ratio of a stock is greater than or less than a certain value.

- You could…filter on anything! How about allowing people to attend a company picnic only if they have not beaten you in Tetris?

Note There is a massive caveat with using `ControlAssembly` and `ControlClass`. In `EditControlBlock`, the menu items are generated in a JavaScript function of `core.js`. That means you cannot use `ControlAssembly` and `ControlClass` to filter ECB menu items.

D'oh!

This applies only to a `CustomAction` using the `ControlAssembly` and `ControlClass` attributes. Normal links using the `UrlAction` child element still work as explained.

However, using a CustomAction is not just limited to menus. The entire Site Settings page uses the CustomAction framework for creating the columns and links to manage a site. The Operations and Application Management pages in Central Administration use custom actions. And, as you have seen, the toolbars located in various places such as in lists use custom actions.

In fact, let's take a look at how the Site Settings page is created and see whether you can add some categories and links. That can be very useful for providing your own management options to site administrators and power users.

The Site Settings page gets its content from the SiteSettings.xml file. Open the [12]\ TEMPLATE\FEATURES\SiteSettings\SiteSettings.xml file, as shown in Figure 5-10.

```
 1  <?xml version="1.0" encoding="utf-8"?>
 2  <Elements
 3      xmlns="http://schemas.microsoft.com/sharepoint/">
 4      <CustomActionGroup
 5          Id="UsersAndPermissions"
 6          Location="Microsoft.SharePoint.SiteSettings"
 7          Title="$Resources:SiteSettings_UsersAndPermissions_Title;"
 8          Sequence="10"
 9          Description="" />
10      <CustomAction
11          Id="PeopleAndGroups"
12          GroupId="UsersAndPermissions"
13          Location="Microsoft.SharePoint.SiteSettings"
14          Rights="EnumeratePermissions,BrowseUserInfo"
15          Sequence="10"
16          Title="$Resources:SiteSettings_PeopleAndGroups_Title;">
17          <UrlAction
18              Url="_layouts/people.aspx" />
19      </CustomAction>
20      <CustomAction
21          Id="SiteCollectionAdministrators"
22          GroupId="UsersAndPermissions"
23          Location="Microsoft.SharePoint.SiteSettings"
24          RequireSiteAdministrator="TRUE"
25          Sequence="20"
26          Title="$Resources:SiteSettings_SiteCollectionAdministrators_Title;">
27          <UrlAction
28              Url="_layouts/mngsiteadmin.aspx" />
29      </CustomAction>
30      <CustomAction
31          Id="User"
```

Figure 5-10. SiteSettings.xml

Ah, this looks quite familiar. There is one new element here, CustomActionGroup. However, when you realize that the CustomActionGroup maps nicely to the GroupId attribute of both FeatureMenuTemplate and CustomAction, I am fairly certain that you can easily understand this new element. In fact, several CustomActionGroup elements match the columns on the Site Settings page.

Let's try adding custom actions to the Site Settings page by using CustomAction and CustomActionGroup. Here is what you could do in the elements file of your feature:

```
<Elements xmlns="http://schemas.microsoft.com/sharepoint/">
  <CustomActionGroup Id="MyCustomSettings"
                     Location="Microsoft.SharePoint.SiteSettings"
                     Description="Custom administration options"
                     Sequence="5"
                     Title="Custom administration"/>
```

```
<CustomAction Id="MyCustomSiteAction"
              GroupId="MyCustomSettings"
              Location="Microsoft.SharePoint.SiteSettings"
              Rights="EnumeratePermissions,BrowseUserInfo"
              Title="Manage something..."
              >
   <UrlAction Url="_layouts/CustomManagement.aspx"/>
  </CustomAction>
</Elements>
```

Figure 5-11 shows the result of this little exercise.

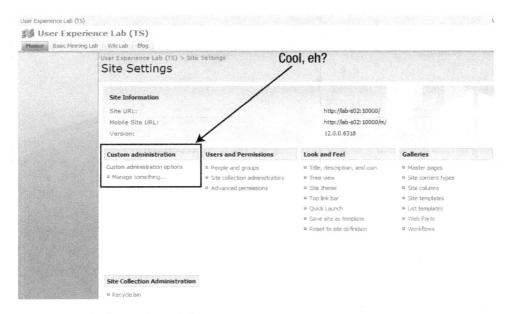

Figure 5-11. *The fruits of your labor*

Now you should begin to understand how to add menu items to virtually any menu in SharePoint. All you need are the Location and GroupId attributes, and you are good to go.

Tip Do you want to find all the possible Location and GroupId values? That is quite difficult. Microsoft does provide a large list in the documentation if you search for *default custom action locations and IDs*. That list is not exhaustive, though, so you may want to dig a bit to find the proper Location and GroupId values if you are missing a position. PersonalActions is an example of a Location and GroupId value that is not listed. Since you can create your own Location and GroupId values as well, no list can ever be exhaustive. A shovel and the will to dig are your best tools.

A final and important element is HideCustomAction. As the name implies, this element can remove existing CustomAction elements. The following code removes the "People and groups" link from the Users and Permissions category on the Site Settings page (and Figure 5-12 shows the result):

```
<HideCustomAction HideActionId="PeopleAndGroups"
    GroupId="UsersAndPermissions"
    Location="Microsoft.SharePoint.SiteSettings"/>
```

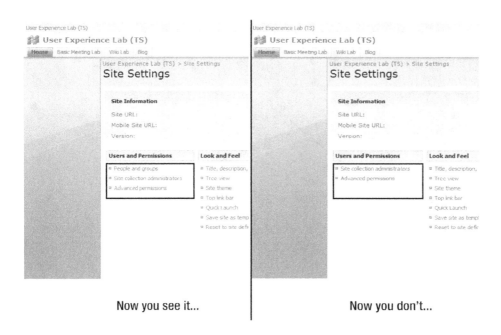

Figure 5-12. HideCustomAction *snatches away "People and groups"*

So if you want to replace any management links on the Site Settings page, just use RemoveCustomAction first, and then use CustomAction to provide your custom link. It's an incredibly powerful option if I ever saw one.

■ **Note** No Microsoft-provided files were harmed during this exercise.

Using Control Templates

When you were searching for examples of where the FeatureMenuTemplate was used, you looked at two .ascx files, welcome.ascx and DefaultTemplates.ascx, located in the [12]\ TEMPLATE\CONTROLTEMPLATES folder. These control files are really just regular ASP.NET controls containing code used to render aspects of the user interface. If you are familiar with the ASP.NET template framework, you know there are no real secrets to the ASP.NET code.

Overview of Control Templates

There are some important things to note about how these controls are used, specifically, regarding the `DefaultTemplates.ascx` file. If you open that file, you will notice that it is composed solely of `SharePoint:RenderingTemplate` tags, each with a unique ID. You may even begin to see, from the `ID` values, what these templates do. Figure 5-13 shows the beginning of the file with the rendering templates collapsed.

```
  6   <%@ Register TagPrefix="wssuc" TagName="ToolBarButton" src="~/_controltemplates/ToolBarButton.asc
  7 ⊞ <SharePoint:RenderingTemplate ID="FieldLabelDefault">...</SharePoint:RenderingTemplate>
 12 ⊞ <SharePoint:RenderingTemplate ID="FieldLabelRequired">...</SharePoint:RenderingTemplate>
 17 ⊞ <SharePoint:RenderingTemplate ID="FieldLabelForDisplay">...</SharePoint:RenderingTemplate>
 20 ⊞ <SharePoint:RenderingTemplate ID="CompositeField">...</SharePoint:RenderingTemplate>
 34 ⊞ <SharePoint:RenderingTemplate ID="DisplayCompositeField">...</SharePoint:RenderingTemplate>
 47 ⊞ <SharePoint:RenderingTemplate ID="ListFieldIterator">...</SharePoint:RenderingTemplate>
 52 ⊞ <SharePoint:RenderingTemplate ID="TwoRowCompositeField">...</SharePoint:RenderingTemplate>
 78 ⊞ <SharePoint:RenderingTemplate ID="TwoRowFieldIterator">...</SharePoint:RenderingTemplate>
 83 ⊞ <SharePoint:RenderingTemplate ID="PropertyIterator">...</SharePoint:RenderingTemplate>
 96 ⊞ <SharePoint:RenderingTemplate ID="GenericForm">...</SharePoint:RenderingTemplate>
104 ⊞ <SharePoint:RenderingTemplate ID="ListForm">...</SharePoint:RenderingTemplate>
142 ⊞ <SharePoint:RenderingTemplate ID="BlogCommentsForm">...</SharePoint:RenderingTemplate>
169 ⊞ <SharePoint:RenderingTemplate ID="BlogForm">...</SharePoint:RenderingTemplate>
207 ⊞ <SharePoint:RenderingTemplate ID="SurveyForm">...</SharePoint:RenderingTemplate>
237 ⊞ <SharePoint:RenderingTemplate ID="AttendeesEditForm">...</SharePoint:RenderingTemplate>
276 ⊞ <SharePoint:RenderingTemplate ID="AttendeeEmailResponse">...</SharePoint:RenderingTemplate>
310 ⊞ <SharePoint:RenderingTemplate ID="AttachmentRows">...</SharePoint:RenderingTemplate>
326 ⊞ <SharePoint:RenderingTemplate ID="AttachmentUpload">...</SharePoint:RenderingTemplate>
378 ⊞ <SharePoint:RenderingTemplate ID="RequiredFieldMessage">...</SharePoint:RenderingTemplate>
383 ⊞ <SharePoint:RenderingTemplate ID="CreatedModifiedInfo">...</SharePoint:RenderingTemplate>
402 ⊞ <SharePoint:RenderingTemplate ID="CreatedModifiedVersionInfo">...</SharePoint:RenderingTemplate>
424 ⊞ <SharePoint:RenderingTemplate ID="CreatedVersionInfo">...</SharePoint:RenderingTemplate>
438 ⊞ <SharePoint:RenderingTemplate ID="DocumentTransformersInfo">...</SharePoint:RenderingTemplate>
443 ⊞ <SharePoint:RenderingTemplate ID="InformationBar">...</SharePoint:RenderingTemplate>
456 ⊞ <SharePoint:RenderingTemplate ID="ApprovalStatus">...</SharePoint:RenderingTemplate>
468 ⊞ <SharePoint:RenderingTemplate ID="ChangeContentType">...</SharePoint:RenderingTemplate>
477 ⊟ <SharePoint:RenderingTemplate ID="InitContentType">...</SharePoint:RenderingTemplate>
```

Figure 5-13. *Beginning of* `DefaultTemplates.ascx`

The "long story short" here is that each of these templates is responsible for creating an aspect of the user interface. Because of this, learning more about this file is incredibly important. I will show a few examples to illustrate what these templates do and then explain how you can use this information to modify the user experience.

Let's start simple, shall we? Look for the rendering template with an `ID` value of `TextField`. It should look something like this:

```
<SharePoint:RenderingTemplate ID="TextField" runat="server">
    <Template>
        <asp:TextBox ID="TextField" MaxLength="255" runat="server"/><br>
    </Template>
</SharePoint:RenderingTemplate>
```

It's nothing too fancy—just a simple text box. I expect you can imagine where this template is used. Try modifying the `asp:TextBox`, and see what happens when you add a new item to a list or library. Remember to reverse your changes, though, because Microsoft Support will eat your head if you modify any default files, as you know.

Here's another example, which is a bit more complex this time:

```
<SharePoint:RenderingTemplate ID="NewFormToolBar" runat="server">
    <Template>
        <wssuc:ToolBar CssClass="ms-toolbar" id="toolBarTbl"➡
                       RightButtonSeparator=" " runat="server">
            <Template_Buttons>
            <SharePoint:AttachmentButton runat="server"/>
            </Template_Buttons>
        </wssuc:ToolBar>
    </Template>
</SharePoint:RenderingTemplate>
```

The NewFormToolBar template references a ToolBar control from the wssuc tag prefix, which, as you can see at the top of the DefaultTemplates.ascx file, is mapped to the ToolBar.ascx control, also residing in the [12]\TEMPLATE\CONTROLTEMPLATES folder. Notice that the ToolBar tag has a child element of AttachmentButton. Now open the ToolBar.ascx file:

```
<table class="<%=CssClass%>" cellpadding="2" cellspacing="0" ➡
       border="0" id="<%=ClientID%>" width="100%" >
  <tr>
<%-- Buttons on the left --%>
<wssawc:RepeatedControls id="RptControls" runat="server">
    <HeaderHtml/>
    <BeforeControlHtml>
        <td class="ms-toolbar" nowrap="true">
    </BeforeControlHtml>
    <AfterControlHtml>
        </td>
    </AfterControlHtml>
    <SeparatorHtml>
        <td class=ms-separator>|</td>
    </SeparatorHtml>
    <FooterHtml/>
</wssawc:RepeatedControls>
    <td width="99%" class="ms-toolbar" nowrap>
        <IMG SRC="/_layouts/images/blank.gif" width=1 height=18 alt="">
        </td>
<%-- Buttons on the right --%>
<wssawc:RepeatedControls id="RightRptControls" runat="server">
    <HeaderHtml/>
    <BeforeControlHtml>
        <td class="ms-toolbar" nowrap="true">
    </BeforeControlHtml>
    <AfterControlHtml>
        </td>
    </AfterControlHtml>
```

```
    <SeparatorHtml>
        <td class=ms-separator>|</td>
    </SeparatorHtml>
    <FooterHtml/>
</wssawc:RepeatedControls>
    </tr>
</table>
```

Note I have left out the directives at the top of the file to save space.

This file, along with its calling rendering template, is responsible for creating the toolbars that appear over the NewForm, EditForm, and DisplayForm forms (see Figure 5-14).

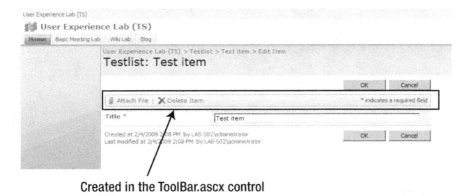

Created in the ToolBar.ascx control

Figure 5-14. *Result of* ToolBar.ascx *in* NewFormToolbar. *Don't mind the list and item names.*

I will suspend the mindless listing of code now; I just wanted to give you a few illustrative examples.

Manipulating the Control Templates

How does any of this help you? Again, you are faced with the agony of not being able to modify any default files. To the rescue comes the ability to overload any rendering template using a seemingly simple technique.

You can override each of the templates in DefaultTemplates.ascx by creating another .ascx file and putting that file in the CONTROLTEMPLATES folder. In the custom .ascx file, you add SharePoint:RenderingTemplate tags using the same Id as the template you want to override. A simple iisreset later, and you have changed which template is actually used to render a user interface element. Take a look at the following code to see an example of overriding the TextField rendering template (Figure 5-15 shows the result):

```
<SharePoint:RenderingTemplate ID="TextField" runat="server">
    <Template>
```

```
    <asp:TextBox BorderStyle="none" BorderWidth="0" ID="TextField"
        MaxLength="255" runat="server"/><br>
  </Template>
</SharePoint:RenderingTemplate>
```

Figure 5-15. *Result of overriding* TextField. *Notice the lack of borders on the text box.*

■**Tip** Get to know the DefaultTemplates.ascx file in more detail; there is gold to be had when you learn where each user interface element gets created.

This is all fine and dandy, but there are some troublesome catches here. First, you can override any template only once. If you attempt to override with a second .ascx file, only one of the overriding templates will take effect.

Second, the override is global, just like any addition to the [12]\TEMPLATE folder. That means there is no scope for a template override, so if you override TextField, you should be prepared to see the effects on every site in every site collection. This may or may not be what you want; just be aware of these caveats, and you should be fine.

If you are looking to modify only a single text field column, you will likely be much better off creating a new field and rendering it the way you want. Chapter 9 details fields and columns.

Using Feature Stapling

Please take a moment and stare into my eyes. You will become sleepy; your eyes will become heavy. Listen to my voice as you slip away into a state of hypnosis. When I snap my fingers, you will wake up.

Features are great. Features are good. Love features. Features are your friends. You want to use features.

Snap!

Good morning, sunshine! (Features are great.) It's time to move on to the next part of this chapter (features are great) that will focus on a wonderful method for modifying the default user experience (features are great).

If you feel a strong urge to use features, then you are indeed a wise developer. Features offer you the best method of adding functionality to a site.

The problem, however, is that if you want to add features to an existing site definition, such as the Team Site definition, you are out of luck. Sure, you can add, install, and activate features after the site has been created, but you cannot modify the site definition itself, both because Microsoft Support will have you flogged but more important because modifying a site definition after a site has been created from the definition is not supported.

Tip Microsoft KB article 898631 details the supported and unsupported methods of modifying site definitions. See `http://support.microsoft.com/kb/898631` for more information.

To solve this problem, Microsoft has added a method called *feature stapling*. In essence, this functionality allows you to add, or *staple* as it is called, a feature to a site definition. This is very useful in some scenarios, especially when you want to abide by the rules of not modifying a site definition after a site has been created from the definition. Feature stapling allows you to bypass this problem by not modifying the site definition but rather appending to it.

To staple a feature, you add a `FeatureSiteTemplateAssociation` element to an elements file of a feature. The `FeatureSiteTemplateAssociation` has two attributes: `Id` is the ID of the feature to staple, and `TemplateName` is the name of the template, for instance, `STS#0` or `MYSiteDefinition#1`. Here's an example:

```
<FeatureSiteTemplateAssociation TemplateName="STS#0" ➥
                    Id="3a79daf8-c5a2-4320-9915-c0df53a10742"/>
```

Now, whenever you create a new site from the `STS#0` definition, the feature with `Id` 3a79daf8-c5a2-4320-9915-c0df53a10742 gets "stapled" to the site. This is particularly useful when sites are created automatically, such as when creating a new Meeting Workspace while adding a new calendar event.

There is one very important thing to know about feature stapling. Feature stapling works when provisioning a site but not on sites that have already been provisioned. So if you create a new Team Site before you staple your fancy new feature to the Team Site template, then your existing Team Site will not get the new feature automatically. You can still activate the feature manually, though.

There really isn't too much more to say about feature stapling except a few tips.

Tip You can have a `FeatureActivated` event handler on the stapled feature and have code executed whenever a site gets created. That way, you can effectively have complete control over the site creation without ever touching the original site definition.

Tip You can also staple a feature to the global site definition to activate a feature on any new site, regardless of which definition is used.

Customizing Application Pages: Master Pages, CSS, and Themes

Have you ever tried to customize the application pages interface? If you have mucked around in `application.master`, you have already broken your supportability. If you search the Web, you will find a lot of creative solutions for handling design on application pages, including adding a custom HTTP module to intercept the page request runtime and change the application page. Sadly, none of these options is supported.

Note The term *application pages* refer to pages that reside in the `_layouts` directory site settings, list settings, user management settings, and so on. The `_layouts` directory is mapped to the `[12]\ TEMPLATE\LAYOUTS` folder.

The problem is that there is only one supported method for modifying the appearance of application pages, and that method is *themes*. When you set a theme for a site, you also set the theme for the application pages. This is great to some level but hardly satisfying when what you want to have is complete control over your management pages.

Using themes is basically just adding another CSS file to the mix. However, CSS deals only with style and visual elements, so you are out of luck if you want to actually focus on the user experience rather than the user interface.

Or are you…?

The fact that Microsoft does not support the editing of any of *its* files does not prevent you from doing exactly what you want to your own files. Adding files to the `[12]\TEMPLATE\LAYOUTS` directory is both supported and encouraged as long as you do not overwrite any of the default files.

So, if you want to have your very own custom application pages, just create your own page. In fact, you can even copy Microsoft's pages and modify the copies to create exactly the management experience you like. We will explore creating custom application management pages in Chapter 14.

Combined with what you learned earlier about modifying the Site Settings page using `CustomAction` and `HideCustomAction`, you can get pretty decent results without breaking any supportability. And the even better part is that if you decide to reverse the changes, then all you need to do is deactivate the feature. As if by magic, your old link to the Microsoft page reappears.

Using Delegate Controls

If you have no idea what delegate controls are, be prepared to learn an incredibly powerful new feature of WSS.

A *delegate control* is actually very simple in concept and works very much like a content placeholder that you know from regular ASP.NET. You create a `DelegateControl` in your page and then, using features, tell SharePoint what you want that delegate control to contain. The idea here is that you modify the page or pages using features, allowing you to deploy a page at one point and then later change how the page works.

Why is this so cool when modifying the default user experience? The `default.master` file that ships with SharePoint includes several delegate controls, meaning that you can modify the contents of `default.master` without even touching it.

Oh…there's more. Listen to this: even the `application.master` file contains three delegate controls. You get to decide what is there. Talk about free ride to customization heaven.

Before you go around adding marquees and modifying CSS on your application pages, let's get the basics down.

A delegate control has at least a `ControlId` attribute that is very important to you. When you want to fill the delegate control with custom goodness, you add a `Control` element to your `elements.xml` file and specify the `ControlId` value of the delegate control using the `Id` attribute.

In addition, you need to specify a `Sequence` number. The sequence is just an ordering integer; in case you have several features that fill the same delegate control, the feature with the lowest sequence number gets priority.

The final requirement of the `Control` element is to specify which control you want to put in the delegate control using the `ControlSrc` attribute. You can use any `.ascx` file that is accessible to the page. Take a look at the following code for an example:

```
<Control Id="AdditionalPageHead" Sequence="5"
        ControlSrc="~/_controltemplates/MyAdditionalPageHead.ascx"></Control>
```

Notice the `Id` attribute? `Id` refers to a delegate control present in the out-of-the-box `default.master` and `application.master` files. I've created a simple control in `MyAdditionalPageHead.ascx` just to illustrate this, but you can go completely bonkers and add basically anything you like. Here's my simple sample:

```
<%@ Control Language="C#" ClassName="WebUserControl1" %>

<script runat="server">
    public override void RenderControl(HtmlTextWriter writer)
    {
        writer.Write("Look, no hands!");
    }
</script>
```

And, what demonstration would be complete without showing the mandatory result? Figure 5-16 should satisfy your wildest dreams of customization options.

Figure 5-16. *That should whet your appetite.*

■**Tip** You can also use `ControlAssembly` and `ControlClass` instead of `ControlSrc` if you have a compiled and strong-named server control that you want to use instead of the user control.

The `application.master` file gives you three delegate controls to fill with your heart's desire. These are `AdditionalPageHead`, `GlobalSiteLink1`, and `GlobalSiteLink2`. If you examine the `application.master` files, however, you will notice that each `GlobalSiteLink` requires a feature scope of `Farm`, meaning you must have your feature scoped at the farm level in order for your control to fill these delegate controls.

The `default.master` file also gives you a few delegate controls for your enjoyment. The most commonly used delegate control is the search box. Microsoft uses this when it modifies the search box when you install MOSS or Search Server 2007. Table 5-1 lists other delegate controls you can use.

Table 5-1. *Delegate Controls in* `default.master`

ControlId	Description
AdditionalPageHead	Part of the HEAD HTML tag; same as for `application.master`
GlobalSiteLink0	Top of page, to the left of Welcome <Username>
GlobalSiteLink1	Top of page, to the right of Welcome <Username>
GlobalSiteLink2	Top of page, to the right of GlobalSiteLink1
SmallSearchInputBox	Search box
TopNavigationDataSource	Navigation data source for top navigation bar
PublishingConsole	Mostly used for MOSS Publishing Pages feature
QuickLaunchDataSource	Navigation data source for QuickLaunch menu

A delegate control, like a content placeholder, can have a default value to be used if no `Control` element is activated. This is the case, for example, for `QuickLaunchDataSource` and `TopNavigationDataSource`, which provide default data sources unless you (or any feature you activate) override the controls.

Cool, eh?

Last Stop

Everyone out! This chapter is finished. You saw a wide range of options you can use to customize the default user experience. Still, plenty more exist, but the ones I have shown here are the options I find most powerful.

A whole book could have been written focusing only on the default user experience, but since I want to cover more ground in this book, I must move on. When you have the time—after reading the remaining chapters, of course—here are some tips you might find useful:

- Never be afraid to explore in your lab environment. If you mess up, you can reinstall or revert to a previous snapshot if you have a virtual environment that supports snapshots. The price to pay for ignorance is far higher than that of the occasional reinstall.

- Be an active participant in online or offline communities. After spending several years in online communities, I can testify that what you learn from your peers far outweighs any effort required to participate.

- Seek to understand, not just perform. If you find a recipe for fixing a problem, understand why that recipe works rather than just performing the steps. Even if you don't have the time to fully explore everything new you encounter, make a mental or physical note to yourself to go back at a later time.

- Oh, and value your designers. Just like we, as developers, might be or will be gurus of making SharePoint dance like a ballerina, designers are really good at making that ballerina look as great as she dances. Appearance is important to the user; *Dirty Dancing* would not have been as good if Dame Edna and Sir David Attenborough starred in it.

Next you'll enter into the forest of lists to explore a very fundamental part of the SharePoint architecture. In the following two chapters, you will go into some very dark places and fight some really scary battles. Inside the forest of lists lurks a monster that has scared SharePoint developers from their senses for many moons. If you do survive, however, you will be rewarded with some very important treasure in the form of knowledge.

If you survive.

CHAPTER 6

What Lurks in the Forest of Lists?

Ripping the Guts Out of SharePoint Dragons, Lists, List Templates, and List Forms

This chapter will lead you toward some of the scariest things that exist for SharePoint developers. In order to survive, you will have to gather up whatever courage you can find and prepare yourself to face demons, monsters, and foul CAML language.

We will begin by examining what lists really are, how they work, and why they make up the foundation of SharePoint. That's nothing too scary, so there is no need to fear anything at this point.

Then we'll move on and start examining the list CAML that you need to master in order to control how lists behave and are experienced by the user. Three parts are relevant here: list instances, list templates, and list forms. Each part will be increasingly more complex and likely outside of what you would normally use in a SharePoint solution. You should begin at this point to see where we are going.

During the course of this chapter, you will gain knowledge used to fight the largest of all SharePoint dragons, the beast that has stricken fear into the hearts of developers for many years, the foul creature that eats men and women alive and yields to nothing but pure knowledge, skill, and plenty of practice.

In the next chapter, it will be time to face...views.

You're not scared? Oh, you will be.

Overview of Lists

I mentioned earlier in the book that lists in SharePoint are not much more than database tables on steroids. Although that is true, I would like to elaborate a bit on what I mean by that.

Lists consist of columns, which I will discuss in much more detail in Chapter 9. Lists are the primary storage facility of SharePoint, and most everything is stored in some kind of list. Even libraries, wiki sites, and web portals are just lists of files, articles, and pages.

If you are SQL savvy, it should be easy to understand how the features of SharePoint lists map to database tables. Table 6-1 shows several of the features and the similarities to a database table.

Table 6-1. *SharePoint Lists Compared to Database Tables*

SharePoint Terminology	Database Terminology
List	Table
Item	Row
Column	Column, sort of
Event receivers	Triggers
Field type	Data type
View	View
List forms	Nothing, really

Although not exhaustive, this table should make it clear that lists can be compared to database tables.

That being said, plenty of factors differ as well. For instance, the concept of referential integrity does not exist in SharePoint. You can have lookup fields that reference other tables, but there is nothing that prevents you from deleting the referenced items or even lists. Another example is CAML vs. SQL. You do have some SQL ideas in CAML, but CAML is nothing near as powerful for data definition and data manipulation.

So, I might actually rephrase the initial statement a bit: a SharePoint list is like a database table on steroids but with a limp.

The Road Ahead

OK, let's get down to the fun parts, the technical stuff. Lists, being the primary storage facility and being compared earlier to database tables, offer surprising amounts of flexibility and customization options. To understand these options, you need to understand the underlying definitions that create and manipulate lists.

But first, as always, let's look at a cool screenshot and some annotations. That way, you can show the book to your boss and say, "Hey, here's a book that shows how SharePoint lists work," and your boss will understand. Bosses like that. See Figure 6-1.

You should make sure your boss is happy.

Bjørn the Elder

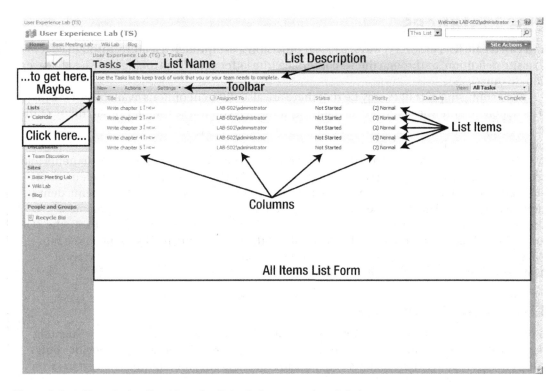

Figure 6-1. *A SharePoint list. Note the "Maybe" annotation; it is important.*

Now, I am not trying to insult your intelligence by showing you this. As SharePoint developers, we are very familiar with this view, but it might still hold some clues that are important.

The page you see in Figure 6-1 is a list form, the AllItems.aspx form actually, and as you will discover later in this chapter, list forms can be highly customized. In fact, they are nothing more than plain ASP.NET pages, and once you know that, you also know you can make them look and behave just as you like. The same applies to other forms that are associated with the list. When you click an item, you go to the DisplayForm. When you edit an item, well, that would be the EditForm. And if I tell you there is a form called NewForm, I am going to credit you with enough brains to figure out what that form does. I'll talk more about forms later.

Another interesting aspect of Figure 6-1 is that it shows most of the components of a list. You have the columns there, the items, a list form, the list name and description, the toolbar...all these components are defined in the list definition, which is basically just a set of CAML files that tell SharePoint how the list should be created.

The list definition consists of a list template as well as a list instance. Compare this to the object-oriented way of thinking, and the list template is the class, while the list instance is the object. As such, the list template defines how the list should look and behave, while the list instance is the actual storage medium for items in the list.

I will cover both list templates and list instances later as well.

List Instances

You can create lists in several ways. You can provision a list through a feature, through code, in a site definition, or through the web interface (the latter actually invoking code just like we can do ourselves).

The confusing part here may be that there are also different options available for creating lists depending on where you create them. So, although you will see similarities in many of the methods, you should be careful to note the differences as well, since you may not have all the options available in a certain scenario.

To make the playing field a little more complex, there are also different List elements that have widely different meanings depending on which file they reside in. The List element of a site definition configuration instantiates a list, while the List element of a list schema definition creates a template. If you search for documentation on the List element, you must therefore pay attention to which List element you find. This confuses even Microsoft; the SDK and MSDN documentation have plenty of links to the wrong element. If your head is a bit dazed by all this, you are in good company (or bad company, depending on your view of Microsoft). I'll try to clear this up a bit here.

Lists in Site Definitions

Since I have just finished my treatise on site definitions, it makes sense to start investigating lists based on what we find in onet.xml. This is the simplest List element and provides only some attributes and child elements you need to learn. You will not require a life vest to swim here.

If you open the STS folder's onet.xml file again (in [12]\TEMPLATE\SiteTemplates\sts\xml) and then go to the configuration element with ID 0, you will see several lists being instantiated in the Lists element, as shown in Figure 6-2. Each List element here creates a list when we provision a site based on said configuration. Let's see how this actually happens.

```
 1    <?xml version="1.0" encoding="utf-8"?>
 2    <Project Title="$Resources:onet_TeamWebSite;" Revision="2" ListDir="$Resources:core,lists_Folder;" xmlns:ows="Microsoft SharePo
 3      <NavBars>...
11      <ListTemplates>
12      </ListTemplates>
13      <DocumentTemplates>...
71      <Configurations>
72        <Configuration ID="-1" Name="NewWeb" />
73        <Configuration ID="0" Name="Default">
74          <Lists>
75            <List FeatureId="00BFEA71-E717-4E80-AA17-D0C71B360101" Type="101" Title="$Resources:core,shareddocuments_Title;" Url="$
76            <List FeatureId="00BFEA71-6A49-43FA-B535-D15C05500108" Type="108" Title="$Resources:core,discussions_Title;" Url="$Reso
77            <List FeatureId="00BFEA71-D1CE-42de-9C63-A44004CE0104" Type="104" Title="$Resources:core,announceList;" Url="$Resources
78              <Data>
79                <Rows>
80                  <Row>
81                    <Field Name="Title">$Resources:onetid11;</Field>
82                    <Field Name="Body">$Resources:onetid12;</Field>
83                    <Field Name="Expires">&lt;ows:TodayISO/&gt;</Field>
84                  </Row>
85                </Rows>
86              </Data>
87            </List>
88            <List FeatureId="00BFEA71-2062-426C-90BF-714C59600103" Type="103" Title="$Resources:core,linksList;" Url="$Resources:co
89            <List FeatureId="00BFEA71-EC85-4903-972D-EBE475780106" Type="106" Title="$Resources:core,calendarList;" Url="$Resources
90            <List FeatureId="00BFEA71-A83E-497E-9BA0-7A5C597D0107" Type="107" Title="$Resources:core,taskList;" Url="$Resources:cor
91          </Lists>
92          <Modules>...
95          <SiteFeatures>...
101         <WebFeatures>...
107       </Configuration>
```

Figure 6-2. Lists *section of* STS *folder's* onet.xml *configuration ID 0*

The `List` element of `onet.xml` has several attributes that can be used to customize the list instance.

The first two attributes of the `List` element are `FeatureId` and `Type`. The `Type` attribute is a reference to a `ListTemplate`, and the `FeatureId` attribute is where that `ListTemplate` is defined. Several list templates ship with SharePoint, such as the Document Library, Custom List, Contacts List, and so on. Each of them is located in a feature. To provision the list, you need to know both the feature ID and the template type. How do you find these values? We'll get to that shortly, but for now there is one thing you should know.

Although many list templates will be defined in features, that is not the case for every one. For instance, the Blog definition's `onet.xml` file defines `ListTemplates` right inside the `onet.xml` file itself, and thus no `FeatureId` is required. You may define templates in the `ListTemplates` section of your own `onet.xml` as well, and in that case you will need the `Type` attribute only. The downside to this, however, is reusability; you will not be able to use your list templates in sites based on other site definitions.

Tip You should strive to put list templates in features whenever possible.

The `Title` attribute gives a name to the list. Note that this is different from the list template name. A library list template may be called Document Library, while your actual library in your site may be called Shared Documents.

The `Description` attribute sets, well, a description for the list. If you refer to Figure 6-1, you see where that description goes in the `AllItems.aspx` list form. We will explore how this attribute gets displayed in the "List Forms" section later in this chapter.

You should also set the `Url` attribute, which determines the site-relative URL of the list. The normal practice is to put anything that is not a library inside a virtual directory, usually named `Lists`. Thus, if your list is called `MyList`, you might want it placed in `http://mysite/Lists/MyList`.

Tip When setting the `Url` attribute, rather than explicitly writing the word *List* as part of the URL, use the resource string `$Resources:core,lists_Folder;` as such:
`Url="$Resources:core,lists_Folder;/MyList"`
That way, you do not need to worry about what language pack might be installed and what *lists* is in Hungarian. You can see an example of how to create and use your own resources in Chapter 3.

You would think that you could enable content types in a site-provisioned list by setting the `EnableContentTypes` attribute to `True`. That would be rather self-explanatory, right? Well, it is not.

What you are enabling is the web interface management of content types. This is really important; content types are the coolest thing since the invention of ice, and you should know that they are always enabled and that you can always use them, even if content types are "disabled" as many people believe they are when they click the check box in the Advanced section of the List Settings page.

I AM NOT USING CONTENT TYPES!

I can hear your question now: "Well, I am not using content types at all, only lists, so how is this relevant to me?"

Actually, you are using content types whether you like it or not. Any list, even if it is not set to allow content types, has the Item root content type enabled. When you create a custom list and add nothing but a new item, you still get the Title column, right? How can this be, if you haven't added the column Title at all?

As you create a new list, SharePoint automatically adds the Item root content type to your list. That content type contains only a single column. Guess what it is called.

NO, REALLY, I AM NOT USING CONTENT TYPES!

If you still think you're not using content types, care to bet $5 on that?

Create a new custom list, and don't add anything; just give the list a name, and click OK. Now stop. You haven't done anything to add any content types, right?

Start SharePoint Manager 2007. If you don't have SPM, get it; it is free and one of the best SharePoint tools that exists. It is available free from CodePlex at http://codeplex.com/spm. Go ahead, I'll wait right here.

Ready? Browse to your newly created list in SPM. In the Properties pane, find the property collection ContentTypes, and click the three little dots. You will see something like this:

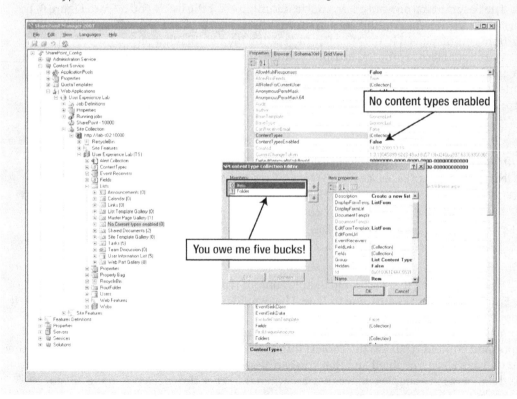

> Notice that ContentTypesEnabled is set to False but that you still are given two content types to the list, Item and Folder. Notice also that the form template names are set to ListForm.
>
> So, you are using ContentTypes, no matter how much you don't want to use it.
>
> Now, hand over that $5.
>
> Actually, I'll settle for a nice and honest review of this book on Amazon.

Content types will have to wait until the next chapter for our enlightened presence, but for now, know that the EnableContentTypes turns on the management of content types through the web interface only.

The EmailAlias attribute is documented as being used to set the incoming address for an email-enabled list; however, it doesn't, which is a real shame actually, if only an inconvenience. I will explain more about this in a moment, but first I'll briefly describe what email enabling lists actually means. In short, you can email content to a SharePoint site and have the email and its contents stored in a list.

This functionality is quite cool and is definitely a user experience feature, so I will take a little time to elaborate on this in the "A Deep Dive into Email-Enabled Lists" section a bit later. I highly recommend reading that section because it contains some wonderful nerdy knowledge.

Oh, and yes, I will explain how to email enable custom lists. And if you are a good reader, I will do it with a single line of code. In the meantime, let's continue exploring the other attributes of site List elements.

Let's get back to the problem of the nonfunctioning EmailAlias attribute. If you examine the STS folder's onet.xml file, you will notice that several of the lists in the configuration with ID 0 have EmailAlias set. However, as much as you would think that would email enable the lists, no such thing happens.

To be honest, that is a good thing, because the email aliases are global to the farm. If you had set the alias for one list in one configuration, you would get an error if you tried to ever use the same configuration again.

If you look at how Microsoft creates new lists on the "create new list" page (new.aspx, which in turn inherits Microsoft.SharePoint.ApplicationPages.NewListPage), you will see that even Microsoft manually sets EmailAlias if you fill in the property.

You can safely ignore the EmailAlias attribute; it doesn't do anything except confuse you.

VersioningEnabled and EnableMinorVersions are closely related. Setting VersioningEnabled will allow you to store multiple versions of a file in a document library or an item in a list. If you additionally set EnableMinorVersions, you will also get subversions to each major version; that is, your versioning will be 1.1, 1.2, 1.3, and so on, with the second number being the minor version and the first number being the major version.

Versioning in SharePoint is a really powerful feature that you can use to track changes and make sure you keep a record of those changes in case you want to revert later. Although a thorough examination of versioning is a bit outside the scope of this book, you should know that major versions are considered the published versions while the minor versions are drafts. If you enable versioning, you can have both a published version visible to everyone and a version visible only to you, list managers, and approvers. Once you are done with your edits, you can publish a new major version, which then becomes visible to everyone.

ForceCheckout forces users to check out a document if they want to edit it. This is useful if you have many people potentially working on the same document at the same time.

Basically, *checking out* a document means that nobody can edit the item until you check the document in again. That prevents situations where two editors modify the same document at the same time. Although useful most of the time, if you forget to check the document in again, it will remain checked out, and nobody will be able to edit the document at all.

Note that you do not need the document to check the document into the library again. If you delete the document on your local hard drive, you can still check the document in to the library by just changing the checked-out status in the library. The version you originally downloaded will then be available again.

QuickLaunchUrl determines to which URL the list name in the QuickLaunch menu should be linked. You must use a relative path here, pointing to a file that actually exists. For example, if you try to set QuickLaunchUrl to http://www.live.com/, it will not work, and the entire link will be removed.

QuickLaunchUrl can be a useful way of setting the link in the QuickLaunch menu, but other methods offer far more flexibility, and I will show you how when we get to list templates later in the chapter.

Remember that "Maybe" annotation from Figure 6-1? Now you know that a link in the QuickLaunch menu might not lead to the All Items view.

RootWebOnly lets you ensure that a list is created only if the site is provisioned as the root site of a site collection. This is useful if you have centrally stored data that needs to exist only once for an entire site, such as global templates, images, or other documents. My preference is to create a separate site definition for the root site of a site collection in any case, so I do not use this much, but that is just me.

A Note on List Instances in Site Definitions

I recommend against using the List element of onet.xml. First, think of reusability. If you create a list instance, you need to replicate the tag for every site in which you intend to provision that list. Putting a list instance in a feature is much more flexible.

Second, using lists in onet.xml is antiquated. It may even be considered obsolete in a future version of SharePoint. The documentation hints at this, stating that the ListInstance element of a feature is the same as the List element *previously* located in onet.xml.

The List element of onet.xml may or may not be removed at some point because of reusability, but even if it will remain supported, list instances in features are much more flexible.

You may wonder why I did not mention this in the beginning of this section. My question to you then is this: would you have read the information if I had warned you against using the element?

Note No out-of-the-box features actually use the ListInstance element in WSS, but several features use it in MOSS.

Lists in Features

As I mentioned earlier, there are other ways to create a list using CAML. I strongly recommend using features to provision lists rather than creating lists as part of the site definition, because features provide you with great flexibility and reusability, and all that power is transferred to list provisioning as well.

Now that you know how to create lists in onet.xml, you will see that provisioning list instances in features is a breeze. Of course, if you have no clue how to work with features, it will seem like riding a bicycle with the seat missing, but then again, reading Chapter 2 will alleviate that.

So, let's get on with the show.

To instantiate a list in a feature, you would add the ListInstance element to your elements.xml file in your feature. The ListInstance element resembles the List element from onet.xml, but there are differences. Here's that breeze I was talking about earlier.

Note The nonfunctioning EmailAlias has been omitted from the ListInstance element. This is yet more evidence that it actually does not work to set that property through CAML code.

The omission virus also struck EnableContentTypes, ForceCheckout, and the attributes to control versioning. If you want to set these attributes, you need to use a FeatureActivated event handler. I will show you how in Chapter 12.

The ListInstance contains the attributes Description, FeatureId, Id, OnQuickLaunch, QuickLaunchUrl, RootWebOnly, TemplateType, Title, and Url. Of these, only OnQuickLaunch and Id were not covered in the "Lists in Site Definitions" section. Some attributes have changed names and meaning, but you should recognize all of these from the previous section.

In ListInstance, the list template type is now, more logically, specified in the TemplateType attribute. The Id attribute is used to uniquely identify the list instance within this feature. The documentation states that Id is both required, which is false, and that it must be an integer, which is also false. Even if you have no Id, pun intended, you will still get the list created. OnQuickLaunch will allow you to decide whether the list should be added to the QuickLaunch menu when the list is created. You can also set this attribute in the ListTemplate for the list, but if you set the attribute in the ListInstance element, the latter will override the ListTemplate attribute.

See how easy that was? I told you it was a breeze.

With that in mind, let's briefly correlate the attributes of lists in site definitions with list instances in features. Table 6-2 lists the attributes in both elements.

Table 6-2. List *vs.* ListInstance *Attributes*

List	ListInstance
Description	Description
EmailAlias	Not available
EnableContentTypes	Not available
EnableMinorVersions	Not available
FeatureId	FeatureId
ForceCheckout	Not available
QuickLaunchUrl	QuickLaunchUrl
RootWebOnly	RootWebOnly
Title	Title
Type	TemplateType
Url	Url
VersioningEnabled	Not available
Not available	OnQuickLaunch

OK, with that out of the way, I think we should take a break from easy street and take a side trip down a deep, deep path to discover something that is a mystery for many developers, email enabling lists. It is also time to cash in on that promise I made about teaching you how to email enable a custom list with only a single line of code. But first, we need some knowledge.

A Deep Dive into Email-Enabled Lists

Caution Deep water ahead. Wear a life vest at all times.

When you set up your SharePoint farm to have incoming email enabled, you can set up certain list types to receive email. What you need to actually make lists able to receive email is to set EmailAlias to the alias part of the incoming email address. The alias would be the part before the @example.com part, such as "documents" in documents@example.com.

Note In the default web interface management of "Incoming email settings," there is an "Allow incoming email" radio button. The only purpose of that button is to allow or disallow you from filling in an email alias. There is no "Enable incoming email" property of the list object; when you set EmailAlias to an alias, the list becomes email enabled.

Only lists based on certain list templates can be email enabled, but sadly not the Custom List template that comes out of the box. If you try creating a custom list in your site and then go to configure the email settings, you will find that no such thing exists. It seems that only a few list template types support incoming email to a list. Many an online developer has asked countless questions about this, but the answer is more or less uniform: you can't do it.

But can you really email enable a custom list? *Building the SharePoint User Experience*'s reporter, Bjørn Furuknap, set out to find the real truth behind the mystery of email-enabled custom lists. What he discovered will shock the SharePoint world. Stay tuned to hear the true story of incoming email in SharePoint.

Note At this point, you are free to imagine some really cool documentary intro, perhaps some action shots of me digging into the SharePoint DLLs and, of course, a whole range of nice women, fast cars, and piles of SharePoint books.

Hello and good evening. My name is Bjørn Furuknap, and tonight we reveal the shocking truth behind email enabling custom SharePoint lists. During the course of the last two… hours…I have been fighting my way through treacherous terrain far behind enemy lines to bring you knowledge of what really goes on with SharePoint lists and incoming email. What you are about to see will blow your mind, but can this elusive beast be caught on tape? Be prepared as we dive deep into the phenomenon of how to email enable custom lists.

The list templates that can be email enabled are defined by a rather curious piece of code in the `Microsoft.SharePoint.dll` assembly, in the `SPList`'s `CanReceiveEmail` property. The code eventually calls an `if` statement in the `SPEmailHandler.HasHandler` method that checks whether the template on which the list is based is one of the `SPListTemplateType` template types that supports email enabling out of the box:

- Announcements

- Events

- DocumentLibrary

- PictureLibrary

- XMLForm

- DiscussionBoard

- Blog

Why only these template types? Actually, there is no technical reason why Microsoft could not allow you to have email-enabled custom lists. The problem arises when you start to think about what a custom list really is. It is custom, right? No predefined columns at all. So, creating a feature to add an email to a list with no columns is rather pointless. At best, you could use the default `Item` content type column `Title` to store the subject, but that would not give you much benefit at all.

So, is there any hope of getting a custom list email enabled? Oh yes, in fact, the CanReceiveEmail property reveals a vital clue. Not only does it check for the template types in the previous list, but it also checks whether the list has the Boolean property HasExternalEmailHandler set to true. To understand what this means, we need to dig a bit deeper.

Tip Even though we cannot directly receive email to a custom list without some custom development, we sure as heck can work around the issue. I have written an online article series on business process automation in SharePoint that details how you can use an intermediary announcement list and a simple workflow to put an email into a custom list. The three-part article series is available at http://www.understandingsharepoint.com/url/10001. Or you could just read on to find out how you can email enable custom lists.

If you need your boss to understand what happens when you send an email to the list, tell her or him that you get a new item created in the list. The title of that item is set to the subject of the email, and the body is set to the contents. For document libraries, including the picture library, you can send files directly to the library, and they will be added to the library.

This explanation should reveal an interesting clue to our problem. If incoming email is handled differently in a library than in another type of list, then there must be some functionality determining how incoming email is handled that differs between these list types.

The handling of incoming email is done by a SharePoint timer job that runs every minute. The job itself eventually calls a method, SPIncomingEmailServiceInstance.ProcessEmail, which iterates through the incoming emails to figure out where that email should be placed. It does so by calling a stored procedure, proc_getEmailEnabledListByAlias, which retrieves the list to which the alias is bound, and then gets a handler that will be responsible for storing the email correctly. The following shows the GetHandler function of the SPEmailHandler class:

```
public static SPEmailHandler GetHandler(SPList list) {
    if (!list.HasExternalEmailHandler)
    {
        switch (list.BaseTemplate)
        {
            case SPListTemplateType.DocumentLibrary:
            case SPListTemplateType.PictureLibrary:
            case SPListTemplateType.XMLForm:
                return new SPDocLibEmailHandler(list);

            case SPListTemplateType.Survey:
            case SPListTemplateType.Links:
            case SPListTemplateType.Contacts:
            case SPListTemplateType.Tasks:
                goto Label_007D;

            case SPListTemplateType.Announcements:
```

```
                return new SPAnnouncementsEmailHandler(list);

            case SPListTemplateType.Events:
                return new SPCalendarEmailHandler(list);

            case SPListTemplateType.DiscussionBoard:
                return new SPDiscussionEmailHandler(list);

            case SPListTemplateType.Posts:
                return new SPBlogPostEmailHandler(list);
        }
    }
    else
    {
        return new SPExternalEmailHandler(list);
    }
Label_007D:
    return null;
}
```

As you can see, there are different types of handlers for the incoming emails, depending on the type of list or library. You will recognize the list template types in the earlier list. Note also that if the list template type is Survey, Links, Contacts, or Tasks, SharePoint will purposely deny any attempt at sending email by returning a null object, which in turn prevents any handling of the email. There's another strange thing, especially when you read on.

If you check the last else bracket in the previous code (snippet), you also see that if no handler can be found, a default SPExternalEmailHandler is returned. So, if there is a defaulthandler called SPExternalEmailHandler, could we utilize that to get our custom list email enabled? Let's see....

The SPExternalEmailHandler class inherits from the SPEmailHandler class. The SPEmailHandler class defines an abstract method called ProcessMessage that will be called for each message in the current batch. The ProcessMessage method is what does the heavy lifting of getting an email message into a list. Although the email handler for libraries is obfuscated in the DLL, we can peek into the other handlers to see what Microsoft was thinking.

Tip I do recommend you take a stroll down the email handler lane with .NET Reflector to see how Microsoft has done its handlers, because you will discover why there are different handlers for each of the different template types. For now, let's keep our goal in view and get our custom list email enabled.

Caution I am sure you read Chapter 5 and remember this, but just in case you were a bit tired and don't remember: do not touch any of the default files that ship with Windows, including the database tables, stored procedures, database views, or anything else. Just don't.

The important thing for us now is the SPExternalEmailHandler and, more to the point, the ProcessMessage of that handler. That method, through some skipping and jumping, checks all the event receivers for a list. If any of those event receivers is of type SPEventReceiverType.EmailReceived, then that receiver is fired.

"Hang on here," I can hear you say, "I have worked with list event receivers before, but there is no EmailReceived method to override!"

And if you actually said that, you would be absolutely right (and I would have hearing that would rival Superman). The SPListEventReceiver class has no such method. However, the SPEmailEventReceiver class does. With that knowledge, we can create a receiver to manage adding items to our custom list. Check out Figure 6-3.

```
1  using System;
2  using System.Collections.Generic;
3  using System.Text;
4
5  using Microsoft.SharePoint;
6  using Microsoft.SharePoint.Utilities;
7
8  namespace EMailEnabledCustomList
9  {
10     public class EmailCustList : SPEmailEventReceiver
11     {
12         public override void EmailReceived(SPList list, SPEmailMessage emailMessage, string receiverData)
13         {
14             SPListItem item = list.Items.Add();
15             item["Title"] = emailMessage.Headers["Subject"];
16             item["sender"] = emailMessage.Sender.ToString();
17
18             item.Update();
19
20
21         }
22     }
23  }
24
```

Figure 6-3. *Sample* EmailEventReceiver *code*

Great, we are getting close, but I don't smell cigar smoke yet. We still need to connect that event receiver to our list. We might use a feature to this, but heck, since we're already in code land, we might as well create a console application to do the work for us. What you would need to add to the basic console application in Visual Studio, besides the rather obvious reference to Microsoft.SharePoint.dll, would be the following code:

```
static void Main(string[] args)
{
    string site_name = "http://lab-s02:10000/";
    string list_name = "emailcustomlist";

    using (SPSite site = new SPSite(site_name))
    {
        using (SPWeb web = site.OpenWeb())
        {
            SPList list = web.Lists[list_name];
            list.EventReceivers.Add(
                SPEventReceiverType.EmailReceived,
                "YOUR ASSEMBLY INFO GOES HERE",
```

```
            "EMailEnabledCustomList.EmailCustList");
        }
    }
}
```

Note that in the code you would replace the site_name and list_name with information from your site and also replace the "YOUR ASSEMBLY INFO GOES HERE" with your five-part strong name for your assembly. But you knew that.

Once we run this application, something strange and wonderful happens. If you go to your list in the web interface, guess which new setting is available on the List Settings page. If you get tired of guessing, check out Figure 6-4.

Figure 6-4. *Voilá!*

We have just solved one of the great mysteries of SharePoint, and with the right knowledge, all it took was a single line of code to register the right event handler. Of course, your actual event handler may be as complex as you need, but you get the point here.

Note If you intend to debug this baby, remember what I said about incoming email handling being done by the timer job. Attach to OWSTIMER.exe rather than w3wp.exe if you want to step through your code.

It's time to move on; we have more secrets to discover.

List Templates

Now that you know how to create lists from templates, it is time to start exploring these templates and how you can use them to customize the user experience.

List templates are defined in two ways, either in the site definition onet.xml file or in a feature. By now you probably know what I recommend, and if not, you haven't been paying attention and should go sit in the corner.

The good news is that creating list templates in onet.xml and in features are very much the same. Although there are trade-offs with creating list instances in features, doing the same with list templates carries no such penalties.

The bad news is that list templates can be quite complex. The ListTemplate element itself holds plenty of attributes, but the true complexity begins when we look at the list template definition file schema.xml.

Let's begin.

Note Do not confuse list templates deployed with features with list templates saved from an existing list through the web interface. In this book we are talking only about list templates in the form of definitions of new lists, not saved list templates from the web interface.

ListTemplate Element

You will find the ListTemplate element in the ListTemplates section of the onet.xml file or in the elements file of a feature. Because the two list templates are similar, I will cover the attributes only once. Also, since complete coverage of all ListTemplate attributes would require too much space, I will focus on the most useful attributes from a user experience perspective.

Tip Quite a lot of the attributes affect the list that is created from the template. Other attributes, such as Category, affect the list template. Pay attention; the devil resides in the minute details.

AllowDeletion affects the list instance and determines whether the list can be deleted. Some lists, such as the User Information list, will cause serious consequences to your site if deleted, so set this attribute to False if you'd like to prevent that with your lists.

If AllowDeletion is set to False, the link "Delete this list from the list settings" will not be present. Also, attempts to delete the list by other means, such as through code or SharePoint Manager 2007, will fail.

AllowEveryoneViewItems is both useful and overlooked. What it does is allow everyone to view items. Duh. Although that may be obvious, the real usefulness of this attribute requires a bit of a demonstration. Let's break your site, shall we?

1. Open your root site in your site collection, and go to the Master Page Gallery. You will find this under Site Settings in the column named Galleries.

2. Verify that owners, members, and guests have access to the `default.master`. Do this by opening the context menu and clicking "Manage permissions."

3. While on the Permissions page for `default.master`, go to the Actions menu, and click "Edit permissions." You will be warned that this may have dire consequences, but we are developers, and we don't listen to such nonsense.

4. Remove all permissions by selecting all the groups' check boxes and then, from the Actions menu, click "Remove permissions." Again, ignore any nagging warning; just click OK and verify that no users now have access to the `default.master` file.

■**Note** If you actually went ahead and did all these steps, I thank you for your blind vote of confidence. The next thing you should do is send all your cash to my PayPal account. Then you should reconsider your policy on trusting strange authors who tell you to do weird things.

You may think that removing all permissions on the master page of a site would crash the site horribly. After all, the `default.master` is used on every page and form. However, since the Master Page Gallery has the `AllowEveryoneViewItems` attribute set to `True`, well, everyone can view items.

This even applies to users from other sites. If a user has access only to subsite B but not to root site A, the user can still access items in any list or library of A that has `AllowEveryoneViewItems` set to `True`.

You still need at least access to the web application, though, so setting `AllowEveryoneViewItems` does not allow anonymous access, since anonymous access is granted on the web application level.

Oh, to reverse the permission changes we made earlier, simply go back to the permissions of the item, and select Inherit Permissions from the Actions menu.

`BaseType` is absolutely required and determines from which of five possible root templates the site template should inherit. These root templates are as follows:

0: Generic list

1: Document library

3: Discussion forum

4: Vote or survey

5: Issues list

These root template types define some very important properties and columns. Although you may get a brief idea of what each type does just by looking at its name, it is important to know where these base types get their settings. The answer is that the base types are defined in the global site definition that we explored in Chapter 4.

If you look into the global site definition at `[12]\TEMPLATE\GLOBAL\XML\onet.xml`, you will find a section that you will not see in any other `onet.xml` files, the `BaseTypes` element. Check out Figure 6-5.

Figure 6-5. BaseTypes *element in the global* onet.xml

As you can see, there is no BaseType element with Type="2". I do not know why.

If you were to investigate these base types in more detail, you would find a mystery revealed. As you have likely noticed, every item you put into a SharePoint list gets a lot of columns apparently from nowhere. For instance, you have columns such as Author, Modified, Version, the EditControlBlock menu (also known as ECB, which appears when you hover over the title of an item), and so on. All these columns and others get added from the BaseType. We will cover fields and columns in great detail in Chapter 9, but for now, take a look at Figure 6-6 to see how the ECB is actually created.

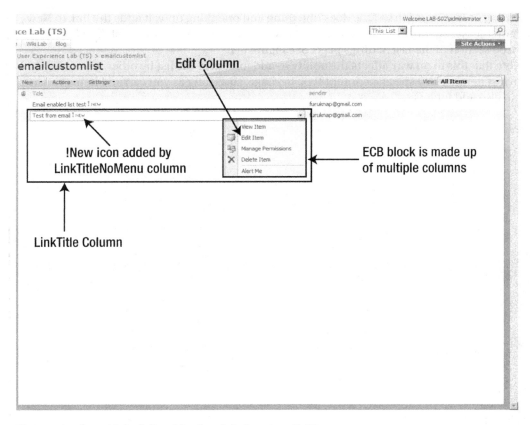

Figure 6-6. *The ECB is defined in the global* onet.xml *file.*

Category defines in which of the four columns on the Create page the template should appear. The possible categories are Libraries, Communications, Tracking, and Custom Lists.

If you omit this attribute, your list will be in the Custom Lists column. Also, there is no way to add other categories; the given categories are hard-coded in the Microsoft. SharePoint.ApplicationPages.CreatePage class from which the create.aspx page inherits.

Description simply gives the list template a description to be displayed when hovering over the list template title on the Create page.

DisallowContentTypes may seem similar to the EnableContentTypes attribute of lists but is in fact very different, even beyond the obvious enabling and disallowing differences. DisallowContentTypes actually removes the possibility of managing content types completely. There will not be an option to turn management of content types on at all.

Not just that, but DisallowContentTypes is actually a protected property of the list, meaning that there is no way to change it on a list if it is set once. Be careful with this attribute; there is no way back if you wander down that road.

DisplayName is the title of the list template, meaning the name users will see when they look at the Create page. Note that there is a difference between the Name attribute and DisplayName. The Name attribute is the internal name of the list template and is rarely seen by users.

Setting FolderCreation to True does one thing and one thing only; it adds the link to New Folder on the New toolbar button in the list. This is the same setting as you will find in the Advanced section of the List Settings page. See Figure 6-7.

Note that this in no way affects the ability to add folders to the list by other means. Folders are just items with a specific content type heritage, so as long as you can add items to a list, you can also add folders.

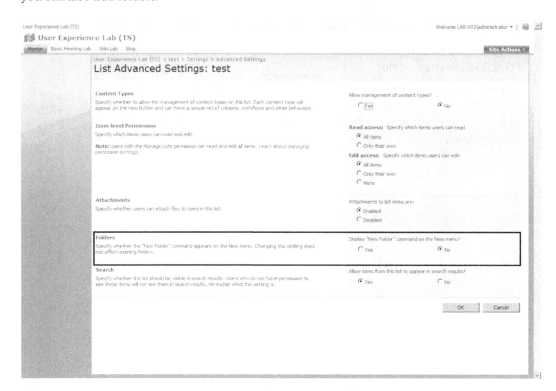

Figure 6-7. *Setting New Folder to be visible through the web interface*

Hidden and HiddenList may appear similar, and are indeed related, but they affect different objects. The Hidden attribute hides the list template from view on the Create page, while the HiddenList attribute hides the list that is created without affecting the display of the template.

Note that hiding the list template in no way prevents lists from being created by other means. You can still create lists using features or code, or you can simply link directly to the New List creation page using the feature ID and list template parameters, for instance like this: http://lab-s02:10000/_layouts/new.aspx?FeatureId={f8dc6818-6fa9-4a5c-a96b-eeb9b7b078c7}&ListTemplate=10002. This particular link will take you to the Create New List page to create a list based on the list template having an ID of 10002 in the feature with the specific GUID.

If you set both Hidden and HiddenList to True, the list template will not be displayed, and the list will be hidden. An example of this is the User Information list, which, despite that you interact with it on a fairly regular basis, is considered hidden. As you can then surmise, hiding the list does not prevent the list from being manipulated either; it just hides it from interface elements that choose to honor the Hidden attribute, such as the View All Items page.

Note The "Hidden and HiddenList set to true" combo also applies to the gallery libraries, such as the Master Page Gallery, List Template Gallery, and Web Part Gallery.

One option that has puzzled me and that I thought would be utterly useless is to have the list template be visible but the list hidden. Thus, you can allow people to create the list, but they will not see it. However, if you intend to create your own separate list management interface for the list, having the list visible for all to see may not be part of your plan.

Image contains a URL, relative to the site, that holds the icon image of the list. You may think this is a waste of time, but consider your users and how much an icon can improve their understanding of what kind of list or library has been created.

Tip You can also place the list icon in the [12]\TEMPLATE\LAYOUTS\IMAGES folder, since that directory is mapped to the virtual path, /_layouts/images, of every site.

Name is the internal name of the list. Most important, this attribute defines the subdirectory in which SharePoint will search for the Schema.xml file. If you set your Name attribute to MyListTemplate in a feature called MyFeature, SharePoint will search in the [12]\TEMPLATE\FEATURES\MyFeature\MyListTemplate directory for the schema.xml file. For a site template, the same applies, but the schema.xml file should be under the [12]\TEMPLATE\SiteTemplates\YourSiteDefinitionName\MyListTemplate folder.

This is not the title of the list template. I repeat: this is not the title of the list template. If I had a dollar for every time I have found developers using Name as the title field, I would have…about $3, but in any case, remember this distinction. The title field of a list template, that is, the name that users will see when selecting a list template, is called DisplayName.

NewPage is also seldom used but is a really cool attribute, especially compared to its sibling EditPage. I will explain EditPage a bit later.

The NewPage attribute is the page that gets displayed when you click the list template title on the Create page. Setting this means that you can create your very own user experience when creating a new list, including gathering additional information, creating a fancy wizard, or pretty much anything you like.

Tip Oh, one thing...SPList objects do not have any property bag like SPWeb and SPListItem have, so you will not be able to store any custom properties or data in the list itself. You still have options for storing custom data about the list, though. For instance, use the RootFolder property of the SPList, which will return to you an SPFolder, which does have a property bag. You can see a practical example of this in the article at http://www.understandingsharepoint.com/url/10007 on my blog.

Is this a best practice? Heck, why not? Microsoft does it all the time to store custom data, so we should be able to do the same. To see this, start SharePoint Manager 2007, and open any of the root folders on your site. Then, expand the Properties node, and you will see a ton of properties that Microsoft sets for you.

Note that you have to do some heavy lifting to create the list. In your code-behind file, you must create the list using code and then customize that list according to your needs. On the default NewPage, Microsoft uses its own class for this, Microsoft.SharePoint. ApplicationPages.NewListPage. Sadly, the NewListPage class is not intended for external use (in other words, by us) and is undocumented. That being said, creating a function to facilitate the creation of a list should not be too much of a problem. A simple SPWeb.Lists.Add() method call should do the trick.

Note I know the documentation states that the NewPage, and its sibling EditPage, should be used to set the name of a custom form that will be used to add new (or edit existing) items on a list.

It doesn't work.

The EditPage attribute would be about the coolest thing since the last ice age if it were a replacement for the List Settings page, but it isn't. Instead, setting this attribute will replace the "Versioning settings" link on the List Settings page.

I am fairly certain that somewhere in Redmond is a developer with a very good idea of why this would be the logical use of the EditPage attribute value. I, on the other hand, am not smart enough to see that kind of logic, so bear with me when I say that this is just the way it is.

Setting the EditPage attribute to a valid and site-relative URL will change the "Versioning settings" link on the List Settings page. Take a look at Figure 6-8.

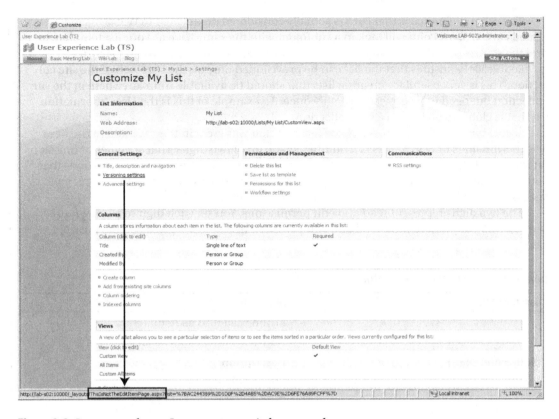

Figure 6-8. *Just so you know I am not crazy. At least not that crazy.*

Another factor makes this attribute even worse. You may be thinking that having a page that you can customize however you like, even if it has an awkward link, may be a good thing, but consider this: since you are overriding the "Version settings" link, you must either handle the version settings yourself on that page, in addition to anything else you might want to customize, or lose the item versioning altogether.

Apart from the AlternateHeader attribute of the Project element we covered in Chapter 4, this has to be the most useless SharePoint feature ever, and that includes future versions of SharePoint.

I mentioned OnQuickLaunch earlier during the discussion on lists, and here it is. Setting OnQuickLaunch to either True or False sets the default value for all lists created from the template. You can override this in the ListInstance element. The effect of setting OnQuickLaunch to True is that you will get a link to the list or library in the QuickLaunch menu. The link itself will, by default, link to the default view of the list, and the link text will be the list title. You can override this on the list instance as well by setting the QuickLaunchUrl attribute.

Path and SetupPath work in much the same way as they do for modules. Both let the list template know where to look for the files to be used for list creation, such as forms pages. The difference is that Path is relative to the list template, while SetupPath is relative to the [12]\TEMPLATE folder.

The other difference is that Path is actually considered deprecated in WSS 3. As mentioned earlier, SharePoint will look in a subfolder with the same Name as your list template to find the schema.xml file. The same goes for other files as well such as custom list forms.

RootWebOnly ensures that the list can be provisioned only on the root web of the site collection. This is very useful for creating lists that should be available from anywhere in the site collection but need to be provisioned only once. An example of this is the User Information list that is global to all sites in a site collection.

SecurityBits concerns one of those features that was great in theory, namely, the item-level permissions of WSS 3. This is a number, made up of two digits, that specifies permissions on individual items in the folder. However, note that this is not the normal permissions that you can set for groups and users from the "Manage permissions" menu. Rather, SecurityBits specifies an additional, and seriously flawed, security layer.

The two digits represent read and edit permissions. You set each digit to a value representing who you want to have read and edit permissions. Table 6-3 gives you the possible values.

Table 6-3. SecurityBits *Digit Values*

Read (First Digit)	Description
1	Anyone can read an item.
2	Only the author can read an item.
Edit (Second Digit)	**Description**
1	Anyone can edit an item.
2	Only the author can edit an item.
4	No one can edit an item.

So, if you want anyone to be able to read and edit items in the list, set SecurityBits to 11. If you want anyone to read but only the author to edit, use 12. If you want a read-only list, set 14.

The thing about SecurityBits, though, is that the value of the feature itself is really limited. What if you have set the read right to 1 but suddenly want your manager to see your new document? You can either let everyone see it or no one except yourself.

I always use normal security and just leave SecurityBits on 11. Managing security can be done with normal permissions, and I fail to see why including another and conflicting security mechanism helps. But you may disagree, so feel free to use it if you think it brings value to your solution.

Type is the attribute identifying the list template within the feature or site definition. The value of the attribute should be an integer that is unique within the feature. When you instantiate a list, the Type attribute would match either the Type attribute or the TemplateType attribute in the list, depending on how you create the list. Figure 6-9 illustrates this.

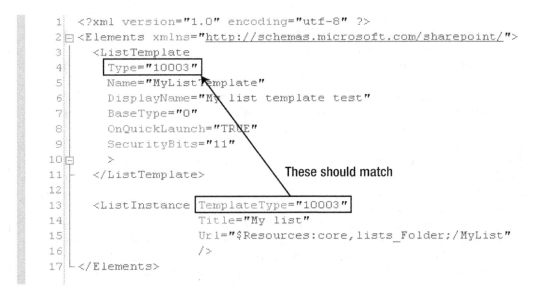

```
 1   <?xml version="1.0" encoding="utf-8" ?>
 2   <Elements xmlns="http://schemas.microsoft.com/sharepoint/">
 3     <ListTemplate
 4       Type="10003"
 5       Name="MyListTemplate"
 6       DisplayName="My list template test"
 7       BaseType="0"
 8       OnQuickLaunch="TRUE"
 9       SecurityBits="11"
10       >
11     </ListTemplate>
12
13     <ListInstance TemplateType="10003"
14                   Title="My list"
15                   Url="$Resources:core,lists_Folder;/MyList"
16                   />
17   </Elements>
```

These should match

Figure 6-9. *List instance* TemplateType *and list template* Type *attribute*

Microsoft recommends using integers greater than 10,000 for Type to avoid possible conflicts with future list templates from Microsoft. Although there is no technical reason why this should be the case, it doesn't hurt to follow this advice, so keep your Type integers greater than 10,000.

If you have worked extensively with SharePoint lists before, you may know that there are a ton of templates that ship with Microsoft that have Type numbers from 100 to around 300 in addition to a few more.

If Unique is set to True, a list based on this template can be created only once for each site. For example, the User Information list or most of the built-in galleries have this attribute set to True.

There is a quirk here, though. If Unique is set, the list template will not appear on the Create page, regardless of whether an instance of the list exists. I believe Microsoft's motivation is that this attribute should be set only for lists created during site provisioning, and thus, there will not be a need to actually let the user manually create the list.

I think that is sad. I mean, this could have been a great feature. Consider having your users be able to create a list, but only once. This would have been an excellent option for creating a sitewide template library or a common images library or a range of other such lists or libraries.

You can still actually create a list, even through the web interface, but you need to give the users a direct link to the New.aspx page with the FeatureId and ListTemplate parameters set manually. Naturally, you can have only one list instance at a time if the Unique attribute is set to True.

`UseRootFolderForNavigation` is also a curious little animal that hops around in the forest without anyone even knowing it is there. When I first read the documentation, it took me several hours to find out how to use the attribute.

The simple idea is that you can use a custom welcome page for a list rather than the default view of all the items in the list. I think this is a marvelous idea; rather than having that dreadful list, you can have a starting page with perhaps some detailed instructions, an introduction to a library, a better interface to library navigation such as an Explorer-style tree view, or even a more intuitive preview using Ajax or Silverlight. Now *that's* a user experience enhancement if I ever saw one.

Sadly, at the time, there were only about five hits on Google for the attribute, and the documentation is at best confusing. I will skip the long story of how I found out (you can read it in my blog at `http://www.understandingsharepoint.com/url/10006` if you are really interested), and I will just explain how it works.

You might actually already have seen this in action. The wiki library uses this feature to display a specific wiki page rather than a list of pages when you enter the library. Basically what you need to do, besides setting this attribute to `True`, is to set the `WelcomePage` property of the root folder of the list. The above explanation is not very enlightening unless you have done this before.

First, take a look at Figure 6-10. I have opened the root folder of a wiki site in SharePoint Manager 2007. Feel free to follow along if you like.

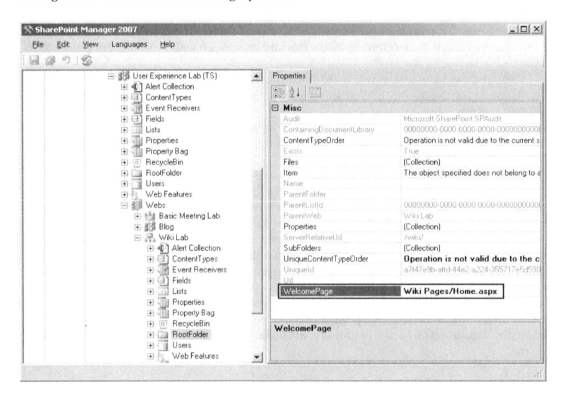

Figure 6-10. `WelcomePage` *property set on wiki site*

If you look at Figure 6-10, you will notice that there is a `RootFolder` located at the root of the site. This folder is the virtual place where files such as `default.aspx` are stored. There will also be a folder, `Lists`, that contains subfolders for all the lists of your site, as well as the root `Folder` objects for all your libraries.

Each of these folders is represented in the object model by an `SPFolder` object. `SPFolder` objects are useful for several reasons. As mentioned earlier, `SPLists` do not have any property bag, so if you want to store custom information about a list, you are out of luck—at least until you remember that there is an `SPFolder` object for each `SPList`, meaning you can store the properties in the `SPFolder` instead.

To use the `UseRootFolderForNavigation` attribute, however, we will use the `WelcomePage` property of the list's `SPFolder` to store the URL to a page that will serve as the front page of our list. The easy choice to set the `WelcomePage` property is to just use a tool like SharePoint Manager to set the property. However, that is not very scalable and certainly not deployable.

Sadly, there is no CAML way to store `SPFolder` properties. This means that in order to set the property, we need to use code. For instance, you can use a `FeatureActivated` event handler to set the property.

OK, that just about completes the `ListTemplate` attributes. Here is what I would call a good news/bad news situation. The good news is that there is little more you should know about the `ListTemplate` element. There are no subelements, and the attributes that we have not covered here are either very easy to understand or very unimportant to understand, at least from a user experience point of view.

The bad news is that there is one more thing you must learn in order to create a list template, and that is `schema.xml`. You may have wondered how the attributes of a list template would be enough to create a list, and the answer is that the `ListTemplate` element is only one part of the solution.

schema.xml

Caution Before we press on into the forest called `schema.xml`, you must know that somewhere inside the forest lies a cave where a mighty monster lives. We must enter that cave if we are to reach the enlightened peaks of SharePoint knowledge. Very few developers are brave enough to face the monster, and even fewer return with their sanity intact. It is said that at night you can still hear the screams of previous developers as they try to claw their own eyes out of their heads.

It is important that you pay attention to what I say. I have walked this forest many times, and although I cannot protect you inside the cave, I can make sure you don't step outside the safe path.

There is still time to walk away; just close the book, put it in your bookshelf, and never think of it again. If you decide to remain here, though, please make sure you have your affairs in order, that you have written a last will and testament, and that you are wearing clean underwear.

I would like to make our trek as easy as possible. After all, a forest is there to be enjoyed, right? We are going to look at an existing and basic `schema.xml` to understand how that file is built. To accomplish this, you need to get the proper gear in place:

1. Start with the Feature template from Chapter 3.

2. Open the [12]\TEMPLATE\FEATURES\CustomList folder in Windows Explorer. Copy the entire CustList folder into your project, under the MyFeature folder. Feel free to rename the MyFeature folder to something a bit more intuitive, such as MyListTemplate. Do the same to the folder you copied. Take a look at Figure 6-11 for how this looks in my solution.

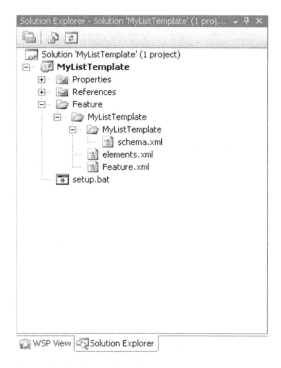

Figure 6-11. *Visual Studio solution for* MyListTemplate

3. Add the following code to the Elements element in elements.xml:

```
<ListTemplate
  Type="10001"
  Name="MyListTemplate"
  DisplayName="My list template test"
  BaseType="0"
  SecurityBits="11"/>
```

■ **Note** Make sure the value in the Name attribute matches the name of the subfolder containing schema.xml. The Name attribute tells SharePoint where to find the schema.xml file.

---

4. Build and verify that your new list template appears on the Create page of your site.

With that out of the way, you should be ready to start exploring. Open the schema.xml file (see Figure 6-12).

Caution Quickly close the Views section of the schema.xml file. That is where the beast resides. We are not going in there before we have had plenty of time to prepare.

Make sure this is closed!

Figure 6-12. *Basic* schema.xml *file*

With the Views section closed, you can see that the schema.xml file is not that horrible. The first thing that you should notice is that there is a List root element. This has nothing to do with the List element of the site definition.

There is only a single subelement, MetaData, which in turn contains just four sections. We will get to all of them shortly.

Note There are actually four other possible sections here in the MetaData section, but these are not important from a user experience view. I wish I could recommend looking in the documentation. Actually, I wish I had more space.

Perhaps if I used shorter words: U may ?: "if dis is all der is to sch.xml, big fuss?". Ah b patient. C the Vu section?

Nah, that didn't work.

You may be asking yourself, "If this is all there is to schema.xml, what's the big fuss about monsters and dark caves?" Ah, be patient. See that View section? Leave it closed, because inside that element are dragons. For now we should focus on the other elements of the MetaData section.

ContentTypes is the declaration of which content types should be added to the list. Inside the content types are two subelements, although only one is shown here, the ContentTypeRef. A ContentTypeRef is a reference to a content type that is defined elsewhere. In this case we are simply adding the default Item (0x01) and Folder (0x0120) content types. You will investigate content types and learn where the Item and Folder content types are defined in the next chapter.

You may notice that there is a folder subelement in the ContentTypeRef for Item. Although not required, this element specifies an SPFolder under the root folder of the site in which you can place resources or set properties to go with your content type. A document template for the content type is a good example.

The Fields section contains any list columns that should be added to the list on creation. You may find it strange that in the custom list this field is empty. However, recall that there are several global settings that add columns to the list, such as the BaseType of the list template as well as the Item content type. There will be plenty more on fields in Chapter 9, but for now just know that this is where you would add list columns to the list.

Note If you want an example of how this is used in a list template, you can look at the PictureLibrary feature. In the folder PicLib resides the schema.xml; just open and enjoy.

You should skip the Views section for now; we will get there in the next chapter. First we must know that we can master the outer parts of schema.xml before we go deeper down and face our demons.

The final element that is part of the custom list schema is Forms. Customizing forms is the most powerful method of enhancing the user experience of lists, basically because forms *are* the user experience of lists. In fact, this is so important to the user experience that I have dedicated an entire section of this chapter to list forms.

List Forms

I would love to tell you that if you understand list forms, you can work miracles. So I will. If you understand list forms, you can work miracles.

In its most fundamental sense, list forms are what users see when they do not see the front page, application pages, or any other page you have made for them (see Figure 6-13). When users look at a calendar in SharePoint, they're looking at a list form. When a user enters data into a task, then that is a list form. When a user sorts the items in a list, that is still a list form.

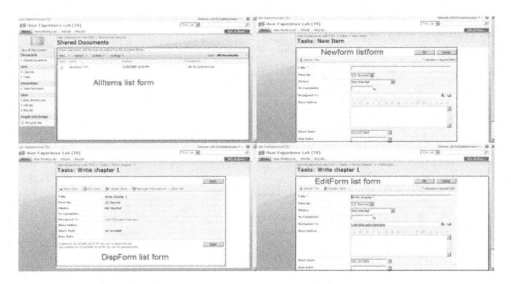

Figure 6-13. *Sample list forms*

To understand how these forms are built, you must first see how they are defined. The following code shows the list form definitions for the display form for the custom list template.

```
<Form Type="DisplayForm" Url="DispForm.aspx" SetupPath="pages\form.aspx"➥
WebPartZoneID="Main" />
```

The other two forms, NewForm and EditForm, are similar, differing in the Type and Url attributes.

The first thing you should notice is the SetupPath that is pointing to a file, pages\form.aspx. As with all SetupPath attributes, this value is relative to the [12]\TEMPLATE directory. So, if you go to [12]\TEMPLATE\pages, you should find a file called form.aspx. Open it. Or squint at Figure 6-14 if you are not in front of your computer.

```
1   <%@ Page language="C#" MasterPageFile="~masterurl/default.master"   Inherits="Microsoft.SharePoint.WebPartPages.WebPartPage,Microsoft
2   <asp:Content ContentPlaceHolderId="PlaceHolderPageTitle" runat="server">
3       <SharePoint:ListFormPageTitle runat="server">
4   </asp:Content>
5   <asp:Content ContentPlaceHolderId="PlaceHolderPageTitleInTitleArea" runat="server">
6       <SharePoint:ListProperty Property="LinkTitle" runat="server" id="ID_LinkTitle"/>: <SharePoint:ListItemProperty id="ID_ItemProperty
7   </asp:Content>
8   <asp:Content ContentPlaceHolderId="PlaceHolderPageImage" runat="server">
9       <IMG SRC="/_layouts/images/blank.gif" width=1 height=1 alt="">
10  </asp:Content>
11  <asp:Content ContentPlaceHolderId="PlaceHolderLeftNavBar" runat="server"/>
12  <asp:Content ContentPlaceHolderId="PlaceHolderMain" runat="server">
13  <table cellpadding=0 cellspacing=0 id="onetIDListForm">
14      <tr>
15       <td>
16       <WebPartPages:WebPartZone runat="server" FrameType="None" ID="Main" Title="loc:Main" />
17       <IMG SRC="/_layouts/images/blank.gif" width=590 height=1 alt="">
18       </td>
19      </tr>
20  </table>
21  </asp:Content>
22  <asp:Content ContentPlaceHolderId="PlaceHolderTitleLeftBorder" runat="server">
23   <table cellpadding=0 height=100% width=100% cellspacing=0>
24   <tr><td class="ms-areaseparatorleft"><IMG SRC="/_layouts/images/blank.gif" width=1 height=1 alt=""></td></tr>
25   </table>
26  </asp:Content>
27  <asp:Content ContentPlaceHolderId="PlaceHolderTitleAreaClass" runat="server">
28  <script id="onetidPageTitleAreaFrameScript">
29       document.getElementById("onetidPageTitleAreaFrame").className="ms-areaseparator";
30  </script>
31  </asp:Content>
32  <asp:Content ContentPlaceHolderId="PlaceHolderBodyAreaClass" runat="server">
33  <style type="text/css">
34   .ms-bodyareaframe {
```

Figure 6-14. *The* form.aspx *form*

Lo and behold! That looks just like a normal ASPX page, and in fact it is just that. And if it is nothing more than a normal ASP.NET page *and* we get to define which ASP.NET page it is, that means we can change and modify it as we please.

To create your own list form page, you can just create any web part page you like and include at least one web part zone. Then, in the Forms section of your schema.xml file, add both the form page file name and the web part zone ID:

```
<Form Type="DisplayForm" Url="DispForm.aspx" Path="MyCustomForm.aspx"➥
WebPartZoneID="MyWebPartZoneId" />
```

I love it when things are easier than I thought.

There is a problem, though—at least if we are to judge by what we have discovered so far. All the default form pages are the same, so how do you get different forms for New, Edit, and Display?

There are a few things to notice here. First, take a look at the PlaceholderMain code in Listing 6-1.

Listing 6-1. *Content from* form.aspx

```
<asp:Content ContentPlaceHolderId="PlaceHolderMain" runat="server">
<table cellpadding=0 cellspacing=0 id="onetIDListForm">
 <tr>
  <td>
 <WebPartPages:WebPartZone runat="server" FrameType="None" ID="Main"➥
Title="loc:Main" />
 <IMG SRC="/_layouts/images/blank.gif" width=590 height=1 alt="">
  </td>
 </tr>
</table>
</asp:Content>
```

Look at the web part zone there. It has an ID of Main, and our list form tags also referenced Main. That simply cannot be a coincidence. But what does it mean?

There is another clue as well. Remember that all the tags had a reference to the same page? NewForm, DisplayForm, and EditForm all used pages\form.aspx. So, how would the page know which form to display?

Form Templates

To answer all of these questions, we need to dig a bit deeper. I will advance you a bit of your knowledge allowance and tell you that it is all related to content types. And if you are still stubborn enough to claim you do not use content types, then please go back a few pages and put your five bucks where your mouth is. Here is definite proof, again.

You see, a list form is not just made up of the form.aspx page. What happens is that when an item form is opened, either DisplayForm, NewForm, or EditForm, SharePoint checks the content type of the item. Then it checks to see which form templates the content type uses for the different form types. The content type form template is then inserted into the list form to make up the complete form.

Let's start with the Item content type. Quite often this is the content type used when users create custom lists through the web interface. To check which form template Item uses, we must first find the definition for Item. Remember the global site definition from Chapter 4? The single base configuration activated two site features, one of them being the ctypes feature. That ctypes feature holds further clues, so next I want you to open the [12]\TEMPLATE\ FEATURES\ctypes folder and then open the ctypeswss.xml file, which is the elements file of the ctypes feature (see Figure 6-15).

```xml
 1  <?xml version="1.0" encoding="utf-8"?>
 2  <!--
 3  -->
 4  <Elements xmlns="http://schemas.microsoft.com/sharepoint/">
 5      <ContentType ID="0x"
 6          Name="$Resources:System"
 7          Group="_Hidden"
 8          Sealed="TRUE"
 9          Version="0">
10          <FieldRefs>
11              <FieldRef ID="{c042a256-787d-4a6f-8a8a-cf6ab767f12d}" Name="ContentType"/>
12          </FieldRefs>
13      </ContentType>
14      <ContentType  ID="0x01"
15          Name="$Resources:Item"
16          Group="$Resources:List_Content_Types"
17          Description="$Resources:ItemCTDesc"
18          Version="0">
19          <FieldRefs>
20              <FieldRef ID="{fa564e0f-0c70-4ab9-b863-0177e6ddd247}" Name="Title" Required="TRUE" ShowInNewForm="
21          </FieldRefs>
22          <XmlDocuments>
23              <XmlDocument NamespaceURI="http://schemas.microsoft.com/sharepoint/v3/contenttype/forms">
24                  <FormTemplates xmlns="http://schemas.microsoft.com/sharepoint/v3/contenttype/forms">
25                      <Display>ListForm</Display>
26                      <Edit>ListForm</Edit>
27                      <New>ListForm</New>
28                  </FormTemplates>
29              </XmlDocument>
30          </XmlDocuments>
31      </ContentType>
32      <ContentType ID="0x0101"
33          Name="$Resources:Document"
34          Group="$Resources:Document_Content_Types"
35          Description="$Resources:DocumentCTDesc"
36          V2ListTemplateName="doclib"
37          Version="0">
```

Figure 6-15. ctypeswss.xml *feature*

The important thing here is the XmlDocuments element in the content type with ID 0x01. That content type is the Item content type, and as you can see, there are three form templates for the three modes of a form, Display, Edit, and New.

I will not go too far into content types here (I still need you to read the next chapter!), but I will reveal that every other content type inherits from the Item content type. And, since all properties are also inherited, the form templates defined in Item will be inherited by child content types if they do not define their own form templates.

Note You may also see that there is a system content type, with ID 0x. Strictly speaking, every content type inherits from System. The only thing System defines is the very existence of an item, the ContentType column, which tells the item or document that it is a content type.

Perhaps this is the creation myth of SharePoint. "In the beginning was System, and System was 0x."

Finding the form templates is an important step on the way, but we still do not know where these templates live. To find them, you can do what I did and search the entire [12] for the string ListForm, eventually finding the right place, or, if you remember from Chapter 5, you can check to see whether this is actually a control template.

Open the DefaultTemplates.ascx file that is in [12]\TEMPLATE\CONTROLTEMPLATES. Scroll down…keep scrolling…a bit more…there! Did you see it? Around line 104 you will find a RenderingTemplate bearing the wonderfully familiar name of ListForm, just like the form template in the Item content type.

Eureka! We found it!

Not just that, but knowing that we can override the control template (see Chapter 5 if you don't remember) means we can completely customize any content type form to fit our needs. No more editing hundreds of list forms to modify the user experience; we can add or modify everything from a single file, just the way we want. Now you know why I called list forms powerful.

Still, we may want more. What if we do not want to modify everything but just add a nice display form to a news article content type? Well, knowing what we now know and having seen what we have seen, we can simply do something like the following to override the default form templates for our own content type:

```
<ContentType ID="0x01002ABA7C4C55F148068095A2E536A5069D"
    Name="News article"
    Group="$Resources:List_Content_Types"
    Description="Publish new news article"
    Version="0">
  <XmlDocuments>
    <XmlDocument ➡
      NamespaceURI="http://schemas.microsoft.com/sharepoint/v3/contenttype/forms">
      <FormTemplates ➡
        xmlns="http://schemas.microsoft.com/sharepoint/v3/contenttype/forms">
        <Display>ListForm</Display>
        <Edit>MyOwnEditForm</Edit>
        <New>ListForm</New>
```

```
        </FormTemplates>
      </XmlDocument>
    </XmlDocuments>
  </ContentType>
```

Notice the `MyOwnEditForm` form template.

Of course, we would have to actually create the template, which we would do by creating an `.ascx` file in the `[12]\TEMPLATES\CONTROLTEMPLATES` directory and adding a rendering template with an `Id` attribute matching our Edit form template name.

Let's take this a bit further with a tip. You can change the form template of a content type even after you have deployed the content type. Not just that, but you can change the form template for a given content type in a given list without affecting every other copy of the content type. To do so, you need to edit the content type on the list using a tool such as SharePoint Manager 2007. You could write your own code to do the exact same thing as well.

The reason why this very cool feature works is that content types get copied to the list when they are deployed. You will explore this more in Chapter 8, but just know that a content type on a list is a copy, not the master. I will demonstrate with a simple exercise:

1. Start by creating two identical task lists. If you use the site structure we created in Chapter 1, just add another task list to your root site.

2. Create a custom form template to use for one of the task lists:

    a. Create a new `.ascx` file in `[12]\TEMPLATE\CONTROLTEMPLATES`. Call it whatever you like; I used `MyCustomListForm.ascx`.

    b. Copy the `ListForm` rendering template tag from `DefaultTemplates.ascx`, including the start and end tags. Remember to include the `Control`, `Assembly`, and `Register` tags from the start of `DefaultTemplates.ascx`.

    c. Edit your new rendering template ID to something else, for instance `MyCustomListForm`. Also, make some kind of random change so you know that you are viewing the modified template later.

    d. Save your new `.ascx` file, and do an `IISRESET` to ensure the new template is picked up.

3. Start SharePoint Manager 2007, and navigate to your site and then to your newly created task list.

4. Expand the Content Types node, and find the Tasks node.

5. In the Properties pane, find the `NewFormTemplateName`, and modify the value to match the ID you set for your custom rendering template in step 2c (`MyCustomListForm`).

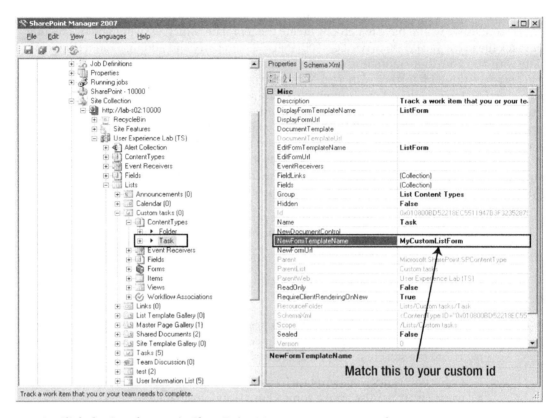

6. Click the Save button in SharePoint Manager to save your changes.

7. Open your customized task list in SharePoint, and click the New Item button to verify that magic has occurred, or just look at Figure 6-16. You may also want to check that the unmodified task list still has the normal template.

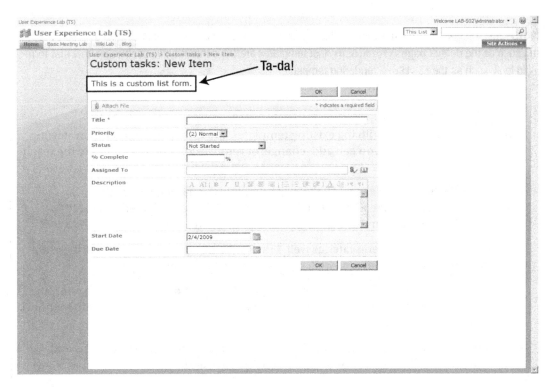

Figure 6-16. *Customized tasks list form template*

In this exercise, you modified the New form of a specific Task content type in a specific list. In a production environment, you would want to make these changes using code rather than manually setting the list templates. If you plan on going down this path, consider creating a feature or solution both to deploy your custom form template and to set the properties in a FeatureActivated handler.

Caution Modifying a content type on a list after the content type has been deployed is not likely to make Microsoft Support happy, but I am not sure on its policy on this. Heavy customization may also cause a maintenance nightmare unless you create a good management solution.

You can also create custom display form templates to use when showing an item or create a custom edit form to enhance the editing experience.

Now that you have seen how to customize the form templates and you know how to change the list form pages, you have even more tools to create a great user experience.

I would love to take the time to explain every detail on how you can create custom forms or modify existing ones, but I believe your imagination should have some freedom. And I am running out of pages in this book. I do want to share some ideas with you, however.

■ Note Just to make sure we are clear on this: list form pages are the ASPX pages used to generate the form, such as the default `pages\form.aspx`. List templates are the content type specifics on how that form should look, such as the `ListForm` rendering template.

- Start by copying and modifying existing templates and form pages rather than starting from scratch. That way, you can add, change, or remove content and compare the result with the default forms.

- Reflect the form template tags. All the `<SharePoint:...` tags come from the `Microsoft.SharePoint.WebControls` namespace that is easily reflected using .NET Reflector. You can learn much from just reading the source code.

- Explore the other form templates as well. `ListForm` is just one form template; there are several other form templates as well, such as the `DocumentLibraryForm`.

- Don't go overboard at first. Completely changing the user experience may be tempting, but remember that your users are used to working with SharePoint in a certain manner and may not approve of massive changes.

- Update your SharePoint installation! There are issues with using custom forms and attachments that have been fixed in the infrastructure update.

Preparing for the Final Battle

OK, we have been putting this off long enough. It is time enter the cave of pain to face what has become the worst fear for many developers.

Even Microsoft is scared of this place. The only map we have is the documentation, which lists only "numerous child elements" but no details beyond that. Most books and articles on this subject recommend only copying what others have done, but very few have even attempted to explain what happens inside. Few people have the courage to think of coming where we are about to go.

Before we go inside, however, there are a few final things you can do to prepare. We are armed with plenty of knowledge, but still there are steps to take:

1. Inform your loved ones what you are about to do. They may never see you again as you are now.

2. Settle your bills, and make sure your life insurance covers fighting mythical monsters.

3. Make sure you have 911 on speed dial. Seconds may count if anything goes wrong.

4. Get a good cup of strong, black coffee.

5. Wear clean underwear.

What lies within? Only what you bring with you.

It is time to face the big, bad monster.

CHAPTER 7

Encountering the Monsters in the Cave

Looking at Views in a Different View

This is it. We are about to enter the cave of monsters and dragons. You will need all your courage, and you will need to muster bravery beyond anything you have ever imagined.

Views are scary beasts. They look all cuddly and sweet when you look at them through the web interface, but beneath the surface they're dragons. Step once in the wrong direction, and you will be spending the better part of eternity trying to figure out what went wrong. And designer support? Hah! Never!

To be honest, views are not all that bad. Granted, they are the most elusive and complex part of any SharePoint solution, but how many gazillion SharePoint installations are there, and how often do you hear in the news that a raging horde of mentally unstable SharePoint developers have stormed Redmond demanding their sanity back?

What most people do not realize is that they fear only the unknown. Having come as far as we have on our journey, we know that once we are armed with the proper amount of knowledge, stoic discipline, a desire to master new things, and a bit of fun, we are able to climb any mountain and face any problem.

So, with those comforting thoughts, I think we are as ready as we will ever be.

Mission Statement

Here is what we want to accomplish. Keep this in mind as we walk deeper into the cave.

Our goal is to understand enough of views to be able to create a list with a custom view from scratch. Because we studied lists in great detail in the previous chapter, we'll focus solely on views here.

The second goal of this chapter is to explore some of the wealth of possibilities that views provide in order to start imagining all the cool things we can do to make SharePoint provide a great user experience. I won't be able to cover every detail of every element, but the topics covered here should get you started and perhaps curious enough to investigate a bit on your own.

The third goal is to keep the complexity down and focus on those aspects of views that yield the highest reward. That means we need to leave some treasure behind, but it also means we are more efficient in our learning.

Our final goal will be to come out alive. That may prove more difficult than you realize.

As I stand before the opening of the cave, I cannot help but feel a bit scared. There are plenty of tracks leading into the cave but few, if any, leading out. The stench of sulfur and rotting flesh feels like a wall, trying to prevent entry, but I know I must go inside and face whatever menace rests within. I take one quick look over my equipment before glancing up at the sun, perhaps for the final time….

What Are Views Anyway?

Views are the display of list data, usually in an HTML page. You know when you click a list and you get a list of all the items in that list? That list of items is a view. The example in Figure 7-1 should be a familiar view to everyone. If not, well, you might be in the wrong book.

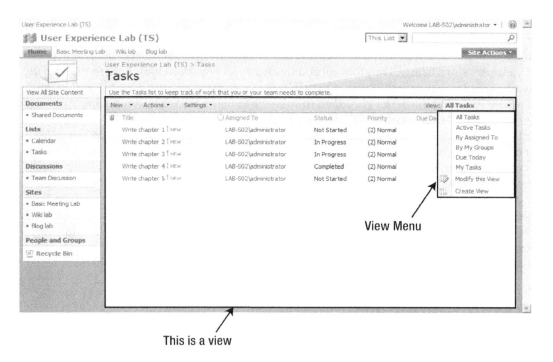

Figure 7-1. *View of a list*

You have probably created some of these views already through the web interface. If not, the following section is a quick run-through of how it's done. Oh, and you might want to pay attention even if you have created views before, because I will be referring to these steps later.

A Web Interface with a View

Start with any list you have created. I'm going with a custom list of books that I created on the Team Site lab of my root site, so any screenshots may be different from what you see if you choose another list. If you want to set up your list like mine, do the following:

1. Create a new custom list.

2. Add a choice column called Genre, and add a few book genres such as sci-fi, horror, mystery, drama, and children.

3. Add a number column titled Sales, and since we do not sell fractions of books, just change the number of decimals to 0. Make no other modifications.

4. Finally, add some sample data. Find some random book titles on the Web, or just make up your own titles. Fill in random data for the remaining columns; we don't need anything fancy.

Now you should be ready to follow the examples. Go into the list or library settings, and scroll all the way down where you will find the views that are already defined for the list or library. Hit Create View. You will be presented with two choices, either to create a view from scratch by selecting a view type or to start from an existing view.

The existing view list is created from all existing views, with a few modifications. Views that have the `Hidden`, `EditorModified`, or `ReadOnlyView` attributes set to `True` or that have an empty `Title` will *not* display.

We want to start from the beginning, so select the Standard view to start with a fresh view. Get it? Fresh view? The view puns will drive you mad.

Note There is no way to add view types, but you can add view styles, which is something completely different—and, might I mention, not particularly fun or practical.

Once you have clicked the Standard view, you get to the Create View page, which, for the simplest examples, requires very little of you. You input a name, decide whether this is a personal or public view, and select the columns to display and their order, and that's basically all you need to do.

The more advanced views require a bit more effort, but not much. If you want to add sorting, just select the columns on which to sort and then the sorting direction. For filtering, you select a column and then enter a value on which to filter the view. You can even add more filtering and sorting columns to make sure you display exactly what you want.

Want to limit the number of items in a view? Look toward the bottom of the available settings, and I am sure you can guess what "Number of items to display" means. Note that you can opt to display items in batches of a size or just limit the total number of items in a view. The latter is useful if you want to make a "Top 10 things to do for your cat" list, where numbers beyond 10 would ruin the point.

Grouping is also a nice option. Let's say you have a list of books, sorted by published date. You might want to categorize the books to list books in a certain genre. To do so, expand the

Group By setting, select the column on which to group items, decide whether to expand groups by default, and finally set how many groups should be present on each page. Figure 7-2 shows a basic view with grouping added.

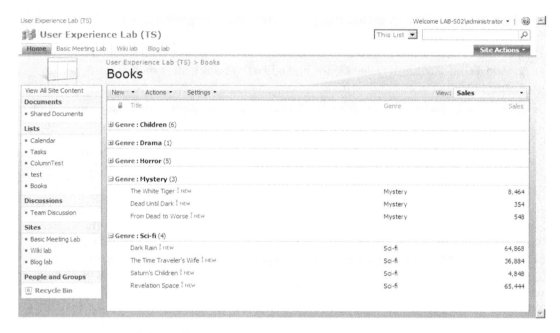

Figure 7-2. *Your run-of-the-mill grouping*

OK, you get the point here, and since you are a somewhat seasoned SharePoint user, these options should be familiar.

> *Somehow the cave didn't seem so dangerous. There were some smaller monsters lurking right inside the entrance but nothing that could warrant the fear that even the bravest warrior had for this place.*

> *What was all the commotion? Perhaps the big dragon at the end was dead. Perhaps no one had tried to enter the cave in a long time. How long could a dragon live without food? There might still be hope....*

The next few settings for a view require a bit more explanation, and because these will be explored in code later, it pays to be attentive right about now.

The Totals setting allows you to create aggregated views. Let's go back to your book list again and look at the Sales column for each of the book titles. By setting up an aggregate view, you will get a sum for all the book sales. This is even more useful if you have a grouped view since the aggregation will sum for each group as well. Take a look at Figure 7-3 for how this would look by default.

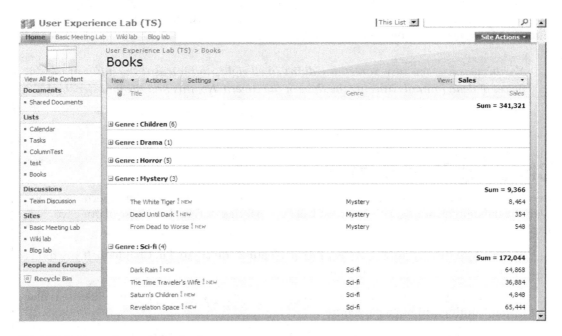

Figure 7-3. *Grouping and totals view*

You are not just limited to sums either; you can do averages, counts, variance, and other aggregations. Note that the available aggregations vary by field type. You cannot average a text field, for instance.

Next up are the view styles. View styles are sort of nice because they allow you to really change the user experience quickly. There are some built-in styles that you might explore, but basically there is little here that we cannot do in normal view development.

Note View styles are a bit old-fashioned and will not be covered in this book.

The folder settings on the view give you an option to not display items inside a folder. If your name is Merlin and you've had dealings with a guy named Arthur, you may recall that we talked about folders being content types in the next chapter. For the rest of us, we will investigate folders more in Chapter 8.

For the impatient, you just need to know that folders are items, just like anything else, that are based on a certain content type. Although it may appear that items are stored in a folder, it is more accurate to say that items are *connected* to a folder. All items, including folders, are stored in the same spot, regardless of folder structure.

Finally, you can choose to make this view a mobile view, which in essence strips away a lot of the navigation and pretty stuff to make a low-bandwidth, low-screen-real-estate version of the view. If you want to make your new view the default mobile view, you can do so.

Fine, we're done. These are the options we have when creating a view through the web interface. How hard can it be to do this in CAML?

No, this was way too easy. Something didn't smell right, and it wasn't the sulfur or the pieces of dead animals littering the floor of the cavern. No, this had the foul stench of trap.

Checking Your Gear

Before we go any further, it can help to have a basic list set up so that we can experiment a bit with the different elements. This basic list will be expanded during the course of our cave exploration.

1. Start with the custom `MyListTemplate` list feature you created in Chapter 6. If you didn't create that feature, you should do so now.

2. Make sure you have IntelliSense working. Developing views without IntelliSense is like parachuting without a parachute.

3. Deploy your list to one of your lab sites. I am using the Team Site lab, but you can choose whichever lab you like. Verify that your list gets created. If not, go back to step 1.

A Simple View of the World

Up to now we have always started out by looking at an existing piece of code from the out-of-the-box SharePoint installation. However, most of the views that ship with SharePoint are so complex that it will probably make you dizzy just looking at the code and trying to make heads and tails of it; so, we should start with something simpler. And what could be simpler than starting out with our own view with nothing but what we really, really need?

Start with the customized custom list template that you should have made by now. In your `schema.xml` file, look at the `Views` section, but ignore the views that are there already. What we want to do is add our own view, so close the existing views, and start with a simple piece of code:

```
<View BaseViewID="2"
     DisplayName="Custom View"
     Type="HTML"
     SetupPath="pages\viewpage.aspx"
     WebPartZoneID="Main"
     Url="CustomView.aspx">
</View>
```

That is really all you need to create a view. Build your solution, which should include a deployment if you have followed the instructions from Chapter 3, and create a new list based on your template if you didn't do this earlier.

The attributes to the view element are not very intimidating either. Your BaseViewId is the Id of the field, used to address this particular view, such as when you want to add your view to a page in a site definition. The DisplayName is, as always, the name shown to users of the view. Type can be set to HTML, Pivot, or Chart to specify, well, what type of view this is.

Tip When adding a view of a list to a web part page directly from the web interface, SharePoint looks for a view with a BaseViewId of 0. As such, if you want your users to be able to add a view of your list to a web part page, make sure you have a view with a BaseViewId of 0.

The next three attributes define how the view will be built into a page. SetupPath works like it does in modules and other places in SharePoint and defines a path, relative to [12], to a file from which the page holding the view will be created. The page itself may be a web part page, but you can also use regular pages. WebPartZoneID specifies in which web part zone on the page the view will be placed. This assumes that you have SetupPath pointing to a web part page.

Url is simply the list-relative URL where the final page will be placed. Note the fact that the URL is relative to the list. So, in our example, we will create a view, called Custom View, that will be placed inside the Main web part zone of a page. That page will be created based on the [12]\pages\viewpage.aspx page and stored at lists/[MyCustomList]/CustomView.aspx.

Of course, our view does not actually contain anything, so it's a rather pointless view at this time. We need to add some content. First, let's add a toolbar to make sure we can add new items and get access to the actions and settings menus:

```
<View BaseViewID="2"
      DisplayName="Custom View"
      Type="HTML"
      SetupPath="pages\viewpage.aspx"
      WebPartZoneID="Main"
      Url="CustomView.aspx">
  <Toolbar Type="Standard"/>
</View>
```

By adding the Toolbar child element, at least now we have an easy way of doing basic list operations. Figure 7-4 shows the result of the previous code.

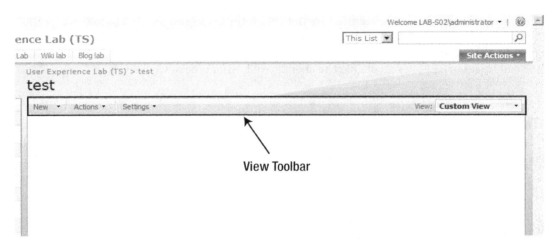

Figure 7-4. *View with a standard toolbar*

The cavern was quiet. Too quiet. The last stretch had been too easy. Not even the smaller monsters were roaming around; even the sound of dripping water had stopped. Now there was only silence.

Wait! What's that noise? Something is coming this way—in a hurry by the sound of it. Time to quaff that potion of high alert.

■**Tip** When you are developing views, you should know that modifying the views is indeed possible without re-creating the list for each change. Update and deploy your new list template, and do an IISReset before reloading your view. This way you do not have to delete sample data and create a new list for each change you make.

Toolbars

It is time to wake up. If you are reading this in a tired state, you might want to take a break. You are about to face your first serious challenge. Get a cup of coffee going. If you don't drink coffee, now would be a great time to start.

View toolbars come in two distinct flavors. The first flavor, the *standard* toolbar, should be well known; you can see it in all standard views, and it contains the New button and Site Actions and Site Settings menus.

The second flavor is called a *freeform* toolbar, and it holds some extremely powerful modification options. However, to tap into all that power, you need to have a deep understanding of CAML. Figure 7-5 shows a very familiar use of the freeform toolbar.

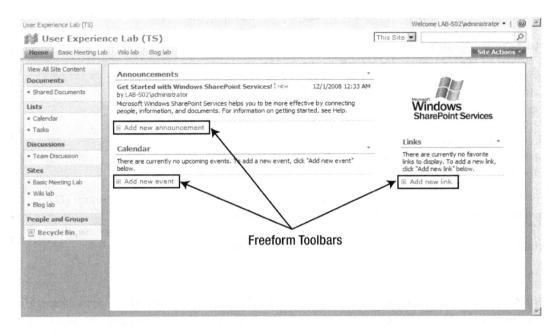

Figure 7-5. *Yup, those are toolbars.*

The nature of the freeform toolbar is that you can do mostly whatever you want. And, to be able to do whatever you want, you need a massive amount of options, which is exactly what freeform toolbars give you.

To start, let's add a link to the site settings for a list. Figure 7-6 shows what our end result should be.

Figure 7-6. *Our sample freeform toolbar*

To accomplish this rather simple task, we need to get into what is called the *view schema*. The view schema is the part of CAML that handles views, including giving us the tools we need to customize our freeform toolbar. We will explore the view schema plenty more later in this chapter, but this little bit of code will get our feet wet.

Replace your `<Toolbar Type="Standard"/>` with the following code:

```
<Toolbar Type="FreeForm">
  <HTML><![CDATA[<A HREF="]]></HTML>
  <HttpVDir/>
  <HTML><![CDATA[/_layouts/ListEdit.aspx?List=]]></HTML>
  <List/>
  <HTML><![CDATA[">List settings for ]]></HTML>
  <ListProperty Select="Title"/>
  <HTML><![CDATA[</a>]]></HTML>
</Toolbar>
```

The HTML element tags are used to output plain HTML. Since XML cannot contain HTML, we need to wrap our HTML code in a CDATA child element.

The HttpVDir element outputs the path to the root of our current site. In my case, that would be `http://lab-s02:10000/` for the root Team Site lab.

Note The HttpVDir documentation includes two attributes that are not present in the schema, meaning you will not get IntelliSense. These attributes, URLEncode and URLEncodeAsURL, will encode the output to a URL-safe string. If you add these attributes, Visual Studio will complain that the attributes are not defined, but you can safely ignore this warning because the attributes do work. Refer to the documentation for more details on these attributes.

The List element outputs the GUID of the current list, in other words, the list to which the view is bound.

The ListProperty outputs various properties of the list. It is used here to output the title of our list.

Together these elements output a string resembling a link to the URL for the list settings:

```
<A HREF="http://lab-s02:10000/_layouts/ListEdit.aspx?List=➡
{0AD6263B-6616-4BEA-850B-F30E18C8E97A}">List settings for Testlist</a>
```

As mentioned, we will get much more experience with the view schema during the course of this chapter. For now just replace your new toolbar with the original standard toolbar:

```
<Toolbar Type="Standard"/>
```

OK, that was a bit worse. That last monster proved that there really is a reason to be attentive in this place. If this was a preview of what is to come, then fighting the dragon at the end may be too hard.

Asking the Right Questions

Before we actually get to fill our new view with wonderful content, we need to know what that content should be. For this we need to look to another schema, the query schema.

You may already be familiar with the query schema if you have worked with extracting list items using the object model. The SPList.GetItems accepts an SPQuery object, which in turn has a Query property. That Query property is a string formatted according to the query schema.

A query schema string resembles SQL in structure and functionality and is used to filter, order, and group items.

All filtering is done in the Where child element inside the Query element. A simple filtering query schema string might look like this:

```
<Where>
 <Eq>
  <FieldRef Name='Title'/>
  <Value Type='Text'>My title</Value>
 </Eq>
</Where>
```

This query string would show items where the Title equals My title. You might remember this sample from Chapter 2.

To use the query schema in our view, we would add a valid query string to the Query element of our view. For example:

```
<View BaseViewID="2"
      DefaultView="TRUE"
      DisplayName="Custom View"
      Type="HTML"
      SetupPath="pages\viewpage.aspx"
      WebPartZoneID="Main"
      Url="CustomView.aspx"
      >
  <Query>
    <Where>
      <Eq>
        <FieldRef Name='Title'/>
        <Value Type='Text'>My title</Value>
      </Eq>
    </Where>
  </Query>
</View>
```

The query string can be much more complex than this. First, we have many more filtering methods. Table 7-1 shows the different comparison operators we can use to filter the items that should appear in our view.

Table 7-1. *Comparison Operators*

Query **Element**	**Description**
Eq	Equals
Neq	Not equal
BeginsWith	Begins with
Contains	Contains
Geq	Greater than or equal
Gt	Greater than
Leq	Less than or equal
Lt	Less than
IsNull	Empty/null value
IsNotNull	Nonempty value
DateRangesOverlap	Used to check whether a recurring event is running at a given date

The IsNull and IsNotNull operators have only a single child element, a FieldRef element, which points to the column name to check:

```
<IsNotNull>
 <FieldRef Name="Title"/>
</IsNotNull>
```

All the remaining elements have both a FieldRef element and a Value element, as shown in the My title samples. The Value element also has an attribute defining the type of value, such as Text or DateTime.

In addition to filtering, you can also sort and group with a query string using the elements OrderBy and GroupBy:

```
<Query>
 <Where>
  <Eq>
   <FieldRef Name='Title'/>
    <Value Type='Text'>My title</Value>
   </Eq>
 </Where>
 <OrderBy>
  <FieldRef Name='Created'/>
 </OrderBy>
 <GroupBy>
  <FieldRef Name='Category'/>
 </GroupBy>
</Query>
```

Both the OrderBy and GroupBy elements take a FieldRef child element, but OrderBy can take multiple FieldRef elements to sort on more than one field. If you add more than one FieldRef to the OrderBy element, the multiple sorting is done in the order the FieldRef elements are defined. For example:

```
<OrderBy>
  <FieldRef Name='Category'/>
  <FieldRef Name='Created'/>
</OrderBy>
```

This example will first sort the items on the Category column and on the Created column.

One thing to be aware of is that logical elements, such as And and Or, work only for two elements at a time. For instance, if you wanted to have three Or elements, you would need to do this:

```
<Query>
  <Where>
    <Or>
      <Eq>
        <FieldRef Name="Title"/>
        <Value>Title 1</Value>
      </Eq>
      <Or>
        <Eq>
          <FieldRef Name="Title"/>
          <Value>Title 2</Value>
        </Eq>
        <Eq>
          <FieldRef Name="Title"/>
          <Value>Title 3</Value>
        </Eq>
      </Or>
    </Or>
  </Where>
</Query>
```

This gets really tricky when you start doing complex queries like Title=t1 OR (Title=t2 AND Date>01.01.2009) OR Title=t3. Tools such as the U2U CAML Query Builder discussed in Chapter 2 can help tremendously in building complex queries.

A Slightly More Complex View of the World

It is time to get serious. If I am to learn the secrets of the cave and defeat both the dragon and my own fear, I need to muster my strength....

At this point, we have a slightly simplified view of the world, so we need to add a bit more complexity to begin getting some tangible results. Your view should look like this:

```
<View BaseViewID="2"
      DisplayName="Custom View"
      Type="HTML"
      SetupPath="pages\viewpage.aspx"
```

```
      WebPartZoneID="Main"
      Url="CustomView.aspx">
  <Toolbar Type="Standard"/>
</View>
```

You may have added your own toolbar or a query string, but these will not affect our further expansion, so feel free to leave them in.

Basics of View Construction

The visual interface of a view consists of three sections: the header, body, and footer, conveniently named ViewHeader, ViewBody, and ViewFooter. In addition, we need to inform the view about which columns should be included in the view, and this is done with the ViewFields element and its child element, FieldRef.

Each ViewHeader, ViewBody, and ViewFooter element contains view schema CAML just like our freeform toolbar, so you should pick up on the basics quickly.

To investigate this, let's create an extremely simple view:

```
<View BaseViewID="2"
      DefaultView="TRUE"
      DisplayName="Custom View"
      Type="HTML"
      SetupPath="pages\viewpage.aspx"
      WebPartZoneID="Main"
      Url="CustomView.aspx"
>
  <Toolbar Type="Standard"/>
  <ViewFields>
    <FieldRef Name="Title"/>
  </ViewFields>
  <ViewHeader>
    <HTML><![CDATA[<table id="testid"><tr><td>My custom view</td></tr>]]></HTML>
  </ViewHeader>
  <ViewBody></ViewBody>
  <ViewFooter>
    <HTML><![CDATA[</table>]]></HTML>
  </ViewFooter>
</View>
```

As you can see, I have added the ViewFields, ViewHeader, ViewBody, and ViewFooter elements. I have also added a DefaultView attribute to the View root element, but that's just because it saves me a few clicks when creating the new list.

The ViewFields sections contain FieldRef elements pointing to the columns with which our view will work. When we later look at the Fields CAML element, you should know that the ViewFields element contains the columns through which Fields and other column iterators will iterate. Note that you do not necessarily display all columns in the ViewFields section; the View part of the element refers to our custom view, not the visibility of columns.

Tip If you add or modify the ViewFields section of your schema.xml file, you may not get your new fields to appear in the view without re-creating the entire list. To fix this, you can simply set up the fields using the web interface.

At this point, the ViewBody is empty. This element will be more complex later, but for now I just wanted to create the outline so that I can refer to the elements rather than posting the entire view all the time.

Before we get into creating the header, body, and footer, I want to mention a couple of supporting elements and concepts that are important for creating the user experience.

ViewEmpty

When you deploy your list template and create a list off that template, you will not see the "My custom view" table cell. This is because the list does not have any items. SharePoint gives us a dedicated element to use when the list is empty, called ViewEmpty. So, if you want to utilize this functionality, and personally I think you should at least let your users know the list is empty, add the ViewEmpty element to your view and compare your results to Figure 7-7:

```
<ViewEmpty>
 <HTML><![CDATA[This view does not contain any items]]></HTML>
</ViewEmpty>
```

Of course, you are free to make this as complex as you like, perhaps adding links for adding new items or detailing information about filters that might prevent your items from appearing.

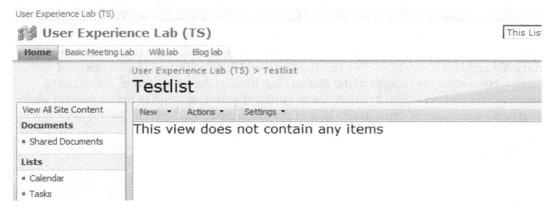

Figure 7-7. *View if empty*

RowLimit and Other Paging Options

When you create a view, you might want to limit the number of items displayed at a time. For this you would use the RowLimit element. This element is the starting point for a range of paging options, but let's keep it simple from the start:

```
<RowLimit>2</RowLimit>
```

This code will limit the number of items in the view to two, which might be useful for showing the top two elements of a view and leaving the remaining items for other views.

If you have set the RowLimit element but the number of items that would otherwise be listed exceeds RowLimit, you have two options. Either you implement paging, meaning people can go the next page or items, or you do not implement paging, meaning there is no way to show the next items in the list.

The latter, no paging, is the simplest option, since all you need to do is add the Paged="False" attribute to your RowLimit element. If you do so, you can also define the RowLimitExceeded element to output information about the existence of more items that will not be shown:

```
<RowLimit Paged="FALSE">2</RowLimit>
<RowLimitExceeded>
  <HTML><![CDATA[Haha, there are more items here, but I'm not going
                to show them to you]]></HTML>
</RowLimitExceeded>
```

Of course, you might opt to not be so cruel, but you get the point.

The other option, implementing paging, requires a bit more effort, but because we are the bold explorers that we are, we shun no hardship to get where we want to go.

By adding the attribute Paged="True" to our RowLimit element, we need to define the PagedRowSet element as well. The PagedRowSet element is shown at the bottom of the view and introduces us to a useful but slightly confusing query schema element, the GetVar element.

The GetVar element allows us to get values from a variable, and the available variables depend on the context. For example, in the PagedRowSet element, we have four values we can get: PageFirstRow, PageLastRow, NextPageData, and PrevPageData. PageFirstRow and PageLastRow return the number of the first and last item on the current page, respectively. NextPageData and PrevPageData are dynamic strings that you can send to the page to get the next or previous page of items. Take a look at the following code:

```
<RowLimit Paged="TRUE">2</RowLimit>
<PagedRowset>
  <HTML><![CDATA[This page displays items from ]]></HTML>
  <GetVar Name="PageFirstRow"/>
  <HTML><![CDATA[ to ]]></HTML>
  <GetVar Name="PageLastRow"/>
  <HTML><![CDATA[.<br/> To get to the next page, <a href="?]]></HTML>
  <GetVar Name="NextPageData" />
  <HTML><![CDATA[">click here</a>]]></HTML>
</PagedRowset>
```

This piece of view schema CAML will render HTML like the following:

```
This page displays items from 1 to 2. To get to the next page, <a
href="?Paged=TRUE&p_ID=2&View=[GUID OF YOUR VIEW]&PageFirstRow=3">click here</a>
```

GET WHAT VAR?

When I just said "the available variables depend on the context," you might have been a bit curious as to exactly what I meant. What context offers what variables?

Sadly, there is no simple answer to this. First, let's all join together for the chorus: "The documentation doesn't say...." Second, much of the code used to render views as HTML has been obfuscated and is thus not open for inspection. Third, well, many of the usages in the schema.xml files that ship with SharePoint are either plain wrong, do not work, or do not seem to have any effect.

So, where does that leave us? Stranded, I'm afraid, which is why the best option is to bring out some suntan lotion, spread out a towel, and fire up some Beach Boys classics. If that does not solve your curiosity, here are a few tips that might help:

- Some documentation exists, so your first order of business would be to check the documentation. Good luck with that.

- Your second chance would be to look at existing out-of-the-box views to see which GetVar variables are used by Microsoft.

- GetVar variables are scoped, meaning that they might work for one part of a view but not in other parts.

- Query string parameters are available as GetVar values. If you add ?MyVar=MyValue to the query string of the view page, you can access MyValue using <GetVar Name="MyVar" />.

Now, you may be tempted to add a link to the previous page to this code. For example:

```
<HTML><![CDATA[<br/><a href="?]]></HTML>
<GetVar Name="PrevPageData" />
<HTML><![CDATA[">Previous page</a>]]></HTML>
```

However, before you do that, consider what happens on the first page; you would have a link to the previous page that would link to only ?, since there is no previous page at all. The PrevPageData would be empty.

So, in order to detect whether we should link to the previous page, it makes sense to check whether the PrevPageData contains anything. To do such checks or any check in view CAML, we can use one of several conditional elements. Let's take a look at how conditional elements work.

Conditional Elements

To render part of the view, such as the link to the previous page of a paged view, only if a specific condition exists, the view schema gives you several options. Table 7-2 lists the conditional elements.

Table 7-2. *Conditional Elements in View Schema*

Element	Child Elements	Description
IfEqual	Expr1, Expr2, Then, Else	Compares Expr1 and Expr2 and performs Then if the values are equal. Otherwise, performs Else.
IfSubString	Expr1, Expr2, Then, Else	Checks to see whether Expr1 is contained in Expr2 and, if so, performs Then. Otherwise, performs Else.
IfNeg	Expr1, Expr2	If Expr1 is a negative value, then Expr1 is displayed. Otherwise, Expr2 is displayed.
IfNew	None	If item is created today, displays view schema contents.
IfHasRights	RightsChoices/RightsGroup, Then	Checks to see whether the current user has certain permissions and, if so, performs Then.
Switch	Expr, Case, Default	Works like a normal Switch/Case. Checks the Expr value against all Case values and performs the Case where the Expr matches. If no Case matches, performs Default.
FieldSwitch	Expr, Case, Default	Same as Switch but Expr is evaluated only once per view display. This is useful if you want to do Switch on a value that does not change during the rendering of the view, such as a column.

These conditional elements all have their uses, and we will see more examples of how these are used during the course of this chapter. For now, let's make some code to display only the Previous page link if the PrevPageData is empty. I will use a Switch element for this, but you might as well use IfEqual.

Add the following to your PagedRowset element:

```
<Switch>
 <Expr>
  <GetVar Name="PrevPageData" />
 </Expr>
 <Case Value=""></Case>
 <Default>
  <HTML><![CDATA[<br/><a href="?]]></HTML>
  <GetVar Name="PrevPageData" />
  <HTML><![CDATA[">Previous page</a>]]></HTML>
 </Default>
</Switch>
```

In the previous code, we check the value of the PrevPageData variable. If that value is empty (in other words, if Value is ""), we do nothing. Otherwise (if the PrePageData does contain something), we display the CAML that is inside the Default element (see Figure 7-8).

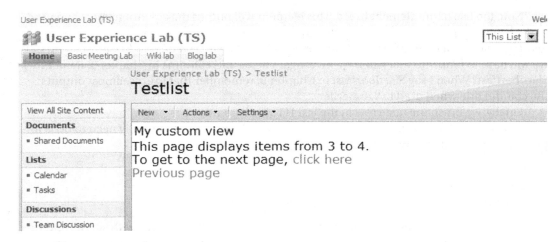

Figure 7-8. *Paging result*

You can of course do the same thing with the Next link; just exchange the GetVar element to check NextPageData instead. That way you remove the Next link from the last page of the row set. For the sake of space, however, I will leave that as an exercise for you.

ViewHeader, ViewBody, and ViewFooter

We are still not seeing any actual data here because we have not added anything to the header, body, and footer elements, at least nothing useful. The time to change that is now upon us.

Your ViewHeader, ViewBody, and ViewFooter are responsible for creating the actual item listings. You use view schema CAML in all of these elements, just like you saw with the other elements this far. Again, let's start simple, just to get the feel for how we will work.

Replace the ViewHeader you have created with the following code:

```
<ViewHeader>
  <HTML><![CDATA[My custom view<br/><table border="1" id="testid"><tr>]]></HTML>
  <Fields>
    <HTML><![CDATA[<td style="font-weight: bold;">]]></HTML>
    <Field/>
    <HTML><![CDATA[</td>]]></HTML>
  </Fields>
  <HTML><![CDATA[</tr>]]></HTML>
</ViewHeader>
```

What we are doing here is adding a table and starting the first row in the first HTML element. Then we use an element called Fields, which is basically a foreach loop for each column defined in the ViewFields element. Whatever code is placed inside the Fields element is repeated for each column.

Note the use of the element Field. This element will output the column name when used in the header or footer of a view but will output the value of the column if used in the body. Actually, that is not completely true; you can decide what will be rendered to some extent, but we will have to look into that when we investigate fields and columns in Chapter 9. Remember Slartibartfast? When I say *Slartibartfast* in Chapter 9, remember that Fields almost outputs the column title when used in ViewHeader.

Finally, we finish the table row in the last HTML element.

Next we want to look at the ViewFooter element. The only thing we really need to do is to finish the table that we start in the ViewHeader:

```
<ViewFooter>
  <HTML><![CDATA[</table>]]></HTML>
</ViewFooter>
```

Finally, to complete our very simple view, we want to fill the ViewBody with some content. What you need to remember here is that the ViewBody is repeated for each item in the view. As such, we need to start a new table row, run the Fields iterator, and then finish the table row.

Add this to your ViewBody element:

```
<ViewBody>
  <HTML><![CDATA[<tr>]]></HTML>
  <Fields>
    <HTML><![CDATA[<td>]]></HTML>
    <Field/>
    <HTML><![CDATA[</td>]]></HTML>
  </Fields>
  <HTML><![CDATA[</tr>]]></HTML>
</ViewBody>
```

Again, the Fields element iterates all the columns in the view, but this time its child Field element outputs the value of the column, not the column name.

That should be it. Build and create a new list based on your list template. You might want to add another FieldRef to the ViewFields section just to better see how your view gets constructed. Figure 7-9 shows a sample output where I have included the Created column in the ViewFields element.

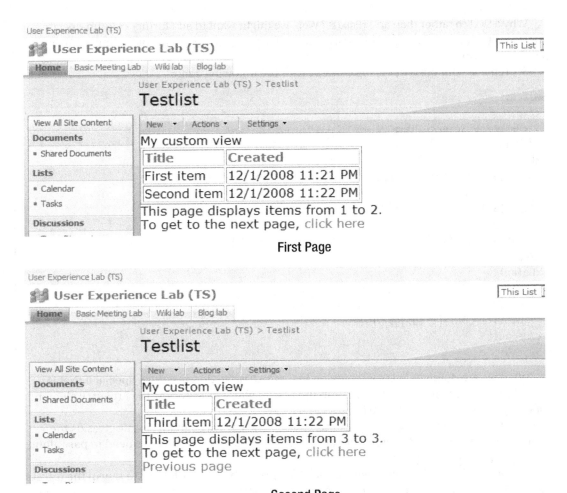

Figure 7-9. *Our first view of the world*

Yeah, I know, it looks horrible. Never hire me to do design work.

For simply listing the items in a list, this view will suffice, at least when you apply some pretty visual design to it. However, we might want to add a bit of functionality, such as being able to click the title to display the item.

To accomplish this, we would need to check for each column if we are currently on the Title column and, if so, add a link. The simple choice here is to use a Switch.

Why a `Switch` rather than an `IfEquals`? Well, we might want to add further column-specific functionality, such as putting a link to a calendar for date/time columns or adding a link to an item in a lookup column.

So, replace your current `Fields` content with the following code:

```
<Switch>
  <Expr>
    <Property Select="Name"/>
  </Expr>
  <Case Value="Title">
    <HTML><![CDATA[<td><a href="dispform.aspx?ID=]]></HTML>
    <Column Name="ID"/>
    <HTML><![CDATA[">]]></HTML>
    <Field/>
    <HTML><![CDATA[</a></td>]]></HTML>
  </Case>
  <Default>
    <HTML><![CDATA[<td>]]></HTML>
    <Field/>
    <HTML><![CDATA[</td>]]></HTML>
  </Default>
</Switch>
```

What we are doing here is switching on `Property Name` to do something special if that is `Title`. Remember that we are doing this in the `Fields` element, meaning the `Property` element is looking at the columns, not the item.

We also introduce a new element here, `Column`. The `Column` element simply gives us the value of a given column of an item, in our case the ID of the item, which we need to pass along to the `dispform.aspx` page.

However, what if we are not using `dispform.aspx` as the display form? We saw in the forest of lists that we can set our display form to any form. Hard-coding the URL is not very flexible.

URL

To help solve our little problem, the view schema includes an ill-titled element called `URL`. The function of the `URL` element is to return the URL of list forms.

The `URL` element has two parameters, `cmd` and `NoID`. The `NoID` attribute can be set to `false` to return the URL without the added ID parameter, but by default it will return the entire string including the ID parameter.

The `cmd` attribute is used to set which form URL should be returned, either `Display`, `DisplayHead`, `Edit`, `New`, `PreviewDisplay`, `PreviewEdit`, or `PreviewNew`. The default is `Display`, so if all you want to do is get the URL of the display form of the current item, all you need to do is add `<URL/>`.

Knowing this, we can improve our previous code by replacing the first three lines of the `Case` element:

```
[…]
<Case Value="Title">
  <HTML><![CDATA[<td><a href="]]></HTML>
```

```
<URL/>
<HTML><![CDATA[">]]></HTML>
<Field/>
[…]
```

And if we wanted to link to the edit form instead, our `<URL/>` element would be changed to this:

```
<URL Cmd="Edit"/>
```

> *The pace quickened. The adrenaline was pumping, keeping me on the tip of my toes all the time. If the dragon didn't kill me, I would probably die of fatigue, and even if I made it out of this alive, I knew I would never be the same again.*
>
> *It was darker here; it was almost like the walls moved closer with every step. I could hear something moving long before I could see what it was. Barely alive now but more confident than ever, I had to learn the truth of what…thing…could dwell in a place like this.*

Advancing Our Perspective

Now that we know how to create a basic view, we'll start exploring some more advanced topics. In this section, I will cover sorting, grouping, permissions, and some other topics that may not be used on every view.

You should consider these topics more like teasers than full disclosures of all the available options. As mentioned, going into detail on every single aspect of views would simply take up too much time and would require a completely separate book.

With that in mind, let's move on to the fun stuff.

Sorting It All Out

We know that we can use the query schema CAML to add static sorting to our view. If you want to do dynamic sorting, however, you need to apply some more effort and learn a few new things.

If you have followed the examples so far, you may have noticed that the `Field` element in the `ViewHeader` does not actually render the field title but rather a much more complex link that includes some code to do sorting by clicking the column name. This code is just plain horrible and, besides including nonvalidating attributes, does not work unless we implement some additional JavaScript code.

This makes sense if you work with the out-of-the-box views, but you didn't buy this book to learn how to leave the user experience alone, now did you? We will look a bit deeper into what actually goes on with the additional code in Chapter 9.

To avoid this approach, we need to modify our column headings in the `ViewHeader` element a bit and utilize a very useful element called `FieldSortParams` that handles the creation of the parameters required to sort the list. Exchange your current `ViewHeader`'s `Fields` element with this piece of code:

```
<ViewHeader>
…
<Fields>
 <HTML><![CDATA[<td style="font-weight: bold;"><a href="?]]></HTML>
 <FieldSortParams/>
 <HTML><![CDATA[">]]></HTML>
 <Property Select="DisplayName" HTMLEncode="TRUE"/>
 <HTML><![CDATA[</a></td>]]></HTML>
 </Fields>
</ViewHeader>
```

A really cool thing about the `FieldSortParams` is that it automatically alternates between sorting ascending and descending when you click to sort. The first click sorts ascending, and the second click sorts descending, and we don't have to lift a finger.

Well, actually, we have to lift a finger to click the mouse button....

Caution Although `FieldSortParams` seems easy to use, remember that what we are doing here is simply linking to `?<FieldSortParams>`, which will give you problems if your current page already includes parameters and thus a `?`. You will want to add some logic to detect this situation in order to create a stable and flexible link.

Tip Pay attention to the earlier caution; if you ignore it, you will get whacked by chaos and errors.

Grouping

Adding grouping to our list is a bit more complex, largely because SharePoint assumes a bit about how we design our views. Check out the sidebar "The Downfall of Fair Play" for more information. Basically, you need to work with tables for your layout.

To add grouping, you need to work with two new elements, the `GroupHeader` and `GroupFooter` elements, which will be displayed before and after each group. You also need to modify your `Query` element to include a `GroupBy` element, which in turn needs a `FieldRef` pointing to the column by which you want to group.

THE DOWNFALL OF FAIR PLAY

Grouping is where SharePoint stops playing fair and commits a grave sin, leading to all those who complain about SharePoint creating horrible HTML being right.

You see, when you start working with grouping, SharePoint assumes that you are presenting your view in an HTML table. In fact, it forcibly adds table code to your already existing view. If you do not use a table to render your view, you get plenty of errors and the nearly impossible task of creating something resembling reasonable code.

Let me show you what I mean with an example. Let's start by continuing our existing table-based layout, so add the following code to your view:

```
<Query>
  <GroupBy>
    <FieldRef Name="Title"/>
  </GroupBy>
</Query>
<GroupByHeader>
  <HTML><![CDATA[<tr><td colspan="3">]]></HTML>
  <GetVar Name="GroupByValue"/>
  <HTML><![CDATA[</td></tr>]]></HTML>
</GroupByHeader>
<GroupByFooter>
  <HTML><![CDATA[<tr><td colspan="3"> Grouped by ]]></HTML>
  <GetVar Name="GroupByField" HTMLEncode="TRUE"/>
  <HTML><![CDATA[</td></tr>]]></HTML>
</GroupByFooter>
```

Yeah, I know, grouping by title doesn't make much sense, but hear me out. When we add this code to our list template and deploy, our view looks like Figure 7-10.

That's right—when you add grouping, SharePoint will add an extra TD element for each of the rows of our view, even if we do not have a table-based layout at all. The result if we are not using a table for our layout is nothing less than a disaster.

My advice? Stick to tables for view layouts, or avoid using grouping at all.

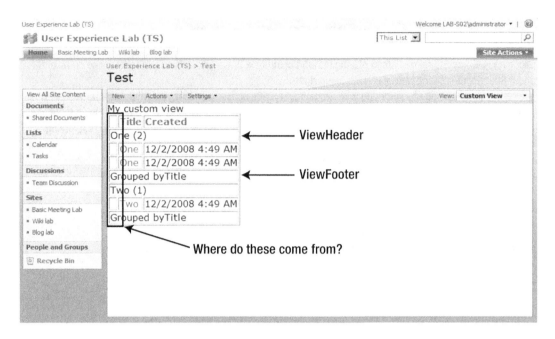

Figure 7-10. *An extra* TD *element?*

When you add grouping to your view, SharePoint handles most of the magic required to group your items together. This magic includes the grouping and intragroup sorting as well as counting and other necessary functions. All we need to do is add descriptive headers and footers to our respective GroupXXX elements.

Try adding this to your view, after adding the GroupBy element to your Query element:

```
<Query>
  <GroupBy>
    <FieldRef Name="Title"/>
  </GroupBy>
</Query>
<GroupByHeader>
  <HTML><![CDATA[<tr><td colspan="3">]]></HTML>
  <GetVar Name="GroupByValue" />
  <HTML><![CDATA[</td></tr>]]></HTML>
</GroupByHeader>
<GroupByFooter>
  <HTML><![CDATA[<tr><td colspan="3"><hr>]]></HTML>
  <HTML><![CDATA[</td></tr>]]></HTML>
</GroupByFooter>
```

Your resulting view should resemble Figure 7-11.

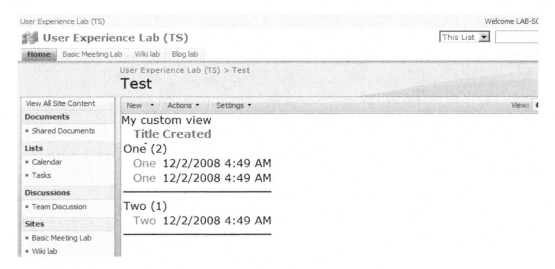

Figure 7-11. *Grouping added to a view*

Note I've removed `border="1"` from the table in Figure 7-11. I just get so sad when I am constantly reminded of the way `GroupHeader` and `GroupFooter` are implemented.

The `GroupHeader` and `GroupFooter` elements have a few noteworthy variables we can get by using the `GetVar` element. The `GroupByValue` that we used in the previous example returns the group value and the number of items within the group. The `GroupByField` returns the name of the field used for grouping. Again, finding all the different `GetVar` variables is a bit of a challenge, and in this case the out-of-the-box SharePoint views are your best bet.

Permissions and Security Trimming

SharePoint 3 is great for security trimming information and links. Compared to previous versions, you no longer see links to items or functions that you cannot access. The truth, however, is that in many cases you, as a developer, need to implement that security trimming yourself.

Let's say we wanted to add a link to edit an item in our view. You might go ahead and add something like this to your `ViewBody`:

```
<HTML><![CDATA[<a href="]]></HTML>
<URL Cmd="Edit"/>
<HTML><![CDATA["> (Edit item)</a>]]></HTML>
```

This would render a link to editing the item, but that link would be present for everyone, regardless of their permissions. Take a look at Figure 7-12 for how this might appear.

Figure 7-12. *Added link to edit item*

If a user does not have permissions, however, the user will get the famous "Error: Access is denied" message when they click the link. Although secure enough, this is hardly a great user experience.

To improve this, we can edit the view CAML and use an element called `IfHasRights` that allows us to show information only if a user has certain permissions. The `IfHasRights` has two child elements, the `RightsChoices` and a `Then`, with the `RightsChoices` element having additional child elements called `RightsGroup`.

I think this will be easier to understand if we look at an example:

```
<IfHasRights>
  <RightsChoices>
    <RightsGroup PermEditListItems="required" />
  </RightsChoices>
  <Then>
    <!-- Your view code here -->
  </Then>
</IfHasRights>
```

You can have multiple `RightsGroup` elements, and you can specify multiple permissions in a single `RightsGroup`. There is a difference; you would use one or the other depending on whether the user must have all or any of the permissions you demand.

If you specify multiple permissions inside a single `RightsGroup`, then the user must have *all* of the rights listed in the `RightsGroup` element:

```
<RightsChoices>
  <RightsGroup PermOpenItems="required" PermViewListItems="required"/>
</RightsChoices>
```

If you specify multiple `RightsGroup` elements, the user must have *any* of the permissions:

```
<RightsChoices>
  <RightsGroup PermOpenItems="required"/>
  <RightsGroup PermViewListItems="required"/>
</RightsChoices>
```

A rule to remember here is that a user must have *all* PermXXX attributes but can have *any* RightsGroup element.

One more thing is important here: when you edit your RightsGroup elements in Visual Studio, or any editor that gives you IntelliSense, you will get only two possible attributes in the RightsGroup element, as shown in Figure 7-13.

```
50      </ViewHeader>
51      <ViewBody>
52        <IfHasRights>
53          <RightsChoices>
54            <RightsGroup />
55          </RightsChoi    PermAddListItems
56        </IfHasRights>    PermEditListItems
57        <HTML><![CDATA[<tr>]]></HTML>
58        <Fields>
59          <Switch>
60            <Expr>
61              <Property Select="Name"/>
```

Figure 7-13. *Lack of* PermXXX *attributes in IntelliSense*

However, the actual list of permissions you can use to filter is much longer. Rather than list them all here, though, I'll refer you to the official documentation at `http://www.understandingsharepoint.com/url/10030`; or you can google *SharePoint rightsgroup*.

Now it's time to get back to our Edit item situation. We can now add a more meaningful link that shows up only if the user can actually edit items in the list. Add the following to your ViewBody:

```
<IfHasRights>
  <RightsChoices>
    <RightsGroup PermEditListItems="required"/>
  </RightsChoices>
  <Then>
    <HTML><![CDATA[<a href="]]></HTML>
    <URL Cmd="Edit"/>
    <HTML><![CDATA["> (Edit item)</a>]]></HTML>
  </Then>
</IfHasRights>
```

Now, when a user does not have permissions to edit items in the list, no link will appear, and your user will be less confused. Good thing!

Providing an Excerpt

When working with views of lists that contain large amounts of text, it may be useful to be able to limit the amount of text displayed. To help us with this, we have the Limit element and its child attribute, Column. Limit helps us by truncating the value of a column or any piece of text at a certain length. We can also add a MoreText attribute, which will be placed right where the text is truncated.

■**Caution** Although the documentation states that the MoreText attribute is optional, I have seen a lot of problems when omitting this attribute. If you do not want any text to be appended, leave the attribute in but set it to an empty value: <Limit MoreText="" Len="30">.

In the following example, I have added a column called Description to the list template along with some sample text to the items in the list. Next, I added the following code:

```
<Case Value="Description">
  <HTML><![CDATA[<td>]]></HTML>
  <Limit MoreText="..." Len="30">
    <Column Name="Description"/>
  </Limit>
  <HTML><![CDATA[</td>]]></HTML>
</Case>
```

The result might look something like Figure 7-14.

Figure 7-14. *Parts of a column*

Wrapping It All Up

OK, we've come this far, and we are still alive. That has to be good, right? Now that you have seen how to build a view from scratch, reading and understanding the out-of-the-box views is suddenly feasible.

And I would advise you to do so. Explore how the default views are created, see how a particular feature is implemented, and allow your curiosity to grant you knowledge. Try to imitate the behavior of a view without copying the code. Try improving on the default views by adding your own functionality.

With your newfound knowledge, I know that you are now ready to…

Face the Dragon

Finally, the last cavern. I knew what was waiting inside. I was prepared, or I was too tired to care. My weapons were as sharp as my attention. No longer did I fear the inevitable. If I never left this cave alive, I knew that I would go out fighting as best as I could.

I walked inside. I could hear the breathing of the beast that called this place its home. The darkness surrounded me on all sides, but I could easily see the contour of the mighty monster that had dealt death and pain to adventurers before me.

I walked forward, sword in hand, waiting for the dragon to notice me. One step at a time, trying to make as little noise as possible. I could feel the sweat on my brow. I could barely sense the pain in my hand from squeezing my sword too hard.

Suddenly the dragon awoke. The wind generated from the wings spreading was almost enough to knock me off my feet. A mighty roar followed as the beast yawned, its eyes glowing red as a setting sun and staring right at me. It opened its mouth as if to spew the fire that would scorch me to a crisp.

'Hello,' it said. 'Nice of you to stop by. My name is Nigel, and I live in this cave. Care for a cup of tea? I am afraid the selection is down ever since the local store stopped delivering, but I can surely whip up at least a cup of Earl Grey.'

I was stunned. Was this a trap? Why was the beast taunting me like this? Why wasn't I dead already?

'You see,' said Nigel, 'people come here to fight and kill me, but that never happens. I cannot be killed; I am immortal.'

'But…but…what happened to all the others who came before me?' I asked, still a bit confused.

'Ah, yes, they are no longer of this world, and you will now join them. Your journey has brought you plenty of knowledge, and now you are leaving your old world behind to rise to a new level, a new plane of existence.'

He continued, 'No longer will you wander among the normal people, wondering how things work. You have faced your fears, and you overcame those fears. You will leave this place only to take your place among the enlightened. You have left your life of ignorance and doubt behind.

'Welcome as a true master.'

■■■

CHAPTER 8

The Liquid Nitrogen of SharePoint

Content Types: The Coolest Thing Since…Cold

I may have mentioned once or twice that the concept of content types is incredibly cool. It is time to see whether you agree, because we are about to enter the fascinating land of the user experience.

You may also recall that everything in SharePoint is a content type. Either directly or indirectly, you are working with content types whenever you add, edit, upload, or in any shape or form manipulate data. So, besides being cool, content types are also fundamental to you understanding SharePoint.

The phrase *content types* means different things in different technologies. In SharePoint, content types are a method of gathering different columns, behaviors, and appearances under a single name, and they have nothing to do with MIME content types.

The concept of content types is nothing new and to a large extent mimics the idea of object orientation in programming languages. In fact, if you read on, you will see how content types in SharePoint are really powerful.

Content Type Basics

Content types are just that—types of content. Consider a solution in which you store accounting and other financial data. You may have different types of content such as invoices, accounts, transactions, employee salaries, and so on. Each of these types requires different sets of data. An invoice would have products or services rendered as well as amounts payable, transactions would require a source and recipient, an employee salary object would have an employee reference, and the salary would have a currency amount.

Note I know very little about accounting and considerably less about accounting in other countries, especially compared to what I know about SharePoint.

Information about these types of data can be encapsulated in SharePoint content types. You would have a content type for each type of content, and the content type would hold fields and columns to describe the information to be stored in each item.

You may be tempted then to compare content types to database schemas. You should yield to that temptation, but keep in mind that content types are far more powerful and have plenty of other features besides just describing pieces of data.

You can also connect behavior to different content types in SharePoint, meaning that you can have a certain piece of data behave in a certain fashion. For instance, if you add an invoice to your invoice collection, you might want to have that automatically trigger updating an account somewhere or asking for approval from someone. Or, when a new employee enters the building, you might want to automatically add them to the payroll.

This may not seem revolutionary—we all probably know that we can have a list of invoices and attach workflow and feature receivers to that list—but the cool thing about a content type is that the behavior follows the type, not the list. If you move an invoice from one library to another, the functionality follows the invoice with no concern for the list in which it is stored.

When it comes to appearance, you can also connect forms such as a display form and edit form to content types. We looked briefly at this in Chapter 6 when we examined the `ListForm` rendering template, so you probably knew that. However, the forms and visual appearance of content types follow the type again, not the list, meaning that where you store the item is of no concern; the appearance remains. For example, you can have an employee salary record displayed in a fancy visual interface, regardless of the list in which the salary record is stored.

As you saw in Chapter 5, on evolving the default experience, you can also attach custom actions that connect user interface elements to certain content types.

In addition, content types are cross-list and cross-site, meaning you can define them independently of any single list or site. If you create a content type once, you can use the same content type several places.

And, now that you are beginning to drool over all the power you will get when you learn how to use content types, here's an added bonus, just for you: content types support inheritance. If you create a base `Document` type to which you add several columns, you can create child content types that inherit from the `Document` base type and thus also all the columns. Add a column to the parent `Document` content type, and you can have every child get that same column added.

Note the word *can*. You don't have to inherit anything. In fact, it is quite difficult to actually get inheritance to work if you manage content types yourself, but we will get back to why in a little while.

But wait, there's more. You can customize a single content type instance as well. If you add a content type X to lists A and B, you can customize X on list A but leave X on B unmodified. This happens for the very same reason that inheritance is a bit fuzzy. Be patient, I will explain shortly.

OK, I need a break and so do you. Sit down, try to calm your mind from exploding, and just relax. By the end of this chapter, you will know plenty about content types.

> ■**Note** Until now I have avoided explaining what is already adequately explained in other books or widely known. Content types are so cool I just have to explain how they work, even if that includes some well-known stuff.

List vs. Site Content Types

There is one very important thing that you must understand. If you do not, pain will mark your advanced content type experience, and you do not want that.

To explain what this means, I need to take a quick trip to the future (in other words, jump ahead to a topic covered later in the chapter) and explain that content type inheritance is based on the content type ID. To inherit from a content type, you just add a formatted value to the content type ID from which you will inherit. For instance, the Document content type (0x0101) inherits from the Item content type (0x01). The same applies to folders (0x0120). We will look deeper into inheritance later in the chapter, but for now this is all you need to know.

Based on this, it is logical to assume that when you add a content type, such as Item, to a list, the content type would have ID 0x01, right? Well, take a look at what SharePoint Manager thinks—see Figure 8-1.

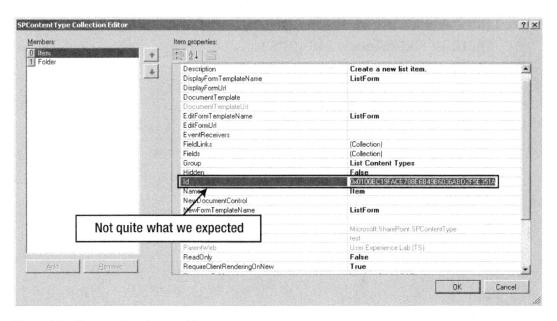

Figure 8-1. *Not exactly what you'd expect*

So, what is going on here?

When you add a content type to a list, you are actually adding a copy of the content type to the list. This introduces several issues and can cause problems if you do not realize that this is happening. Or rather, it can cause opportunities, if you are the "glass is half full" kind of person like me.

The effect of this copying is that you are in fact creating a separate content type that can be manipulated independently from the source. This is actually an absolute requirement if content types are going to be any good. Think of the basic `Item` content type, which you use for every list you create. If you were to modify the `Title` field of the content type of a single list, you would in effect modify every `Item` content type, which would be bad. Copying the source content type to the list prevents this and allows you to modify a single content type instance rather affect the whole site collection. Check out the following exercise if you want to investigate this for yourself:

1. Start with your Team Site lab, and create a new list. I've called mine `testlist`.

2. On the List Settings page of your new list, go to Advanced Settings, and allow the management of content types.

3. Back on the List Settings page, you now see that both the `Item` and `Folder` content types have been added. Actually, they've been there all along, but now you see them in the interface.

4. Click the `Item` content type, and change the name of the content type; I've used `Testlist Item`.

5. Verify that your change has taken effect.

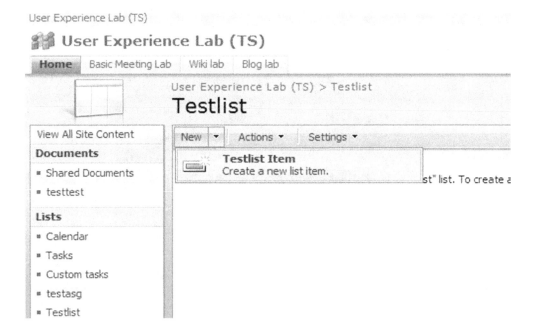

At this point, you might think that since you updated the name of the `Item` content type, the changes should be reflected wherever the `Item` content type is used. However, if you create a new list by following steps 1–3, you will see that the new list will get the original name of `Item` on the content type. The same thing would have happened even if you had created both lists before changing the name.

So, if you want to change all the `Item` content types, how would you do that? Simple! The source `Item` content type is a site content type, meaning that you need to modify it from the site settings. In the Galleries column of the Site Settings page, you will find site content types. If you want to modify every instance of a content type, this is where you would go.

There are also some things to know about site content types. Again, confusion will be certain if you don't get these seemingly minor concepts, so, please, pay attention.

The first thing to note is that site content types use direct references to site columns; you cannot add any columns except for site columns. When editing columns in a site content type, you are editing the site column. Thus, if you change the name of the `Title` column in the `Item` site content type, you will actually be changing every occurrence of the `Title` column throughout the site. That may not be what you want.

Caution If you change the site column `Title` by mistake, you may be unable to change it back without some extra work. Check out the sidebar "Ouch! My Title Has Changed" for one method of changing this back.

The second thing to note is that when you make changes to a site content type, you have the option of propagating changes to child content types. This choice is important because some changes may not easily be propagated again later. For instance, if you add a site column and do not propagate the changes to child content types, you need to remove and add the column again from the parent to be able to propagate again.

This may or may not be what you want. You can use this to your advantage, for instance, when you want to differentiate which child content types inherit all or only some columns. If you are not aware of this, however, this feature may bite you in the butt. In fact, when you add columns through the object model, be prepared to do the propagation yourself; there is no automatic propagation from parent to child in code.

To be honest, I like to control my own propagation. That way, I remain in complete control over what and how propagation works, and I can be much more granular than "everything or nothing."

We will look more into inheritance later, so for now, let's move on.

OUCH! MY TITLE HAS CHANGED

Have you ever modified the default title by mistake (or on purpose) and wanted to change it back? You face a couple of problems.

First, the `Title` column is stored in the `_Hidden` group, which is not shown on the Site Columns page at all. You can circumvent this problem by going to the `Item` site content type, clicking the `Title` column there, and then clicking "Edit site column in new window."

However, when you try to set the column name back to `Title`, you may be faced with an error message stating that "The column name that you entered is already in use or reserved. Choose another name."

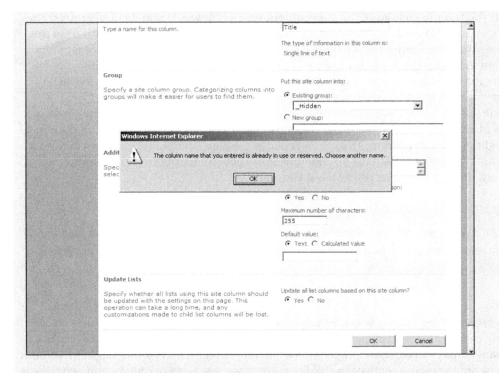

D'oh!

This is caused by the SharePoint web interface checking every `InternalName` property of existing fields to see whether there will be a conflict with the new name.

A workaround here requires modifying the column through the object model. The shortcut is to use a tool such as SharePoint Manager 2007 to edit the column directly. Doing so will update the column to `Title`. Start SPM, navigate to your site, and open the `Fields` node. Then follow these steps:

1. Find the `Title` field that has its `InternalName` property set to `Title`.

2. Modify the `Title` property back to `Title`.

3. Hit the Save button in SPM.

This circumvents the JavaScript-based error checking in the web interface.

Next you might want to propagate this change to every list to completely reverse the effects. To do so, go back to editing the site column `Title` from the `Item` content type as described earlier. This time, since you have changed the title outside of the web interface, the existing fields check is not performed. Make sure the Update Lists option is set to Yes, and hit OK.

Voilà—problem solved.

So, in short, set the `Title` property of the `Title` field to `Title`. And if I ever hear the word *Title* again I think my head will explode.

Keep Your Parents Happy

Content types support inheritance, with a bit of a peculiar method of defining inheritance. In simple terms, this means you can create a hierarchy of content types, just like a class hierarchy, and have child content types inherit properties from parents and grandparents.

■**Caution** Do not confuse content type inheritance with content type scope. These are very different. Misunderstandings may be your doom should you choose to ignore this warning.

Let's say that you want to create a document management system in which company documents are organized into legal, customer, and financial reports, with the financial documents being separated further into quarterly financial reports and annual reports.

There may be commonalities to all the documents. For instance, who is responsible for the document? What kind of company policy applies to the document? These common information details may be stored in a root company document type.

In turn, the financial documents, regardless of whether it is an annual or a quarterly report, will be relevant to a reporting period, while a time period makes no sense to a customer document. Thus, you can have the financial report type, from which the quarterly and annual reports inherit, have a period metadata column.

Finally, for the quarterly report, you might want to include the quarter as separate metadata. With my vast financial expertise, I have no idea why you would want this, but play along and take a look at the chart in Figure 8-2.

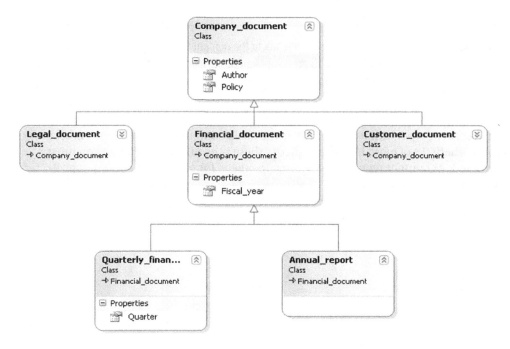

Figure 8-2. *Content type inheritance diagram*

You noticed that I used the class diagram of Visual Studio to make this figure, did you? Well, that is because content type inheritance works very much like class inheritance. It makes you want to create a class to mimic a SharePoint content type, doesn't it? The joys, the joys....

What differs significantly from other hierarchical systems is a rather awkward method for describing inheritance in SharePoint content types. Every content type in SharePoint has a unique identifier, the content type ID. You may remember that we touched briefly on this in the "Form Templates" section in Chapter 6 when talking about lists.

When you create a content type, you define a content type ID that is of the format 0xNNNNNNN, where NNNNNNN is a number. That number not only identifies this content type but also identifies from which parent content type we should inherit. That's right, no kidding—inheritance is hidden inside the identifier string.

All you need to do to inherit from a content type is to include the parent content type ID in your content type ID and then add a few numbers. I will explain what these numbers may be in the "Content Type Authoring" section a bit later.

Caution Content type ID crafting is a delicate art, so pay attention.

To investigate content type IDs and inheritance further, start by opening your site content types in your Team Site lab. You will find the site content types on the Site Settings page. On the Site Content Type Gallery page, you should see several out-of-the-box content types. For now, click the `Item` content type, and look at the URL. You will notice the `ManageContentType.aspx` file has a parameter `ctype=0x01`. Yeah, the `ctype` part is the content type ID.

Tip You can also hover your mouse pointer over the link to the content type to get the `ctype` parameter in the status bar. Or you can use a tool such as SharePoint Manager to investigate the content type. Do what thou wilt—the important thing is to pay attention to the content type IDs.

The `Item` content type, with its ID of `0x01`, is the basic content type from which most other content types inherit. I say *most*, because in theory there is no absolute rule that you must inherit from the `Item` content type, so you are free to create, for example, a content type `MyItem` with a content type ID of `0x02`.

In any case, the Item content type inherits from a root content type called System that has a content type ID of 0x. On the other hand, if you examine the Document content type, you will see that it has a content type ID of 0x0101. Compared to Item, being 0x01, you now know that Document inherits from Item since its ID includes 0x01. Table 8-1 shows the most commonly used content types.

Table 8-1. *Common Content Types*

ID	Content Type
0x	System
0x01	Item
0x0101	Document
0x0120	Folder

Folders Are Content Types?

Yes, folders are content types. I am happy you are paying attention to details. Now, be patient for a few more moments, and I will explain. First, we need to complete the description of content type inheritance.

OK, Back to Content Type Inheritance

The concept of inheritance becomes a bit more complex when you realize that not all properties of a content type are actually inherited by children. In fact, the only things that *are* inherited are columns and forms. As you will learn later in this chapter, content types can be set up with behavior as well as appearance, but neither workflows nor event receivers are inherited.

Also, remember what I said about propagation of changes. If you make a change to a parent content type, you need to decide whether you want those changes to be propagated to the children. If you do not propagate your changes, the changes will need to be manually added to the children later.

Let's see how this could look in your site content type gallery—see Figure 8-3.

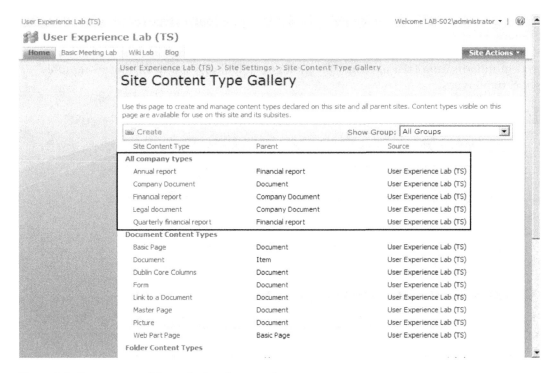

Figure 8-3. *Content type hierarchy implemented*

The Site Content Type Gallery page provides a less than optimal overview of the hierarchy. Now you see another reason why I opted to illustrate the inheritance using the class designer in Visual Studio.

So, how do the content type IDs look? Look at Table 8-2, and keep in mind that these are my results and that your actual codes may be different.

Table 8-2. *Content Type ID Inheritance Samples*

Content Type	ID
Company document	0x010100B88CA477A46A6146A1E82817745A8915
Legal document	0x010100B88CA477A46A6146A1E82817745A891501
Financial report	0x010100B88CA477A46A6146A1E82817745A891502
Quarterly financial report	0x010100B88CA477A46A6146A1E82817745A89150201
Annual report	0x010100B88CA477A46A6146A1E82817745A89150202

Notice that company document inherits from Document (0x0101) by the "00 + GUID" method, while the other types inherit from the respective parents using the two-digit method.

Note Yeah, I know, there is no customer document there. This example is for illustrative purposes, but it's nice to see that you are still paying attention.

So, What About Those Folders?

When working with a SharePoint list or library, you can sort your items and documents in folders and subfolders. On the surface, it may then seem that items are stored inside folders in some manner.

However, this is not the case. Folders are in fact little more than regular list items. Granted, they are treated differently than normal items, but they do not store items in any way. There is no actual hierarchical storage mechanism in lists or libraries. All items are stored on the same level, regardless of whether items appear to be stored inside a complex folder structure.

The easiest way to realize this is to open SharePoint Manager 2007 and see how a list with folders appears. In Figure 8-4 I have created a simple custom list and added a folder on the root (Test folder 1) and another folder inside that folder (Subfolder 1). Inside each level folder, including the root, I have added an item.

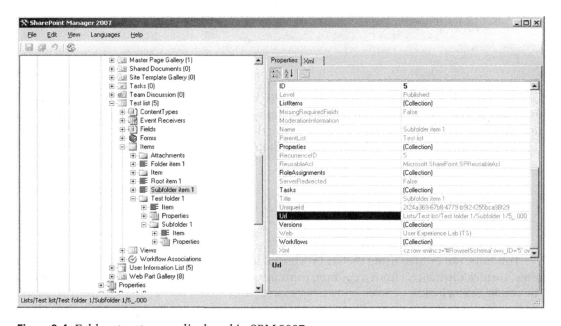

Figure 8-4. *Folder structure as displayed in SPM 2007*

Notice that the folders I created are displayed with a folder icon. If you were to check, you would see that the folders are actually represented by SPFolder objects. However, don't let that fool you. If you look really closely at Figure 8-4, you will see that the ID property of the Subfolder item 1 is 5, even though there are only three items in the list. You may still think that I've just deleted two items to make it appear like folders get their own IDs in the list. Care to make that bet again?

To check whether I am just pulling your leg here, re-create the folder structure I did, and then run the following code in a console application where you have referenced Microsoft.SharePoint.dll:

```
class Program
{
    static void Main(string[] args)
    {
        using (SPSite site = new SPSite("http://lab-s02:10000/"))
        {
            using (SPWeb web = site.OpenWeb())
            {
                SPList testlist = web.Lists["Test list"];
                SPListItemCollection items = testlist.Items;

                foreach (SPListItem item in items)
                {
                    Console.WriteLine(item.Title);
                }
                Console.ReadKey();
            }
        }
    }
}
```

You should not be surprised that iterating a list such as this will give you all items, regardless of where in the folder structure they are seemingly stored. But we don't get any folder items here, so how would I be able to prove to you that folders are actually items?

Try exchanging the foreach loop with a for loop as such:

```
for (int i = 1; i<=testlist.ItemCount; i++)
{
    SPListItem item = testlist.GetItemById(i);
    Console.WriteLine(item.DisplayName);
}
```

This time, rather than using the SPListItemCollection, which contains only "regular" items, we pick the item ID from a counter, running up to the max number of items in the list. The result? Take a look:

```
Test folder 1
Folder item 1
Root item 1
Subfolder 1
Subfolder item 1
```

I won't go into too much detail here, but take with you a few pointers:

- Folder types can be created just like any other content type, including adding columns.

- Because folders are items, you can treat them as items, including updating column values, setting permissions, and attaching workflows.

Yes, you can attach workflows to folders. No, folder-attached workflows are not inherited by items that seemingly are stored in the folder. Check out Figure 8-5. Because there is no default interface, you would have to associate the workflow using other means, such as .NET code.

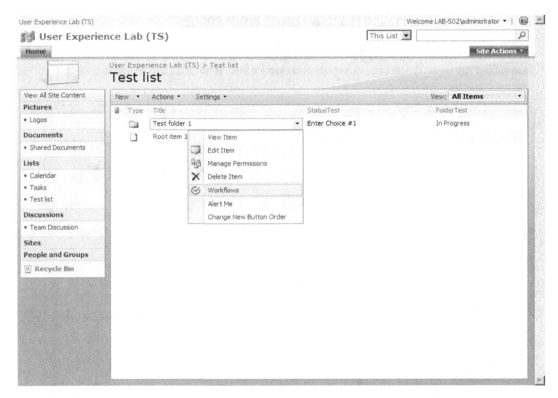

Figure 8-5. *Workflow attached to a folder*

I told you content types were cool!

Content Type Scope

Caution Do not confuse content type scope with content type inheritance. These are very different. Misunderstandings may be your doom should you choose to ignore this warning.

Content types are scoped, meaning that they are available from the site in which they are defined and any child site below that site. If you create your content type at the root site of a site collection, every site in the site collection can use the content type. However, if you add the content type to a subsite—for instance, the Basic Meeting Lab if you are using the setup I suggested in Chapter 1—only sites below the Basic Meeting Lab will have access to the content type.

There are two issues with this—one simple workaround issue and one major bummer class issue. Check out the sidebar "Subsites in Meeting Workspaces?" for the simple workaround issue.

SUBSITES IN MEETING WORKSPACES?

Although it has absolutely nothing to do with content types, I thought I would mention this anyway. You may have noticed that on the Create page of a meeting workspace there is no "Sites and workspaces" listed where it should be.

I do not know why Microsoft has chosen to not include web sites and pages on this list, but I suspect it has to do with pages being managed differently in meeting workspaces than other site definitions.

The sad thing, of course, is that in Microsoft's eagerness to remove the option to add pages like we are used to, creating subsites has been removed as well. Talk about tossing the baby out with the bath water. Luckily, you can still add sites from the Site Settings page. Just check out Site Administration and click the "Sites and workspaces" link; or just go to http://yoursite /_layouts/mngsubwebs.aspx where you will find a Create link to add new subsites.

"Scoping Content Types for Webs? Hah, That's Not Possible!"

Oh, I beg to differ, and I'll take your $5 bet on that also.

There is a major issue with deploying content types using features or site definitions. You see, the only feature scope that allows content types is the site scope. As you certainly remember from Chapter 3, site scope means site collection. Web scope is what we need when we want to deploy a feature scoped for a site. And of course, web-scoped features cannot include content types.

So, we face a bit of a problem. If we want a content type to be available only for a certain web, we are actually out of luck deploying content types in features. That's a major bummer! It's such a nice feature, but there's no way to implement it, at least not without deploying the content types across the entire site collection.

There is a very good reason for this. Content type inheritance works across the entire site collection, so content types need an ID that is unique to the entire site collection. What would happen if you deployed a web content–type feature on two different subsites? You would deploy your content type twice but with the same ID. And SharePoint would have no way of knowing from which content type a child content type would inherit. So, web-scoped content type features don't seem possible.

So, have I lost the bet? No way! Content types can be created in more ways than one. My approach is to use a feature event receiver attached to a web-scoped feature and create the content type using code:

```
public override void FeatureActivated(SPFeatureReceiverProperties properties)
{
 using (SPWeb web = (SPWeb)properties.Feature.Parent)
 {
  SPContentType parentType = web.AvailableContentTypes["Company document"];
  SPContentType newType = ➥
   new SPContentType(parentType, web.ContentTypes, "Basic meeting web scoped type");
  web.ContentTypes.Add(newType);

  …

  newType.Update();
 }
}
```

By creating the content type in code, SharePoint generates a unique ID for us, so the problem of conflicting IDs is solved.

Of course, you may want to do more with your content type, perhaps even reading in an elements file and mimicking the complete content type creation experience in code, but I will leave that to your experimentation.

This is somewhat more cumbersome than just creating a content type in CAML but shows that you can indeed create web-scoped content type features. I believe that puts you back another $5.

Your Best Behavior

Another cool aspect of content types is the ability to attach behavior to a content type. This allows you to have an item derived from a content type behave in a certain manner. You can do this in one of two ways, event receivers or workflows.

Event receivers are pieces of code that get fired when something happens. We looked briefly at event receivers earlier, but I would like to take a moment to go a bit deeper here.

Note I will not be covering workflows in this book. Sorry.

Event receivers are fired by SharePoint during specific events. You can attach an event receiver to a certain object, such as a site, list, or content type.

For content types, the most relevant event receivers are the item event receivers located in the `SPItemEventReceiver` class. By having your class inherit from `SPItemEventReceiver`, you can override the methods you want to handle. The method names match the event being fired. The following are the available method names:

```
ItemAdded
ItemAdding
ItemAttachmentAdded
ItemAttachmentAdding
ItemAttachmentDeleted
ItemAttachmentDeleting
ItemCheckedIn
ItemCheckedOut
ItemCheckingIn
ItemCheckingOut
ItemDeleted
ItemDeleting
ItemFileConverted
ItemFileMoved
ItemFileMoving
ItemUncheckedOut
ItemUncheckingOut
ItemUpdated
ItemUpdating
```

The method names should be self-explanatory, but you may notice that there are matching ed and ing method names, for example `ItemAdded` and `ItemAdding`. The difference is because of when the event is fired. ed events are fired after the fact and are called *asynchronous* events, while ing events are fired during the fact and are called *synchronous* events.

The difference is important. If you want to prevent an item from being added if certain criteria are not met, you need to use an ItemAdding event receiver and cancel the adding of the item. You would do so by setting properties.Cancel to true as such:

```
public override void ItemAdding(SPItemEventProperties properties)
{
 if (SomeCriteriaDoesNotMatch())
 {
  properties.Cancel = true;
 }
}
```

Caution Although you could delete the item again in an ItemAdded event, doing so is messy. Consider what would happen if you have an automatically launched workflow that alerts users of a new item and the item itself is deleted right after the workflow is started.

We will get back to how we actually attach our event receiver when we examine crafting content types.

Content Type Authoring

At this point, you should have enough information about how content types work to be able to understand the details of how content types are created.

You already saw the programmatic method of adding a content type, and you will revisit that method in Part 3 of the book. At this point, we should explore using CAML in features to create content types.

Let's start with a content type that is provided for us by SharePoint, the Document content type. Open the [12]\FEATURES\ctypes\ctypeswss.xml elements file, and scroll down past the System and Item content types until you reach the Document content type at around line 32.

Tip Check out the comments. These comments give a glimpse into SharePoint development thinking.

Figure 8-6 shows the XmlDocuments element closed. We will look at XmlDocuments more shortly.

```
<ContentType ID="0x0101"
    Name="$Resources:Document"
    Group="$Resources:Document_Content_Types"
    Description="$Resources:DocumentCTDesc"
    V2ListTemplateName="doclib"
    Version="0">
    <FieldRefs>
        <RemoveFieldRef ID="{67df96f4-9dec-48ff-a553-29bece9c5bf4}" Name="Attachments" /> <!-- Attachments -->
        <RemoveFieldRef ID="{f1e02obc-ba26-443f-bf2f-b68715017bbc}" Name="WorkflowVersion" /> <!-- WorkflowVersion -->
        <RemoveFieldRef ID="{bc91a437-52e7-49e1-8c4e-4698904b2b6d}" Name="LinkTitleNoMenu" /> <!-- LinkTitleNoMenu -->
        <RemoveFieldRef ID="{82642ec8-ef9b-478f-acf9-31f7d45fbc31}" Name="LinkTitle" /> <!-- LinkTitle -->
        <RemoveFieldRef ID="{ae069f25-3ac2-4256-b9c3-15dbc15da0e0}" Name="GUID" /> <!-- GUID -->
        <RemoveFieldRef ID="{de8beacf-5505-47cd-80a6-aa44e7ffe2f4}" Name="WorkflowInstanceID" /> <!-- WorkflowInstanceID -->
        <FieldRef ID="{5f47e085-2150-41dc-b661-442f3027f552}" Name="SelectFilename" /> <!-- SelectFilename -->
        <FieldRef ID="{8553196d-ec8d-4564-9861-3dbe931050c8}" Name="FileLeafRef" Required="TRUE"/> <!-- FileLeafRef -->
        <FieldRef ID="{8c06beca-0777-48f7-91c7-6da68bc07b69}" Name="Created" Hidden="TRUE" /> <!-- Created -->
        <FieldRef ID="{fa564e0f-0c70-4ab9-b863-0177e6ddd247}" Name="Title" Required="FALSE" ShowInNewForm="FALSE" ShowInEditForm="TRUE"/>
        <!-- TODO hailiu: The old display name was 'DisplayName="$Resources:core,Created_Date;">__LDisp(camlionet37)' We may need to spe
        <FieldRef ID="{28cf69c5-fa48-462a-b5cd-27b6f9d2bd5f}" Name="Modified"  Hidden="TRUE" /> <!-- Modified -->
        <!-- TODO hailiu: The old display name was: 'DisplayName="$Resources:core,Last_Modified;">__LDisp(camlionet36)' We may need to sp
        <FieldRef ID="{822c78e3-1ea9-4943-b449-57863ad33ca9}" Name="Modified_x0020_By" Hidden="FALSE"/> <!-- Modified_x0020_By -->
        <FieldRef ID="{4dd7e525-8d6b-4cb4-9d3e-44ea25f973eb}" Name="Created_x0020_By" Hidden="FALSE"/> <!-- Created_x0020_By -->
    </FieldRefs>
    <XmlDocuments>...
</ContentType>
<ContentType ID="0x010101"
```

Figure 8-6. Document *content type definition*

To add a content type using a feature, we would add a `ContentType` element to the `elements.xml` file of our feature. Then we would fill that `ContentType` element with all sorts of goodies, just like a Christmas stocking.

ContentType Element

The `ContentType` element has several attributes and child elements. The only required attributes are `Name` and `ID`. `Name` is the name you want to give your content type. `ID` is a unique string that defines not only content type inheritance, as you just learned, but also identifies each content type uniquely in a site collection. Getting the `ID` value right requires a bit of knowledge.

You can craft your content type ID in two ways. You may start to see a pattern in the examples you have examined so far. Looking at the parent and child content type IDs, the inherited IDs of `Item` and `Document` added the number 01 to the parent type. Adding two numbers—for example, 01, 02, or 99—is one way of inheriting from a parent type. If you wanted to inherit directly from `Item`, you could have your content type have an ID of `0x0102`, `0x0193`, and so on.

The other method for crafting content type IDs is to add 00 and then a GUID string without the hyphens. For example, you may have an ID that inherits directly from `Item` as such:

`0x01001A48C1A2B071432EACA85A0A35FF5185`

Break that ID down, and you will see `Item` (`0x01`), two zeros (`00`), and a GUID.

The `Description` attribute is rather simple. The text you add here is displayed below the name on the New button. If you look at Figure 8-7, you will see that the description for the `Document` content type is "Create a new document in this library."

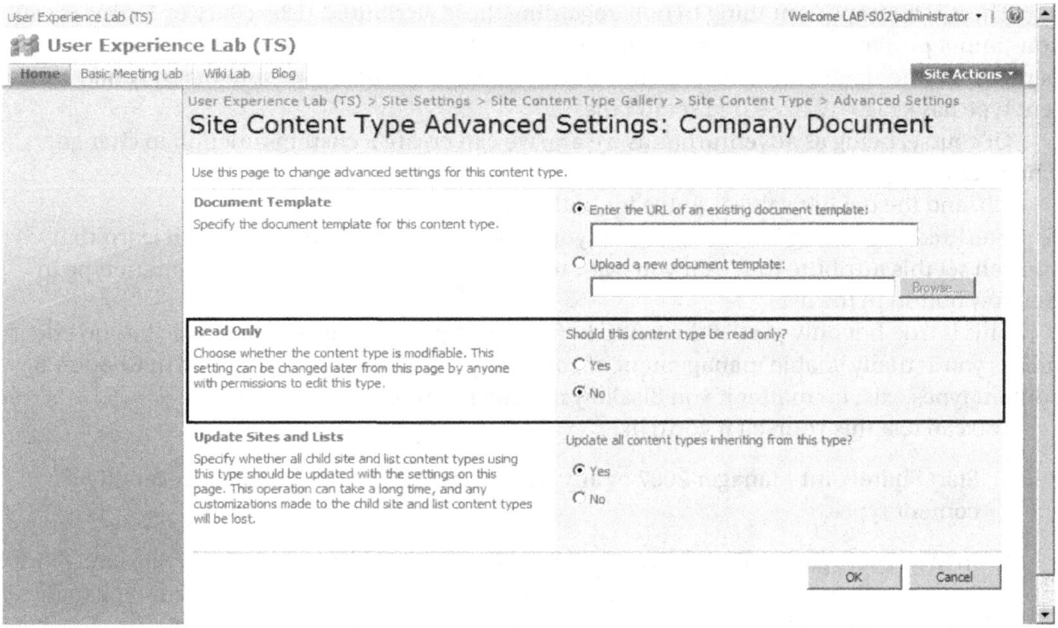

Figure 8-7. *Advanced settings of the content type settings*

Content types can optionally be arranged into groups. Most notably this is used in the Site Content Type Gallery. The Group attribute states under which subheading the content type should appear. The string value of Group is just an arbitrary value. You can enter whatever you like, and SharePoint will create a new group for you; or you can use an existing group name to group content types together.

Tip If you remove all content types from a group, the group is automatically deleted.

V2ListTemplateName is used to map our content type to a WSS 2 list template and is rarely used in new sites. On the other hand, Version is not used at all, since the attribute is reserved for future use.

OK, we have looked at the attributes used in the document content type, but there are still more attributes we can use in our own content types.

If you set the ReadOnly attribute to True and note that its default value is False, you cannot make changes to the content type after it has been deployed—at least not until you change the ReadOnly attribute to False. You can set or unset this value in the advanced settings of the content type settings. Actually, you would need to have list management permissions to change the setting, but if you do, you can turn on and off ReadOnly from the interface.

The Sealed attribute is related to ReadOnly but is more permanent. First, you need to be a site collection administrator to unseal a sealed content type. Second, you would need to do so either using a tool such as SPM 2007 or using your own code. There is no web interface by default that will allow you to change the Sealed attribute.

There is an important thing to note regarding these attributes. If ReadOnly or Sealed is set, you cannot propagate changes from a parent content type. If you need to make changes to a parent type and update the descendant content types, you must make sure that no child content type has ReadOnly or Sealed set to True.

Of course, being as adventurous as we are, we can create a custom function to change whatever we like.

Oh, and the default value is False for both attributes.

The Hidden attribute is a bit strange. If you read the documentation, you will learn that you can set this attribute to True if you want to prevent the availability of the content type in the New button in the list.

This is true but only part of the truth. In fact, setting a content type to Hidden has no effect unless you actually enable management of content types as well. As I explained in Chapter 6, content types exist no matter if you disallow management of content types.

You can test this yourself if you'd like:

1. Start SharePoint Manager 2007 or any other tool that allows you to easily modify content types.

2. In SPM 2007, go to a list, such as the Shared Document list in your Team Site lab, and open the Content Types section. Make sure your list does *not* have content type management enabled.

3. Locate the Document content type, and set the Hidden property to True.

Note Do this on the List content type to avoid affecting every Document content type available. In any case, you can always revert this step to make the content type unhidden again.

---

4. Open your shared document in a web browser, and check out the options on the New button (see Figure 8-8).

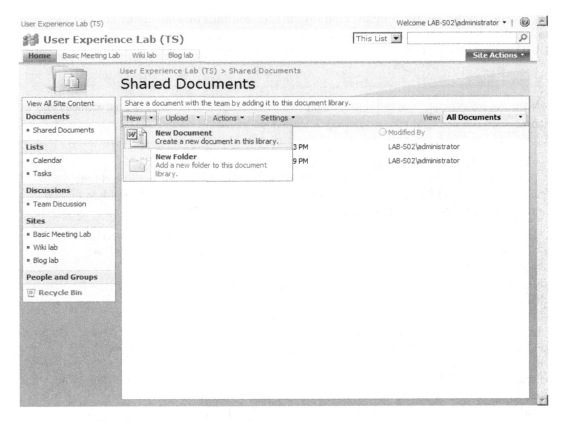

Figure 8-8. *Hidden document content type?*

5. Go to the advanced settings on the Shared Documents list settings page, and allow the management of content types.

6. Check out the New button again. Your Document content type should be gone.

ContentType Child Elements

With that little curiosity out of the way, let's move on to the child elements. Staying true to our original plan, we should look at the child elements from the default Document content type.

FieldRefs

Usually your reason for using content types is to collect certain columns that are common to types of content, right? To configure which columns are connected to a content type, you use the FieldRefs element. The FieldRefs element contains either FieldRef or RemoveFieldRef child elements.

Content types can use only site columns, that is, columns that are defined on the site rather than on a list. Each if these site columns have a GUID that is unique to the site, and that GUID is what you use to add a reference to the site column to your content type.

■**Note** We will examine fields and columns more in the next chapter, so for now this is all you need to know.

Take a look at the `FieldRefs` element of the `Document` content type excerpted here. Each `FieldRef` has an ID that points to a field defined somewhere in the site. The fields specified here are parts of the fields feature that gets installed with SharePoint.

```
<FieldRef ID="{5f47e085-2150-41dc-b661-442f3027f552}" Name="SelectFilename" />
<FieldRef ID="{8553196d-ec8d-4564-9861-3dbe931050c8}" Name="FileLeafRef"➥
 Required="TRUE"/>
<FieldRef ID="{8c06beca-0777-48f7-91c7-6da68bc07b69}" Name="Created"➥
 Hidden="TRUE" />
<FieldRef ID="{fa564e0f-0c70-4ab9-b863-0177e6ddd247}" Name="Title"➥
 Required="FALSE" ShowInNewForm="FALSE" ShowInEditForm="TRUE"/>
<FieldRef ID="{28cf69c5-fa48-462a-b5cd-27b6f9d2bd5f}" Name="Modified"➥
 Hidden="TRUE" />
<FieldRef ID="{822c78e3-1ea9-4943-b449-57863ad33ca9}" Name="Modified_x0020_By"➥
 Hidden="FALSE"/>
<FieldRef ID="{4dd7e525-8d6b-4cb4-9d3e-44ee25f973eb}" Name="Created_x0020_By"➥
 Hidden="FALSE" />
```

You may notice that the `Title` field is included here. Now, if you have been particularly attentive, you may remember that the `Title` field is also included in the `Item` content type, from which `Document` inherits. By virtue of inheritance, `Title` should already be included, so why is it added to the `Document` content type as well?

The reason is quite simple. `FieldRef` not only adds references to new columns but also modifies existing columns. If you examine the `Title` `FieldRef` from `Item`, located just above the `Document` content type in `ctypes.xml`, you will see that it is different from the `Title` `FieldRef` in `Document`.

Here's the `Item` `Title` `FieldRef`:

```
<FieldRef ID="{fa564e0f-0c70-4ab9-b863-0177e6ddd247}" Name="Title"➥
 Required="TRUE" ShowInNewForm="TRUE" ShowInEditForm="TRUE"/>
```

Here's the `Document` `Title` `FieldRef`:

```
<FieldRef ID="{fa564e0f-0c70-4ab9-b863-0177e6ddd247}" Name="Title"➥
 Required="FALSE" ShowInNewForm="FALSE" ShowInEditForm="TRUE"/>
```

As you can see, the `Required` attribute is `False` in `Document`, because you don't need to title your documents, and the `ShowInNewForm` is also `False`, because you only need to upload a file, not give it a title, when you add a new `Document` to a library.

Thus, the `Document Title FieldRef` is used to modify the behavior and appearance of `Title`, not to add it.

You can override many attributes in this fashion. I will cover fields, columns, and field references in the next chapter.

RemoveFieldRef

If you decide you really do not need a column inherited from a parent, you can use the `RemoveFieldRef` element to get rid of the parent columns. The documentation is also a bit confusing here, since it lists plenty of attributes such as `ReadOnly`, `ShowInNewForm`, and `Required`, but in fact, none of these attributes is required or even used. The only attribute you need is the `ID` attribute, and that attribute references the ID of a parent field you want to remove.

Maybe the documentation is confusing, but the extra attributes are helpful. Tell me, which field is removed here?

```
<RemoveFieldRef ID="{922551b8-c7e0-46a6-b7e3-3cf02917f68a}"/>
```

You may keep a record of all field IDs in your head, but for me, adding an extra attribute saves me some headache:

```
<RemoveFieldRef ID="{922551b8-c7e0-46a6-b7e3-3cf02917f68a}" Name="ImageSize"/>
```

Note For some unknown reason, the `wss.xsd` schema includes a `DocumentTemplate` entry in the `FieldRefs` element. You may see this when you use IntelliSense to author your content type. You may also forget the entry is there; it doesn't do anything.

XmlDocuments

The next part of the document `ContentType` entry is `XmlDocuments`. Sadly, very little documentation exists on this element. Luckily, that has never stopped a determined developer like you, especially when you realize what the prize is. And it is grand. Let me just make sure you understand this: `XmlDocuments`, horribly underused in SharePoint custom development, redefines the definition of *grand prize*. From now on, every other use of the term *grand prize* should be reduced to "great prize—not as grand as SharePoint's `XmlDocuments`."

OK, I may be exaggerating a bit, but `XmlDocuments` can be really cool.

What the `XmlDocuments` element does, or rather, what its children `XmlDocument` elements do, is store custom information about your content type. You may actually store anything you like; as long as you follow correct XML syntax, you can add your own custom information to use however you see fit.

If that does not blow your mind, let me give you a few examples.

One use of XmlDocument is to customize the forms of content types. You may recall from Chapter 6 that new, edit, and display form templates are actually tied to the content type. The XmlDocument element to support custom form templates is FormTemplates and is laid out as such:

```
<FormTemplates xmlns="http://schemas.microsoft.com/sharepoint/v3/contenttype/forms">
 <Display>DocumentLibraryForm</Display>
 <Edit>DocumentLibraryForm</Edit>
 <New>DocumentLibraryForm</New>
</FormTemplates>
```

This is an XmlDocument type that is included with SharePoint and supported by the content type framework. You have another option as well, the FormUrls type of XmlDocument, which is used to redirect to a separate URL for the form, rather than just update the form template:

```
<FormUrls xmlns="http://schemas.microsoft.com/sharepoint/v3/contenttype/forms/url">
 <Display>$Resources:core,lists_Folder;/$Resources:core,blogpost_Folder;/Post.aspx
 </Display>
</FormUrls>
```

This is from the Blog content type, with content type ID 0x0110.

There is also a third included XmlDocument type, Receivers, which is used to attach event handlers to content types. You'll learn more about that later in the chapter.

Oh, and XmlDocuments elements are inherited when you create a new child content type. If you further examine the other content types in ctypeswss.xml, you will notice that many, if not most, do not specify a FormTemplates XmlDocument at all. This is because they inherit from a parent content type, for example the Item or the Document content type, which defines the FormTemplates section.

Caution Although XmlDocuments elements are inherited for *new* child content types, updates to existing child content types have a quirk. Basically, if a content type is in use—in other words, it is deployed to a list or items have been created based on the content type—updates to the parent XmlDocuments element are not propagated. To force updates, you can update the child content type manually or ensure that no lists or items currently use the child content type.

Of course, I am still a "glass is half full" kind of guy, so please read on for how you can use this to your advantage.

You may still not yet see how this is incredibly cool, so let me give you a custom example. Let's say that you have a legal statement that you need to include with every item based on a certain content type, such as something about the release of liability to your financial documents in our hierarchy example. You have a few options.

First, you can modify the forms or pages to display a static legal disclaimer, but sadly, since a content type–based item can move around, you would need to modify every single page. Besides, if you have different legal statements for each content type you are out of luck.

Second, you can store the legal statement in the item itself. Of course, this would mean updating every single item if you change the statement, not to mention that you would be storing the statement about a gazillion times.

The perfect solution is to use a custom XmlDocument element. Not only would every child element get the statement, but you could have different statements for each child. When you add the information in the earlier caution to the mix (you did read that, right?), you know that updating the parent statement will not affect the children, unless you want it to do so.

Tip To put this in a language programmers will understand, think of XmlDocument elements as static properties of a content type class.

To add such a custom XmlDocument to your content type, you would add something like this:

```
<XmlDocuments>
 <XmlDocument NamespaceURI="http://example.com/legal/statements/document">
  <Statement NamespaceURI="http://example.com/legal/statements/document">
   <Text>Don't try this at home</Text>
   <Contact>legaldepartment@example.com</Contact>
   <Version>1.0</Version>
  </Statement>
 </XmlDocument>
</XmlDocuments>
```

Then, when you want to use this information, you can access it like this:

```
SPList list = web.Lists[<YOUR LIST NAME>];
SPListItem item = list.GetItemById(<YOUR ITEM ID>);
string xmlString =➥
 item.ContentType.XmlDocuments["http://example.com/legal/statements/document"];
XmlDocument xmlDoc = new XmlDocument();
xmlDoc.LoadXml(xmlString);
string statementText = xmlDoc["Statement"]["Text"].InnerText;
string statementContact = xmlDoc["Statement"]["Contact"].InnerText;
```

How you actually get a hold of the SPListItem will of course vary, but once you have an SPListItem, you can easily get a hold of the XmlDocument of the content type of that item.

Caution Pay careful attention to the use of the NamespaceURI. SharePoint relies heavily on having correct namespaces, and using the wrong NamespaceURI values can cause much grief.

I don't know about you, but I think XmlDocuments is a really cool feature of an already cool feature, possibly making this thing the coolest thing on Earth. It is so cool it will make cold freeze.

Content Type Forms

A natural next step is to further explore content type forms. You have two options, both defined in the XmlDocuments node.

First there is the FormUrls type of XmlDocument, briefly mentioned earlier. You would use the FormUrls method if you want your content type to have completely separate pages for the user experience.

The second method is to use the FormTemplates type of XmlDocument which, in contrast to the FormUrls, will use the default list form pages and insert your respective FormTemplate into the web part zone specified in the list form page.

Both methods share the child elements Display, New, and Edit. The FormUrls child elements specify the URL of a form page, while the FormTemplates child elements specify just the name of a rendering template.

Note See Chapter 5 for more information on RenderingTemplates.

We will explore more details on how to actually build the forms and form templates in Part 3 of this book.

Remember that, like all XmlDocuments, both FormUrls and FormTemplates are inherited, but once a content type has been used, changes to the parent XmlDocument will not be automatically propagated.

Declaratively Adding Event Receivers to a Content Type

We need to attach the event receiver to our content type. This is a bit more complex than it needs to be, and I will take a short detour to explain why.

Attaching Event Receivers to List Templates Using Features

Yes, I said detour. Back into the forest we go, but no monsters this time.

When you want to attach an event receiver to a list, you can do so using a feature. Start with the basic feature as explained in Chapter 3. In the elements file, make sure you have the Elements root element in place, and then add a child element called Receiver. As you will notice, Receiver is indeed a supported child element, as evident in the IntelliSense support.

Now, in the newly create Receivers element, add an attribute. If you get IntelliSense, you will see that there are two legal attributes, called ListTemplateId and ListTemplateOwner. So, to add a receiver to a list template, simply set the value of the ListTemplateId attribute to the list template ID of your list template.

Then, inside your `Receivers` element, you add a `Receiver` child element and some more child elements to the `Receiver` element. Deploy your feature, activate, and boom—Bob's your uncle.

A sample elements file to deploy an item event receiver to a list template may look like this:

```xml
<?xml version="1.0" encoding="utf-8" ?>
<Elements xmlns="http://schemas.microsoft.com/sharepoint/">
  <Receivers>
    <Receiver>
      <Assembly>YOUR STRONG NAME HERE</Assembly>
      <Class>YOUR CLASS NAME HERE</Class>
      <Data></Data>
      <Filter></Filter>
      <Name>My event receiver</Name>
      <Type>ItemAdded</Type>
      <SequenceNumber>10</SequenceNumber>
    </Receiver>
  </Receivers>
</Elements>
```

A few things are worth noticing about this element. You can add custom data to your receiver inside the `Data` element, which is useful if you want to have the same receiver code but make it behave differently. For example, you may have a verification receiver that checks whether values are valid for a wide range of lists. You can customize the error message or the verification procedure itself using custom data, while maintaining just a single piece of code.

There is also a `Filter` element in the `Receiver` schema. I have yet to find any documentation, information, or examples regarding this element.

Yes, this is indeed undocumented, but as far as anyone seems to know, it is also unused. It is safe to ignore this element completely; perhaps it is reserved for future use.

The `Sequence` element is used to decide the order in which multiple event receivers run. The `Name` element is just for your convenience, and you can call your event receiver element "Johnny Fartypants" if that makes you happy. As for `Assembly` and `Class`…well, I'll leave you to figure out what those do.

Attaching Event Receivers to Content Types Using Features

The important thing with attaching event receivers like we just saw is to notice that there is no way to bind a receiver to a content type, only to a list template.

No, there are no ways to add receivers to individual lists either. However, as you saw in Chapter 6, you can programmatically add event receivers using code. You can use the same technique to add event receivers to a content type as well, but there should be a way to do this using CAML in a feature. After all, that is where you define the content type, as you will see later in the chapter.

The answer? Event receivers in content types are defined in a different section of the elements file.

Again, you can look to XmlDocuments and the third built-in XmlDocument type Receiver. The Receiver XmlDocument resides in the http://schemas.microsoft.com/sharepoint/events namespace. If you want to see a Receiver XmlDocument in your default SharePoint installation, search the ctypeswss.xml file for the content type 0x010107, the DocumentWorkflowItem:

```
<XmlDocument NamespaceURI="http://schemas.microsoft.com/sharepoint/events">
 <spe:Receivers xmlns:spe="http://schemas.microsoft.com/sharepoint/events">
  <Receiver>
   <Name>Workflow Library Item Added</Name>
   <Type>ItemAdded</Type>
   <SequenceNumber>1</SequenceNumber>
   <Assembly>Microsoft.SharePoint, Version=12.0.0.0, Culture=neutral,➡
    PublicKeyToken=71e9bce111e9429c</Assembly>
   <Class>Microsoft.SharePoint.Workflow.SPWorkflowLibraryEventReceiver</Class>
   <Data />
   <Filter />
  </Receiver>
… (snipped for space-saving purposes
 </Receivers>
</XmlDocument>
```

■ **Note** The example uses a prefix spe: for the Receivers element. This is not necessary from a technical point of view but can add clarity to your code.

As you can see, the Receiver element follows the structure of a regular item event receiver as defined in elements—except, of course, that the receiver is defined in the XmlDocument section of the content type.

The End of the Ice Age

It is time to call it a night—or early morning if you stay up all night to read SharePoint stuff like I do. Some useful tips to take away are in order:

- Content types require some getting used to. However, as programmers, we should be familiar with the concept. What took the most time for me was wrapping my head around thinking of content types as classes, but once I realized that, the true power of content types was clear.

- Convincing your project manager about the usefulness of content types can also be a challenge. For nontechnical people, using the class analogy doesn't work.

- As always, start simple when learning. Don't try to implement a complex content type hierarchy with plenty of behavior, appearance, and metadata structures if you have never worked with them before. Inheritance, for example, can be a cruel beast until you learn all the quirks.

- Also, start thinking content types from the beginning. If you start out thinking which lists you want to implement, you are likely to have more problems later when you want to harness the power of content types.

- Managers as well love to hear that you can map business objects to content types; after all, thinking of a contact as a contact rather than a predefined set of columns makes more sense for a nontechnical user.

- And, when working with content types, always wear a sweater, because you will likely be the coolest spot in your entire team, and you risk getting a cold.

I'll stop the bad jokes now.

CHAPTER 9

■ ■ ■

Strolling Through Fields of Gold

I Think…Yes, There It Is…Our Goal Is in Sight

We have been traveling a long time, but we are closer than ever to our destination. Our final trek will take us across a wonderful golden field—or, rather, a whole range of fields, to be precise.

This chapter is all about fields and columns, the minute parts of SharePoint that make up the most basic units of storage.

Now, before we go any further, I should explain the use of the phrase *fields of gold*, because those few words hold a few secrets. First, mastering fields and columns is very important to understanding how to customize the user experience in SharePoint.

Second, when you think of fields of gold, except perhaps the best song ever written, you may think of massive fields with billions of individual grains of barley. Fields are somewhat like that; there are no less than 100 attributes to the Field element, with a staggering amount of possible child element combinations.

Perhaps handcrafting DNA is not such a bad job after all.

We will focus primarily on the attributes and elements that matter to the user experience, but still this will be a very technically detailed chapter.

Columns and Properties of Gold?

The terms *fields*, *columns*, and *properties* are often used interchangeably, and they often refer to the same thing. All the terms refer to the storage device in which data about an item is actually stored. Examples of this are the Title, Author, Modified, Due Date, and Assigned to columns, as well as other similar pieces of information storage units.

There are minute differences, however, between the three terms. Fields and columns, being the same thing, usually refer to columns in a site, list, or content type. Properties are often used on items or documents. So, your Quarterly Reports library may have a Department column, but the Quarterly report for Q1 2009.pdf file has a Department property.

During the course of this book, I have tried to consistently use the term *column* when referring to list and content type columns and to use *property* when referring to item or document metadata. Because of the similarity of the terms *field* and *field type*, I have refrained from using the term *field* at all, but you should know that, in general, *field* refers to the same thing as *column* or *property*.

Caution Throughout the CAML files, the term *field* is used for columns. For the duration of this chapter I will sometimes use the term *field* when referring to columns.

Wait! What Are Field Types?

Ah, yes, *field types* are the type of data. If you are familiar with database terminology, think data types, such as integers, text, and so on.

Unlike databases, however, SharePoint allows us to create our own data types. In fact, as with may other things, the default field types, such as single line of text, date/time, number, and person, are defined using regular CAML.

This gives us a massive amount of power. If you need to improve on a text field perhaps to add autocomplete or you need to create a drop-down list that retrieves data from an external data source, you can accomplish that by creating a custom field type.

A common scenario is to create cross-list, cross-site, and cross-site collection lookup fields. We will create our very own field type in Chapter 10.

...and Field Type Controls?

A field type has two elements, a storage element and a method of displaying the stored data. The *field type control* is responsible for handling the visual interface of a field type, such as an HTML text box for the text field type and a calendar for the date/time data type.

You can change the existing field type controls as we briefly saw in Chapter 5, and if you decide to create your own field type, you can do pretty much anything you want.

Note When I say "if," I really mean "when." Custom field types are incredibly powerful, and you would do wisely to learn how to create them. If nothing else, we will create custom field types in Part 3 of this book.

With those definitions out of the way, let's move on to see how columns are used.

Site Columns vs. List Columns

You can define columns on two levels, either on the site level or on the list level. Site columns are useful if you intend to use a column in multiple lists. Rather than having to define all the settings for every list, you can define a site column with all the settings and add that site column to the lists.

Site columns are your only option if you intend to use your columns in content types. List columns are available only for a particular list.

For lists, you can use either site columns or list columns. Or, actually, you can use list columns only. Or, actually, you can add site columns, but they become list columns. Let me explain.

On the list or library settings page, you have the option to either create a new column or add an existing site column. If you choose the latter, a copy of the site column is made using the same field ID as the site column. The copy becomes a list column.

The use of similar ID values for both the site column and the list column maintains the parent-child relationship. This relationship means you can make changes to the site column and optionally have all child columns inherit those changes.

This is a good thing, because it means that the list column is detached from the site column when you want it to be, but it can still maintain its relationship to the parent site column. An example might clarify this.

Let's say you have a site column named Recipient used to store who will receive reports from different departments. You add that field to a new list for a new department, but then the department head comes to you and says that the column needs to be named "Target manager" instead.

In this situation, you can simply go to the list settings and change the name of the column on that list. Had you changed the site columns, every occurrence of the Recipient column would be changed, and other departments might not like that.

What might spin your head a bit later is when we start to consider how content types work in this scenario. As I mentioned, content types use only site columns, so if we want to change a column for a content type on a list, we might be in trouble. And, if content types are so cool and we should use them as often as we can, how can we have such a limitation?

The answer is that content types also create list column copies of their respective site columns. When you add a content type to a list or library, all the site columns of that content type are copied into list columns on a list.

Problem solved.

Site Columns in CAML

To add site columns using the web interface, you simply go to the site where you want to add a column, then go to the Site Settings page, and finally select the site columns. Create your site column by clicking Create, fill in the form, submit it, and live happily ever after. You can do this on any site.

Creating a basic field using a feature is slightly more complex, but not much. First, start with your basic feature as explained in Chapter 3, and make sure your feature scope is set to site, not web.

As with content types, site column features are site scoped, and of course you remember that *site* in this feature context means site collection. The ID of the field needs to be unique to the entire site collection to support content type inheritance and to allow site columns to be used in child sites.

Yes, that's correct. Columns have scope just like content types. If you define a site column in one site, all child sites will also be able to use that column. Site columns and content types are closely connected.

Let's get back to your feature now—in your elements file, add a `Field` element as such:

```xml
<?xml version="1.0" encoding="utf-8" ?>
<Elements xmlns="http://schemas.microsoft.com/sharepoint/">
```

```
<Field Name="Recipient" DisplayName="Recipient"
        ID="{053EC00E-D451-4733-8CA0-31532C974E91}" Type="Text" >
</Field>
</Elements>
```

Caution Unlike other GUID examples, you must use brackets in the GUID ID value when defining site columns. Do not forget this.

All you need to do to deploy your new column now is to deploy the feature and then activate the feature from the Site Collection Features page on the root web in the site collection.

INVISIBLE FIELDS?

Don't forget the DisplayName attribute. The DisplayName attribute is what is visible to you when you want to add, edit, or remove the column. If you skip the DisplayName attribute, you will have a rather annoying problem—an invisible field in the site columns. Not just that, but since the field does not have a name, you cannot click it to remove it either. Figure 9-1 shows this situation.

Your solution, as for many problems, is your trusty copy of SharePoint Manager 2007. Open your site, and browse to the fields of the site. Your unnamed column should be right at the top. Either change the name to enable deletion and modification from the web interface or delete the column before reactivating the feature.

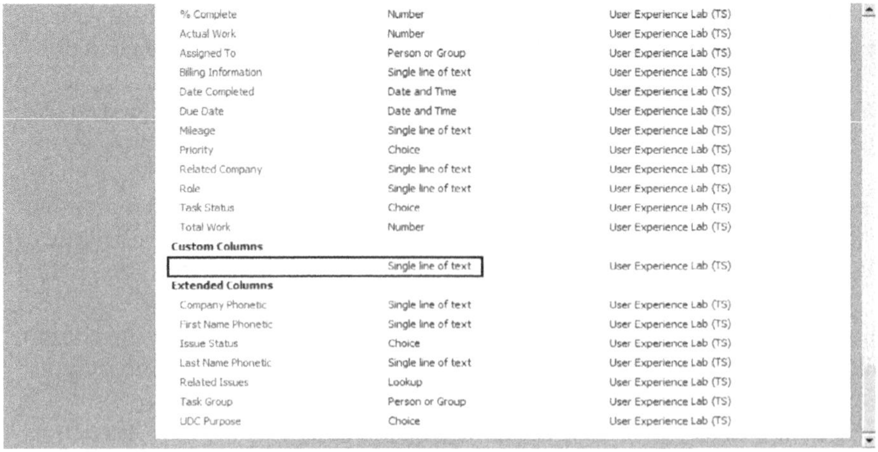

Figure 9-1. *Nothing to click*

Let's take a look at how this is done in some of the default fields installed with SharePoint. Open the [12]\TEMPLATE\FEATURES\fields\fieldswss.xml file.

The fieldswss.xml file holds all the default site columns that are installed when you set up SharePoint. The fields feature containing all these fields is activated through the global site definition at [12]\GLOBAL\XML\onet.xml, as you saw in Chapter 4.

Your first impression of the fieldswss.xml file might be "Wow!" It is a huge file, and I bet you never imagined so many columns were installed. When you start to investigate, however, the file is quite manageable. What will really stun you is the sheer amount of options you have when you want to create your columns.

We should investigate some of the common columns used throughout SharePoint, but we can't ignore the lesser known columns either. I'll show you some columns, and then we will explore the different attributes and elements afterward.

ContentType

You know that all items in SharePoint are based on a content type. At least you know that if you have been paying attention, especially in Chapter 7. All items, regardless of content type inheritance, have a ContentType property. This is facilitated through the System root content type, defined in [12]\TEMPLATE\FEATURES\ctypes\ctypeswss.xml, which contains a single field reference to the ContentType site column:

```
<ContentType ID="0x"
    Name="$Resources:System"
    Group="_Hidden"
    Sealed="TRUE"
    Version="0">
    <FieldRefs>
     <FieldRef ID="{c042a256-787d-4a6f-8a8a-cf6ab767f12d}" Name="ContentType"/>
    </FieldRefs>
</ContentType>
```

The site column referenced in the system root content type is the second column or field defined in fieldswss.xml:

```
<Field ID="{c042a256-787d-4a6f-8a8a-cf6ab767f12d}"
    Name="ContentType"
    SourceID="http://schemas.microsoft.com/sharepoint/v3"
    StaticName="ContentType"
    Group="_Hidden"
    RowOrdinal="0"
    Type="Text"
    DisplayName="$Resources:core,Content_Type;"
    ReadOnly="TRUE"
    Sealed="TRUE"
    ColName="tp_ContentType"
    PITarget="MicrosoftWindowsSharePointServices"
    PIAttribute="ContentTypeID">
</Field>
```

Some of the attributes shown here require further explanation. ID is a GUID that uniquely identifies a site column within a site collection. Note the minor detail of being unique with a site collection.

Next, the name attributes—as you can see, there are actually four names in use here: Name, StaticName, DisplayName, and ColName. In addition, there are two more attributes that denote a column's name in different scenarios. Luckily, we need to concern ourselves with only two of these names, the Name and DisplayName attributes.

Name is the internal name of a field and is rarely, if ever, shown to a user. Name cannot be changed for a column; once it is set, that's the name with which you are stuck. This is in contrast to DisplayName, which is shown as the name of the field to users in the web interface. Users, or you, can change the DisplayName attribute without messing up the column.

You should use this distinction to your advantage. When you are working with fields in code, you often reference fields by Name, which makes sense since this value never changes. However, if you have a column titled "Things to do," the Name value would have to be accessed as Things_0x0020_to_0x0020_do, which is inconvenient. Instead, you can set DisplayName to Things to do and set Name to Tasks or ThingsToDo. That way, you maintain the best of both worlds: you get a descriptive title and a convenient internal name for use in code.

Tip If you create a column with spaces in the name using the web interface, SharePoint autogenerates the name with the 0x0020 notation for spaces. To avoid this, create the column using the name you want to use internally, and then rename the column to the descriptive name you want the user to see. Only the DisplayName will be changed when you modify a column's name in the web interface. This also applies to other special characters that cannot be used by SharePoint internally. My first name, Bjørn, would be translated to Bj_x00f8_rn if I were to use that as a column name.

Here's a quick explanation of the other name attributes. The ColName attribute is used to specify the name that should be used when storing the column in the SharePoint database. A related and similarly seldom used attribute is JoinColName, which is used in place of ColName when doing SQL joins. XName is used only internally and is related to handling changes in XML forms.

You will never use any of these three attributes yourself; they are related to how SharePoint stores your columns in the database, but you should know what they do.

StaticName is a bit bewildering. The documentation states that you can use this attribute to get or set the internal name of a field. Knowing that there is no way we can change the internal name of a column after it has been provisioned, this may seem a bit strange.

The confusing bit here is that StaticName is a semihidden attribute that defaults on get requests to the internal name of a field, which is the Name attribute we must set. However, you can change the StaticName attribute to another value, and in that case, that value is returned instead of the Name value of the column. See Table 9-1.

Table 9-1. StaticName *vs.* Name *Return Values*

StaticName	Name	SPField.StaticName **Returns...**
[Nothing]	MyField	MyField
MyStaticName	MyField	MyStaticName

Most developers (and Microsoft in its default out-of-the-box site columns) just set StaticName to the same value as Name.

Next, the Type attribute defines the field type used to store and optionally display the data stored in the column. There are several built-in types, such as text, integer, computed, date/time, yes/no, and choice, and you can create your own types as well. We will explore this a bit later in Chapter 11. (A *bit* in that sentence is the same bit as "there is a bit of water in the sea.")

The Group attribute of the Field element serves the same function as the Group attribute in content types in that it is used to group columns in some fashion. The string is completely arbitrary, and you can write whatever value you want. SharePoint will create a new group if no matching groups exist and remove the group if no columns belong to a group anymore.

The grouping serves no technical purpose other than helping you arrange columns in a logical group structure. There are no parent-child groups either. The grouping is most frequently seen on the Site Column Gallery page, as shown in Figure 9-2.

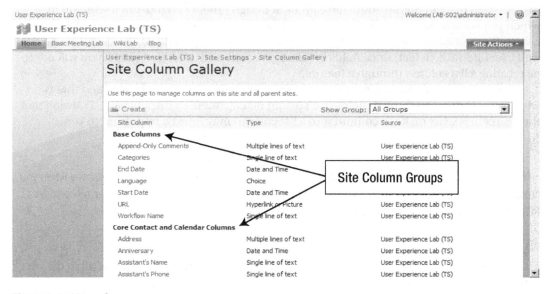

Figure 9-2. *Site column groups*

The ReadOnly and Sealed attributes work in the same way as with content types. The ReadOnly attribute can be turned off in the interface, while Sealed requires direct object model access from a site collection administrator. See the descriptions for the ReadOnly and Sealed attributes in Chapter 8 for more information.

One more thing requires our attention, and that's the SourceID attribute. This attribute serves two purposes that may be a bit tough to understand right away. First, the SourceID attribute defines the namespace in which the column resides, most often http://schemas.microsoft.com/sharepoint/v3.

Second, the SourceID may hold the GUID of the list in which a list column is defined. When you add a column to a list, the only thing that ties that column to that specific list is that the default namespace is replaced by the GUID of the list in the SourceID property.

So, if you want a site column, leave the SourceID attribute blank, or add http://schemas.microsoft.com/sharepoint/v3 namespace, and if you want a list column, add the GUID of the list in which you want to column to appear.

That may not puzzle you now, but consider this question: how would you know the GUID of a list at design time? You can't, since the GUID is autogenerated when the list is created and you have no way of controlling that GUID.

Note This is the same chicken-and-egg problem you face when you want to create lookup columns through a feature: you need to know in advance the GUID of a site or list that doesn't exist yet. We will solve the lookup problem in Chapter 12, though.

So, what use can this attribute have for us at design time? I can think of a scenario in which you want to add a specific field to an existing list. However, creating a feature for such a list column would incur massive overhead compared to simply adding the field through the web user interface. In fact, since fields in features require site collection scope, you will never be creating a list column through a feature.

There is one situation where you might want to use this attribute, though, and that is when you are iterating through fields in a custom management or display page. Knowing that the SourceID is what makes a column into a list column may thus be important to you.

Note At this point, you might be thinking that you can manipulate the SourceID through code when you create a list column through code in the object model. The SourceID is set for you, however, so consider this a read-only value that is handled for you.

The remaining attributes in the ContentType site column are not relevant at all to the user experience.

Title

The next site column I want you to see is the `Title` site column. This is perhaps the most used publicly editable column there is. The `Title` site column is defined in `fieldswss.xml` at around line 452:

```
<Field ID="{fa564e0f-0c70-4ab9-b863-0177e6ddd247}"
    Name="Title"
    SourceID="http://schemas.microsoft.com/sharepoint/v3"
    StaticName="Title"
    Group="_Hidden"
    Type="Text"
    DisplayName="$Resources:core,Title;"
    Required="TRUE"
    FromBaseType="TRUE">
</Field>
```

The `Title` site column is added to every item everywhere by being added to the `Item` content type in `ctypeswss.xml`:

```
<ContentType ID="0x01"
 Name="$Resources:Item"
 Group="$Resources:List_Content_Types"
 Description="$Resources:ItemCTDesc"
 Version="0">
 <FieldRefs>
  <FieldRef ID="{fa564e0f-0c70-4ab9-b863-0177e6ddd247}" Name="Title"➥
 Required="TRUE" ShowInNewForm="TRUE" ShowInEditForm="TRUE"/> <!-- Title -->
 </FieldRefs>
 <XmlDocuments>
(XMLDocuments omitted to save space)
 </XmlDocuments>
</ContentType>
```

Now that we have investigated the `ContentType` attributes, most of the attributes here will be simple to understand. Still, a few new attributes require our scrutiny.

The `FromBaseType` attribute, besides its obvious use of telling us that this column derives from a base type, has one important function. When you set `FromBaseType`, you also prevent the column type from changing.

Now, `BaseType` here refers to the columns defined in the list templates in the global site definition. As you may recall from Chapter 4, the global site definition contains a set of base list types, which in turn contains several fields or columns. This is where the `Title` column and any other column with `FromBaseType` have their roots.

In the `Title` case, all the attributes of the base type `Title` field are overridden, so there is actually nothing left of the root `Title` column. This was a far more useful technique in WSS 2 where content types did not exist.

More relevant for us, however, is the second effect of `FromBaseType`. You may have noticed that some columns allow you to slightly modify the type of column, for instance from text to multiline text or from number to text, and so on. If you set `FromBaseType` to `true`, it becomes impossible to change the column type. Take a look at Figure 9-3.

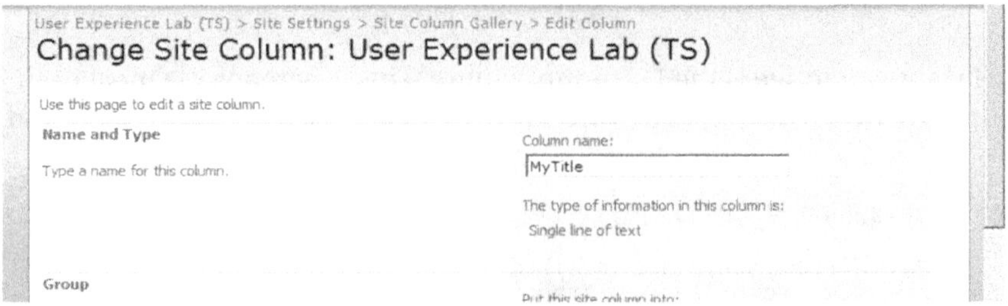

FromBaseType="true"

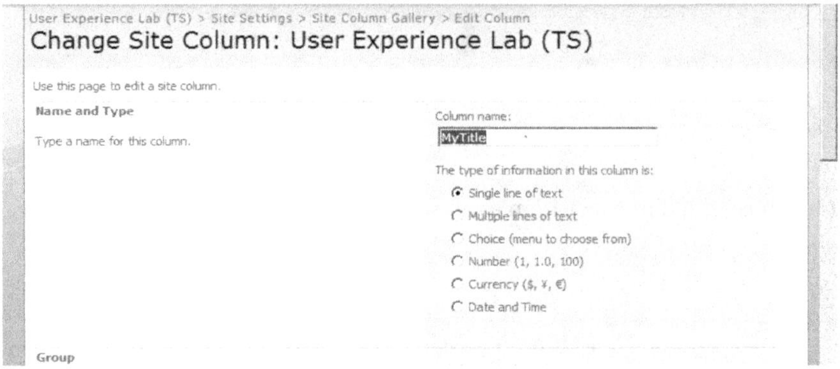

FromBaseType="false"

Figure 9-3. *Effect of* FromBaseType

Finally, notice the reference to the Title site column in the Item content type. This reference includes ShowInNewForm="TRUE" and ShowInEditForm="TRUE". We touched briefly on this in Chapter 8 when you learned how the Document content type modified the behavior of the Title column in list forms.

The ShowInXXXX attributes control when a column is displayed in various list form pages. The "sister" attributes are ShowInDisplayForm, ShowInEditForm, ShowInListSettings, ShowInNewForm, ShowInVersionHistory, and ShowInViewForms. Note that the attributes are relevant only when you use the default methods of creating list forms. If you create your own custom list forms or you use other data input, edit, or display methods such as a Windows application or a custom RSS feed, you must make sure you honor or disregard these settings yourself.

Picking Up the Pace

So far, we have seen simple examples of how columns are defined using a feature. None of these examples should pose much of a challenge, except perhaps by the amount of possible attributes to the Field element.

Now it is time to pick up the pace, because we have only scratched the surface of what fields can do. Remember that cave of monsters called views? Well, we are going back, at least to some extent, to the view schema that we explored in views. This time, we should be much more prepared for what lies ahead.

LinkTitle

The next column I want to show you is a much more complex example—a computed column named LinkTitle. This column is responsible for creating the contents of the EditControlBlock drop-down menu when you hover over the title of an item.

Note That's actually only part of the truth, because the functionality and at least some of the content in the ECB is created using JavaScript. But that's another show….

In my fieldswss.xml file, it is located at line 535. Search the file for Name="LinkTitle", and you should find it. Figure 9-4 shows the field CAML code.

```
533          </DisplayPattern>
534     </Field>
535     <Field ID="{82642ec8-ef9b-478f-acf9-31f7d45fbc31}"
536          Name="LinkTitle"
537          SourceID="http://schemas.microsoft.com/sharepoint/v3"
538          StaticName="LinkTitle"
539          Group="$Resources:Base_Columns"
540          ReadOnly="TRUE"
541          Type="Computed"
542          DisplayName="$Resources:core,Title;"
543          DisplayNameSrcField="Title"
544          ClassInfo="Menu"
545          AuthoringInfo="$Resources:core,Linked_Item_With_Menu;"><!-- _locID@DisplayName="camlionet60" _l(
546          <FieldRefs>
547               <FieldRef ID="{fa564e0f-0c70-4ab9-b863-0177e6ddd247}" Name="Title"/>
548               <FieldRef ID="{bc91a437-52e7-49e1-8c4e-4698904b2b6d}" Name="LinkTitleNoMenu"/>
549               <FieldRef ID="{3c6303be-e21f-4366-80d7-d6d0a3b22c7a}" Name="_EditMenuTableStart"/>
550               <FieldRef ID="{2ea78cef-1bf9-4019-960a-02c41636cb47}" Name="_EditMenuTableEnd"/>
551          </FieldRefs>
552          <DisplayPattern>
553               <FieldSwitch>
554                    <Expr><GetVar Name="FreeForm"/></Expr>
555                    <Case Value="TRUE"><Field Name="LinkTitleNoMenu"/></Case>
556                    <Default>
557                         <Field Name="_EditMenuTableStart"/>
558                              <Field Name="LinkTitleNoMenu"/>
559                         <Field Name="_EditMenuTableEnd"/>
560                    </Default>
561               </FieldSwitch>
562          </DisplayPattern>
563     </Field>
564     <Field ID="{b1f7969b-ea65-42e1-8b54-b588292635f2}"
```

Figure 9-4. LinkTitle *field*

The first thing you should notice is that there are two child elements to the Field element, FieldRefs (lines 546–551) and DisplayPattern (lines 552–562). FieldRefs references other columns, including the Title column that we explored earlier. These referenced columns are used when rendering the LinkTitle column.

The rendering is done in the DisplayPattern element. You may recognize the look and feel of the code here; it is the same schema as we used in views. Thus, we should have the proper weapons to understand what's happening. Let's take a look.

The DisplayPattern element contains a FieldSwitch (553), which you may remember is the same thing as a Switch, except it is evaluated only once per view. The column here checks whether we are in FreeForm mode (554), meaning we are not in a list view, and if we are, it renders the output of one of the referenced columns, called LinkTitleNoMenu (555). If we are not in FreeForm mode, we should also render two more columns, _EditMenuTableStart and _EditMenuTableEnd, in addition to the LinkTitleNoMenu (lines 556–560).

So, where are these three columns defined? A quick search in fieldswss.xml for Name="_EditMenuTableStart" reveals the answer; they're around line 1001, in the form of a massively complex Field element. It has no less than 16 references to other columns and a DisplayPattern—that would scare even the bravest of developers.

Don't let the complexity overwhelm you. On closer inspection, you will find that most of the FieldRef references are just references to simple elements, and the display pattern is just used to output some extraordinarily ugly HTML in a fairly simple HTML table:

```
<table height="100%" cellspacing=0 class="ms-unselectedtitle" ➥
 onmouseover="OnItem(this)" CTXName="ctx1" Id="1" ➥
 Url="/Shared%20Documents/MyDocument.docx" DRef="Shared Documents" ➥
 Perm="0x7fffffffffffffff" Type="" Ext="docx" ➥
 Icon="icdocx.gif|Microsoft Office Word|SharePoint.OpenDocuments" ➥
 OType="0" COUId="" SRed="" COut="0" HCD="" CSrc="" MS="0" CType="Document" ➥
 CId="0x0101008AD77C1A367C63479F46C59787295E88" UIS="512" SUrl="">
```

Now you know where those people who say SharePoint renders noncompliant HTML get their arguments. Most of the attributes here have nothing to do with HTML and will likely make any HTML validator explode. Twice.

Still, there's no need to worry, because we can change this if we like, but for now we should move on.

If we continue to look at the LinkTitleNoMenu column referenced in our original LinkTitle column, starting at around line 502 in my file, we find a much more agreeable sight: two referenced columns and a rather understandable DisplayPattern.

Here's the whole DisplayPattern. Note that I have removed some comments for formatting purposes.

```
<DisplayPattern>
 <IfEqual>
  <Expr1><LookupColumn Name="FSObjType"/></Expr1>
  <Expr2>1</Expr2>
  <Then><Field Name="LinkFilenameNoMenu"/></Then>
  <Else>
   <HTML><![CDATA[<a onfocus="OnLink(this)" href="]]></HTML><URL/>
   <HTML><![CDATA[" ONCLICK="GoToLink(this);return false;" target="_self">]]>➥
   </HTML>
   <Column HTMLEncode='TRUE' Name="Title" Default='$Resources:core,NoTitle;'>➥
   </Column>
   <HTML><![CDATA[</a>]]></HTML>
   <IfNew>
    <HTML><![CDATA[<IMG➥
```

```
SRC="/_layouts/[%=System.Threading.Thread.CurrentThread.CurrentUICulture.LCID%]➥
/images/new.gif" alt="]]></HTML>
    <HTML>$Resources:core,new_gif_alttext</HTML><HTML><![CDATA[">]]></HTML>
  </IfNew>
 </Else>
</IfEqual>
</DisplayPattern>
```

The `DisplayPattern` uses an `IfEqual` element that basically checks whether the item is a document and, if so, links to the document file instead of the display form of the item. The link to the display form is rendered using the URL CAML element we used in Chapter 7.

And, to wrap the whole `LinkTitle` column up, look at the `_EditMenuTableEnd` column, which is really simple and just finishes up the table that started in `_EditMenuTableStart`:

```
<DisplayPattern>
 <HTML><![CDATA[</td><td><img src="/_layouts/images/blank.gif" width=13➥
 style="visibility: hidden" alt=""></td></tr></table>]]></HTML>
</DisplayPattern>
```

Columns in List Templates

Columns in list templates are defined in the `schema.xml` file of a list template feature. There is a `Fields` element, which you saw briefly during our exploration into lists.

It is time for some good news. Columns in list templates are exactly the same as columns in features, like we have just explored. Really, there is nothing more to learn about columns. Well, that's not exactly true; even with our fairly comprehensive investigation, we have still seen only a fraction of the columns available and what they can do.

However, columns behave the same in features as they do in list templates. The only difference is scope. List template columns are available to a list only, while feature columns are site scoped and available to all sites and subsites from where we deploy the feature.

Tip If you want to use your column with a content type, you must deploy it as a site column using features.

Columns in Content Types

As we saw in Chapter 8, you can only use site columns in content types. Also, remember that you do not define columns in content types; you can reference only existing site columns.

Phew, that was quite a ride just to do something as simple as creating a link on an item title. Still, understanding how these columns are built is important for understanding how the complete user experience is built.

When we start creating our own columns in Part 3 of the book, we will use much simpler code, so rest assured that the worst is behind us. Our final stretch in exploring the SharePoint user experience is just ahead: field types.

Field Types

With your newly found knowledge of columns, you can probably see a lot of potential power here. You can use different columns to store basic data and then use a computed column to create vastly complex renderings of that data.

Still, with all that power, there is still one thing you need to learn in order to truly understand the power of SharePoint customization: the field type.

The field type can be considered the atom of a SharePoint solution. It is the smallest piece of storage we can use. When harnessed, we get access to immense power, and although there are smaller pieces still, those smaller pieces belong to a completely different system and are rarely available to us.

Oh, enough of the analogies. I know you are eager to complete our journey. Be patient, and you will be rewarded.

Caution If you open a list with columns based on custom field types in the Datasheet view, the custom field type–based columns will not appear. The same applies for the built-in Excel export. But of course, we can create our own custom views now, and exporting data to an Excel worksheet is not really that difficult.

Before we start, I would like to get a few basics down first. Field types are the type associated with a certain column, such as text, choice, date/time, or integer. These types define the storage and optionally the rendering of data.

In the object model, all field types eventually inherit from the SPField class, usually through one of its descendant classes such as SPFieldText and SPFieldChoice. In addition to providing storage, a field type also optionally allows you to define how to render a column based on the field type you develop.

Note We will revisit these field types and look at all the default types in Chapter 11. If you are impatient, Table 11-1 lists all the possible values.

The really powerful thing here is that you can create these field types yourself to create your very specific custom type of data, including the visual appearance, storage, validation, and other behavior. In short, the custom development of field types is exceptionally powerful as a customization technique. We will try this in Chapter 11.

To create a custom field type, you *need* to do two things, and you *should* do a few more. The absolute requirements are to have a field type definition, which is CAML, and to have a field type class, which is .NET code.

Now, if there are still some nonprogrammers reading the book at this point, you might feel a bit relieved to know that although a field type class is definitely required, several default classes exist in SharePoint, and you can use them for your custom field type.

Field Types in CAML

To start (and since we are already in CAML land), we should look at the field type definition first. These definitions handle the process of telling SharePoint how our field type should be treated.

The field type definitions are stored in [12]\TEMPLATE\XML and are called fldtypesXXXXX.xml, where XXXXX is anything you like. This works like the webtempXXXXX.xml files—you need to make sure your file name is unique, starts with fldtypes, and ends in .xml. Oh, and remember that when you add or edit .xml files, you need to do an IISReset to have the changes picked up by SharePoint.

The default or out-of-the-box field types are stored in a file called fldtypes.xml. Open that file now, and let's take a look at the text field type. It should be the second FieldType element.

Note The requirements for a custom field type are different from the requirements for a built-in field type. As such, you will see different elements when exploring the out-of-the-box field types than when you create your own field types.

The first thing you may notice is that there are only two types of child elements, the Field and RenderPattern elements. There is one additional child element called PropertySchema that is not present in any of the default field types.

Although the number of child elements may seem simple, the complexity is hidden in the different use of these two elements. It's hardly a perfect XML implementation, but it's what we get.

Field

The Field elements are the most interesting to us at this point, because they define most of the field type properties required to get a field up and running. Each Field element has a Name attribute that defines which property to set, and the value of the Field element defines what value to set to a given property. Here are the Field elements for the Text field type:

```
<Field Name="TypeName">Text</Field>
<Field Name="TypeDisplayName">$Resources:core,fldtype_text;</Field>
<Field Name="InternalType">Text</Field>
<Field Name="FieldTypeClass">Microsoft.SharePoint.SPFieldText</Field>
<Field Name="SQLType">nvarchar</Field>
<Field Name="FieldTypeClass">Microsoft.SharePoint.SPFieldText</Field>
<Field Name="ParentType"></Field>
<Field Name="Sortable">TRUE</Field>
<Field Name="Filterable">TRUE</Field>
```

The TypeName property is required and defines a name used when referencing the field type in code. This is not the displayed name of the field type but rather what you would use in the Type attribute of the Field element when creating columns. See Figure 9-5 for an illustration of how these values map.

FLDTYPES.XML

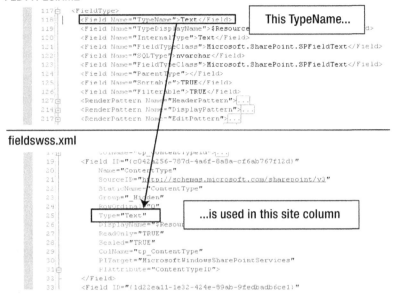

Figure 9-5. TypeName Text *used in site column*

■**Note** At this point, you might realize that both columns and field type definitions use the element `Field`. That's OK; it had me confused for a while too.

Although the `TypeName` is used only in code, the `TypeDisplayName` is what you would see when you add a new column. And where the `TypeName` has strict rules for what is allowed, the `TypeDisplayName` allows more freedom. Just don't confuse them, and you should be OK.

The `InternalType` property is used only for the out-of-the-box types and refers to the internal base type of a column. When developing your own custom field type, you should never set this value.

The `FieldTypeClass`, however, is much more important. When creating your own custom field type, you would add your five-part strong-named field type class here. Yes, it's five-part, because you need to add the class name before your normal four-part strong name. So, if your assembly is `MyCustomField` and your field type class is called `MyCustomFieldClass`, your `FieldTypeClass` might look like this:

```
<Field Name="FieldTypeClass">MyCustomField.MyCustomFieldType, MyCustomField,➡
 Version=1.0.0.0, Culture=neutral, PublicKeyToken=d9d34608fcd1f7a8</Field>
```

Note Yes, in the built-in `Text` field type, the `FieldTypeClass` is added twice. There is no need for that. Microsoft is obviously capable of mistakes too.

The `SQLType` property is used to define what data type should be used when storing information in SQL Server. You do not need to set this in your custom field type, and, in fact, you should not do so.

The `ParentType` is used when you inherit from an existing field type, which is always the case when creating your own field types. The base field types, however, do not inherit, and thus this value is empty for the `Text` field type. It's mandatory in your custom field type; otherwise, it's optional.

The two final values set in the `Text` field type, `Sortable` and `Filterable`, are Boolean values that define whether the columns based on the field type can be sorted and filtered, respectively. You might not want to filter on an image, for instance.

This is only partially true, however. Columns are sortable or filterable only if they are placed in a view that takes sorting and filtering into account. As we saw when creating our own view, if our view does not support sorting, no amount of property setting will make our view sortable.

These `Field` elements are used in the `Text` field type, but there are other `Field` elements we should at least give a cursory glance while we are here. I will just explain these here; they are used in multiple field types throughout.

You may think that the `Field` elements were too easy, and you are right thinking that. There are many more fields we can use to set properties for a field. I'll cover some of these when we start building our own fields in Part 3, so I will postpone any further mention here.

And I have another surprise in store for you. The documentation for the `Field` name values is quite good. That's right—I just commended the documentation. No, I am not completely crazy, and the sky isn't going to fall down tomorrow; the documentation on custom field types and especially the `Field` element states clearly and with good explanations what the different `Name` attribute values mean.

I highly recommend taking the time to look through the documentation.

RenderPattern

The `RenderPattern` elements define how the field should appear. Now, before you go ahead and mention that this could be handled with a custom field type control (which is correct and also a bit premature since we haven't covered that yet), check out the "I'll Handle My Rendering in Code, Thanks" sidebar.

Regardless of where you put your rendering logic for displaying or editing a field, there is still some rendering logic that should be placed in a `RenderPattern`. For example, the header pattern that is responsible for rendering the column header in a list view should be added in CAML.

As with `Field`, there is no real strongly typed schema for `RenderPattern` elements, and the single attribute `Name` controls the usage of the value. The `RenderPattern` has seven possible values for `Name`, all referring to a different rendering pattern:

- `HeaderPattern`: Used to render the column header in list views

- `DisplayPattern`: Used to display the column, either in list views or in display forms

- `EditPattern`: Used to render the column for editing an existing item

- `NewPattern`: Used to render the column when adding a new item

- `PreviewDisplayPattern`: Used to preview the display of the column in visual editors such as SharePoint Designer 2007

- `PreviewEditPattern`: Used to preview the editing of a column in visual editors such as SharePoint Designer 2007

- `PreviewNewPattern`: Used to preview the adding of a column in visual editors such as SharePoint Designer 2007

The `RenderPattern` contains CAML based on the view schema. Now, if you had not fought the dragon in the cave, you might go "Oh no" just about now, but since we are now enlightened developers, running through the rendering patterns used in the `Text` field type should be a walk in the park. If you felt like skipping the cave, well, it should still be a walk in the park, but the park will be littered with broken glass and you will be barefooted.

Note See how that dragon keeps coming back? See how important it was to fight our way through to the end of the cave? You can thank me by email to `furuknap@gmail.com`.

I'LL HANDLE MY RENDERING IN CODE, THANKS

I know we are developers. We like to do things in code or in a user control. And that is fine, but consider this. If you create a field type for storing a telephone number, how would you display that number if it were a US number? How about a German or even a Norwegian phone number? If you were to create all rendering logic inside a custom control class, you would have to recompile and redeploy that class each time you added a new country to your supported list. If, instead of storing your rendering logic inside a compiled assembly, you stored the `RenderPattern` in an XML field definition, you can add extra field definitions if you need to make post-compile changes to how a field is rendered.

First, let's take a look at the DisplayPattern, because it is so incredibly simple:

```
<RenderPattern Name="DisplayPattern">
  <Column HTMLEncode="TRUE" AutoHyperLink="TRUE" AutoNewLine="TRUE"/>
</RenderPattern>
```

This just adds the column value to the output and does some automatic linking magic if the text resembles something that you would normally click, such as a URL or an email address. Also, if present, newlines will be replaced with <br>, and multiple space characters will be replaced with . The latter is facilitated by setting AutoNewLine to TRUE, by the way. We'll also want any HTML code to be translated into HTML entities, meaning, for example, that < is replaced with < to avoid our browser going completely bonkers. This is handled by setting HTMLEncode to TRUE.

OK, that was too easy. No broken glass for the cave-skippers yet. Time to break out the heavy artillery. Open the HeaderPattern.

At first, the HeaderPattern may seem incredibly complex, but once you apply a bit of selective reading and closing of tags, you can see that it is actually fairly simple. The header checks to see whether the column is sortable and filterable and outputs various content depending on these conditions.

One small and curious thing you may learn from reading the header code for the Text field is that it does a switch if a variable called Filter is set to 1:

```
<Switch>
  <Expr>
    <GetVar Name='Filter'/>
  </Expr>
  <Case Value='1'>
[…]
```

The variable in question here is set from the query string, but there are no links to the view with Filter=1 as the parameter. If we add that manually, however, we do get something new, except it is really old—filtering in SharePoint 2003 style. See Figure 9-6.

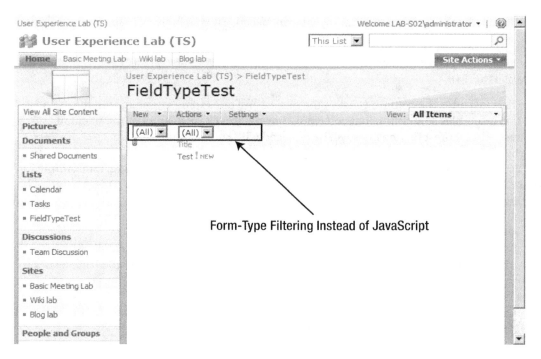

Figure 9-6. *Ever seen this before? Old-style filtering from back in the day*

You may at this point be a bit confused. Back when we fought dragons, you learned that the header was actually produced using an element called ViewHeader. Why would we have an extra pattern for the fields? You may recall that when we added the column to the ViewHeader, I said to remember *Slartibartfast*. Now is the time.

When we add the Field to the ViewHeader, we got a whole lot of additional code instead of just the title of the column. When we looked at sorting, we circumvented this by grabbing a Property rather than using the Field, and I promised we would look into what actually went on.

When you add a column to a ViewHeader using the Field element, what is actually added is whatever is defined in the HeaderPattern of the field type. If you go through the code generated when adding the Field element to a ViewHeader and compare that to the HeaderPattern of the field type, you will see exactly how this code is generated.

The remaining DisplayPattern elements follow the same pattern, pun intended, as the HeaderPattern and DisplayPattern, so I will leave it to you to read the rest of the code as an exercise.

We Made It!

Finally, we are here! We have dug through the SharePoint architecture from top to bottom, learning tons of material along the way. Well, at least I did—your mileage may vary.

Now that you have seen how all the various bits and pieces of SharePoint tick, you should take a break and rest a bit before moving on. As such, I have written a short chapter on the mentality of a SharePoint developer that I hope you will enjoy.

We are far from done, however. Now that we have journeyed through SharePoint land and explored, it is now time to begin touching. In the next part of this book, we will begin building and thus get more experience by trying what we have learned in this part.

You have done well! You have my sincerest congratulations for coming a long way.

CHAPTER 10

Intermission: The Mentality of a SharePoint Developer

Use Your Noodle the Right Way and Be a Better Developer

So far, we have focused on learning new technical skills. Our journey has taken us from site exploration boot camp through forests of lists, demons in dark caves, glaciers of content types, and fields of gold, all while keeping a goal in mind—that of understanding how SharePoint architecture works from a user experience perspective.

During the next part of this book, we will use a series of exercises to apply what we have learned to create a completely new SharePoint site, from the bottom pits of fields and up toward the surface of seeing our site in all its glory. There is plenty in store on that journey as well. Our new goal will be to create a publishing site for a newspaper with a completely new interface and experience for both the end users and the authors.

Before we start on that journey, however, I would like to take a short break here to share with you some of my thoughts on the mind-set of a SharePoint developer. There is little technical skill building here; it's just a short break to give our minds a little rest before we head on home. No screen shots, no code listings, no tables of reference—just you and me sitting down with a cup of coffee and talking about a developer's life.

Well, actually, I'm doing the talking, at least for the next few pages.

These ideas are just my personal opinions, and your opinions will vary. If you do not agree, good! Let me know so I can learn from you. Shoot off an email, hook up with me the next time we meet, or just write a blog post and curse my ancestors.

SharePoint Is a Platform, Not a Product

You may be starting to realize this now, but SharePoint is a lot more than team sites, meeting sites, publishing portals, and blogs. The site definitions that ship with SharePoint show off some of these features, but we have a wide range of other options.

In fact, many of the coolest features of SharePoint, such as content types and event handlers, are hardly used at all in the default setup. As such, many developers have no idea about the potential that SharePoint has and stick only to using the default and simple features that ship out of the box.

Sadly, this also means that very few people take the time to learn and practice more advanced development options, which in turn leads the community as a whole to shift toward simpler and simpler customization options. I have read from very prominent SharePoint community leaders that the best thing to do to deliver a great SharePoint experience is to just trust what Microsoft has created and adapt your customer to SharePoint and what is offered by default. "Fix some logos and some style sheets perhaps, but otherwise just use the default lists, libraries, pages, and workflows."

If I were to put my disagreement with statements like that on a scale of 1 to 10, I believe the rest of this book would support the number on that scale. Suffice to say it would be far closer to infinity than 1.

I fear that the art of hard-core SharePoint development may become a rare commodity.

I am not saying you should create something from scratch just because you can. SharePoint ships with a lot of ready-to-use features that will greatly enhance any collaboration or publishing solution. There is no reason to create a document library from scratch if all you want to do is change a single library form. If the default QuickLaunch menu and top navigation bar fulfills 90 percent of your navigation requirements, you should consider carefully whether the last 10 percent is worth re-creating the remaining 90 percent. Perhaps that time is better spent on another part of the project.

Some good advice often heard is to know the default features (features as in the literal sense and not the SharePoint technical sense) and then base your customization on those default features.

The reason why I am stressing the need to be able to build features from scratch is that you should know very well how these features work. You never know what your next project will require from a customization perspective. If you have deep knowledge of a certain feature, you will likely see how you can utilize default features better and save a ton of time.

In short, know how to modify absolutely everything you can. And then don't.

To Boldly Go...

Learning is exploring. Don't be afraid to try something that doesn't work; there is no failure. Either you learn or you succeed.

When you are working with a virtual environment, you have a Save option that allows you to revert to a previous state at the click of a button. By taking regular snapshots of your virtual machine, especially before trying something risky, you lose very little time or effort if everything goes kaboom. Now, if only real life could be virtualized...I would go skydiving this instant.

Be adventurous; there is so much cool stuff to learn about SharePoint. Exploration is the key. Try stuff out, and eventually you will know how it works. It may take time and effort, but the kick you get from learning something completely new is well worth what you put into the adventure.

Don't be afraid of reflecting code; you can learn massive amounts of information by looking at `Microsoft.SharePoint.dll`. I often wander for hours inside DLLs just to find out more about a program or system. Put .NET Reflector on speed dial, and your understanding and confidence will rise with each launch.

Do all this from a learning perspective. When you hit the real world where you start putting all your skills into production systems, your development experience will change. You'll face source control, rigorous testing, code revisions, and a lot of other production development topics. However, you will know your SharePoint like you know the back of your hand.

This Time It's Personal

Another piece of advice is to look at what others have done before you, but rather than copying what they have done, learn from them. Try to put yourself into the mind of the girl or guy who wrote a piece of code. What was that person thinking? What particular style is used? Can you see similarities in other pieces of code?

Remember, every piece of code you see—every feature, every page, every workflow—was at some point designed and developed by someone, perhaps just like you. If you manage to think of code in that fashion, development becomes a much more personal art. No longer will you think that "Microsoft did this" or "Oracle wrote that"; rather, you will begin to see the person sitting in some office somewhere on the globe with a task, just like you, of creating just that piece of code.

When you write code, consider your own style as well. You are an artist. You create code; you don't just produce solutions. Whether you are aware of this, you have a very particular style of writing code. Perhaps you picked up a pattern in an old book back in the ages, perhaps you are inspired by a particular blogger and mimic their style, or perhaps you just add up bits and pieces of code you find online.

Your code is not dead after you deploy it and wrap up the project. The code will remain for a very long time, and it carries your signature. Someone may at some point open your solution or reflect your assembly to see how you were thinking and try to understand what made you make a certain decision.

Think of the posterity of your code when writing, and consider the welfare of those who come after you.

Use the Right Tools

I know I have said I prefer that you use a nail, two wires, and a battery to magnetize your own hard disk plates. That is a joke. Feel free to laugh. If you don't, you seriously need to reconsider your approach to tools.

You can do quite a lot of fancy SharePoint development in Notepad, and doing so in some cases is the best thing. For the sake of productivity, however, consider learning about the different tools that can speed up your development time.

Learn how to create a feature (in the technical SharePoint sense, not the literal) by hand. Do so for your first five features just to add variety to your learning experience. After you have become a bit familiar with the authoring experience, switch to tools. Use WSPBuilder, VSeWSS, or STSDEV; find out what you like, save tons of time, and still have the experience required to debug a faulty elements file.

Blow open a WSP solution file in WinZip, pull the bowels out, and put it back together. Create a .wsp file yourself, including all the solution manifests, features, and files you need. Then switch to a tool that does the job for you.

Tip WSP files are just `.cab` files with a funny name. Rename the `.wsp` file to `.cab`, and you can open it with any decompression tool.

The problem is that starting out with tools will subtract from your learning. If all you want is to produce a solution, fine, but you will never learn what you are doing beyond "click here to create something."

I will not recommend any particular tool, because finding out which tool works best for you is also a learning experience. My preferences are stated throughout this book, but you should not take these as any kind of best practices or even any endorsement of one tool over another.

Take solution building in Visual Studio. If you are using Visual Studio to develop Share-Point solutions, you have at least four good alternatives; using no helper tools, you have the Microsoft Visual Studio Extensions for WSS, STSDEV, and WSPBuilder. I have used all these tools and landed on my preference of WSPBuilder only after spending weeks finding out what fits my development style.

Your style will be different. Each tool has strengths and weaknesses, and you must find out what you like. There is no best or worst, only preference.

The Most Important Tool of All

OK, I'll reveal the biggest secret to SharePoint development I know. You may want to sit down, grab a cup of your favorite brew, relax, and try to prepare yourself.

The most important tool to SharePoint development is...

SharePoint.

That's right. SharePoint is a tool. Nothing more. Granted, it is a rather advanced tool, much more advanced than, say, a hammer, but it is still just a tool.

It doesn't matter how good you are with a hammer. You may be able to hit nails in your sleep with both hands tied behind your back and hanging upside down from your toes. All you are doing is striking nails into wood. That is useful, of course, but it will never get you a house.

If you want to build a house, you need to learn a ton of other skills. You need to learn design, architecture, and how to use other tools such as saws, screwdrivers, and blowtorches. As you probably realize by now, I have no idea how to build a house, but I know that you need far more than a hammer and a skilled nail barbarian.

So, try to see beyond SharePoint and see how SharePoint fits into the bigger picture. Teach your team, your boss, your customer, or whoever pays your salary how they can utilize your wonderful hammer-wielding talent. Show them how user experience, workflows, business intelligence, and all the other aspects of SharePoint development can bring peace and har-mony to the world.

Don't be good at hammering. Be good at building houses, including being proficient with a hammer. Do that, and you have yourself a first-class ticket to job security nirvana for the rest of your natural life.

Enough Already!

OK, that's it! No more intermesso.

PART 3

■■■

Building an Empire

It is time for a new era of your SharePoint adventure. Having traversed the deepest depths of SharePoint knowledge in the previous part, it is now time to put some of that knowledge to practical use.

In this part of the book, we will create a new site, from bottom to top, using the skills and techniques learned in Part 2. There will be plenty of exercises to hone your new skills, and in the end you will have a new site made with nothing but your own sweat, blood, and perhaps some tears.

The site we will be creating is a publishing site, a newspaper to be precise. That does not matter much, however, since the goal will be to practice creating a great SharePoint user experience. Each chapter will build on the previous chapters, so you will likely get more out of the process if you follow along in all the chapters.

With that said, here is a very important warning.

Caution   What you are about to see is extremely dangerous. Never try this at home. The stunts performed here are done by professional stunt developers and are for illustrative purposes only. Do not launch a newspaper web site based on the code provided here.

Seriously, I am not joking. The code in this chapter is illustrating different aspects of SharePoint development. You will likely break every best practice for software development ever created. Your server will implode and take the entire building with it if you ever put this in a production environment. Your spouse will be very angry and make you sleep on the couch for a week. The sun will not rise tomorrow. Christmas will be canceled next year. Bob will not be your uncle or even acknowledge being in your family. In fact, Bob will likely disown you.

Be very clear on this: do not use this code in production.

So, grab a shovel, a hammer, and whatever nails you can find, because it is time to build an empire!

■ ■ ■

CHAPTER 11

Starting Field

Getting Fields and Field Types to Behave

Fields are the smallest bits of information and so easy to overlook. Fields are as important to the user experience as anything, so you need to make sure you know how to build that experience.

Unlike Einstein, who sought to split the smallest known parts in the universe, you want to learn how to create these atomic storage units. These units will then be used when we build our empire in later chapters.

In this chapter, you will learn about custom field type development. You may have heard people talking about how difficult the process of custom field type development is. However, after you have completed the exercises in this chapter, you will likely be very surprised at how easy this can actually be.

In the second part of the chapter, we will create site columns to deploy to our new site. We will create several column types, including one approach for creating lookup columns that uses a feature receiver.

And I'll give you some parenting advice….

Mission Statement

Our goal for this chapter is to create a custom field type that will be used as the title of articles in our newspaper web site. We will create a field type that resembles the normal "single line of text" type but then add custom displaying and input of the data to see how to do this in a full-scale implementation.

Next we will create several site columns to be included in the articles. We will explore different field types for our columns and find a solution to the problem of nonworking lookup columns.

A Note on Custom Field Types

Before we dive into the deep end, I want to take a few paragraphs to talk a bit about custom field types. It seems that, right after custom views in CAML, custom field type development is among the tasks SharePoint developers fear most. A lot of web sites demonstrate how to develop custom field types, but most are either directly based on or derivatives of the custom field walkthrough example from MSDN (`http://www.understandingsharepoint.com/url/10032`). Even seasoned SharePoint veterans seem to be elusive about just how custom field types work and especially about how to develop one.

During this chapter you may be surprised how incredibly easy custom field type development can be, if done right. Many of the exercises here will show you, using illustrative examples, of course, how you can change a custom field type in just one or two steps while utilizing the parent field type that has already done most of the hard work for you.

Don't get me wrong, custom field type development is a complex topic, and online documentation and examples are scarce. At the time of this writing, a full eight hits are returned when googling *SharePoint BaseTextField*, even when this is one of the simplest (and should be most inherited) classes for explaining how custom field types can be developed.

So, even after reading this chapter and understanding how all the pieces of custom field type development work, don't just run off to your team and start evangelizing custom field type development. Yes, custom field type development is a really cool method of customizing how users interact with data. Yes, custom field type development allows you to give your designers a plain-vanilla ASP.NET control to add whatever goodies designers like to add and have it still work.

However, also consider how people will maintain your solution. Being the only person on your team who understands a particular component may make you indispensable, but it also makes your solution quite more complex and can increase the cost of maintenance. Consider whether there are alternatives among the methods you have learned in this book before you go to the somewhat drastic step of creating a custom field type.

Your First Field Type

For the exercises in this chapter, I'm going to assume that you have considered the issues in the previous section, because it would be a very short chapter if we decided that a standard Team Site would be OK. So, it is time to bring out the proverbial shovel and get to work.

■**Note** For this exercise, I will assume that you are using WSPBuilder extensions for Visual Studio. The code should still be usable with other development tools, but you will have to set up the deployment on your own.

Exercise 11-1. Setting Up Your Solution

In this exercise, you are going to set up the solution with which you will be working for the rest of the book. You will use WSPBuilder as the basis because WSPBuilder speeds up development and testing by offering a lot of nice tools and shortcuts. If you need a recap of how WSPBuilder works, check out Chapter 1.

1. Create a new Visual Studio project. Your project type should be a WSPBuilder project. Name the project EmpireTimes or use a name you like. Your Solution Explorer should look something like Figure 11-1.

Figure 11-1. *Initial setup of Visual Studio*

At this point, WSPBuilder has done a lot of work for you. First, notice the 12 folder. WSPBuilder will deploy anything you put inside this folder. You remember that [12] refers to the install path of SharePoint, usually C:\Program Files\Common Files\Microsoft Shared\web server extensions\12, right?

Second, notice that you have one .snk file, a signing key. WSPBuilder has set up the project to be signed and generated that key for you so that when you build you get a strong-named assembly.

There are a few things WSPBuilder will not do for you when you create a new project. One thing is to add a reference to the Microsoft.SharePoint.dll, and another is to output the four-part strong name for you. You need both, so step 2 is a little trick I'll mention a few times.

2. Add a new item to your project of type Feature with Receiver. Name the feature TimesSiteColumns, and make the scope Site.

You may at this point raise your hand to say, "I thought we were doing custom field types, not columns." This is a good point, but as I said, this is a little trick, so for now, don't think too much about this feature. We will return to this later in this chapter.

When you add a Feature with Receiver feature to the project, WSPBuilder will add the correct reference to Microsoft.SharePoint.dll for you. More importantly, the newly created feature.xml file will hold the strong name that you will need for your custom field type in the next exercise.

For now, you should be ready to start your custom field type development.

What we just did in the previous exercise is to set up the groundwork for a new solution. We will use this solution to create a complete site including all of the elements we learned in Part 2 of the book.

■**Tip** Having WSPBuilder sign your assembly and create the strong name is a real time-saver. However, should you need to find the strong name from another assembly, just go to the JustAsk web site (http://www.understandingsharepoint.com/justask) and search for *How do I find the strong name of an assembly.*

Next you'll begin the custom field type development.

Exercise 11-2. Defining the Field Type

In this exercise, you will create the field type definition file for your custom field type. This file, as you learned in Chapter 9, is responsible for telling SharePoint about your custom field type.

1. In your Solution Explorer, add a new folder under the 12\TEMPLATE folder called XML.

2. Add a new XML file in the XML folder. Naming is important, so call it fldtypes_TimesFieldType.xml.

The naming of field type definition files must follow a certain pattern. As with webtemp files, you should use fldtypes_XXXXXXX.xml, where XXXXXXX is an arbitrary string. This is how SharePoint will recognize the file as a field type definition.

Also, remember that adding files in the 12 folder in your solution will deploy these files to the [12] folder when you deploy your solution.

3. To the fldtypes_TimesFieldType.xml file, add the following code:

```
<?xml version="1.0" encoding="utf-8" ?>
<FieldTypes>
  <FieldType>
    <Field Name="TypeName">TimesType</Field>
    <Field Name="ParentType">Text</Field>
    <Field Name="TypeDisplayName">Times Type</Field>
    <Field Name="TypeShortDescription">Times custom type</Field>
    <Field Name="UserCreatable">TRUE</Field>
    <Field Name="Sortable">TRUE</Field>
    <Field Name="AllowBaseTypeRendering">TRUE</Field>
    <Field Name="Filterable">TRUE</Field>
    <Field Name="FieldTypeClass">[FIVE-PART STRONG NAME]</Field>
  </FieldType>
</FieldTypes>
```

Refer to Chapter 9 for a detailed explanation of the different Field elements here. However, I'll take you through creating the five-part strong name for your class, which you need to substitute for the token in the previous code. This is where that Feature with Receiver comes in handy.

4. Substitute the [FIVE-PART STRONG NAME] token with the text EmpireTimes.TimesFieldType , including the comma and the final space.

This is the beginning of the five-part strong name. Remember that a five-part strong name includes the namespace and the class. You haven't created that class yet but will in the next exercise.

5. Open the `TimesSiteColumns` folder and then the `feature.xml` file.

Notice that inside the `ReceiverAssembly` attribute is the four-part strong name of your assembly.

6. Copy the value of the `ReceiverAssembly` element, and paste that value after the `EmpireTimes.TimesFieldType` text in the `FieldTypeClass` value of the `fldtypes_TimesFieldType.xml` file.

Your field type definition is now complete.

The field type definition tells SharePoint the metadata about your custom field type. The remaining parts of the custom field type are .NET classes and .NET user controls and in this example comprise the two classes and one user control you need to create.

I'll take a moment to explain how these classes work and their purpose.

Field Type Classes

For the `Times` field type, we will utilize two classes to build a field type where we can customize the user experience. These two classes are the field type class and the field control class.

The field type class is the only required class in a custom field type. The field type class is the heart and soul of the field type and connects the other optional classes together. The field type control class is responsible for the visual representation of the field type.

You'll also want to add two user controls to your field type. One user control, containing a rendering template, will be part of the visual rendering of the input form, and one user control will be used to configure your field type when you add new columns.

So, these are the elements of the field type:

- Field type definition (`fldtypes_TimesFieldType.xml`)

- Field type core class (will be created as `TimesFieldType.cs`)

- Field type control class (will be created as `TimesFieldControl.cs`)

- Field type rendering template user control (will be created as `TimesTextField.ascx`)

Another class that you may use, but that is less important to our example, is the field type value class, responsible for storing your data if you need a custom storage format. Using a field type value class means you get to decide how your data gets stored in the SharePoint database. If you need to store complex data, this would be the way to do so. In theory, you could easily store any kind of data within a single field type value.

However, because this is a user experience book, I will limit the scope to not include custom field type values. Instead, you will rely on the default value type of the text field type, which basically stores just a string of text.

It is easy to get confused with the different classes. After all, the field type class is actually in control, even though you do have a field type control class, so you need to keep your head really cool when you begin to include the rendering of values in the input states, in the display forms, and in the list views.

To avoid confusion, I will build the required classes with a bare minimum of required code and make very sure you have the basics down before adding some flair. As such, when you have completed creating your custom field type, it will actually just be a plain copy of the "single line of text" type. We will change that afterward, though.

Custom Field Type Class

The only class that is mandatory for a custom field type is the field type class. This is the class you reference in the field type definition. In Exercise 11-2 you named this class TimesFieldType. Let's make that class now.

Exercise 11-3. Creating a Custom Field Type Class

In this exercise, you will create the TimesFieldType class and add the minimum required code to get your class to work.

1. In your Solution Explorer, add a new class file to the EmpireTimes project. You can add this to the root of the folder or wherever you like. Name the file TimesFieldType.cs.

2. Add a using Microsoft.SharePoint; statement, make your class public, and then make your class inherit from the SPFieldText class. Your class should look like this:

```
using System;
using System.Collections.Generic;
using System.Text;
using Microsoft.SharePoint;

namespace EmpireTimes
{
    public class TimesFieldType : SPFieldText
    {
    }
}
```

3. Next, add the following two constructors to your class:

```
public TimesFieldType(SPFieldCollection fields, string fieldName)
    : base(fields, fieldName)
{
}

public TimesFieldType(SPFieldCollection fields,
    string typeName, string displayName)
    : base(fields, typeName, displayName)
{
}
```

That's it. Nothing more. You're done. You've created your first custom field type.

OK, OK, hold on just one minute. People threaten to leave their jobs from fear of having to learn that? Surely you must be joking, Mr. Norwegian. All those hours of fighting? The therapy our team leader went through to prepare for custom field type development? And you're saying that was it?

Yup, that's what I'm saying. You're done. You've made your own custom field type. Yes, there is plenty more you can do, but those three steps are all the steps you have to do (and the field type definition you created earlier, of course).

Here's the deal: you inherit all the functionality of the parent field type text. As with all .NET classes, if you just inherit from the parent and don't add any functionality yourself, you get a copy, more or less, of the parent.

If you still don't believe me, build your solution and deploy it. The easiest way to do this is to select the Tools ➤ WSPBuilder ➤ Build WSP menu in Visual Studio and then select WSP-Builder ➤ Deploy. Wait for solution deployment to complete, and go to your site. Create a new custom list, and add a new column to that list. The first thing you should see is what is in Figure 11-2.

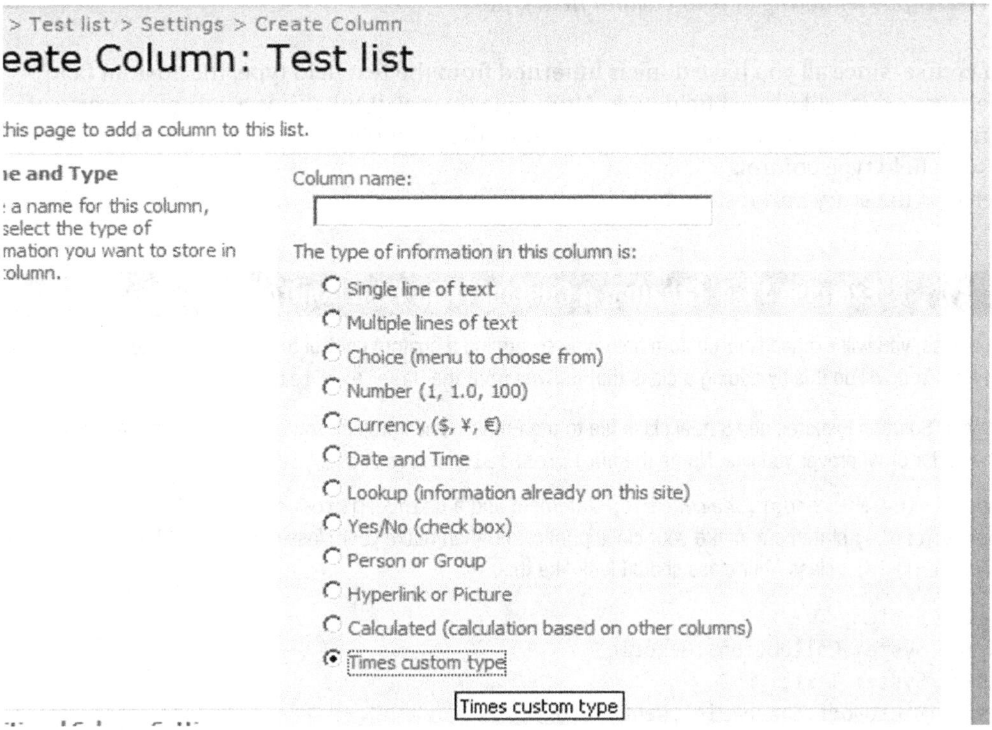

Figure 11-2. *Your first custom field type available*

However, getting a new entry in the list of available column types requires only a field type definition. If you want to test that your custom field type actually works, go ahead and create that new column based on your type, and then go to the list.

Add a new item, and lo and behold, look at Figure 11-3 to see the result, if you did everything correctly.

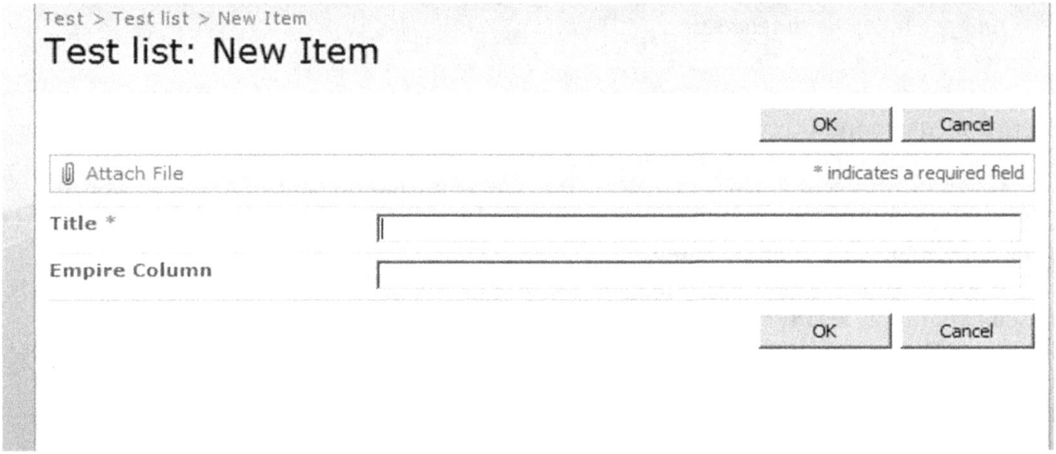

Figure 11-3. *Input rendering of your custom field type*

Of course, since all you have done is inherited from the text field type, the custom field type behaves exactly like a text field type. Although you may think this is a complete waste of time and energy, rest assured that you will advance the example in the next exercise when you create your field type control.

Perhaps the scary part resides here.

Exercise 11-4. Creating a Custom Field Type Control Class

In this exercise, you will expand your custom field type by adding a custom control to handle the rendering of the field type. You will do this by adding a class that derives from the `BaseTextField` parent class.

1. In your Solution Explorer, add a new class file to the EmpireTimes project. You can add this to the root of the folder or wherever you like. Name the file `TimesFieldControl.cs`.

2. Add a `using Microsoft.SharePoint;` statement and a `using Microsoft.SharePoint.WebControls;` statement, make your class public, and then make your class inherit from the `BaseTextField` class. Your class should look like this:

```
using System;
using System.Collections.Generic;
using System.Text;
using Microsoft.SharePoint.WebControls;

namespace EmpireTimes
{
    public class TimesFieldControl : BaseTextField
    {
    }
}
```

3. This is the tricky part: return to the `TimesFieldType.cs` file, and override the `FieldRenderingControl` property as such:

```
public override Microsoft.SharePoint.WebControls.BaseFieldControl
    FieldRenderingControl
{
    get
    {
        TimesFieldControl c = new TimesFieldControl();
        c.FieldName = this.InternalName;
        return c;
    }
}
```

What you are doing by overriding the `FieldRenderingControl` property is overriding which control will be used to render the field rather than using whatever the parent class wants you to use. You are returning a new instance of the `TimesFieldControl` class you just created and making sure your control gets the name of your field type, which would be `EmpireType`, which you defined in the `fldtypes_TimesFieldType.xml` definition earlier.

Oh, and by the way, the part about this being tricky? Irony.

Again, you're done. And again, yes, I am being serious.

OK, so what did you just do? First you created a new field control class that you can use to define custom rendering of the field type. You haven't really done any custom rendering yet, but you have the class in place.

Next you connected that field control to the field type class by overriding the `FieldRenderingControl` property, effectively saying to the parent class that, yes, you appreciate the years of upbringing, love, and support, but now you want to stand on your own feet. You just took the first step to break the tight bonds to our parents, so to speak. Compare this to getting your own place to stay when you turn 18 but not moving in just yet.

This way of building a custom field type is really a perfect transition into adulthood for the field type. You maintain close ties with the parent class and only slowly do what you need and want to get your own independence. And, being the perfect parent, the parent class happily continues to supply you with whatever functionality you choose not to implement yourself, allowing you to move out at just the pace you want.

And now I'm giving out parenting advice. It's time to get back to the bits and bytes, but keep the parent-child relationship in mind; it makes development a lot more manageable.

For the basic outline of a custom field type, this really is all you need to do, but it is time to take your first step into custom rendering and explore how you can make the display of the column a bit more interesting. First, take a look at Figure 11-4, just to make sure you see what the default value looks like. As you can see, it is exactly like a regular text field. `

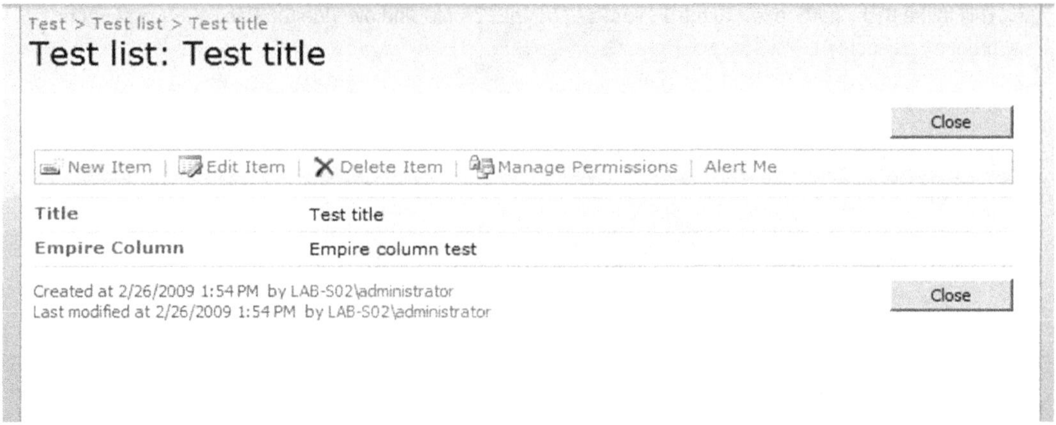

Figure 11-4. *Baseline for rendering. You don't want this.*

Exercise 11-5. Modifying the Display of a Custom Field Type

In this exercise, you'll modify the rendering of your custom field type. You will first focus on one method, rendering in code, for changing the display of data before you modify the input experience using a custom user control in the next exercise.

1. Open the `TimesFieldControl.cs` file. Inside the class, override the `RenderFieldForDisplay` method as such:

```
protected override void
    RenderFieldForDisplay(System.Web.UI.HtmlTextWriter output)
{
    output.Write("<span style=\"font-size:18pt;background-color:red;\">");
    base.RenderFieldForDisplay(output);
    output.Write("</span>");
}
```

2. Find a Post-it note, and write the following message: "Never, ever hire Bjørn Furuknap as a designer."

3. Glue the Post-it note to your monitor. In fact, engrave your monitor with the message.

4. Build your solution and deploy. Once deployed, run `IISRESET` to make sure your assembly is reloaded.

5. Observe the changes to your display form. Or check mine, in Figure 11-5.

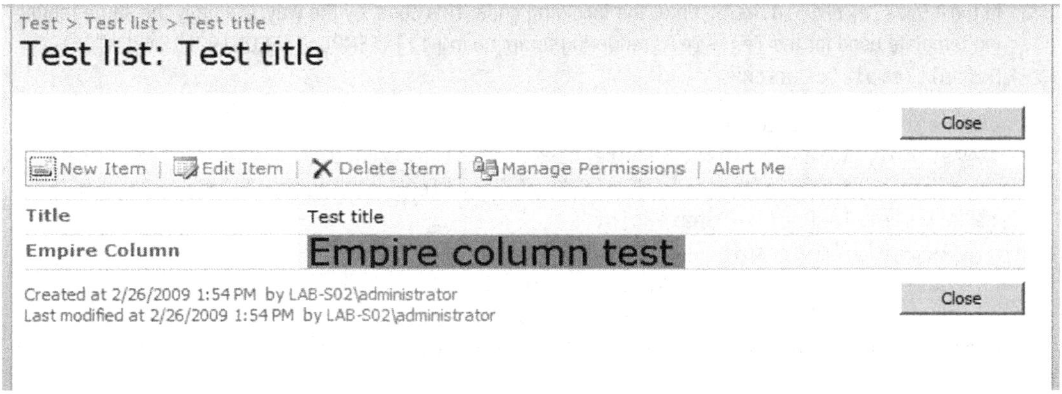

Figure 11-5. *If this were a full-color book, you would see a red background.*

Remember that about never hiring me as a designer.

With that massive undertaking out of the way, we should stop for a moment and think about what we have done.

Overriding the RenderFieldForDisplay is the first available method for changing the rendering of a field. Because this is .NET code only, you have full control over exactly what you do, which is a level of control that is sometimes necessary if you need to do complex operations.

The sample you just made can hardly be considered a complex operation; in fact, all you do is surround the parent's RenderFieldForDisplay method with a simple span tag to modify the display style. As I said, it's for illustrative purposes; I'm not a designer.

However, sometimes we cannot afford ourselves complete control over rendering in code. For example, if you are smart enough to hire a good designer, he or she might not be allowed or even capable of writing .NET code. This is where creating an ASP.NET user control and using that as the rendering mechanism makes sense.

Let's take a look, shall we?

Exercise 11-6. Using an ASP.NET User Control for Rendering

In this exercise, you will modify the input experience of your custom field type. This is where users enter or edit the data of our field. You will accomplish this by creating a rendering template and connecting that rendering template to your control class.

1. In your Solution Explorer, add a new folder to the TEMPLATE folder, called CONTROLTEMPLATES.

2. In the CONTROLTEMPLATES folder, add a new text file, and name it TimesTextField.ascx.

Creating a text file but naming the file TimesTextField.ascx will cause Visual Studio to treat the file as a web control, even if you do not have a web project.

3. In the `TimesTextField.ascx`, enter the following code. This code, by the way, is simply the same rendering template used for the `TextField` rendering template in `[12]\TEMPLATE\CONTROLTEMPLATES\DefaultTemplates.ascx`:

```
<%@ Control Language="C#"%>
<%@Assembly Name="Microsoft.SharePoint, Version=12.0.0.0,
         Culture=neutral, PublicKeyToken=71e9bce111e9429c" %>
<%@Register TagPrefix="SharePoint"
    Assembly="Microsoft.SharePoint, Version=12.0.0.0,
    Culture=neutral, PublicKeyToken=71e9bce111e9429c"
    namespace="Microsoft.SharePoint.WebControls"%>
<SharePoint:RenderingTemplate ID="TimesTextField" runat="server">
    <Template>
        <asp:TextBox ID="TextField" MaxLength="255" runat="server"/><br>
    </Template>
</SharePoint:RenderingTemplate>
```

Notice that the code is plain-vanilla ASP.NET with references to the SharePoint assembly.

4. Hand that file over to your designers, and let them go bananas. However, tell them to keep the `asp:TextBox` with the `ID="TextField"` intact. I will explain why in a moment.

5. In your `TimesFieldControl.cs` file, override the `DefaultTemplateName` property as such:

```
protected override string DefaultTemplateName
{
    get
    {
        return "TimesTextField";
    }
}
```

I bet you are itching to do the Build and Deploy dance. Before you do, however, you need to be aware of one thing. By default, WSPBuilder will upgrade a solution when you hit Deploy rather than redeploying the solution. However, in an upgrade, only existing files are replaced, and no new files are added. You added an `.ascx` file in this exercise, which would not have been deployed had you simply upgraded the solution.

So, to do the Build and Deploy thing, you must first uninstall your solution. Luckily, uninstalling a solution is just as easy as deploying; select WSPBuilder ➤ Uninstall first.

Now you can deploy again, and your results, depending on how wild your designers got, may resemble Figure 11-6.

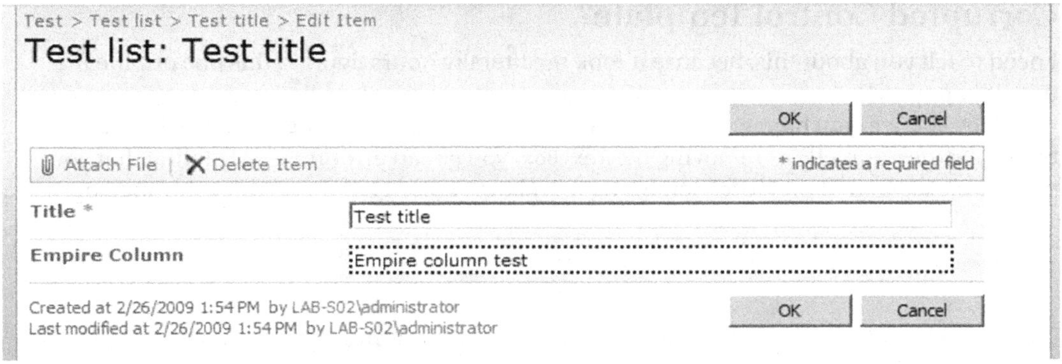

Test > Test list > Test title > Edit Item
Test list: Test title

| OK | Cancel |

📎 Attach File | ✖ Delete Item   * indicates a required field

Title *   Test title

Empire Column   Empire column test

Created at 2/26/2009 1:54 PM by LAB-S02\administrator | OK | Cancel |
Last modified at 2/26/2009 1:54 PM by LAB-S02\administrator

Figure 11-6. *Look! I made a nice border!*

Now, before you start drooling over all the possibilities, let's take a look at what just happened.

First, you created a new user control containing a SharePoint:RenderingTemplate tag, having a specific ID property. As you learned in Chapter 5 when we explored the default user interface, rendering templates is a method by which SharePoint utilized standard ASP.NET controls to render content.

Second, you overrode the DefaultRenderingTemplate of the TimesFieldControl class. As was the case with RenderFieldForDisplay, you just take over that function from the parent class and handle it yourself, returning your own rendering template name for use in your field.

Now, there is some magic going on here. Adding such a rendering template usually entails spending a lot of time in the CreateChildControls method to hook up the value of the column to the text box and reading it back out again when the user submits the form. In fact, most examples on the Wide World Web and in books usually start by making all kinds of advanced code to hook up the value with the controls in the .ascx file. So why don't we?

The secret to the trick is that you maintained the TextBox with ID="TextField". You see, the parent CreateChildControls method looks for a TextBox with that ID, and if it finds it, it will handle all the plumbing for you. Since you don't override the CreateChildControls method, the parent method looks through the rendering template for the same TextBox, and—poof!—out with a lot of plumbing code, all because you inherited from a very nice parent.

This may or may not be sufficient for your needs. You may have a project that requires you to do more complex operations, but what I'm trying to say here is that if you listen to your parents and learn how they do their thing, you might save yourself a lot of hassle.

And now I'm giving advice to teens.

Some Advice on Custom Field Types

Before we move on to the next topic of this chapter, columns, I would like to share with you some general tips and some small cool ideas you may want to explore.

Corrupted Control Template?

I need to tell you about this, because it took me literally hours figuring this one out the first time it happened.

If, by chance, you happen to make a mistake with your rendering template, for example by adding the wrong ID or removing the TextBox, you get an error message stating that you need to check your "TextField" rendering template. Figure 11-7 shows this error message.

Server Error in '/' Application.

Corrupted control template. Please check RenderingTemplate of "TextField" in the control template ascx file.

Description: An unhandled exception occurred during the execution of the current web request. Please review the stack trace for more information about the error and where it originated in the code.

Exception Details: System.ArgumentException: Corrupted control template. Please check RenderingTemplate of "TextField" in the control template ascx file.

Source Error:

Figure 11-7. *Error in error message*

This, however, is not entirely accurate, since you may have created your own rendering template. The reason why "TextField" is used, however, is that you are inheriting the CreateChildControls from the parent, and the parent has hard-coded the name of its rendering template into the error message.

Custom DisplayPattern in List Views

Remember that we discussed render patterns in Chapter 9? You may or may not want to edit these patterns for your field type. If you do, you can opt to just override the default DisplayPattern by adding a RenderPattern element to your field type definition:

```
<Field Name="TypeName">TimesType</Field>
<RenderPattern Name="DisplayPattern">
  <HTML><![CDATA[<span style="font-size:large;color:red;">]]></HTML>
  <Column/>
  <HTML><![CDATA[</span>]]></HTML>
</RenderPattern>
</FieldType>
```

However, you will quickly find that you get no IntelliSense. I know that being hard-core is sometimes a cool thing, but writing CAML view schema without IntelliSense is just madness.

To help out, however, open one of your list templates, and write your code inside a view where the IntelliSense will work and give you plenty of support.

Custom Field Properties

Creating custom field types is not really hard once you know the basics like you do now. However, what if you wanted to have a different background color for your display rendering? You would need to create a new field type, even if your change is a small one.

One option to solve this is to use custom field properties. You may have noticed that when you create certain types of columns you get a set of configurable options in the Additional Column Settings section on the Create Column page. Figure 11-8 shows the typical lookup column additional settings.

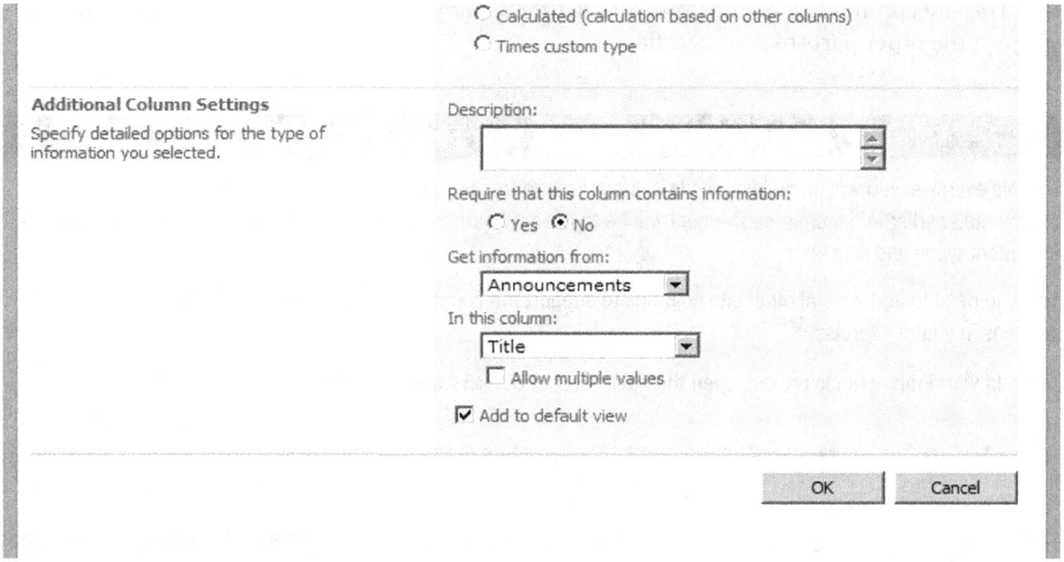

Figure 11-8. *Custom field properties*

These options may be stored in custom properties on the column itself when you create a new column, and you can use these options to configure your column, increasing the reuse of your class significantly.

However, the custom field property handling is riddled by bugs that will make using custom field properties very difficult.

There is some good news, though, and again WSPBuilder comes to our rescue. The WSP-Builder project list includes a custom field type item template that includes code to fix most of the problems related to storing custom properties on field types. If you want to create reusable field types, I encourage you to explore the field type template that ships with WSPBuilder.

Even if you handle the storage of custom properties, you are still faced with a problem related to deploying site columns with custom properties through features. Where would you add the custom field property values? You only have access to the elements Field and RenderPatterns, and neither of these can be used.

To solve this, you can use a custom namespace. Although a thorough example is beyond the scope of this book, I'll point you to an online article that explains how to do this: http://www.understandingsharepoint.com/url/10033.

With these few tips out of the way, we should move on and actually start using our fancy new field type.

Columns

Now that we have a custom field type up and running, we should put it to work. Our next task will be to create a site column from our field type and see what options we have for working with that column.

The site column will be the news article title. Later you will also add more site columns to support the other parts of a news article.

Exercise 11-7. Creating Your First Site Column

For this exercise, you will be building a site column feature for your project. You will use the `TimesSiteColumns` you created earlier in the chapter. The goal will be to have a feature deploy your site column so you can include it in content types and lists later.

You also need to add several other site columns to support the complete newspaper site, but you shall add these columns in a later exercise.

1. In your EmpireTimes project, open the `TimesSiteColumns` feature folder.

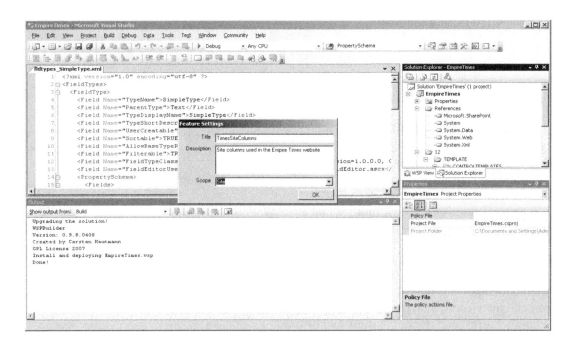

The name you chose for your feature will also be the name used in the feature folder. That folder will be placed alongside all other features in the `[12]\TEMPLATE\FEATURES` folder. Having a good naming policy, for example by adding an identifier to the front of the feature name, means less chance of having conflicting features. Naming your feature `Feature` is not likely to be your wisest move.

2. Open the `elements.xml` file.

Note that WSPBuilder adds the correct namespace to the `Elements` element. If you have set up your IntelliSense as described in Chapter 1, you will immediately get IntelliSense support for all CAML files in this namespace.

3. Add the following code to your `elements.xml` file:

```xml
<?xml version="1.0" encoding="utf-8" ?>
<Elements xmlns="http://schemas.microsoft.com/sharepoint/">
  <Field ID=""
         Name="ArticleTitle"
         StaticName="ArticleTitle"
         DisplayName="Article title"
         Group="EmpireNews news articles"
         Type="TimesFieldType"
         />
</Elements>
```

4. Create a new GUID value to use for the ID attribute. The easiest way to do so is to select Tools ➤ Create GUID in Visual Studio. Select the registry format, and hit Copy to put the new GUID value on your clipboard. Then paste the value into the ID attribute.

Caution For site columns, you must use the full registry format, including the brackets and hyphens.

---

5. Open the feature receiver code file located in the `FeatureCode` folder of your solution. It should be named `TimesSiteColumn.cs` if you named your project `TimesSiteColumns`. This file is added by WSPBuilder when you add a Feature with Receiver item. The code throws an exception when the feature is activated, so you need to delete the exceptions for the feature to be deployable. As such, delete the four lines that say this:

```csharp
throw new Exception("The method or operation is not implemented.");
```

6. Build and deploy your solution.

7. When deployment has finished, go to the root site in your site collection, then to Site Settings, and then to Site Collection Features. Activate your feature, and verify on the Site Columns page that your new column has been added.

If everything went as planned, you should now see your new column in the list, and the column is ready for use from your lists or content types.

Adding More Columns

Of course, having articles with only a title makes no sense. You want to add more columns and at the same time explore some of the other field types and also other methods of creating fields.

We want to add four more columns for use in our articles. You want an introduction, a body text, a picture, a category, and a publishing date. These columns will offer you a variety of field types to create. Table 11-1 shows the columns and their field types.

Table 11-1. *Article Columns and Field Types*

Column	Field Type
Introduction	Multiple lines of text
BodyText	HTML/rich text
Category	Lookup
PublishingDate	Date/time

Note I have no idea what data newspapers really use for their articles. I chose these columns for the sake of illustrating different field types.

Exercise 11-8. Adding More Columns

This exercise will show how different field types require different attributes. You will add three more site columns using the CAML `Field` definition schema.

1. Open your `elements.xml` file again, and in your `Elements` element, add the following three columns:

```
<Field ID="{A9D43B6B-F6D8-4938-B545-0465AB696F97}"
        Name="Introduction"
        StaticName="Introduction"
        DisplayName="Introduction text"
        Group="EmpireNews news articles"
        Type="Note"
        RichText="FALSE"
        NumLines="4"
        />
<Field ID="{7439066B-E58A-448a-9BF7-73BE426150DD}"
        Name="BodyText"
        StaticName="BodyText"
        DisplayName="Body text"
        Group="EmpireNews news articles"
        Type="Note"
        RichText="TRUE"
        RichTextMode="FullHtml"
        NumLines="10"
        />
<Field ID="{B3A86425-7C09-4574-B181-B94E2DA3A07D}"
        Name="PublishingDate"
        StaticName="PublishingDate"
        DisplayName="Publishing date"
        Group="EmpireNews news articles"
        Type="DateTime"
        Format="DateTime"
        />
```

Tip If you are reading this text electronically and have the option of cutting and pasting the text, don't. Exploring the attributes of an element using IntelliSense is a great way of learning about new attributes as well.

---

2. Build and then deploy or upgrade your solution.

3. Activate the feature from the Site Collection Features page. If the feature is still activated from the previous exercise, deactivate first.

4. Verify that your site columns appear, and feel free to check the settings to make sure you got everything correct. See Figure 11-9 for how this should look.

Role	Single line of text	User Experience Lab (TS)
Task Status	Choice	User Experience Lab (TS)
Total Work	Number	User Experience Lab (TS)
EmpireNews news articles		
Article title	SimpleType	User Experience Lab (TS)
Body text	Multiple lines of text	User Experience Lab (TS)
Introduction text	Multiple lines of text	User Experience Lab (TS)
Publishing date	Date and Time	User Experience Lab (TS)
Extended Columns		
Company Phonetic	Single line of text	User Experience Lab (TS)
First Name Phonetic	Single line of text	User Experience Lab (TS)
Issue Status	Choice	User Experience Lab (TS)
Last Name Phonetic	Single line of text	User Experience Lab (TS)
Related Issues	Lookup	User Experience Lab (TS)
Task Group	Person or Group	User Experience Lab (TS)
UDC Purpose	Choice	User Experience Lab (TS)

Figure 11-9. *Almost all the site columns in place*

You might be wondering why we have not added the Category column. We will get to that in a moment.

Lookup Columns

At this point, we have most of our site columns in place. However, we still need to add the Category site column, and that column is a lookup column.

What we are going to do, in the next chapter, is to create a list called Categories, which will hold the different news categories in which we link articles. Categories include Local, Weather, Lifestyle, Sports, and so on. The reason why we want to have a lookup rather than a choice field is that lookup columns are more dynamic.

The problem is that it is not possible to add a lookup column declaratively. Lookup columns have a List attribute in their Field element that points to the list from which the lookup values are gathered.

You might think that simply adding the name of a list to the List attribute would suffice, but unfortunately the List attribute requires the GUID of a list. The GUID of a list in turn is automatically generated when the list is created, meaning it is unique every time you create a list. Either you have to edit the field after the list is created or you must find another solution.

The good news is that modifying a lookup field to connect it to the correct list is relatively easy. The bad news is that finding the correct GUID can be a little awkward at best.

Let's see whether we can find a solution.

Exercise 11-9. Adding a Lookup Column

What you are doing in this exercise is creating a lookup column through a combination of CAML and feature receiver code.

1. In your elements file, add the following site column definition:

```
<Field ID="{79292857-5275-4f45-8A3C-AF482F9FC565}"
        Name="ArticleCategory"
        StaticName="ArticleCategory"
        DisplayName="Article category"
        Group="EmpireNews news articles"
        Type="Lookup"
        List="Categories"
        ShowField="Title"
    />
```

If you were to deploy this solution now, you would indeed get a lookup column, but it would not be mapped to any list or column. Check out Figure 11-10.

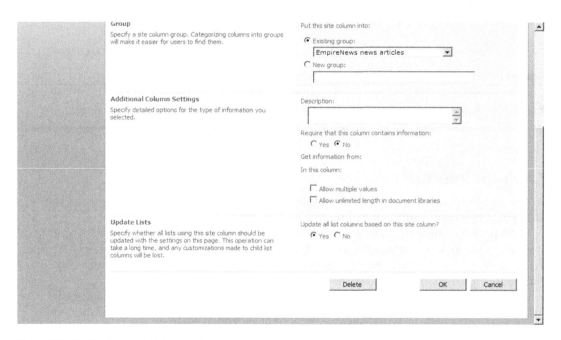

Figure 11-10. *No dice. Or list. Or column.*

"Ah!" you might say. "That is because the Categories list does not exist." That would indeed be a valid suggestion, but no amount of Categories list adding will make this solution work, regardless of whether you create the list before or after provisioning the column.

No, you need to do a bit more work and set the list name in the feature receiver code.

2. In your `FeatureActivated` method, still located in the `TimesSiteColumns.cs` file, add the following code, right after the `articleField.Update()` line:

```
// articleField.Update(); would be just before this
SPFieldLookup categoriesField = (SPFieldLookup)web.Fields["Article category"];
categoriesField.LookupList = "{" + ➥
 web.Site.RootWeb.Lists["Categories"].ID.ToString() + "}";
categoriesField.LookupWebId = web.Site.RootWeb.ID;
categoriesField.Update();
```

3. On your site, create a new custom list called Categories. You do not need to do anything with the list at this point; you are only adding the list to test the lookup column.

4. Build and then deploy or…oh, for crying out loud, you know the drill, right? Make sure your column looks something like Figure 11-11.

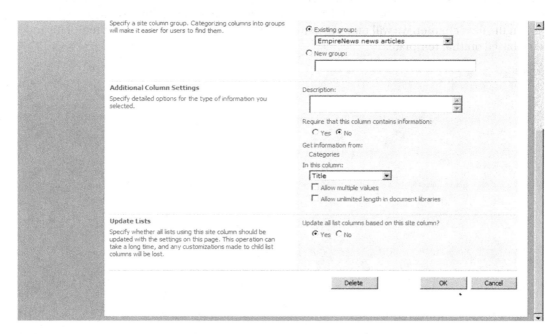

Figure 11-11. *Three simple lines of code make all the difference in the world.*

In the next chapter, you will be creating the Categories list through a feature, so for now, feel free to delete the list. When you do your lookup column will stop working and you will be back to Figure 11-10.

What we are doing with this code is getting a reference to our newly created column and attaching that column's `LookupList` property to the ID of a list in the root web of our site collection. Note that the ID of a list is a GUID, while the `LookupList` expects a string.

You also set the `LookupWebId` to the root web ID. This allows you to use the lookup column correctly in child sites regardless of where in the site hierarchy you add the column.

Note You are adding { and } to the `LookupList` string to enable the site column to properly reference the list in child sites. Omitting the curly brackets will cause the lookup to fail in child sites.

This code is not very dynamic, but it serves the purpose, which is to understand what you need to do to get a `LookupField` to work.

Our Empire So Far

OK, we have started building the *Empire Times* newspaper's web site and created a field type and some site columns. Although these columns may not be the most exiting or sexy aspects in the world of SharePoint, they are still vital to getting a site working the way you want.

In the next chapter, we will take our solution one step further and add a list template and a list based on that template.

CHAPTER 12

Creating Your First Content Factory

Using Content Types As Part of Our User Experience

With our first building blocks in place, we should now start looking at what content we should include in our newspaper. No, I'm not talking about which articles would provide the best readership but rather how the content is built.

Structuring content is a lot easier with content types, but we also get a lot of other benefits, as you saw in Chapter 8. Now it is time to see how you can harness the power and coolness of content types to create a great user experience.

Mission Objective

In this chapter, we will practice creating content types and create a simple content type hierarchy for use in our *Empire Times* web site. We will create three different content types to hold a root NewsArticle type, and we'll have two child types, a "Series article" and "Stand-alone article," derive from that root type. We will utilize the site columns we created in the previous chapter.

We will also discover a few gotchas for content type deployment. Finally, we will add an event receiver to our content type to make sure editors do not delete or modify the news in any way we do not approve.

Content Type Startup

We established in Chapter 8 that content types are exceptionally cool. Or rather, I told you, and you are of course free to disagree, but I will assume that you at least want to explore how to build content types so you can make up your mind.

So, let's get down to business.

Exercise 12-1. Creating Your First Content Type

In this exercise, you'll create a content type for the news articles we will be publishing on our *Empire Times* web site. We will be building on the Visual Studio solution from the previous chapter.

1. Open your existing EmpireTimes solution.

2. Add a new item of type WSPBuilder ➤ Feature with Receiver. Add a name and a description, and make sure you set the scope to Site. I have called my feature `TimesContentType`.

Remember the tip from the previous chapter of prepending the name with a token to easily identify features in the `[12]\TEMPLATE\FEATURES` folder.

Also, since we are adding a feature with a receiver, you *must remember to remove* the exception thrown on `FeatureActivated` like we did in the previous chapter.

3. Your `elements.xml` file in the new feature should open automatically. If not, open the `elements.xml` file. Edit the file as such:

```
<?xml version="1.0" encoding="utf-8" ?>
<Elements xmlns="http://schemas.microsoft.com/sharepoint/">
  <ContentType ID=""
               Name="News Article"
               Group="EmpireTimes"
               >
  </ContentType>
</Elements>
```

You need to add an ID value to the content type to make it work. You may remember from Chapter 8 that the ID of a content type also denotes the content type inheritance. This means the ID requires a bit of crafting.

To craft the content type ID, you first need to include the `Item` content type ID. Next you should add a GUID value to the `ID` string.

4. In the `ID` attribute, add `0x0100`. This denotes that you will be inheriting from the `Item` root content type and will be adding a complete GUID to make your content type unique.

5. Add a GUID value after the `0x0100` string. The easiest way to do this is to go to the Tools menu and click Create GUID. Click Copy, close the window, and paste the value.

6. In the `ID` attribute, remove any brackets and hyphens to leave only the numbers and letters. Your ID should look something like this:

```
0x0100F2525ACE8DE54912A7A10724466A6A80
```

7. Build and then deploy or upgrade your solution.

8. Go to your site collection features from the Site Settings page on the root site in your site collection. Activate your feature.

9. Verify that your content type appears in the list. Figure 12-1 shows the result.

Picture	Document	User Experience Lab (TS)
Web Part Page	Basic Page	User Experience Lab (TS)
EmpireTimes		
NewsArticle	Item	User Experience Lab (TS)
Folder Content Types		
Discussion	Folder	User Experience Lab (TS)
Folder	Item	User Experience Lab (TS)
List Content Types		
Announcement	Item	User Experience Lab (TS)
Contact	Item	User Experience Lab (TS)

Figure 12-1. *Content type installed*

At this point, our content type does not contain anything, but, hey, you got it to appear, so something must be right. Right?

What we just did was add the base of a content type. In itself this is quite worthless, but I wanted to show you a few basic things first, before we dive into the heavier stuff.

The most challenging aspect so far is to create the content type ID. As you may remember from Chapter 8, we basically have two options for crafting the ID value. The first method is to use the parent content type, 0x01 for Item in our example, and then add a two-digit number for our content type. Any two-digit number goes, except for 00, which is used in the second method.

The second method is to use the parent content type, still 0x01 for Item in our example, and then add 00 followed by a GUID value where the hyphens and brackets have been removed. This method yields a guaranteed unique ID for our content type but also a rather long ID.

You may likely want to combine the two methods when you are developing a content type strategy. One of the cool features of content types is inheritance support, and you may want to take advantage of this feature in your strategy. In this case, you may want to use the second method to create your root content type and then use the first method to create child content types.

Let's take a look at how this might work.

Exercise 12-2. Creating a Content Type Hierarchy

In this exercise, you will create a simple content type hierarchy where you will create two specialized child article content types for a stand-alone article and a series article.

1. Open your `element.xml` file in the `TimesContentTypes` feature.

2. Add the following CAML code after the existing `NewsArticle` content type:

```
<ContentType ID=""
             Name="Stand-alone article"
             Group="EmpireTimes"
             >
</ContentType>
<ContentType ID=""
```

```
              Name="Series article"
              Group="EmpireTimes"
              >
</ContentType>
```

3. For the ID attributes, copy the ID of the `NewsArticle` content type, and paste it into the ID of the child content types. Then, add `01` and `02` to the end of the ID value in the child content types. In my example, where the ID of the parent content type is `0x0100F2525ACE8DE54912A7A10724466A6A80`, the completed `elements.xml` file now looks like this:

```
<?xml version="1.0" encoding="utf-8" ?>
<Elements xmlns="http://schemas.microsoft.com/sharepoint/">
  <ContentType ID="0x0100F2525ACE8DE54912A7A10724466A6A80"
              Name="NewsArticle"
              Group="EmpireTimes"
              >
  </ContentType>
  <ContentType ID="0x0100F2525ACE8DE54912A7A10724466A6A8001"
              Name="Stand-alone article"
              Group="EmpireTimes"
              >
  </ContentType>
  <ContentType ID="0x0100F2525ACE8DE54912A7A10724466A6A8002"
              Name="Series article"
              Group="EmpireTimes"
              >
  </ContentType>
</Elements>
```

4. Build and then deploy or upgrade. Deactivate and then reactivate the feature from site collection features. Verify that your new content types appear in the Site Content Types Gallery. Your result should be like Figure 12-2. Notice that each of the child content types is correctly shown to inherit from the `NewsArticle` parent type.

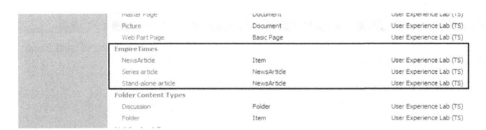

Figure 12-2. *Simple content type hierarchy*

Still, the content types do not actually do anything. Patience. We will get there shortly.

As of now, we have a semiworking content type hierarchy for our solution, but we still have a long way to go. Next we want to add our previously created site columns to our content types and discover some gotchas for content type deployment.

■Tip At this point, you may want to set the `Hidden="True"` attribute on the root `NewsArticle` content type. We will not be using that content type directly but rather focusing on the child content types. This is completely optional.

Content Type Columns

Now, by the sheer power of logic, we should be able to add some fields and some content to our parent types and then have the child content types inherit those properties. Let's give that a try, shall we?

Exercise 12-3. Adding Content Type Content

What you will do now is add the site columns you created in the previous chapter to the parent content type and see what happens. If you haven't created the site columns in the previous chapter, now would be a good time.

1. Open the `elements.xml` file from the site columns feature created in the previous chapter.

2. In your `elements.xml` file for the `TimesContentTypes` feature, add a child element `FieldRefs` to the parent content type `NewsArticle`:

```
<ContentType ID="0x0100F2525ACE8DE54912A7A10724466A6A80"
             Name="NewsArticle"
             Group="EmpireTimes"
             >
  <FieldRefs>
  </FieldRefs>
</ContentType>
```

3. Inside the `FieldRefs` element, add `FieldRef` child elements for each of the site columns we created in the previous chapter. You should end up with five `FieldRef` elements something like this:

```
<FieldRefs>
  <FieldRef ID="{D4A9AEE0-5559-47a5-A8A7-019D5150556C}" />
  <FieldRef ID="{A9D43B6B-F6D8-4938-B545-0465AB696F97}"/>
  <FieldRef ID="{7439066B-E58A-448a-9BF7-73BE426150DD}"/>
  <FieldRef ID="{B3A86425-7C09-4574-B181-B94E2DA3A07D}"/>
  <FieldRef ID="{79292857-5275-4f45-8A3C-AF482F9FC565}"/>
</FieldRefs>
```

The ID values may vary if you created your own GUID values for the site columns. Just make sure your ID values correspond to the site columns you created in the previous chapter.

4. Build, deploy...yada, yada...check to see what has happened to the NewsArticle content type. Figure 12-3 shows my results.

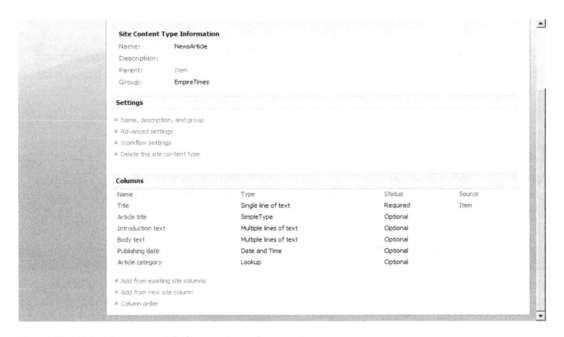

Figure 12-3. *Woo-hoo, we added some site columns. Go, you.*

Everything looks just as it should. You are hereby awarded the title of "content type deployer"—a highly sought title, I am sure.

Our base article content type has gotten the site columns we wanted. If you did everything correctly in the previous chapter, you should also find that the columns reference the right list and field and that everything is peachy.

Now let's check to see what has happened to the child content types. Excited? Don't be, there is disappointment ahead. You see, with the code we have now, there is very little inheritance, at least for the sake of site columns.

Figure 12-4 may throw some cold water in your blood. Don't worry; there is an easy fix—our first gotcha for SharePoint content type deployment.

Figure 12-4. *What? Where are the "inherited" site columns? I want my money back!*

As you can see, we didn't get any of the columns that the parent content type NewsArticle defines, even if we set up the correct content type ID. Let's take a look and see whether we cannot fix this.

Exercise 12-4. Fixing Broken Inheritance

In this exercise, you will fix the broken content type column inheritance.

1. Modify your child content types, and add an empty FieldRefs element to each:

```
<ContentType ID="0x0100F2525ACE8DE54912A7A10724466A6A8001"
             Name="Stand-alone article"
             Group="EmpireTimes"
        >
   <FieldRefs></FieldRefs>
</ContentType>
<!--Repeat for Series article content type-->
```

That's it. Nothing more. Do the build, deploy, deactivate, reactivate cycle, and, kaboom, Bob's your uncle. Again. He might even reinstate your inheritance.

I made this error quite a lot when I started out doing content type inheritance through code. Now you don't have to.

Check out Figure 12-5.

Figure 12-5. *Now that's more like it!*

Time to Get Serious: Content Type Forms

We need to take a trip down memory lane. You should recall from Chapters 6 and 8 that the data editing, entry, and display experience is closely tied to content types. Each content type is connected to a set of form templates that define how data should be presented to users. The default form templates are inherited by the Item content type, and all point to the ListForm rendering template.

However, the default display of data doesn't really suit us. After all, we want to create a newspaper, not a data sheet web site. The default form templates do not resemble any newspaper I have seen, so let's get medieval on the default interface.

Exercise 12-5. Changing the Default Form Templates

In this exercise, you will create a new rendering template for the content types you created earlier in the chapter. Then you will attach that rendering template to the various forms used to render the content type data. WSPBuilder will handle correct deployment of the code as long as you place it in the correct structure in your solution.

1. You should have a folder called 12\TEMPLATES\CONTROLTEMPLATES in your solution already. If not, create it.

Mimicking the [12] structure will help WSPBuilder place your files in the correct directories when you deploy.

2. In the CONTROLTEMPLATES folder, add a new text file called TimesListForms.ascx.

Why a text file? Well, the project is not a web project, so you don't have the option of adding a web user control. Naming the file `.ascx` will still tell Visual Studio that you want a control, however.

3. From the `[12]\TEMPLATES\CONTROLTEMPLATES` directory in your SharePoint installation, open the `DefaultTemplates.ascx` file.

4. Copy the directives at the top of the `DefaultTemplates.ascx` file, and paste them into your own `TimesListForms.ascx`. That would be all the lines starting with `<%@`.

5. In the `DefaultTemplates.ascx` file, locate the `ListForm` rendering template. Copy the rendering template, starting with the `<SharePoint:RenderingTemplate ID="ListForm" runat="server">` tag and ending with the next `</SharePoint:RenderingTemplate>` tag. Paste it into your `TimesListForms.ascx` file.

6. In the `TimesListForms.ascx`, modify the ID of the rendering template from `ID="ListForm"` to `ID="EmpireTimesNewsDisplayForm"`. Figure 12-6 shows an excerpt of what the final code should look like.

```
1   <%@ Control Language="C#"   AutoEventWireup="false" %>
2   <%@ Assembly Name="Microsoft.SharePoint, Version=12.0.0.0, Culture=neutral, PublicKe
3   <%@ Register TagPrefix="SharePoint" Assembly="Microsoft.SharePoint, Version=12.0.0.0
4   <%@ Register TagPrefix="wssuc" TagName="SPHttpUtility" Assembly="Microsoft.SharePoint, Version=12.0.
5   <%@ Register TagPrefix="wssuc" TagName="ToolBar" src="~/_controltemplates/ToolBar.as
6   <%@ Register TagPrefix="wssuc" TagName="ToolBarButton" src="~/_controltemplates/Tool
7   <SharePoint:RenderingTemplate ID="EmpireTimesNewsDisplayForm" runat="server">
8       <Template>
9           <SPAN id='part1'>
10              <SharePoint:InformationBar runat="server"/>
11              <wssuc:ToolBar CssClass="ms-formtoolbar" id="toolBarTbltop" RightButtonS
12                  <Template_RightButtons>
13                      <SharePoint:NextPageButton runat="server"/>
14                      <SharePoint:SaveButton runat="server"/>
15                      <SharePoint:GoBackButton runat="server"/>
```

Figure 12-6. *Rendering template excerpt*

7. Modify the rendering template to match the design of your favorite newspaper web site. Remember to include relative image references and download all supporting scripts and CSS files. Build, deploy, and test.

Yeah, that last item was a joke.

The point is, adding the listing of a complete design of a web site to a book like this makes no sense, and we are short on space already. As such:

8. If you are reading this while offline, make some kind of random change to the rendering template. If you are reading this while online, you can go to the book's downloads and download a sample design. The URL for this sample is `http://www.understandingsharepoint.com/url/20002`.

OK, next you update the content types to use your new display form.

9. Open the `elements.xml` file of the `TimesContentTypes` feature. In the `NewsArticle` content type, add the following `XmlDocument` content after the `FieldRefs` element:

```
<XmlDocuments>
  <XmlDocument ➥
NamespaceURI="http://schemas.microsoft.com/sharepoint/v3/contenttype/forms">
    <FormTemplates ➥
```

```
xmlns="http://schemas.microsoft.com/sharepoint/v3/contenttype/forms">
      <Display>EmpireTimesNewsDisplayForm</Display>
      <Edit>ListForm</Edit>
      <New>ListForm</New>
   </FormTemplates>
 </XmlDocument>
</XmlDocuments>
```

10. Reactivate, deactivate, deploy, and build your solution. In reverse order. While blindfolded. You should know this routine by now.

Right, that should be it.

___

Note We haven't modified or created a custom `NewForm` or `EditForm`. These forms follow the same principles as the `DisplayForm`. I will leave modifying them as an optional exercise for you.

___

We now actually have a working content type that uses our new forms, but we haven't actually added the content type anywhere. You could of course trust me, but then you wouldn't heed the warning I gave you about not trusting strange authors. So, to verify, do the following optional exercise.

Exercise 12-6 (Optional). Testing the List Custom Display Form

In this optional exercise, you will test the content type and make sure it displays correctly.

1. Create a new custom list. Enable content type management from the Advanced settings on the List Settings page.

2. (Optional) After enabling content type management, go back to the List Settings page. Click the `Item` content type, and then delete it.

Yes, I said delete it. Remember, list content types are just copies of the parent type. Deleting the `Item` content type here affects only the current list.

3. Click "Add from existing site content types." Find the "Stand-alone article" content type, and add it to the list before clicking OK. If you select EmpireTimes from the drop-down list above the lists, you may find the correct content type faster (see Figure 12-7).

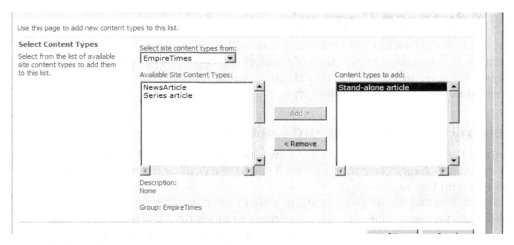

Figure 12-7. *Adding a content type to a list*

4. Go back to the list, and add a new item. Note that you have not yet edited the NewForm or our content type, so you just get the standard SharePoint ListForm template.

5. Open your new item. Depending on whether you downloaded the sample design, you should see something like Figure 12-8.

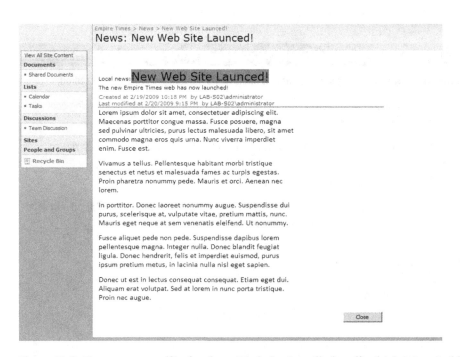

Figure 12-8. *Your great new display form. Yeah, I misspelled stuff, which is inevitable proof that even I make mistakes. It has happened before; once, in 1998, I took a wrong turn at an intersection.*

Cool, eh? Let's get moving again.

More Advanced Concepts

You may wonder why I asked you to create a feature with a receiver earlier, rather than just a blank feature. Rest assured that your time of wondering is now over; you are about to be enlightened. What we are going to do here is explore some advanced concepts in order to learn more about the coolness of content types.

Preventing News Deletion and Category Change

The editor of *Empire Times* has decided that news should not be deleted. In addition, news articles should not change categories. I mean, if you have a weather report, chances are it will not be a sports update any time soon.

To accomplish this, we are going to utilize an item event receiver. Event receivers are important tools for making sure that the user experience feels right and is secure. In short, an event receiver is a piece of code that fires whenever a certain event happens in SharePoint.

Note A thorough investigation of event receivers is a bit outside the scope of this book. Luckily for you, I have a Business Process Management series on my blog that explains event receivers and workflows. Check it out at `http://www.understandingsharepoint.com/url/10001`.

Exercise 12-7. Creating Event Receivers in Content Types

In this exercise, you will create two event receivers and attach them to the content types you have created.

1. Add a new class file, for example, in the `FeatureCode` folder of your solution. Name it something cool, such as `TimesNewsEventReceivers.cs`. Open the file.

Note that if you add the class file to the `FeatureCode` folder, Visual Studio will add `FeatureCode` to your namespace. You do not want that.

2. Add a `using Microsoft.Sharepoint;` statement to the file.

3. Have your class inherit from the `SPItemEventReceiver` class. Oh, and make the class public. It sort of works best that way. At this point, your file should look something like this:

```
using System;
using System.Collections.Generic;
using System.Text;
using Microsoft.SharePoint;

namespace EmpireTimes
{
    public class TimesNewsEventReceivers : SPItemEventReceiver
    {

    }
}
```

4. Override the `ItemUpdating` method. Add the following code to your overridden method:

```
public override void ItemUpdating(SPItemEventProperties properties)
{
    SPListItem item = properties.ListItem;
    SPFieldLookupValue newValue =
        new SPFieldLookupValue(item["ArticleCategory"].ToString());

    if (newValue.LookupId.ToString() !=
        properties.AfterProperties["ArticleCategory"].ToString())
    {
        properties.ErrorMessage = "You cannot change category";
        properties.Cancel = true;
    }

}
```

This method handles the changing of article category. Now we want to avoid deletion of news.

5. Override the `ItemDeleting` method. Add the following code to your overridden method:

```
public override void ItemDeleting(SPItemEventProperties properties)
{
    properties.Cancel = true;
    properties.ErrorMessage =
        "Cannot delete news. If it happened, it happened.";
}
```

That takes care of deleting news. Feel free to argue that the editor is an idiot for refusing to delete items, but, hey, I didn't make the rules.

Next we need to attach the event receiver to the content type. To do so, as you may remember, we need to add an XML document to the content type.

6. Update the `NewsArticle` root content type, and add an XML document to the `XmlDocuments` element as such:

```
<XmlDocument NamespaceURI="http://schemas.microsoft.com/sharepoint/events">
  <spe:Receivers xmlns:spe="http://schemas.microsoft.com/sharepoint/events">
    <Receiver>
      <Name>Updating news article</Name>
      <Type>ItemUpdating</Type>
      <SequenceNumber>1</SequenceNumber>
      <Assembly>EmpireTimes, Version=1.0.0.0, Culture=neutral,➡
  PublicKeyToken=[YOUR PUBLIC KEY TOKEN]</Assembly>
      <Class>EmpireTimes.TimesNewsEventReceivers</Class>
      <Data />
      <Filter />
    </Receiver>
    <Receiver>
      <Name>Deleting news article</Name>
```

```
            <Type>ItemDeleting</Type>
            <SequenceNumber>1</SequenceNumber>
            <Assembly>EmpireTimes, Version=1.0.0.0, Culture=neutral,➥
     PublicKeyToken=[YOUR PUBLIC KEY TOKEN]</Assembly>
            <Class>EmpireTimes.TimesNewsEventReceivers</Class>
            <Data />
            <Filter />
          </Receiver>
        </spe:Receivers>
      </XmlDocument>
```

Note that `[YOUR PUBLIC KEY TOKEN]` must be replaced with the public key token for your solution. If you're using WSPBuilder, the easiest way to get this value is to check the `Feature.xml` file of your feature because this will contain the public key token.

7. Build and then deploy or upgrade your solution. Deactivate and reactivate the feature.

Note that if you added the content type to a list in the optional exercise earlier, you must remove and re-add the content type to the list for the changes to take effect.

What we just did was bind a feature receiver to a content type using an XML document. The cool thing about this is that no matter where you now add the content type, the feature receiver will follow.

We can still do more. Content types can be tied to other functionality as well. For example, you might want to connect special user actions only to documents or items of a particular type.

One method of doing so is with a custom action, which we discussed briefly in Chapter 5. Custom actions are the method by which links and items are added to menus and lists in SharePoint. We will explore this further in Chapter 13 as well, but I wanted to show you how to connect a custom action to a specific content type.

Exercise 12-8. Connecting a Custom Action to a Content Type

In this exercise, you will create a Submit for Editor action that is connected to the stand-alone news article content type. You will do this by creating a `CustomAction` element and connecting that to the content type using the `RegistrationType` and `RegistrationId` attributes of the `CustomAction` element. You will then make the `CustomAction` appear on the EditControlBlock of items based on the stand-alone news article content type.

1. In the `feature.xml` file of `TimesContentTypes`, add the following line to the `ElementManifests` element:

```
<ElementManifests>
  <ElementManifest Location="elements.xml"/>
  <ElementManifest Location="customaction.xml"/>
</ElementManifests>
```

I'm having you put the custom action in a separate elements file to keep things tidy and to point out that you can indeed have several element files in the same feature.

2. Create a new XML file in the `TimesContentTypes` folder, called `customaction.xml`.

3. In the `customaction.xml` file, add the following code:

```
<?xml version="1.0" encoding="utf-8" ?>
<Elements xmlns="http://schemas.microsoft.com/sharepoint/">

</Elements>
```

4. Add a `CustomAction` element inside the `Element` element of your new element's `customaction.xml` element file. And if you mention element again....

```
<CustomAction Location=""
               RegistrationType="ContentType"
               RegistrationId=""
               Title="Submit article to editor"
               >
    <UrlAction Url="submitarticle.aspx"/>
</CustomAction>
```

Notice that as you complete typing the `RegistrationType` attribute, you get IntelliSense for the values, as shown here.

```
1    <?xml version="1.0" encoding="utf-8" ?>
2    <Elements xmlns="http://schemas.microsoft.com/sharepoint/">
3    <CustomAction GroupId=""
4                   Location=""
5                   RegistrationType="║"
6    </Elements>
                                        ▤ List
                                        ▤ ContentType
                                        ▤ FileType
                                        ▤ ProgId
```

As you learned in Chapter 5, `GroupId` and `Location` are the attributes that decide where your `CustomAction` will appear. However, for the EditControlBlock, we do not need a `GroupId` at all. So:

5. Update the `Location` attribute as such:

```
Location="EditControlBlock"
```

6. Enter the content type ID for your stand-alone article in the `RegistrationId` attribute. You'll find the content type ID in your other `elements.xml` file in the `TimesContentTypes` feature.

You have added a `UrlAction` child element pointing to `submitarticle.aspx`. This page doesn't exist, so the link won't actually work. We will explore how you can create such custom pages in Chapter 14.

However, to know which article you actually want to submit, you need to pass an argument to the `submitarticle.aspx` page. To do this, you can include tokens as part of the `Url` attribute or `UrlAction`.

7. Update the `Url` attribute of the `UrlAction` element as such:

```
<UrlAction Url="submitpage.aspx?Article={ItemId}&amp;List={ListId}"/>
```

The {ItemId} token will be replaced at runtime with the item's ID. This ID, however, is unique only within a list. So, to make sure you know exactly which item is submitted, you also need to include the {ListId} token.

Since the submitpage.aspx page does not exist, you will get an error if you try to click the "Submit to editor" link in the context menu. One tip to test that you have actually entered the correct values in the Url action before the page is complete is to surround the Url with a javascript:alert().

8. (Optional) Edit the UrlAction element as such:

```
<UrlAction
  Url="javascript:alert('submitpage.aspx?Article={ItemId}&amp;List={ListId}');"/>
```

Build but pause for a second. When you add new files to a solution, as is the case here, you cannot upgrade the solution, because upgrading a solution will upgrade only existing files. Instead, uninstall your existing solution before you install. Then, activate the content types feature as you did before.

Figure 12-9 shows my results.

That's really how easy this is. Of course, everything is easy when you know how, and now you know. Good, you!

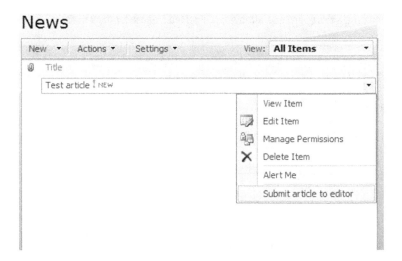

Figure 12-9. *EditControlBlock* CustomAction *tied to a content type*

Binding the Pieces Together

One more important task remains. What happens if we activate our content types feature without having already activated the site columns feature? Disaster I tell you, disaster!

Fortunately, SharePoint gives us an opportunity to prevent such accidents through the FeatureActivationDependency element. This element, when placed in a feature.xml file, will prevent features from being activated if the dependent features are not activated already.

Note that FeatureActivationDependency does not activate the dependent features for you. You must still activate these, so consider this feature as a reminder, not as any form of automation. We will look at a better solution in Chapter 14.

To enable feature activation dependency, add the following to your feature.xml file in the TimesContentTypes feature, right inside the Feature element:

```
<ActivationDependencies>
  <ActivationDependency FeatureId="[FEATURE ID OF SITE COLUMNS FEATURE]"/>
</ActivationDependencies>
```

Substitute the FeatureId attribute with the feature ID of your TimesSiteColumns feature. You will find this value in the feature.xml file.

Stop Being Cool

I hope these small exercises have inspired you to start developing your own content types from scratch. You may even have picked up a tip or two on a few pitfalls that lurk, waiting for the next haphazard developer who assumes that everything works just like they hope.

You can now remove your sunglasses, take off your leather jacket, and step off the Harley. Just remember to bring it all back when you start doing content type development in your production environment. You'll be the star of any show.

Unless they bring a straitjacket, that is. Either way, you should have a great time.

CHAPTER 13

Accounting Gone Haywire
List, Forms, Reports, Views…Ah, the Bean Counters Will Go Mad!

Lists: either you love them or you need to reconsider SharePoint as your platform of choice.

Everything that is SharePoint revolves around lists of some sort. As good developers, we must thus learn how to work with and develop these lists. After reading this chapter, you will have covered the basics of both list template creation and list instantiation using features.

Mission Objective

In this chapter, we will create a list template from scratch. Actually, we will skip the view construction and just borrow code from the Custom List template.

Next, we will attach our previous content types to that list template and discover some caveats to content type deployment. Finally, we will instantiate two new lists, the "News article" list and the "Article category" list, before we add some logic to make sure our list infrastructure gets created the right way.

List Templates

Our first step is to create the list templates we will use for the news articles. So, without further delay, here is the first exercise.

Exercise 13-1. Creating the First List Template Feature

In this exercise, you will create a list template from scratch. This list template will be expanded in later exercises so that here we focus on what is required to get the template up and running.

1. In your EmpireTimes solution, add yet another Feature with Receiver item. Remember to remove the exception from the .cs file as before. Name the feature something you like, such as TimesLists.

2. Your new `elements.xml` file should open; if not, open it. Add the following `ListTemplate` element:

```
<ListTemplate Name="TimesArticleList"
              Type="10001"
              DisplayName="Article list"
              Description="List to hold Empire Times news articles"
              BaseType="0"
              Category="Custom Lists"
              OnQuickLaunch="TRUE"
              SecurityBits="11"/>
```

3. Build, deploy, and then go to the site settings and site features. Activate the `TimesLists` feature. Check your Create page. Your result should resemble Figure 13-1.

If you do not see the `TimesList` feature, remember that when you add a feature to a solution, you must redeploy rather than upgrade the solution. If this happens, just retract (uninstall from the WSPBuilder menu), and then deploy the solution again.

	Communications	Tracking	Custom Lists	Web Pages
ibrary	▫ Announcements	▫ Links	▫ Custom List	▫ Basic Page
/	▫ Contacts	▫ Calendar	▫ Custom List in Datasheet View	▫ Web Part Page
brary	▫ Discussion Board	▫ Tasks	▫ Article list	▫ Sites and Workspaces
ıry		▫ Project Tasks	▫ Import Spreadsheet	
		▫ Issue Tracking		
		▫ Survey		

Figure 13-1. *First list template installed*

Don't try to create a new list from the template yet, though, because we haven't added anything to the template besides the element definition. That means more work ahead, I'm afraid.

Exercise 13-2. Creating Your Basic Schema.xml File

In this exercise, you will create the first basic `Schema.xml` file and see whether you can make it dance.

1. In your `TimesLists` folder, create a new folder. Name it exactly the same as the `Name` attribute of the `ListTemplate` element, which would be `TimesArticleList` if you followed the previous example.

2. In the newly created `TimesArticleList` folder, create a new XML file called `Schema.xml`, and then open that file.

3. Add the following to the `Schema.xml` file:

```
<List xmlns="http://schemas.microsoft.com/sharepoint/"
      Name="TimesArticleList"
      Title="Article list"
      BaseType="0"
      Url="$Resources:core,lists_Folder;/Articles"
      DisableAttachments="TRUE"
      Type="10001"
      >
  <MetaData>
  </MetaData>
</List>
```

Note the use of `$Resources:core,lists_Folder;` in the `Url` attribute. The resource string will make sure that the list can be deployed to the correct URL regardless of the language installed.

4. Inside the `MetaData` element, add two child elements, `Views` and `Forms`, as such:

```
<MetaData>
  <Fields>
  </Fields>
  <Views>
  </Views>
  <Forms>
  </Forms>
</MetaData>
```

This is actually all you need to create your list. Not just that, but if you did try to create your list now, it would in fact be created. You will get an error message if you do, but the list will get created. To get something useful out of our list when created, we need to fill the child elements with some more content. Let's start with the simplest addition, and for that we need to borrow a bit of code.

Note Even if we will not be adding columns to this list in the `Fields` element, the empty element must be present to avoid a "Cannot complete this action" error message. Confusingly, the error log in that case will state "Failed to retrieve the list schema for feature [YOUR FEATURE ID], list template 10001; expected to find it at:…" and will state the path to the list directory, even if both the directory and the `schema.xml` file are present.

---

5. Go to the `CustomList` feature in the `[12]\TEMPLATE\FEATURES` folder. In the `CustList` folder inside the `CustomList` feature, open the `schema.xml` file.

Yup, that's right; we will be borrowing some XML from the default Custom List template. Don't worry—we'll be giving it back later.

6. At the very bottom of the custom list `schema.xml`, locate the `Forms` element. The element contains three `Form` child elements. Copy all three lines into your own `Forms` element in the `schema.xml` file of your own list template. You may also just type in the `Form` child elements yourself:

```
<Form Type="DisplayForm" Url="DispForm.aspx"➥
 SetupPath="pages\form.aspx" WebPartZoneID="Main" />
<Form Type="EditForm" Url="EditForm.aspx"➥
 SetupPath="pages\form.aspx" WebPartZoneID="Main" />
<Form Type="NewForm" Url="NewForm.aspx"➥
 SetupPath="pages\form.aspx" WebPartZoneID="Main" />
```

We will customize these forms later, so for now these forms just serve to allow us to test our list and our initial configurations.

Next we need a basic view to help verify list functionality. Again, we borrow code from the Custom List template.

7. In the CustList feature's schema.xml file, locate the view that has BaseViewId="1". In my version, that view starts at line 1019. This is the All Items view, which is set to be the default view for our list.

Note We will not be creating a new view from scratch. View construction was covered in Chapter 8. You can relax now.

---

8. Copy the entire View element, and paste it into your own Views element.

Tip You might want to close the View tag to make copying the entire element easier. Check out Figure 13-2.

Also, if you want to put your new lists in a web part, such as on the front page, include the View element with BaseViewId="0" as well. This is the default view used when adding a list as a web part to a web part page.

```
   1  <?xml version="1.0" encoding="utf-8"?>
   2  <List xmlns:ows="Microsoft SharePoint" Title="Basic List" FolderCreation="FALSE" Direction="$Resour
   3    <MetaData>
   4      <ContentTypes>
   5        <ContentTypeRef ID="0x01">
   6          <Folder TargetName="Item" />
   7        </ContentTypeRef>
   8        <ContentTypeRef ID="0x0120" />
   9      </ContentTypes>
  10      <Fields>
  11      </Fields>
  12      <Views>
  13        <View BaseViewID="0" Type="HTML">...>
1019        <View BaseViewID="1" Type="HTML" WebPartZoneID="Main" DisplayName="$Resources:core,objectiv
2149      </Views>
2150      <Forms>
2151        <Form Type="DisplayForm" Url="DispForm.aspx" SetupPath="pages\form.aspx" WebPartZoneID="Main" />
2152        <Form Type="EditForm" Url="EditForm.aspx" SetupPath="pages\form.aspx" WebPartZoneID="Main" />
2153        <Form Type="NewForm" Url="NewForm.aspx" SetupPath="pages\form.aspx" WebPartZoneID="Main" />
2154      </Forms>
2155    </MetaData>
2156  </List>
```

Figure 13-2. *Copying the All Items view from the Custom List template*

9. Build, deploy or upgrade, and check out your Create page. You should now be able to create a new "Article list." Figure 13-3 shows the results.

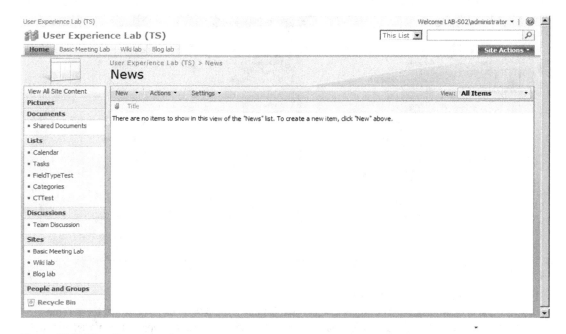

Figure 13-3. *First list created*

Congratulations! You have just created a new list template almost from scratch. Of course, we borrowed some of the hard work from the custom list, but we will get back to that in a few moments. For now, pat yourself on the back if everything worked as expected, and retrace your steps if something went wrong.

CONTENT TYPE MYSTERY

You may have noticed that we did not add any content types to our list. If you remember our previous bet regarding whether or not you were using content types, you may recall that you always get Item and Folder content types added to your list if you create a default custom list. Now that we didn't use the custom list, the Item and Folder content types are not present.

Before you run over to Amazon to retract your book review or cancel the $5 payment to my PayPal account, check out your list in SharePoint Manager 2007. Specifically, check out the ContentTypes node and see that you still get a default content type, named after your list.

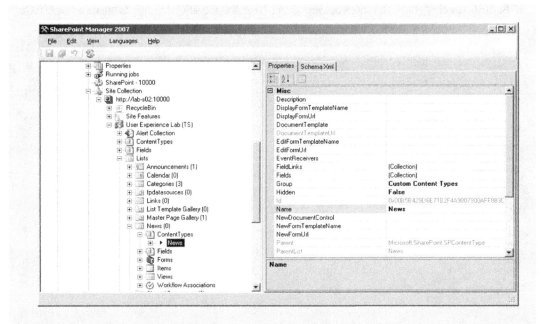

So, yes, you still owe me that review.

Oh, and in case you are wondering where the Title, Created By, and Modified By originate, these come from the `BaseType` 0 list, defined in the global site definition. The default content type added to a list without any specific content type gets columns added from the `BaseType` from which the list is generated.

Adding Content Types to Our List

We haven't added any content types to our list yet, and we want to do that, so let's try the most obvious thing first, the `ContentTypes` element of our list template.

Exercise 13-3. Adding Content Types, Take 1

In this exercise, you will add content type references to the list template using the `ContentTypes` element.

1. In your `MetaData` element of your list template, add the following code, right after the `<MetaData>` start tag:

```
<ContentTypes>
  <ContentTypeRef ID=""/>
  <ContentTypeRef ID=""/>
</ContentTypes>
```

2. In the first `ID` attribute, paste the ID of the "Stand-alone article" content type you created in the previous chapter. In the second `ID` attribute, paste the ID of the "Series article" content type.

At this point, my `MetaData` element looks like this:

```
<MetaData>
  <ContentTypes>
    <ContentTypeRef ID="0x0100F2525ACE8DE54912A7A10724466A6A8001"/>
    <ContentTypeRef ID="0x0100F2525ACE8DE54912A7A10724466A6A8002"/>
  </ContentTypes>
</MetaData>
```

Your content type IDs may be different.

3. Build, deploy or upgrade, and then deactivate and reactivate your list feature.

4. Try creating a new list, which will succeed if you did everything correctly, and then check out the columns on the List Settings page. Figure 13-4 shows my results, which should be close to your results.

Figure 13-4. *No columns added? How strange!*

You will notice that none of the columns of your content types are added. Take 1 didn't work as expected. How disappointing.

The problem here is that the child content types do not inherit the parent type's properties correctly. If you had added the `NewsArticle` root type instead, all the columns would be added as expected, but of course this is not what we want, so we need to look for alternative solutions.

You have a few options for making content types work as expected using the `ContentTypes` element in the list template:

- Update the content type manually through the web interface. Just go into any column on the content type and hit OK without making changes.

- Add the content type manually to the list. Remember to enable content type management from the advanced settings of the List Settings page.

- Add all the content type columns to the `Fields` element in your list template.

These options aren't any good, though. The first two options rely on manual labor after creating a list. Imagine the overhead of instructing users to go through the hoops. The last option is a terrible approach because it relies on adding your columns in two places, first in the content type and then in any list using those content types.

No, we need a better approach. Read on....

Note   I am going to annoy you a bit. Now that you have created the list, try deleting it. Not successful? I'll show you why later and provide you with a fix.

Exercise 13-4. Adding Content Types, Take 2

In this exercise, you will be adding content types using a separate feature and the `ContentTypeBinding` element.

1. Add a new feature to your solution, and give it a temporary name and web scope. We will be deleting this feature later, so don't worry about naming it.

2. In the elements file, add the following code:

```
<ContentTypeBinding ContentTypeId="" ListUrl="Lists/News"/>
<ContentTypeBinding ContentTypeId="" ListUrl="Lists/News"/>
```

3. In the `ContentTypeIds`, add the ID of the "Series article" and "Stand-alone article" content types. In the `ListUrl`, substitute the URL of the list to which you want the content types to be added.

4. Build, deploy, and activate your new feature.

Your list should now have the content types added. You may now safely delete the new feature.

This approach does solve a few of our problems. First, we do get our content types added. Second, we also automatically enable content type management. Third, the columns from the content types are added correctly to the list.

The downside, however, is that we need to know the list URL prior to creating the feature. Since we have no way of modifying the feature after it has been deployed, this method is useful only when we also deploy the list instance using features and thus know the URL prior to creating the content type bindings feature.

Still, this may be useful, especially if you create lists as part of site creation. Next, let's see whether we can find an even better approach.

Exercise 13-5. Adding Content Types, Take 3

In this exercise, you will utilize the feature activation handler of the content type feature to forcibly update the content type on activation.

1. Open the class file of the feature activation handler for the content type feature. In my solution, this file is called SiteContentTypes.cs.

2. Add the following code to the FeatureActivated method:

```
SPSite site = (SPSite)properties.Feature.Parent;
using (SPWeb web = site.RootWeb)
{
    web.ContentTypes["NewsArticle"].Update(true);
}
```

3. Build, deploy, or upgrade. Deactivate and reactivate the content types feature from the Site Collection Features page.

The code we have added here calls the Update method of the newly added content type. The True parameter forces the content type to also update any child content types. This is essentially the same as updating the content type through the web interface, which, as we learned, will fix the adding of content type columns when creating our list.

Although this method will allow us to add child content types and make them behave as we want, it still has issues. First and foremost, we do not enable management of content types using this method, and thus we will always be given the default content type when adding a new item through the web interface. Second, since management of content types is not enabled, there is no way to change a content type for an existing item.

The benefit of this approach is that we are fixing the inheritance issue at the source. Because of this, we do not need to know the URL of any lists that will use the content type in advance.

Sadly, there is currently no "best-of-both-worlds" solution to the issue of deploying child content types, so you need to take the approach that best fits your needs.

We should move on; there's plenty of work still to be done.

List Forms

Previously we borrowed the Forms section from the default Custom List template. This may or may not be what you need. If it is what you need, feel free to use that method, but if not, here's how to add your own list forms to customize the editing and displaying of list data.

Remember that a list form is only one part of the content type/user experience picture.

Exercise 13-6. Adding Custom List Forms

In this exercise, you will create and add your own list form to the list template. The process is similar for all three types of list forms, so for now, you will modify only the DisplayForm page.

1. In your TimesList/TimesArticleList folder, create a new text file, and name it DisplayForm.aspx. The file should be located next to the Schema.xml file.

Using a text file and naming it .aspx will make Visual Studio recognize the file as an ASP.NET file even if the original file type is text.

2. Copy the contents of the [12]\TEMPLATE\Pages\form.aspx file into your new file.

Note that the ASPX file uses the default.master page, and thus you are limited to editing the ContentPlaceHolder content.

3. Make a modification to the code in your own file. For example, add a comment to the <td> HTML element inside the PlaceHolderMain content placeholder at line 15.

Copying the out-of-the-box code may seem meaningless. As with the display form template for our content type, I have avoided pasting pages and pages of ASP.NET and kept the sample design code in a downloadable file. You can get that code from http://www.understandingsharepoint.com/url/20003.

4. Open your Schema.xml file. Go to the Forms element, and modify the Form element for the DisplayForm as such:

```
<Form Type="DisplayForm" Url="DispForm.aspx" Path="DisplayForm.aspx" ➥
WebPartZoneID="Main" />
```

5. Build, deploy, and so on. Create a new list from the "Article list" template. Add an item, and then click the item to go to the display form. If you have downloaded the sample code and added the included master page, you should see something resembling Figure 13-5.

Figure 13-5. *Custom display form page quite unlike regular SharePoint*

Note that in the previous example you do not see the fancy, red background rendering of the article title. This is because the sample in the download uses `DataFormWebPart`, which in turn uses XSLT to extract just the value, and not the rendering, of the column.

If you like, repeat the process for the `NewForm` and the `EditForm` of your list.

Note When creating your own custom list form pages, remember to match any changes in the `WebPartZoneId` of the `Form` element to the web part zone in your page.

List Instances

Although it is extremely simple, we now have a working list template from which we can create our new list. We need to create two lists actually, both the article list and the category list to which the `Article Category` lookup column will be linked.

Let's start with the article list, because the category list will cause us a bit of a problem.

Exercise 13-7. Adding a List Instance

In this exercise, you will add a list instance based on the "Article list" template to our solution.

1. In the `TimesLists` folder, add a new XML file called `ArticleList.xml`.

This list will hold the list instance element for our new article list.

Tip To get CAML IntelliSense, remember that you can go to the Properties pane of the XML file and add the `wss.xsd` schema to the `Schemas` property. Refer to Chapter 1 for specific instructions.

---

2. Open the `Feature.xml` file of the `TimesLists` feature. Add the following line to the `ElementManifests` element:

```
<ElementManifest Location="ArticleList.xml"/>
```

This line will include our new XML file in the feature.

3. In the `ArticleList.xml` file, add the following `Elements` and `ListInstance` elements:

```
<Elements xmlns="http://schemas.microsoft.com/sharepoint/">
  <ListInstance TemplateType="10001"
                FeatureId=""
                Title="News"
                Url="$Resources:core,lists_Folder;/News"
                />
</Elements>
```

4. In the `FeatureId` of the `ListInstance` element, add the ID of the `TimesList` feature. You will find this in the `Feature.xml` file.

5. Build and then deploy or upgrade. Deactivate and reactivate the `TimesList` feature. Verify that the new list gets created. Also check out the list settings to verify that the correct columns are added. Figure 13-6 shows your first list.

Figure 13-6. *Your first list. Woo-hoo!*

Right! That wasn't too painful, was it?

Adding the Categories List

The Categories list is where we will store news categories. The site column `Article Category`, which we created in Chapter 11, is linked to this list. We can create this list from the Custom List template, so we don't need to create a new list template for the Categories list.

It would seem that adding the category list would be really easy now. It is, but there is also a caveat. Let's take a look at what does not work.

Exercise 13-8. Adding the Categories List, Take 1

In this exercise, you will expand the TimesList feature by adding the Categories list.

Caution Pay close attention to the last step in this exercise, or you will get in trouble.

---

1. In the TimesLists folder, add a new XML file called CategoriesList.xml.

This list will hold the list instance element for our new Categories list.

2. Open the Feature.xml file of the TimesLists feature. Add the following line to the ElementManifests element:

```
<ElementManifest Location="CategoriesList.xml"/>
```

3. In the CategoriesList.xml file, add the following Elements and ListInstance elements:

```
<Elements xmlns="http://schemas.microsoft.com/sharepoint/">
  <ListInstance TemplateType="100"
                FeatureId="00BFEA71-DE22-43B2-A848-C05709900100"
                Title="Categories"
                RootWebOnly="TRUE"
                Url="$Resources:core,lists_Folder;/Categories"
                >
    <Data>
    </Data>
  </ListInstance>
</Elements>
```

The FeatureId points to the CustomLists feature that ships out of the box with SharePoint. The TemplateType 100 is the CustList template within that feature. So, we are basically just creating a new list instance based on the out-of-the-box Custom List template (just so you know).

Also note the addition of the RootWebOnly="TRUE" attribute. This prevents the list from being created on subwebs. We need the Categories list only on the root web to support the site column Article category.

4. Inside the ListInstance element, add a Rows element and then some Row elements as such:

```
<Data>
  <Rows>
    <Row>
      <Field Name="Title">Local news</Field>
    </Row>
    <Row>
      <Field Name="Title">Weather</Field>
    </Row>
    <Row>
```

```
        <Field Name="Title">Sports</Field>
      </Row>
    </Rows>
  </Data>
```

Each of these `Row` child elements adds a new item to the list. We set `Title` because this is the only visible column of the custom list. You can add more items if you feel like it; just repeat the `Row` element and add different `Title` values.

5. Do not build, deploy, or upgrade. I am *not* joking—do not build, deploy, or upgrade after this exercise.

This is important: you cannot deploy your solution at this point. Read on, and I will explain why.

It All Depends on This…

So, why can we not deploy the solution now? At this point, we have three main components in our solution. First, there are the site columns, one of which is a lookup column to a list, and then there's the Categories list, which we are about to create. So, to activate the site columns feature, we must first make sure we activate the lists feature.

Now, the lists feature adds a content type, or two actually, to the list. So, it makes sense to have the list dependent on the content type being activated. You may see where this is going.

The content type is utilizing the site columns we added, including the lookup column. So, now the content type depends on the site columns feature, which depends on the list feature, which depends on the content type feature. Circular references and madness ahead. But we are smarter than that, aren't we?

Exercise 13-9. Adding the Categories List, Take 2

In this exercise, you will solve the circular dependency by creating a separate feature for the Categories list.

1. Add a new WSPBuilder `Blank` feature to your project. Call it something like `TimesArticleCategoriesList`. Make it web scoped, and add a nice description. "Cool list" is not a nice description.

2. Open the `Feature.xml` file of the `TimesArticleCategoriesList` feature file, and add the following `ElementManifest`:

```
<ElementManifest Location="CategoriesList.xml"/>
```

You can also delete the existing element manifest pointing to the `elements.xml` file, as well as the `elements.xml` file of the feature folder. We will not be using those.

3. Move the `CategoriesList.xml` file from the `TimesLists` feature to the `TimesArticleCategoriesList` feature. You can do this by dragging and dropping the file in the Solution Explorer.

4. In the `Feature.xml` file of the `TimesLists` feature, remove the corresponding `ElementManifest`.

That's it. We have now separated out the Categories list into a separate feature so our site columns can depend on the new feature and avoid circular references.

Fixing the List Deletion Problem

You may have been surprised by a small issue with the News list. If you try to delete the list, regardless of whether you have items in the list, you will get a message saying "Cannot delete news. If it happened, it happened." Of course, you remember that we set up an event handler to give us this message in the previous chapter.

This may be surprising because there are no items in the list and the event handler that causes this error is connected to the `ItemDeleting` event. Even if you have no items in the list, the `ItemDeleting` event handler prevents you from deleting the list. Why?

The answer becomes clear after a bit of SharePoint Manager investigation. Open your list in SPM, and look at the items there (see Figure 13-7).

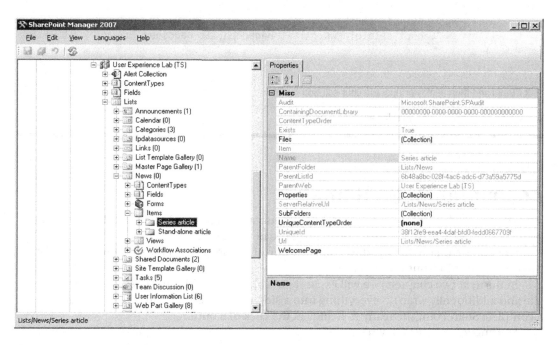

Figure 13-7. *Mystery solved.*

When we add a content type to a list, SharePoint creates two folders to hold content type resources for us. And, as we remember from Chapter 8, folders are nothing but normal items with a specific content type inheritance. Thus, the `ItemDeleting` event is fired for these two folder items, preventing us from deleting the list.

Let's see whether we can fix this annoyance.

Exercise 13-10. Fixing the ItemDeleted Event Handler

In this exercise, you are going to update the `ItemDeleted` event handler created in Chapter 12.

1. Open the `TimesNewsEventReceivers.cs` file.

2. Modify `ItemDeleting`, and update the code as such:

```
public override void ItemDeleting(SPItemEventProperties properties)
{
    if (properties.ListItem != null) // Fix to delete empty lists
    {
        properties.Cancel = true;
        properties.ErrorMessage =
            "Cannot delete news. If it happened, it happened.";
    }
}
```

3. Build and then deploy or upgrade your solution.

You should be able to delete your list as normal now.

Accountants, Go Home!

We're done with lists for now. No more. The accountants may have had a field day, but we are going home. Or, at least, we are going to go to the next chapter.

Our empire is growing steadily. Using the current code, we are able to get our news web site up and running. But we want more….

In the next two chapters, we will expand our solution to add some custom pages to our site and additionally wrap up everything into a single site definition. After that, we will have a complete SharePoint site ready to deploy at the click of a button.

You know that's just a saying, right?

See you on the next page.

CHAPTER 14

Pages and Pages of Fun!
Creating Custom Editing, Management, and Presentation Pages

Custom page development is important to the user experience. After all, everything the user sees is a page, right? So, if we are able to customize the pages, we have maximum control over the user interface.

This chapter will work both with the EmpireTimes solution and with separate and stand-alone solutions. I'll show a range of options for creating pages, including pages that are not tied to any particular solution. So, without further ado, let's get started.

Mission Statement

In this chapter, we'll explore page construction in SharePoint. We will create two types of pages: an application page and a site page. We will also use two different methods for adding code to our pages, both using inline code and using a code-behind assembly. The application page will be a content type hierarchical list, while the site page will be a list of the categories we have put in our Categories list.

Finally, we will use a custom action to add a link to the Site Settings page so that we get a link to the content type hierarchy application page.

Sound good? Let's go!

Basics of Page Authoring in SharePoint

SharePoint is nothing but a relatively standard ASP.NET solution. So, we should be able to create custom pages as much as we like.

We need to consider a few things, however. First, SharePoint uses a common _layouts virtual directory that is mapped to the [12]\TEMPLATE\LAYOUTS folder. This virtual directory is shared between all sites in the entire farm, so it is a very useful place to put pages that are going to be used in all or most sites.

If you want your page to be accessible only to a certain site or site collection, it makes sense to package the pages as a module and make that module part of a feature. That way, you can deploy or retract the page or pages on a site-by-site basis.

Let's start with the latter and create a basic page for our *Empire News* web site.

Exercise 14-1. Creating a Site Page

In this exercise, you will add a custom page to the EmpireTimes solution. This page will just display the categories you've created and any articles in that category. First you will set up the custom page framework just to make sure the page works.

1. In your EmpireTimes solution, add a new blank feature. No need for a receiver this time. Name the new feature something like `TimesCategoryPage`. I did, and you want to be like me, right? Also, make the feature web scoped.

2. In the feature folder for `TimesCategoryPage`, add a new folder called `CategoryPage`.

This folder will remain inside `TimesCategoryPage` when deployed, so naming is less important here.

3. In the `CategoryPage` folder, add a new text file, and name it `categories.aspx`.

4. In your elements file, add the following code:

```
<Elements xmlns="http://schemas.microsoft.com/sharepoint/">
  <Module Name="CategoryPage" Path="CategoryPage">
    <File Url="categories.aspx">
    </File>
  </Module>
</Elements>
```

This code will place our file in a module for deployment. The `Path` attribute refers to the folder inside `TimesCategoryPage` we just created. The `File` element's `Url` attribute tells SharePoint we want to place the file at the URL `categories.aspx`, which will be relative to the root of the site in which the feature is deployed. Also, the `Url` attribute doubles as the file name in this case.

Refer to Chapter 4 for more information about modules.

5. In the `categories.aspx` page, add the following code:

```
<%@ Assembly Name="Microsoft.SharePoint, Version=12.0.0.0, Culture=neutral,➡
PublicKeyToken=71e9bce111e9429c" %>
<%@ Page
 Language="C#"
 MasterPageFile="~masterurl/default.master"
 Inherits="Microsoft.SharePoint.WebPartPages.WebPartPage"
%>
<asp:Content runat="server" ContentPlaceHolderID="PlaceHolderMain">
</asp:Content>
```

This code simply adds the `Microsoft.SharePoint` namespace and declares that we are making a web part page that uses the `default.master` master page.

We will explore the other classes from which you may inherit later in this chapter.

Note The string `MasterPageFile="~masterurl/default.master"` is not a URL. The `~masterurl/default.master` part is a token that SharePoint translates to the current master page URL of our site. If we change the master page for the site, all pages will get the new master page. Very convenient.

You can read more about master page tokens on MSDN at `http://www.understandingsharepoint.com/url/10033`.

6. Add a random control to the `asp:Content` control. If you are in a particularly noncreative mood this day, here is a suggestion:

```
<asp:Label Text="Custom content" runat="server" />
```

The control doesn't really matter at this point; we just want to set up the framework.

7. Build, deploy, and then activate your new feature on the site you use for the *Empire Times* example. Go to the page `siteurl/categories.aspx`. For my example, that would be `http://lab-s02:10000/categories.aspx`.

Check out Figure 14-1 for how this looks on my server.

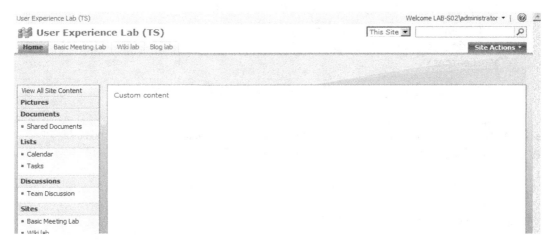

Figure 14-1. *Custom site page*

That's it. It's nothing too fancy for the moment. We will return to the more elaborate examples in a moment.

The custom page you just created can serve as a template for creating other site pages. From this point on, we will add page-specific content, so I thought it would be wise to just pause here for a moment so you can admire your creation.

Note that most of the content in our page is still housed in the default master page. To maintain a consistent user experience, this makes sense. I am not saying you should keep the standard SharePoint master page; after all, we are here to learn how to customize the user experience, not re-create the existing experience. However, if you stick to using the ~masterurl/ default.master token, then updating the user experience for all pages is a lot easier.

Also note that we are inheriting the Microsoft.SharePoint.WebPartPages.WebPartPage class. In a later exercise, we will create our own class to serve as the code-behind class, but for now we will make do with the basic functionality that WebPartPage provides.

I think we should move on and start adding some interesting stuff to our page.

Exercise 14-2. Adding Some Content to the Page, Take 1

In this exercise, you will add content directly to the asp:content control. You will manipulate the page using inline code to archive an article listing grouped by categories.

1. (Optional) Start from the page you created in Exercise 14-1, and add the following line to the top of the categories.aspx page:

```
<%@ Register TagPrefix="SharePoint" Namespace="Microsoft.SharePoint"
 Assembly="Microsoft.SharePoint, Version=12.0.0.0, Culture=neutral,➥
 PublicKeyToken=71e9bce111e9429c" %>
```

Adding those lines makes code writing a lot easier because you do not have to prefix all your SPXXXX objects with Microsoft.SharePoint.

2. Add a script tag below the ASP:Content control you added earlier:

```
<asp:Content ID="Content1" runat="server" ➥
ContentPlaceHolderID="PlaceHolderMain">
</asp:Content>

<script runat="server">
</script>
```

3. Inside the script tag, override the OnLoad method, and remove the base.OnLoad method call:

```
<script runat="server">
    protected override void OnLoad(EventArgs e)
    {
    }
</script>
```

Note The rest of our code will happen inside the OnLoad method, so I will refrain from mentioning that fact every time.

---

4. Add some objects, and get some proper web and list references to the OnLoad method:

```
EnsureChildControls();

SPWeb web = SPContext.Current.Site.RootWeb;
SPList categoryList = web.Lists["Categories"];
```

```
ContentPlaceHolder cp =
    (ContentPlaceHolder)Master.FindControl("PlaceHolderMain");
cp.Controls.Clear();

Table table = new Table();
// Whoops, better not, or we'll have the entire
// HTML TABLES ARE BAD crowd on our tails.
```

Yeah, we'll stay away from the table-based layout, just to please the CSS geeks out there. Skip the last three lines if you like.

Next we want to iterate over the category items and place the correct items in a list beneath the category name.

5. Add the following code after the object initialization in step 4:

```
foreach (SPListItem categoryItem in categoryList.Items)
{
    Panel p = new Panel();
    p.CssClass = "empirenews-categorylist";
    Label lb = new Label();
    lb.CssClass = "empirenews-heading";
    lb.Text = categoryItem.Title;
    p.Controls.Add(lb);

    foreach (SPListItem articleItem in web.Lists["News"].Items)
    {
        SPFieldLookupValue articleCategory =
            new SPFieldLookupValue(articleItem["ArticleCategory"].ToString());

        if (articleCategory.LookupValue == categoryItem.Title.ToString())
        {
            LinkButton linkbutton = new LinkButton();
            linkbutton.CssClass = "empirenews-articleitem";
            linkbutton.Text = articleItem.Title;
            p.Controls.Add(linkbutton);
        }
    }

    cp.Controls.Add(p);
}
```

As stated, this code iterates the category items, adds a nice `<div>` tag for each category, and then iterates all the items in the news list to check whether the item belongs to the category.

■ **Note** If your current thought at this point includes the acronym WTF, you are not alone. Iterating every single item in the news list for every single category is a highly unoptimized way of generating a list. We will improve this later.

---

6. (Optional) Since we added the `.CssClass` property to our controls, we might as well add the CSS code to our page. Add the following code outside the `script` tag and existing `asp:Content` controls:

```
<asp:Content runat="server"➥
ContentPlaceHolderID="PlaceHolderAdditionalPageHead">
    <style type="text/css">
.empirenews-heading
{
 font-size: medium;
 font-weight: bold;
 display: block;
}

.empirenews-articleitem
{
 display: block;
}
</style>
</asp:Content>
```

Yeah, I know, that is CSS. There won't be much more, I promise. This is just done to pretty things up a bit.

7. Build and then deploy or update. You changes should be immediate; there's no need to reactivate the feature. Your result should resemble Figure 14-2.

Figure 14-2. *Custom site page deployed*

It's cool but not very efficient. We should work to improve our example a bit.

■**Note** We are adding inline code to our site page, which must present a security problem. After all, if you can just upload an .aspx page and have code run inside, anyone could upload code to a page library and run the page. The answer to this mystery is that we are not running our page from a library at all. If you try the same trick with a page stored in a library or even if you customize the page we have created here using SharePoint Designer, you get an error message stating that you are not allowed to run inline code in this page.

■**Tip** If you need to specify paths where you will allow inline code to run, you need to modify the web.config file and set the PageParserPaths element inside the SafeMode element of the SharePoint element in web.config. MSDN has an article describing this issue at http://www. understandingsharepoint.com/url/10035.

When you deployed your updated categories.aspx page in the previous exercise, you did not need to reactivate the feature. The reason for this is that you are updating the source of the module created in the first exercise. SharePoint maintains the link to the source file in a module as long as we do not customize the page further using tools such as SharePoint Designer. As such, any edits made to the source file will immediately affect any page that has been provisioned from that source file.

Here comes a cool thing about WSPBuilder: in your Solution Explorer, you copy a file directly to [12] using a context menu shortcut. Developing this is extremely handy because you do not need to rebuild the WSP file, deploy, wait for solution retraction, and deploy for every minor change you do to your page. All you do is right-click the file, hit "Copy to 12 hive," and refresh the page. Figure 14-3 shows where this option is located.

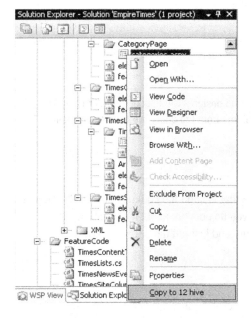

Figure 14-3. *"Copy to 12 hive" option in WSPBuilder*

OK, it is time to fix that horrible iteration code from the previous exercise.

Exercise 14-3. Improving the Site Page Code

In this exercise, you will improve the code from the previous exercise and utilize an SPQuery object to optimize the page.

1. Replace the code you added in step 5 of Exercise 14-2 with the following code:

```
foreach (SPListItem categoryItem in categoryList.Items)
{
    Panel p = new Panel();
    p.CssClass = "empirenews-categorylist";
    Label lb = new Label();
    lb.CssClass = "empirenews-heading";
    lb.Text = categoryItem.Title;
    p.Controls.Add(lb);

    SPQuery query = new SPQuery();
    query.Query = @"<Where><Eq>
        <FieldRef Name=""ArticleCategory"" LookupId=""True"" />
        <Value Type=""Lookup"">"
        + categoryItem.ID +
        "</Value></Eq></Where>";

    foreach (SPListItem articleItem in web.Lists["News"].GetItems(query))
    {
            LinkButton linkbutton = new LinkButton();
            linkbutton.CssClass = "empirenews-articleitem";
            linkbutton.Text = articleItem.Title;
            p.Controls.Add(linkbutton);
    }

    cp.Controls.Add(p);
}
```

The major changes here are that we now use an SPQuery object and design a CAML query to return only the relevant items from the news list. Since we get only the relevant items from the query, we have also simplified the foreach loop that iterates the news list.

■Note Look at the FieldRef element of our query, and note that we add the LookupId="True" attribute. This ensures that we query the Id part of the lookup value. If you do not care about the possibility of duplicate names in a lookup list, you can skip the LookupId attribute and just put the SPListItem.Title property in the Value element.

That should be it. Running your code should yield exactly the same result as shown in Figure 14-2.

By using the SPQuery object, we get a lot more control over what is displayed. For example, you might want to add RowLimit to your SPQuery object to just get the first five items within each category:

```
query.RowLimit = 5;
```

Or, knowing that the default sort is by ID, you might want to sort the items in a different order. You could sort the news by the modified date to bring the latest news first by adding a few elements to the query:

```
<OrderBy>
<FieldRef Ascending="False" Name="Modified" />
</OrderBy>
```

Look, this exercise is about creating pages, so I don't want to get too deep into the list querying stuff. In any case, doing this using a custom view is likely to be much more efficient and will also add the benefit of being able to modify the view using the web interface rather than updating compiled code.

As such, let's move on.

Adding a Global Page and a Code-Behind

Sometimes you want to improve or expand the management experience, and this is a situation where placing files in the [12]\TEMPLATE\LAYOUTS folder would be a wise choice. As mentioned before, files placed in this folder are available to all sites in all site collections.

For this example, I have chosen to do a simple content type hierarchy page. For the sake of brevity, the example will be extremely simple and just add the content types to a TreeView control. I will leave any expansion beyond that, such as adding fancy icons for sealed or read-only content types or linking to other custom or out-of-the-box management pages, for your exploration.

For this exercise I want you to create a new solution. This solution will be globally available and not dependant on the EmpireTimes solution.

Note There are probably way smarter methods of creating the tree. This is not an exercise in tree building but in global page development.

Exercise 14-4. Adding a Global Page

In this exercise, you will create and deploy a global page that will display the content type hierarchy.

1. Start by creating a new Visual Studio solution based on the WSPBuilder project template. Call it whatever you like; I have called mine CustomPages.

If you like to maintain full control, feel free to start with a class library and make scripts to deploy the pages on your own. WSPBuilder will help out with certain aspects of the page creation but is in no way an absolute requirement for page development.

2. (Optional) Add a Feature with Receiver item to your solution.

Adding a Feature with Receiver will make WSPBuilder create some of the folder structure for us, sign our assembly, and output the strong name in the `Feature.xml` file. It just saves a bit of time.

3. Add a folder structure as shown in Figure 14-4. If you performed step 2, this will be just a matter of adding the `LAYOUTS` folder. If you did not perform step 2, just ignore the `FeatureWithReceiver1` folder; the important thing is to mimic the `12/TEMPLATE/LAYOUTS` structure as shown.

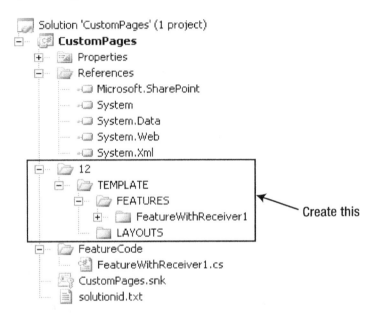

Figure 14-4. *The folder structure for* Layouts *deployment*

4. In the `LAYOUTS` folder, create a new text file, and name it `ContentTypeHierarchy.aspx` or something you like better.

Again, using a text file but naming it `.aspx` will give us a plain file that Visual Studio will interpret as an ASPX file.

5. Open the ASPX file. Enter the following code at the very beginning of the page:

```
<%@ Assembly Name="" %>
```

6. Inside the `Name` attribute, put the strong name of your assembly.

If you performed step 2, this is as easy as opening the `Feature.xml` file of your Feature with Receiver feature and copying the strong name from there. If you did not perform that step, you need to add a key file from the project properties, build your solution, and get the strong name manually. I recommend using .NET Reflector for this task; refer to Chapter 1 for detailed instructions.

■Note If you followed step 2, we have now gotten all we need from the Feature with Receiver we added, so you are free and encouraged to delete the feature folder as well as the `FeatureCode` folder holding the class file of the receiver.

---

7. Add a new class file to your solution. This will be your code-behind file. I have called mine `ContentTypeHierarchy.cs`, but you can call it whatever you like.

8. Add a reference to the `Microsoft.SharePoint.dll` file if it is not already present.

9. In your new class file, named `ContentTypeHierarchy.cs` in my example, add the following `Using` statements:

```
using Microsoft.SharePoint.WebControls;
using System.Web.UI.WebControls;
using Microsoft.SharePoint;
```

`Microsoft.SharePoint.WebControls` is used for the `LayoutsPageBase` parent class, `System.Web.Ui.Webcontrols` holds the TreeView control, and `Microsoft.SharePoint` gives us access to the content types.

10. In the class file, make your class inherit from the `LayoutsPageBase` class as such:

```
public class ContentTypeHierarchy : LayoutsPageBase
```

Inheriting from the `LayoutsPageBase` ensures that we can limit access to our page based on SharePoint permissions. The alternative is to inherit from the `UnsecuredLayoutsPageBase`, which effectively gives us a global open-for-all page.

At this point, your class file should look like Figure 14-5.

```
 1  using System;
 2  using System.Collections.Generic;
 3  using System.Text;
 4  using Microsoft.SharePoint.WebControls;
 5  using System.Web.UI.WebControls;
 6  using Microsoft.SharePoint;
 7
 8  namespace CustomPages
 9  {
10      public class ContentTypeHierarchy : LayoutsPageBase
11      {
12      }
13  }
14
```

Figure 14-5. *Class file after initial setup*

11. In your `ContentTypeHierarchy.aspx` page, or whatever you chose to call it, add the following code after the `Assembly` statement:

```
<%@ Page Language="C#"
        MasterPageFile="~/_layouts/application.master"
        Inherits="" %>
```

You may, of course, change the language if you are writing your code in a different language. My examples are in C#, though.

12. In the `Inherits` attribute, add the namespace and class name of your class. In my example, this would be `Inherits="CustomPages.ContentTypeHierarchy"`.

At this point, we have connected our code-behind file with our page, so we are ready to add some content. Let's take a short break first.

What we have created up to this point is the outline of a custom layouts page, often referred to as an *application page*. You basically have the stem cell of a SharePoint layouts page; from here on, the page can be turned into virtually any page you need. Note that `System.Web.UI.WebControls` is not strictly necessary, but you will be using this so often I thought it made sense to include it in this example.

We are also using the `~/layouts/application.master` master page. As you learned in Chapter 5, this page is global to the farm, and modifications to the `application.master` page are not supported by Microsoft. You may want to create your own master page, and if so, a good starting point is to copy the existing `application.master` from the `[12]\TEMPLATE\LAYOUTS` folder and place it into your solution. However, the default `application.master` contains a lot of nonvalidating code and certain...features...that will break the Visual Studio rendering engine and display errors. As such, you might want to just start from scratch, especially if you are developing a master page for your solution anyway.

I will leave custom application master page development as an exercise for you to do on your own.

Note Starting down the path of custom `application.master` development should not be done without considering the consequences. Maintaining a separate `application.master` includes both operations and development maintenance, because you need to update your `application.master` as part of your regular update cycle.

We should get back to our regularly scheduled page development.

Exercise 14-5. Adding Content to the Page

In this exercise, you will add some content to your application page. Because this is for illustrative purposes only, the actual content will be very simple.

1. In your `ContentTypeHierarchy.aspx` page, add the following code:

```
<asp:Content ID="Main" contentplaceholderid="PlaceHolderMain" runat="server">
    <asp:TreeView ID="tvContentTypes" runat="server">
    </asp:TreeView>
</asp:Content>
```

2. In your code-behind file, `ContentTypeHierarchy.cs`, add the following code to the `ContentTypeHierarchy` class:

```
protected TreeView tvContentTypes;
protected override void OnLoad(EventArgs e)
{
    SPContentTypeCollection cts = this.Web.AvailableContentTypes;
    Dictionary<SPContentTypeId, TreeNode> ctsNodes = new
  Dictionary<SPContentTypeId, TreeNode>();
    TreeNodeCollection nodes = tvContentTypes.Nodes;

    foreach (SPContentType ct in cts)
    {
        TreeNode ctnode = new TreeNode(ct.Name, ct.Id.ToString());
        if (ctsNodes.ContainsKey(ct.Parent.Id))
        {
            TreeNode parent = ctsNodes[ct.Parent.Id];
            parent.ChildNodes.Add(ctnode);
        }
        else
        {
            nodes.Add(ctnode);
        }
        ctsNodes.Add(ct.Id, ctnode);
    }
}
```

This code essentially builds the node tree of the TreeView control.

Note that simply adding a protected TreeView object with the same name as the ID of the TreeView in our ASPX page will cause ASP.NET to map our object to the correct control.

3. Build your solution and deploy it. There are no features to activate, and WSPBuilder will make sure your file gets placed where it should inside [12]. Also, WSPBuilder puts the assembly in the GAC for you. If you have chosen not to use WSPBuilder, you must perform these steps manually.

4. Go to any site in your site collection, add /_layouts/ContentTypeHierarchy.aspx to the URL of your site (for example http://lab-s02:1000/_layouts/ContentTypeHierarchy.aspx), and see your new application page in all its glory.

If something didn't work, you can see my results, in all their glory, in Figure 14-6.

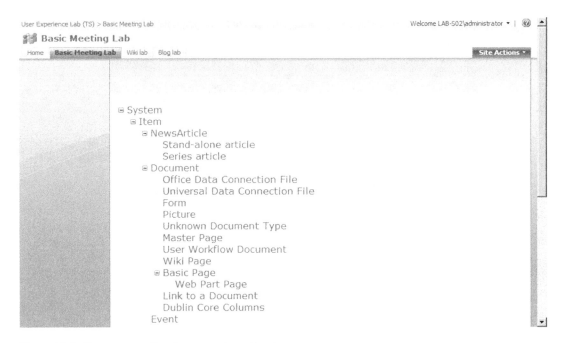

Figure 14-6. *Custom application page in action!*

Another pat on the back for you. Let's see how we can make access to our page a bit easier.

What we did in our previous example was to add some content in the form of an asp: Content control and a standard TreeView control to display our content type hierarchy. Then we added some code in our code-behind file to fill the tree with the content types. It wasn't anything fancy; it was just to show you the outline of how you can create a custom page.

Note There are many more content placeholders you may want to utilize to make a better-looking page. I highly recommend reading through the application.master page to learn about the different placeholders.

Next we want to add our page to the site settings. After all, we don't want to type the _layouts/ContentTypeHierarchy.aspx string every time we want to see our page. For this we need to use a CustomAction feature.

Exercise 14-6. Adding Links to the Custom Page

In this exercise, you will create a farm-scoped feature to add links to your page from the Site Settings page. You will do this in two ways, first as a separate column on the Site Settings page and then as part of the Galleries column on that page.

1. Add a new Blank Feature WSPBuilder item to your CustomPages solution. Yes, that's right, no receivers this time either.

2. Add the following code to the elements file:

```
<Elements xmlns="http://schemas.microsoft.com/sharepoint/">
  <CustomActionGroup Id="MyCustomSettings"
                Location="Microsoft.SharePoint.SiteSettings"
                Description="Custom administration options"
                Sequence="5"
                Title="Custom administration"/>
  <CustomAction Id="MyCustomSiteAction"
                GroupId="MyCustomSettings"
                Location="Microsoft.SharePoint.SiteSettings"
                Rights="ManageWeb"
                Title="Content Type hierarchy"
                >
    <UrlAction Url="_layouts/ContentTypeHierarchy.aspx"/>
  </CustomAction>
</Elements>
```

■**Note** You may recognize this code. It is very similar to the example used for custom actions in Chapter 5.

3. Build and deploy your feature. Go to the Site Settings page to verify that you do have a new column, as shown in Figure 14-7.

■**Tip** Remember that our new feature is farm scoped, so if you need to deactivate it, you need to go to the Central Administration web site. You will find farm features on the Operations tab.

Figure 14-7. *Custom column for page links*

I realize this looks horrible, so let's modify our `elements.xml` file a bit to put our custom link in the Galleries column instead.

4. (Optional) Modify your elements file as such:

```
<Elements xmlns="http://schemas.microsoft.com/sharepoint/">
  <CustomAction Id="MyCustomSiteAction"
                GroupId="Galleries"
                Sequence="22"
                Location="Microsoft.SharePoint.SiteSettings"
                Rights="ManageWeb"
                Title="Content Type hierarchy"
                >
    <UrlAction Url="_layouts/ContentTypeHierarchy.aspx"/>
  </CustomAction>
</Elements>
```

Your content type hierarchy should now be moved to the Galleries column, just below the "Site content types" link. Check out Figure 14-8 if you don't believe me.

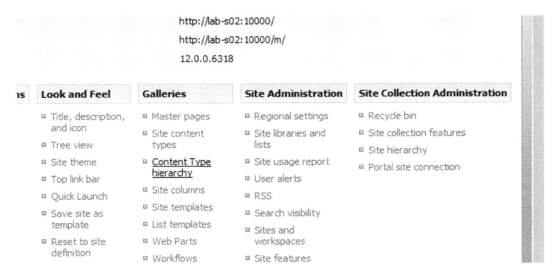

http://lab-s02:10000/

http://lab-s02:10000/m/

12.0.0.6318

	Look and Feel	Galleries	Site Administration	Site Collection Administration
	▫ Title, description, and icon	▫ Master pages	▫ Regional settings	▫ Recycle bin
	▫ Tree view	▫ Site content types	▫ Site libraries and lists	▫ Site collection features
	▫ Site theme	▫ <u>Content Type hierarchy</u>	▫ Site usage report	▫ Site hierarchy
	▫ Top link bar	▫ Site columns	▫ User alerts	▫ Portal site connection
	▫ Quick Launch	▫ Site templates	▫ RSS	
	▫ Save site as template	▫ List templates	▫ Search visibility	
	▫ Reset to site definition	▫ Web Parts	▫ Sites and workspaces	
		▫ Workflows	▫ Site features	

Figure 14-8. *Told you!*

I think that's it!

You may ask yourself how I knew about the GroupId and Sequence values. Go ahead, ask yourself. No answer? I'll provide one for you.

Look in the [12]\TEMPLATE\FEATURES\SiteSettings folder, specifically in the SiteSettings.xml file. Inside you will find all the links on the Site Settings page. Just search for the CustomAction tag with Id="ManageCType", and you have your answer.

If you need a refresher, check out Chapter 5 for the details on CustomAction.

Last Page

Well, at least it is the last page of this chapter. And, since this chapter was about pages…well, you get the pun.

Anyway, we've explored a few different methods for page creation in SharePoint. You should consider this an introduction, however, because the topic is a massive one, and your possibilities are endless. Needless to say (but I'll say it anyway), custom page creation is a very powerful user experience feature. I'd encourage you to experiment and keep exploring, but I may have mentioned this a few times already.

We still have one more chapter to go, in which we will wrap up everything into a single site definition. We will create a site definition, dabble with the site navigation, and explore methods to improve our site creation. Oh, and the killer won't be revealed on this last page. There will be another.

I love these little teasers….

■ ■ ■

CHAPTER 15

Our Empire United

Wrapping All Our Hard Work into a Single SharePoint Solution

Now we are nearing the end of our empire building, but there are still important tasks to accomplish. We want to wrap all our hard work into a complete SharePoint solution that can be used to set up a complete SharePoint site, including all the custom fields, list templates, lists, content types, and pages we have developed.

Unlike certain MMORPGs I play, however, the end game in this book is far from lacking. We still have more tasks to accomplish, such as adding our own custom navigation and ensuring that everything is set up as expected. Oh, and our story takes a strange turn later, so read on.

Mission Statement

In this chapter, we will create our final pieces of our puzzle and put those pieces together to form a new site. We will create a basic site definition and then add the pieces we have created. We will then add navigation and explore how we can create navigation options that fit our needs.

Creating the Site Definition

After reading Chapter 3, you may know that I am biased toward using features for most of our functionality deployment. Let's take that notion to the extreme by removing any superfluous functionality from our site definition.

Exercise 15-1. Creating a Bare-Bones Site Definition

In this exercise, you will create a site definition containing only what is absolutely required to get the site running.

1. In your Solution Explorer, under the `12\TEMPLATE` folder, add a new folder corresponding to the four-digit LCID of your language.

The LCID defines for which language the site definition will be created. These LCIDs correspond to the language packs you have installed, so check the `[12]\TEMPLATE` folder to see which language pack LCIDs are installed. For English, the LCID is 1033. I will be using 1033.

2. In the `1033` folder, create a new folder called `XML`.

3. In the `XML` folder, add a new XML file, and call it something like `webtempEmpireTimes.xml`.

The important thing about the file name is that it must start with the string `webtemp` and must end in `.xml`. In the previous step, you can change *EmpireTimes* to whatever you like as long as you adhere to the other two naming rules.

Note I will refer to this file as the *webtemp* file later.

---

4. Back in your `12\TEMPLATE` folder in the Solution Explorer, add a new folder called `SiteTemplates`.

5. Under `SiteTemplates`, add a new folder called `EmpireTimes`.

Unlike with the webtemp file, the naming of this folder is important and should match the configuration we will add to the webtemp file later. You may change this, but you also need to update the webtemp file. I'll talk more about that a bit later in this chapter.

6. In the `12\SiteTemplate\EmpireTimes` folder, add a new folder called `XML`.

7. In the new XML folder, add an XML file called `onet.xml`.

Note I will refer to this file as the *onet* file later.

Look at Figure 15-1 for how the final structure should appear.

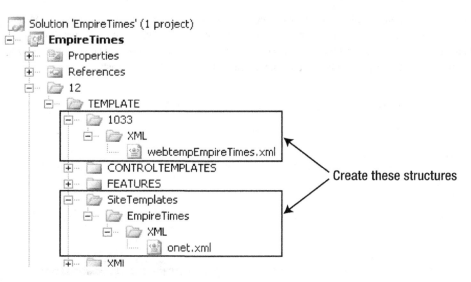

Figure 15-1. *Final site definition structure*

It's time to add some content to these files.

8. In the webtemp file, add the following XML code:

```xml
<?xml version="1.0" encoding="utf-8"?>
<Templates xmlns="Microsoft SharePoint">
  <Template Name="EmpireTimes" ID="20000">
    <Configuration
      ID="1"
      Title="Empire times web site"
      Hidden="FALSE"
      Description="Empire times web site, including all our creative effort."
      ImageUrl="/_layouts/images/[image].png"
      DisplayCategory="Empire Times" >
    </Configuration>
  </Template>
</Templates>
```

The Template element is discussed in Chapter 4, so I will only outline the important bits here.

The ID of the single Template element must be unique in your farm and should be greater than 10,000. Microsoft has reserved site template IDs below 10,000 for future expansion. Of course, Microsoft is not very consistent in this. If you have access to MOSS, check out the template ID of the Records Center. It is 14483, so stay away from that number as well if you have MOSS installed.

The template Name attribute is what maps to the folder we created to hold the onet.xml file earlier. If you change the folder name, you also need to update the Name attribute of the Template element.

Finally, the ID of the Configuration element must be unique within a Template element, but not much else. The number is used when you create new site using code where you would address this particular site configuration as EmpireTimes#1.

At this point, you can deploy your solution and see your new site definition appear when you go to one of the site creation pages, either from Central Administration or from the root site itself. You may want to do this just to test that the webtemp file is working as expected. Or take a look at Figure 15-2, which shows my result. Don't create a site yet, though, because the lack of content in the onet file will cause the creation to crash.

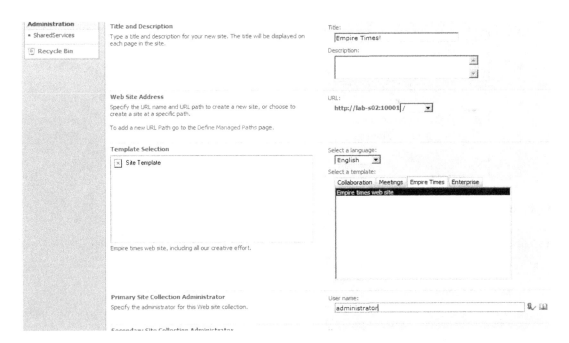

Figure 15-2. *Site definition added to the Create site collection page*

On to the onet file.

9. In your onet.xml file, add the following code. We will expand this code later, so for now it is extremely crude:

```xml
<?xml version="1.0" encoding="utf-8" ?>
<Project xmlns="http://schemas.microsoft.com/sharepoint/">
  <Configurations>
    <Configuration ID="1"
                   Name="EmpireTimesWebSite"
                   Title="Empire times web site"
                   >
    </Configuration>
  </Configurations>
  <DocumentTemplates></DocumentTemplates>
  <NavBars></NavBars>
</Project>
```

By adding this XML code, we now have a creatable site definition. Of course, it is still empty, so going to the front page will yield a 404 error. We'll add more cool stuff later, but first we should take a look at what we have done up to this point.

Note There are two empty elements here, DocumentTemplates and NavBars. The NavBars element is there for validation only; it is required by the wss.xsd schema. The DocumentTemplates element must exist, but may be empty, for the default Document Library template to work. If the DocumentTemplates element is not present, attempting to create a document library will cause an exception to be thrown.

Oh, and you might want to call me a liar in a little while.

Our site so far really has no content. No default.aspx page, no lists or even list templates, no data, no nothing. It's not very useful, is it?

What we can do, however, is to go to the Site Settings page and activate all the glorious features we have created. Go ahead—do that now.

Not very easy, you say? How do you get to the Site Settings page without the Site Actions menu? Oh, yeah, if you manage to wrangle that _layouts/settings.aspx URL from memory, now all you have to do is remember in which order to activate the different features. Remember that if you do this wrong, your site may be permanently damaged and even at best will simply not work as expected.

There must be a better way. And, knowing me as you do after reading this entire book, you also know that an answer will be presented shortly.

Exercise 15-2. Improving the Site: Step 1

In this exercise, you will add to your site definition and make it easier to implement the EmpireTimes solution.

1. Open the onet file. Inside the Configuration Id="1" element, add a new child element:

```
<ExecuteUrl Url="_layouts/settings.aspx"/>
```

This addition makes sure that when we create a new site, we automatically end up on the Site Settings page of the new site. However, this works only for sites created from an existing site, in other words, from the Create page. If you create a new site collection from the Central Administration web site, you still get sent to the root URL of the new site collection.

We can make this a bit better, however. In Chapter 6, we looked at the UseRootFolderForNavigation property of the list template element. This property relied on the WelcomePage property of the folder for a list. If that property is set, links to the root of the list—in other words, http://lab-s02:10000/lists/News—will go to the address stored in WelcomePage instead of the default view for the list.

It turns out that we can use this property on the root folder as well. You can test this by setting the WelcomePage property using SharePoint Manager. Look at Figure 15-3. The effect is that going to the root of the site, as in http://lab-s02:10000/, will send the user to the welcome page instead of the normal default.aspx.

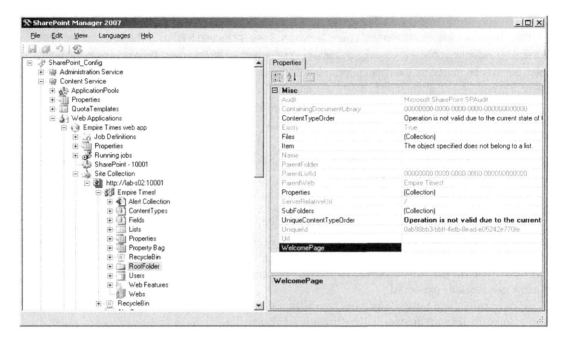

Figure 15-3. `WelcomePage` *property of root folder*

Let's set this property to a custom page as part of our setup.

2. In the `FeatureAdded` method in your `TimesSetup.cs` class, add the following piece of code:

```
// Set custom home page
SPFolder root = web.RootFolder;
root.WelcomePage = "categories.aspx";
root.Update();
```

It's not perfect, but it's better than nothing. We still need a better way of activating features so we do not have to remember the correct order or risk problems related to missing features.

3. In your EmpireTimes solution, add a new Feature with Receiver item. Make it web scoped, and name it something like `TimesSetup`. As usual, remove all the `throw new Exception` lines from the methods in `TimesSetup.cs`.

4. In the `FeatureActivated` method of the `TimesSetup.cs` file, add the following code:

```
SPWeb web = (SPWeb)properties.Feature.Parent;
Guid g;
g = new Guid("[FEATURE GUID OF TimesArticleCategoriesList]");
web.Features.Add(g);
```

```
g = new Guid("[FEATURE GUID OF TimesSiteColumns]");
web.Site.Features.Add(g);
g = new Guid("[FEATURE GUID OF TimesContentTypes]");
web.Site.Features.Add(g);
g = new Guid("[FEATURE GUID OF TimesLists]");
web.Features.Add(g);
g = new Guid("[FEATURE GUID OF TimesCategoryPage]");
web.Features.Add(g);
```

Replace the string in the GUID constructors with the feature ID of the respective features.

OK, this at least ensures that we get our features activated in order. Now all we need to do is activate the single TimesSetup feature, and all should be well.

In the previous exercise, we made a few improvements so that most of our setup is now done semi-automatically. First, we made sure that when a new site is created from within the site collection, we are sent to the Site Settings page to complete the setup of features and other...features.

Second, we set the WelcomePage property to a custom page. You can, of course, set this to any page, but note that the address is relative to the current site.

With a complex feature dependency scheme like the one we have in our solution, the built-in activation dependencies will not work. One important reason why activation dependencies will not help is that one of the site-scoped features, the fields feature, depends on a web-scoped feature, specifically, the "Article category" list feature. Site-scoped features cannot depend on web-scoped features.

And even if activation dependencies did work, you will only be warned that you need to activate other features first. The "dependee" features will not get activated when a depending feature is activated. We need to either activate manually or write code as we have done here.

Still, our solution is not elegant or flexible. If you add new features, you need to build and deploy a new assembly. If you change the order of activation, you need to build and deploy the new assembly. These issues, however, can be overcome, for example, by reading the order of features from a config file. I will leave that as an exercise for you, because we have more pressing matters that require our attention.

At this point, we have a site that resembles Figure 15-4 after we have created a new site collection and hit the Activate button on the TimesSetup feature.

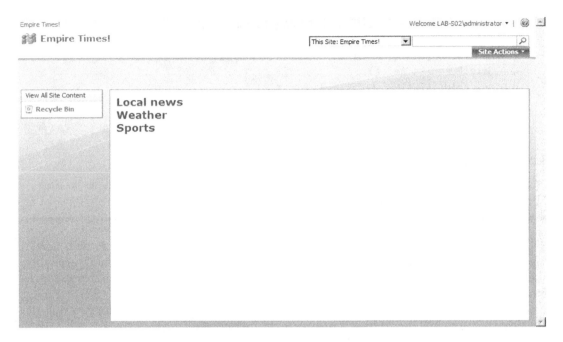

Figure 15-4. *Our site so far*

Although I know that this is massively impressive and your mind can barely grasp the power you now possess, we still need to do more. For example, we have no navigation yet. Let's fix that.

Exercise 15-3. Improving the Site: Step 2

In this exercise, you will manipulate the built-in QuickLaunch menu and the top navigation bar. You will do this using .NET code because it gives you nice insights into how the navigation works. Plus, it is more flexible to do this through code.

1. In the `FeatureActivated` method of the `TimesSetup.cs` file, add the following code after any existing code:

```
// Quicklaunch navigation
SPNavigationNodeCollection quickLaunch = web.Navigation.QuickLaunch;
for (int i = 0; i < quickLaunch.Count; i++)
{
    quickLaunch[0].Delete();
}
```

This code removes any existing QuickLaunch menu items.

2. Continue by adding a root menu item as such:

```
SPNavigationNode aboutUs = new SPNavigationNode("About us", "/");
quickLaunch.AddAsFirst(aboutUs);
```

The SPNavigationNode constructor in this case takes two parameters. The first is the text to be linked, and the second is the URL to which the link will go. The constructor may also take a third parameter, a Boolean that is set to True to signify that the link is an absolute URL rather than a relative URL.

Note If you use a relative URL like we are doing here, SharePoint will check whether the URL goes to an existing page and will throw an exception if the page does not exist.

Next we simply add the SPNavigationNode to the QuickLaunch menu. But we want more, right? Let's add some child elements.

3. Add the following code after the previous lines:

```
SPNavigationNode contact = new SPNavigationNode("Contact form", "/");
aboutUs.Children.AddAsFirst(contact);
SPNavigationNode map = new SPNavigationNode("Map", "/");
aboutUs.Children.Add(map, contact);
```

Note the use of two different methods for adding the first and second nodes. In the Add method of SPNavigationNodeCollection, like the Children property is here, you need to specify both the node to add and the preceding node. Here we add the contact node first, but since it is the first node, we can use the AddAsFirst method.

The same applies to the quicklaunch object we got in step 1. The first item is added with quicklaunch.AddAsFirst, and any subsequent items are added using the Add method. Go ahead and explore this if you like.

For now you can build, deploy or upgrade, and then recycle IIS. Yes, you need to recycle IIS to avoid assembly caching. Then deactivate and reactivate the setup feature.

Can't reactivate the feature? Getting errors about already existing features? I know, I know, we have already activated the feature that in turn activated all the other required features of our solution. Not just that, but if you deactivate the features, you still get an error since one of the features, TimesArticleCategoryList, will try to create a list that already exists.

There is a simple fix. Just modify your feature activate code, and check to see whether the feature is already activated:

```
if (web.Features[g] == null) web.Features.Add(g);
```

Similarly, for site-scoped features, you can use this:

```
if (web.Site.Features[g] == null) web.Site.Features.Add(g);
```

You may wonder why I did not tell you about this right away. Well, it is easier to remember a fix for a problem you experience than just an explanation that something will go wrong if you don't do something.

Now you can try to reactivate your setup feature and see what happens. Back on your front page, you should now see something resembling Figure 15-5.

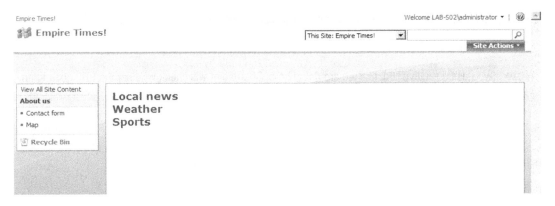

Figure 15-5. *QuickLaunch in place*

We should move on. Let's see whether you can guess what's up next.

Exercise 15-4. Improving the Site: Step 3

Yeah, that's right campers; it is time to put the final piece of our puzzle in place, the top navigation bar. I can hear you all crying that we are almost finished and there is no more book left. Well, dry your eyes, matey; this ship is coming to port.

1. In the `TimesSetup.cs` file, in the same place as the previous two exercises, add the following code:

```
SPNavigationNodeCollection topNavigationBar = web.Navigation.TopNavigationBar;
for (int i = 0; i < topNavigationBar.Count; i++)
{
    topNavigationBar[0].Delete();
}
```

As for the QuickLaunch example, this simply makes sure we empty any existing items in the menu.

2. Continue with this code, which is again rather similar to the previous example:

```
SPNavigationNode newsNode = new SPNavigationNode("News", "categories.aspx");
topNavigationBar.AddAsFirst(newsNode);
```

Note that I have linked the News item to the `categories.aspx` page. I'll show you why in a moment.

3. You'll want more items. Add some! Such as:

```
// Horizontal items
SPNavigationNode localNews = new SPNavigationNode("Local news", "/");
newsNode.Children.AddAsFirst(localNews);
```

```
SPNavigationNode weather = new SPNavigationNode("Weather", "/");
newsNode.Children.Add(weather, localNews);
SPNavigationNode sports = new SPNavigationNode("Sports", "/");
newsNode.Children.Add(sports, weather);
```

The comment is optional; the rest is not.

■**Note** Yes I realize hard-coding links like this is bad practice. I am doing this to show you how to modify the navigation, not to be a saint. That train left the station a long time ago, and the ticket was too expensive for me.

---

4. (Optional) Did you know that the menus also support child elements? Try this:

```
// Child items
SPNavigationNode soccer = new SPNavigationNode("Soccer", "/");
SPNavigationNode golf = new SPNavigationNode("Golf", "/");
SPNavigationNode football = new SPNavigationNode("Football", "/");
sports.Children.AddAsFirst(soccer);
sports.Children.Add(golf, soccer);
sports.Children.Add(football, golf);
```

Now, for the last time, build, deploy or upgrade, recycle IIS, and then...poof! The object reference is not set to an instance of an object. No menu. So close but no cigar. Let's see what went wrong.

Come on, you knew I was kidding, right? We're not done yet. There are still a great many things we should do, but for now, let's fix up the problem we just discovered.

The problem in our case is simple; there is no TopNavigationBar defined in our site. Remember back to our site definition? We left the NavBars element empty. However, in order to add items to the menu, the menu must exist. Now you know why you might want to call me a liar for saying that the empty NavBars element was there for validation only. I feel very ashamed if that makes you feel better.

So, our solution seems simple enough; just modify your site definition NavBars element in the onet file as such:

```
<NavBars>
  <NavBar ID="1002"/>
</NavBars>
```

And you would think that everything is in order, right? Wrong. If you modify your site definition, your supportability takes a nosedive that would bring a blush to the face of Stuka pilots.

This is important. Because your site definition in effect is set in stone once you create your first site off that definition, you need to think very carefully what you put into that definition. If you forget a vital element, such as the TopNavigationBar element, you are basically out of luck and must re-create all your sites.

However, for our development environment, we don't care. And, because of our massive developer genius, we know that we can simply delete our site completely, redeploy our fixed `onet.xml`, create a new site collection, and hit our magic Setup button to get the whole show running again.

But let's really explore brilliance. While in the onet file, add the following element to your single configuration element:

```
<WebFeatures>
  <Feature ID="[FEATURE ID OF TIMESSETUP FEATURE]"></Feature>
</WebFeatures>
```

See where this is going?

Exercise 15-5. Marveling at Your Creation

This one is the simplest exercise. This is where you brand yourself with the proverbial crown of glory, raise your hands toward the sky, and feel the rush of success.

1. Delete your current site collection. Create a new site collection based on the EmpireTimes site definition.

And now, to make the crowd go wild...

2. Go to the root of your new site. Yeah, just click the link from the site collection creation receipt.

I will let the applause from the audience, along with Figure 15-6, speak for itself.

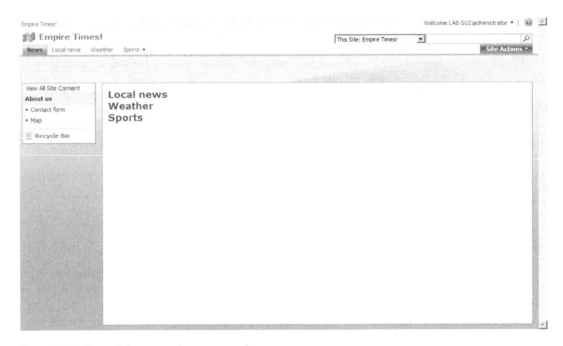

Figure 15-6. *Something to make you proud*

OK, there are a few details left. And I promised I would explain why I added the categories.aspx URL to the News navigation node.

First, though, some more glory. Figure 15-7 shows what your TopNavigationBar looks like with the child menu open.

Figure 15-7. TopNavigationBar *open...and another detail*

Notice anything in particular? At least two things might spring to mind. The News tab is highlighted. That is because we are on the page to which the News tab links. If you add nodes directly to the TopNavigationBar navigation node collection, you will, as a free bonus, get tab highlighting when you are on the page to which a tab links.

You can try this by modifying your node creation code in TimesSetup.cs as such:

```
SPNavigationNode newsNode =
 new SPNavigationNode("News", "Lists/Categories/AllItems.aspx");
topNavigationBar.AddAsFirst(newsNode);
SPNavigationNode localNews = ➥
 new SPNavigationNode("Local news", "categories.aspx");
topNavigationBar.Add(localNews, newsNode);
SPNavigationNode weather = new SPNavigationNode("Weather", "/");
newsNode.Children.AddAsFirst(weather);
SPNavigationNode sports = new SPNavigationNode("Sports", "/");
newsNode.Children.Add(sports, weather);
```

I have put the modified lines in bold. The changes simply remove the link to categories.aspx from the News node and place it on the "Local news" node instead. Now, if you go to the front page, you will get Figure 15-8 as your result. Needless to say, going to the All Items view of the Categories list will highlight the News node.

Figure 15-8. *Highlighting of different tab*

Figure 15-8 also reveals another feature. Note that in the latest modification we added two nodes directly to the TopNavigationBar node collection, but we added two child elements to the News item and even some grandchild elements to spice up the navigation. Notice that the nodes now are ordered differently than Figure 15-7, for example. That is because the root nodes, News and "Local news," in our example, get all their child elements added before the next root node. If we add child elements to the "Local news" node, SharePoint will add these to the end of our menu.

To be perfectly honest, and I think I should be after that NavBars prank I pulled, the number of element levels displayed horizontally depends on the StaticDisplayLevels property of the AspMenu control that is added by the default.master page. By default this is set to 2, meaning the first two levels of elements are added as horizontal tabs.

The number of fly-out levels is determined by the MaximumDynamicDisplayLevels property of the same control. So, changing these values to StaticDisplayLevels="1" and MaximumDynamicDisplayLevels="2", we get a result resembling Figure 15-9.

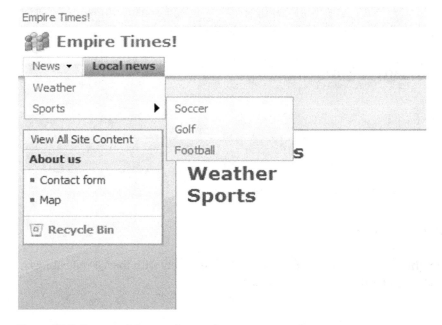

Figure 15-9. *Less static, more dynamic*

OK, there is one last thing I want to reveal before we end. The highlighting issue is a bit more complex. You see, the highlighting is actually done on the root node if you are on a page from which any of the descendant elements of that node links. For example, if you were to modify the Soccer node to the following code:

```
SPNavigationNode soccer = new SPNavigationNode("Soccer", ➥
"/Lists/Categories/NewForm.aspx");
```

then the News node would light up if you were on the NewForm of the Categories page. This is because the Soccer node is a child, or rather a grandchild, of the News node. I have done this; Figure 15-10 shows how this works.

Figure 15-10. *Highlighting root node*

Of course, you might already know this if you worked extensively with the ASPMenu object before. Yeah, those menus are little more than regular ASP menus.

Enough talk.

Your Empire Is Complete

You're done! Yeah, really. Done. No more. You have created, from scratch, a complete site while learning how to manipulate the user experience in a ton of different ways.

You have explored deep forests. You have traversed mountains and glaciers of ice so cold that any other mortal would succumb. You have fought dragons and monsters in dark, damp caves. You have investigated massive fields of technical challenges down to details so small that quarks look like planets. You have built an empire from scratch, from virtually nothing, until a massive and majestic site emerged. Your empire will stand the test of time.

You want to know what that empire really is? It is your knowledge. The site will be gone when you reinstall your computer. Your knowledge of how you built the site will remain forever.

Congratulations. You are done. Now it is time to get started.

Oh, and by the way, in case you're reading only the last page of this book: there is only one fictional character here (except the dragon, of course). Remember that annoying editor who wanted to prevent you from deleting news articles? Well, since no other character is part of our story, it is logical to assume that the killer is the editor.

Now, the real mystery is to figure out who was killed. Perhaps I need to write a new book....

■ ■ ■

Fast Track to Feature Generation
Tricks and Tips for Speeding Up SharePoint Development Time— a Lot

Writing CAML is like being an alcoholic—it's not writing XML that's the big problem; it is when you stop writing and look at what you have done that you realize how much trouble you're in. Sadly, no "Recovering CAML Abusers" support group exists as far as I know.

I will share with you a technique I use a lot when developing custom features for SharePoint. Actually, there are several techniques, but they are based on the same topic, namely, getting SharePoint to do most of the work for you.

Tools of the Trade

Being an efficient developer is not about having the most tools but about having the right tools. More important, it is about learning how to apply those tools in the right fashion. I'll give you a few tips here—tips that enable me to create features that have complex columns, content types, and list views within minutes rather than hours.

I am going to assume that you have a copy of Visual Studio that you like. Visual Studio 2005 or 2008 will do; I'll use Visual Studio 2005 here to make sure I support you either way. If you don't have Visual Studio, you should get that now; the Express versions will do.

The following sections show what you'll need in addition.

WSPBuilder

WSPBuilder is the coolest little tool for SharePoint developers. The main function of WSPBuilder, as the name implies, is to build WSP files. If you do not know already, WSP files are installable solution packages for SharePoint.

WSPBuilder makes building WSP files a lot easier, but its true beauty lies in an extension that you can install to Visual Studio. Doing so gives you a set of tools that we will explore in a moment. If you have not already done so during the previous chapters, get WSPBuilder and its Visual Studio Extensions plug-in from CodePlex at http://www.codeplex.com/WSPBuilder.

SharePoint Manager 2007

SharePoint Manager 2007, or SPM for short, is a SharePoint object model browser that allows you to inspect your SharePoint installation. Not just that, but SPM allows you to perform basic manipulation of your SharePoint sites, lists, content types, and columns.

Oh, and to make SPM even more perfect, it is absolutely free. You can download it from `http://www.codeplex.com/spm`. Don't wait. Go get it now. I'll wait right here until you get back.

Let's start learning how to utilize these tools to become a SharePoint development superstar.

WSPBuilder

I covered a bit of WSPBuilder's Visual Studio Extensions in Chapter 1, so consider this a short refresh before I show you a bit more on how this tool can improve your development experience.

WSPBuilder extends Visual Studio by adding several new project and item types. You will see this when you create a new project in Visual Studio after installing WSPBuilder. Figure A-1 shows the New Project dialog box in Visual Studio.

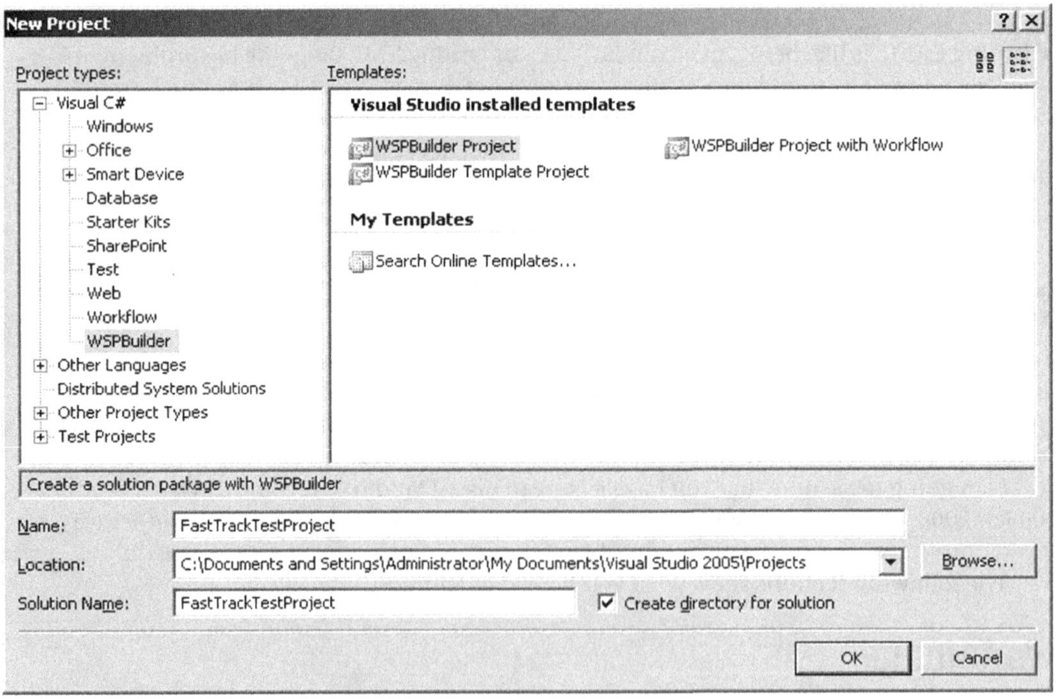

Figure A-1. *WSPBuilder project types*

You will develop most of your projects based on the default WSPBuilder Project template. Start by creating a new project based on this template, and give it a nice name, such as FastTrackTextProject. We will use this project for the rest of the demonstrations and exercises in this appendix. The project name will be used as the solution name for your SharePoint solution as well.

Note You should also know that using the WSPBuilder Project with Workflow project template requires MOSS, or at least references the MOSS DLLs. If you want to use the workflow template with WSS, you need to remove these references, including the related `using` statements.

Once your project is created, you will see that you get a few items in your Solution Explorer. Most notably, you have a 12 folder. This 12 folder will map to the [12] hive when you deploy your solution later. This in itself will save you a lot of time when deploying components that are not features, such as custom application pages, images, site definitions, and custom field types. (We explored adding content to the 12 folder and thus to the [12] hive in Part 3 of the book.)

For our demonstrations here, we will focus on creating features. After all, this is a fast track to feature generation, right?

Your first task is to create a feature with an event handler attached. Of course, feature receivers require you to deploy an assembly to the GAC, meaning you need to strong name your assembly, which entails setting the project to be signed, creating a new signing key, and building the assembly. Then, to tie the assembly to the feature receiver, you need to build the `feature.xml` file, reflect on that assembly to get the strong name, and get the right class name before you pass all that stuff into the `feature.xml` file. Then you need to build your solution and deploy the assembly to the GAC before you copy all your feature files into the 12 hive. Or you could build a DDF file and create a WSP solution file, which is about as fun as watching grass grow in real time—and that's before you create your class file and remember the correct assemblies to reference and the class from which to inherit.

Or, you could simply right-click your WSPBuilder project, add a new item, and select Feature with Receiver from the WSPBuilder node as your item type. Select which scope your feature should have, optionally give it a nice name and description, and hit OK. In one single and short operation, you have done the following:

- Created a new feature

- Configured your project to be signed (which, by the way, WSPBuilder did even before you added the feature)

- Extracted the strong name from the assembly

- Written the `feature.xml` file

- Created the class file that inherits from the correct class

- Overridden all the right methods in the class

- Created an empty, ready-to-use, just-add-water `elements.xml` file.

I get exhausted just telling you about all the time you saved, but Figure A-2 speaks volumes.

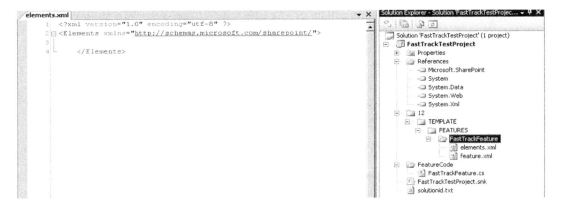

Figure A-2. *Feature created*

Neat, eh? Oh, you ain't seen anything yet.

Note By default, WSPBuilder will create a class file that just throws an exception whenever you try to do anything with the feature in SharePoint, so your first order of business is usually to open the class file and remove the exception throwing from all four methods.

Of course, creating the feature is only the first part of the job. Next you need to actually deploy the feature. This, it is rumored, is a very complex operation, requiring you to master the art of DDF file building. That in itself may be a useful skill, but if you're not in the mood, it can be a tiresome exercise.

With WSPBuilder, however, all you need to do is right-click your project and choose WSPBuilder ➤ Build WSP, and you suddenly have a WSP file ready to deploy. And if you can't be bothered to actually install and deploy the solution yourself, WSPBuilder handles that for you as well by simply giving you a Deploy menu item inside the same WSPBuilder menu you used to build the WSP file. Figure A-3 shows the WSPBuilder menu options.

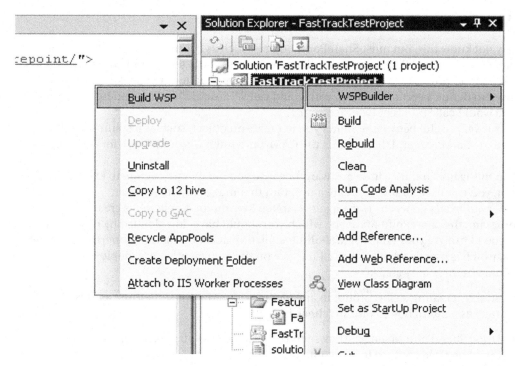

Figure A-3. *WSPBuilder context menu*

You will also notice that you have several other options on the WSPBuilder menu. Upgrading and uninstalling your solution is quite a time-saver, but you can also very easily copy files to [12] or deploy your assembly to the GAC if you need to do these steps manually for some reason. Also, what really saves me time when debugging SharePoint code is the ability to quickly attach the debugger to the IIS Worker processes. I know, this is quite fast using the regular menu in Visual Studio, but I just like to have this option a bit more conveniently located.

The only thing I'm missing from this menu is IIS Reset. Some changes are not picked up by AppPool recycling alone, so Carsten, if you are reading this, please add IIS Reset to the WSPBuilder context menu.

Note Carsten Keutmann is still a genius. And still Danish, which is sad, since Norway is so much better.

I am tempted to take a few pages and explain about all the different features of the command-line WSPBuilder as well, but we are here to speed up things, and frankly, starting up cmd.exe takes about one second too long. However, I strongly, strongly encourage you to look in the install folder for WSPBuilder and look through the documentation for all the wonderful things WSPBuilder can do for you.

Now, let's see how fast we can create a new feature that actually contains something.

Make SharePoint Work for You

You may not know this, but most SharePoint objects, such as columns, content types, and lists, can export the CAML used to create them. To get this XML, you would grab the contents of the SchemaXml property of the object using code. So, for instance, if you want to extract the XML used to define a certain column, you would call SPField.SchemaXml, and for a content type you would call SPContentType.SchemaXml.

This is very useful because it allows you to create an object, such as a column, in the web interface of SharePoint and then extract the CAML and put it in your feature for later deployment.

And this is fine, but it's a little awkward because you need to write code to extract the code. Or, you can have someone create a program that makes this a lot easier.

Enter our overly generous Dane again, Carsten Keutmann. Carsten has created another nice program, the SharePoint Manager, which you should have downloaded by now. SPM allows you to browse your entire SharePoint installation and view all the properties of all the objects, which is exactly what we need. I'll walk you through creating and deploying a custom site column in three easy steps:

1. Start by creating a site column in any of your sites. Make it something a bit complex, such as a multichoice column (check boxes).

2. Using SharePoint Manager, browse to your site where you created the column, and open the Fields note to locate your column.

3. Copy whatever XML is in the Schema Xml tab of SPM, less the XML declaration, and paste it into your elements.xml file of the feature you created earlier. Check out Figure A-4 to see how SPM displays the XML for you.

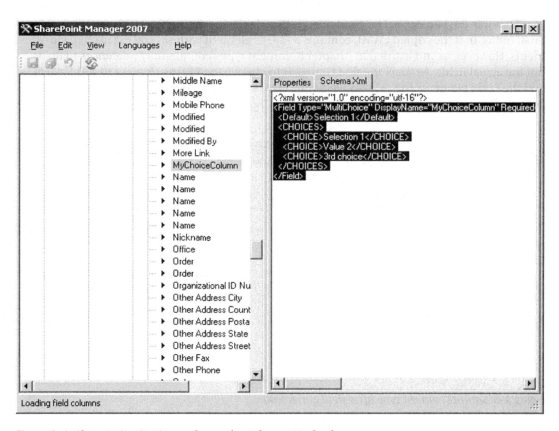

Figure A-4. *SharePoint Designer shows the Schema Xml tab.*

Deploy, and you're done.

Content Type Generation

Around this moment, some wise guy will storm up to the microphone and state that this little exercise is indeed possible with other tools as well. And that wise guy would be correct. So, why use the WSPBuilder+SPM combination? Let's take our exercise a bit further and tackle content types:

1. Create a new site content type, and add some columns.

2. Open SharePoint Manager again, and browse to the site in which you created the content type. Open the content type you created.

3. Copy the content of the Schema Xml tab again into your `elements.xml` file.

This would have been a perfect story if I could now just tell you to build and deploy, but alas, it's not that simple with content types. The schema that SharePoint uses, which is the one you see in SharePoint Manager or by calling the `SPContentType.SchemaXml` method, is not the same schema used for defining new content types.

That was the bad news. The good news is that the changes you need to make are simple. First, notice that the copied CAML contains a Fields element with several Field child elements. However, as you learned in Chapter 8, content types contain only references to fields, not the actual fields. As such, the first change is to change the Fields element to a FieldRefs and the Field elements to FieldRef elements. Figure A-5 shows how this looks for my sample content type.

```
1   <?xml version="1.0" encoding="utf-8" ?>
2   <Elements xmlns="http://schemas.microsoft.com/sharepoint/">
3
4     <ContentType ID="0x0100F1350C42A60BD149AACAAF1AC928BFAC" Name="My Content Type" Group="Custom
5       <Folder TargetName="_cts/My Content Type" />
6       <FieldRefs>
7         <FieldRef ID="{c042a256-787d-4a6f-8a8a-cf6ab767f12d}" Name="ContentType" SourceID="http:/
8         <FieldRef ID="{fa564e0f-0c70-4ab9-b863-0177e6ddd247}" Name="Title" SourceID="http://schem
9         <FieldRef ID="{fc2e188e-ba91-48c9-9dd3-16431afddd50}" Name="WorkAddress" SourceID="http:/
0         <FieldRef ID="{0FC9CACE-C5C2-465d-AE88-B67F2964CA93}" Name="_Category" Group="Core Docume
1         </FieldRef>
2       </FieldRefs>
3       <XmlDocuments>
4         <XmlDocument NamespaceURI="http://schemas.microsoft.com/sharepoint/v3/contenttype/forms">
5           <FormTemplates xmlns="http://schemas.microsoft.com/sharepoint/v3/contenttype/forms">
6             <Display>ListForm</Display>
7             <Edit>ListForm</Edit>
8             <New>ListForm</New>
9           </FormTemplates>
0         </XmlDocument>
1       </XmlDocuments>
2     </ContentType>
3   </Elements>
```

Figure A-5. *Sample content type after field correction*

When you change the Field elements to FieldRef elements, you will notice that several of the remaining attributes in the former Field elements are invalid. Your next task will thus be to remove all invalid attributes from the FieldRef elements.

While you are at it, you should also delete the entire ContentType FieldRef element as well as any references to Fields inherited from the parent from which your content type inherits. Of course, as you remember from Chapter 12, you need at least the empty FieldRefs element for inheritance to work. If you have not added any columns to your content type and you have opted to remove the parent columns, leave at least the empty FieldRefs element.

Finally, you may optionally want to remove the XmlDocument element containing the FormTemplates element. The downside to leaving the FormTemplates element in place is that you will override the parent settings for content type forms. Removing is completely optional, though, and if you want to make changes to the content type forms, you should leave it in place.

Next you are ready to build and deploy if you like. Simple, eh?

The Fast Track to Custom Views

Let's take this technique a bit further and go for gold by simplifying the most complex task known to SharePoint developers: custom view development. Yeah, that dragon again. Although I am fairly certain that your newly acquired skills will more than suffice to create custom views from scratch, there is no reason not to save development time when we can.

Before going into the details, however, notice that as we start working with more complex features, we require more manual labor to get our feature working. This is the case also for custom view development, which requires quite a bit of manual labor.

In this demonstration, I will show you how you can create a custom view for lists templates in minutes. I'll use the most basic of lists, the Custom List template, since it is a good starting point when you want to create your own list templates later. As such, you should create a copy of the `CustomList` feature in your Visual Studio solution or create a new list template as explained in Chapter 13 and copy the `schema.xml` file from the `[12]\FEATURES\CustomList\CustList` folder.

1. First, create a new list based on the Custom List template.

2. To your newly created list, add a view, and customize it as you want. This is key—you want to design your view in the web interface.

3. Open up your trusty SharePoint Manager again, and browse to your site in question. In the Lists node you will find your list, and under the list you will find the Views node, including the view you just created.

4. This time, rather than copying the contents of the Schema Xml tab, go to the CAML tab, and you will find your entire view code, ready to be added to your Custom List copy. Just paste the entire contents into the Views section of your `schema.xml` file.

As with content types, you need to make some corrections to the view you just copied. Several of the attributes are plain wrong, while some attributes must be added.

Start by changing the `BaseViewId` attribute into a unique value. Second, change the URL into the list-relative URL where you want your new view created. Third, you need to specify the web part zone to which the view will be added using the `WebPartZoneId` attribute. For the default view page, this would be `WebPartZoneID="Main"`.

Finally, add the `Path` or `SetupPath` attribute pointing to the file from which the list page should be created. For the default custom views, the attribute would be `SetupPath="pages\viewpage.aspx"`, but you may want to create your own page and use that instead.

You should now be able to deploy your list template and create new lists from that template, including the new custom list view you just created.

Time to Slow Down

I hope the techniques shown in this chapter will help you speed up your development time. True, you will not get 100 percent perfect results, but you might get 90 percent, and that leaves a lot more time to fiddle around with final tuning and configuration.

■ ■ ■

Questions from the Audience
Real Questions from Real People

During the time it has taken to write this book, I have received countless emails asking questions and asking whether the sender's particular issue will be addressed. And, as a good author, I always answer:

Yes, of course! Just buy the book, and it will be on page 93. Contents subject to change.

Now, to make sure at least some of those people do not sue me for all my earthly possessions, I have included this chapter to answer a few of those questions. What you are about to read are real questions from real people....

Good evening, ladies and gentlemen. My name is Bjørn Furuknap, and I will be here to answer all your questions regarding SharePoint. To make sure we proceed in an orderly fashion, I will take one question at a time. Please raise your hand and wait for me to address you before you speak.

Before we begin, I would like to direct your attention toward the screen behind me. Alas, the moving bits of my presentation came down with the flu, so all we have are static illustrations, but you are free to imagine a properly running demonstration of all the topics discussed here.

Question 1

SharePoint branding is difficult because of the excessive HTML that is generated by SharePoint. What solutions do you recommend to solve this problem?

—Kanwal Khipple, SharePoint consultant and founder of SharePointBuzz.com

Throughout this book, close to every single element is examined and explained, and with the noted exception of grouping in views, I show how everything is generated and how you can exchange the horrible default HTML. Grouping in views is a sad chapter of SharePoint that forces you to rely on HTML tables for output. What's even worse is that there is no way to change this.

My recommendation depends a bit on how much time you want to put into branding, the complexity of your solution, and which features you actually need to brand. If you have limitless time, I recommend re-creating the entire interface. If you have a complex site and utilize nearly every available feature and in addition run on a limited budget, I recommend swapping out the master page and just doing the best you can with CSS.

Question 2

Working with SharePoint, I have found myself increasingly annoyed at the little bugs or errors that seem to want to prevent me from doing my job. Am I missing something, or is SharePoint development so annoying?

—Debbie, Illinois

I think I know what you mean. To me, every project is a learning experience. Even after seven years developing for SharePoint, I still find new areas to discover. The complexity is massive, and this is a source of problems.

I have gotten used to most of the little issues, such as the documentation errors, the bugs in wss.xsd and IntelliSense, the problems with custom field types, and the strange unknown errors that seem to pop up whenever I want to do something trivial. However, the "getting used to" has taken quite some time, and I have been extremely frustrated at times, especially when I learned to make custom views and field types for the first time.

My advice is to look at your learning experience as a journey, and that is also why I have structured this book as a journey. Getting your project done may very well be your short-term goal, but for each project you complete, you learn something new that makes the next project more interesting. If you focus on learning SharePoint as your goal rather than just keeping your boss happy to have a job, I think you will find the entire SharePoint experience a lot more satisfying.

Question 3

How do I get started with SharePoint development? Do I need to buy a server, or can I work on my home computer? I have worked with ASP, PHP, HTML, and CSS, but I have never developed anything for SharePoint.

—Anonymous

Learning to develop for SharePoint is no different from learning any other platform development. You mention experience from different languages, and having wide experience from different languages is always a good idea. Remember that language is just a tool; learning a programming language does not make you a developer any more than learning English or German makes you an author.

How you should learn to develop for SharePoint depends a lot on your learning style. Do you prefer to read? If so, get a good book. For starting out learning SharePoint, I am afraid this book is not your best choice, but you have a wide range of other good choices. I have compiled a list of books I recommend on `http://www.understandingsharepoint.com/url?/20010`.

If you prefer other methods of learning, you will find a wide variety of online and offline resources using Google. Microsoft has an excellent SharePoint developer training site at `http://www.mssharepointdeveloper.com/`. You can also check out the training resources on the Understanding SharePoint web site at `http://www.understandingsharepoint.com/training`.

Regardless of how you want to learn, I do have one advice: be patient. Learning a new technology takes time, and you will get frustrated at times. Stick with it; the rewards of the journey are well worth the effort.

Question 4

Having seen the table of contents before the book was released, I was surprised that there doesn't seem to be a web part chapter. Why is that?

—Claire, United Kingdom

Good question! Web part development is a very popular method for developing functionality for both SharePoint and other web applications. The web part framework in ASP.NET is rich and provides a lot of opportunities for creating very nice interfaces and experiences for users.

However, web parts are essentially part of ASP.NET, just like master pages. I have tried to focus on SharePoint-specific topics. Getting up to speed with web parts in SharePoint is not too different from regular ASP.NET. With the knowledge you have learned in this book, you will be far along the path of creating SharePoint web parts just by applying regular ASP.NET web part skills, without any special training.

A related question is "When should I develop a web part, and when should I rely on standard SharePoint user experience development?" I'm not sure that there is a straight answer that will apply to all scenarios. Think of web parts as little web applications that may or may not interact with SharePoint. Web parts are separate entities that encompass some kind of functionality whether it is interacting with the user or simply displaying data in a certain way. If you require that separation, use a web part.

Question 5

While developing, I keep getting error messages, but I cannot find where WSS logs the errors. The logs in `12-hive/Logs` *are confusing. Can you help?*

—Anonymous

SharePoint allows for great flexibility in logging. The default setup might not give you exactly what you need, but you can easily adjust the logging level. To do so, go to Central Administration, and check out the Diagnostic Logging link where you can adjust logging and error reporting with fine granularity. From then on, your new settings will apply to the log files stored in [12]\LOGS.

Reading these logs, however, can be a pain since the file is just a plain-text file with very long lines. The SharePoint 2007 Features package on CodePlex will help you, though, because it contains the Log Viewer feature. That feature will add a log-viewing page to Central Administration that greatly enhances your log-viewing experience. You can download the feature from the CodePlex site at http://www.codeplex.com/features on the Releases tab.

I have also written a blog post on debugging SharePoint, available at http://www.understandingsharepoint.com/url/10008. That article details how to set up and work with logging as well as how to set up SharePoint to display improved error messages.

Question 6

I have developed a custom field type but cannot store any custom properties. After googling the problem, I came across a workaround that I couldn't understand. Using GetCustomProperty doesn't work.

—Anonymous

I'm not sure exactly what your question is from this. However, as it relates to custom properties in custom field types, I can understand if you're bewildered. This is a "good news, bad news" situation—or, rather, it's a "good news, bad news, worse news, horrible news, and news of impending doom" situation.

The bad news is that custom properties in field types work in mysterious ways. Some people call it a bug, but it is not really a bug but rather an inherent problem with the way that adding columns work. Your custom field type code actually serves two distinct purposes when creating new columns. One is to provide the interface where you add your custom field type properties, and the other is to actually store the column after it is created.

The worse news starts when you realize that there are actually two object instances that serve these two purposes, one that holds the custom properties and another that creates the column. Of course, these two objects do not know about each other and cannot communicate directly, so there is no simple way to get the new custom properties from the object that holds the user input into the object that creates the column.

The horrible news is that the problem isn't really a bug but rather just a design issue that follows as a result of how adding new columns is implemented. And since this isn't a bug, the problem will likely remain throughout the life span of the current SharePoint. Brace yourself, and be prepared to live with it and work around it; or, don't implement custom properties in your field types.

Oh, but your day has just started in the bad news category. The impending doom news is that there isn't any good news after all. Nope, no last-minute stay of execution, no white knight or knightess riding in to save the day, no brave sacrifice in the last scene.

If you want to know more about custom properties in field types, the third issue of *Understanding SharePoint Journal* explains how this problem works and also suggests one workaround that may at least bring some sunlight to an otherwise horrible day. You can read more about that issue and download the code to see how that workaround works at http://www.understandingsharepoint.com/journal.

WSPBuilder implements another widely used workaround in the WSPBuilder Field Type project item. I advise you to add such a custom field type and then study the code that WSPBuilder generates for you.

Question 7

How can I circumvent developing on a server? SharePoint will not install on XP, and I don't want to run Windows Server 2003 on my laptop.

—Multiple askers

This question is asked very frequently and is likely one of the first questions that a SharePoint developer will ask.

I talked about this in Chapter 1 and explained why I don't recommend developing anywhere else but on a server. Not just that, but developing on a server gives you many benefits that you would not get if developing on a workstation. For example, Visual Studio integration will very easily attach to the process running SharePoint, so you can get step-by-step debugging while developing .NET code. You could set this up to work on a remote machine, but it is a hassle.

Second, the object model exposed through the SharePoint DLLs, one of the most powerful development tools you have, is available only locally on the server. You could circumvent this by referencing the SharePoint DLLs, but you would not be able to test your features without deploying your code to the server in any case, and you would still have to tackle the debugging issues.

My recommendation is to develop on a server—a virtual server to be precise. You can download Virtual PC or VMware Server for free, and with an MSDN subscription you get developer licenses of Windows Server. Worst case, you can use the evaluation version of Windows Server. Install a new virtual machine with Windows Server and then install Visual Studio or any other development tools you need.

There's no need to install anything except the virtual machine software on your laptop, and you gain all the benefits of working directly on the server.

Question 8

Some people advise against writing .NET code and just work with the default function-
ality, since upgrading code later will be a problem. When should I develop my own code,
and when should I work with the default features?

—Jagadeep

I'm a developer by heart, so if you ask me, I'd write everything in code. However, I'll buy several arguments for not doing so for everyone.

First, consider the nondevelopers who may need to maintain your features. Visual Studio may not be available, and in any case, recompiling and deploying an assembly every time you want to change a feature is more of a hassle than working with CAML definitions.

Second, some tasks are more difficult to accomplish in code than in CAML, such as creating list views. Even though technically possible through code and even though code would actually allow you to create dynamic views, if all you need to do is create a simple All Items–style view, doing so through CAML is a lot easier, especially when you use the technique I explain in Appendix A.

With that said, again, I love programming, and I use .NET code whenever I think the default features are too limiting or nonexistent. For example, the trivial task of finding out the number of current users on a site is virtually impossible through default features. Add some code, a few delegate controls, a custom action, and a custom administration page, and suddenly you have a very nice solution such as as SPCurrentUsers on CodePlex: http://www.codeplex.com/SPCurrentUsers.

I am probably the wrong person to ask because I like to test the boundaries of technology and focus less on production code.

Index

Numbers and symbols

You Need the Companion eBook

Your purchase of this book entitles you to buy the companion PDF-version eBook for only $10. Take the weightless companion with you anywhere.

We believe this Apress title will prove so indispensable that you'll want to carry it with you everywhere, which is why we are offering the companion eBook (in PDF format) for $10 to customers who purchase this book now. Convenient and fully searchable, the PDF version of any content-rich, page-heavy Apress book makes a valuable addition to your programming library. You can easily find and copy code—or perform examples by quickly toggling between instructions and the application. Even simultaneously tackling a donut, diet soda, and complex code becomes simplified with hands-free eBooks!

Once you purchase your book, getting the $10 companion eBook is simple:

❶ Visit **www.apress.com/promo/tendollars/**.

❷ Complete a basic registration form to receive a randomly generated question about this title.

❸ Answer the question correctly in 60 seconds, and you will receive a promotional code to redeem for the $10.00 eBook.

THE EXPERT'S VOICE™

2855 TELEGRAPH AVENUE | SUITE 600 | BERKELEY, CA 94705

All Apress eBooks subject to copyright protection. No part may be reproduced or transmitted in any form or by any means, electronic or mechanical, including photocopying, recording, or by any information storage or retrieval system, without the prior written permission of the copyright owner and the publisher. The purchaser may print the work in full or in part for their own noncommercial use. The purchaser may place the eBook title on any of their personal computers for their own personal reading and reference.

Offer valid through 10/09.